A FINAL VALIANT ACT

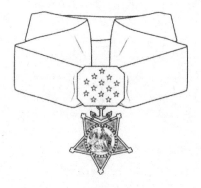

A FINAL VALIANT ACT

The Story of Doug Dickey, Medal of Honor

LtCol John B. Lang, USMC (Ret.)

CASEMATE

Philadelphia & Oxford

Published in the United States of America and Great Britain in 2020 by
CASEMATE PUBLISHERS
1950 Lawrence Road, Havertown, PA 19083, USA
and
The Old Music Hall, 106–108 Cowley Road, Oxford OX4 1JE, UK

Hardcover Edition: ISBN 978-1-61200-757-1
Digital Edition: ISBN 978-1-61200-758-8

A CIP record for this book is available from the British Library

Printed and bound in the United States by Integrated Books International

Typeset by Versatile PreMedia Services (P) Ltd

For a complete list of Casemate titles, please contact:

CASEMATE PUBLISHERS (US)
Telephone (610) 853-9131
Fax (610) 853-9146
Email: casemate@casematepublishers.com
www.casematepublishers.com

CASEMATE PUBLISHERS (UK)
Telephone (01865) 241249
Email: casemate-uk@casematepublishers.co.uk
www.casematepublishers.co.uk

To the Gold Star Mothers
of the Vietnam War

"And you yourself a sword will pierce."

Luke 2:35

Contents

Maps and Illustrations

MAPS

ILLUSTRATIONS

Maps and illustrations by Mark Franklin Arts: www.markfranklinarts.co.uk

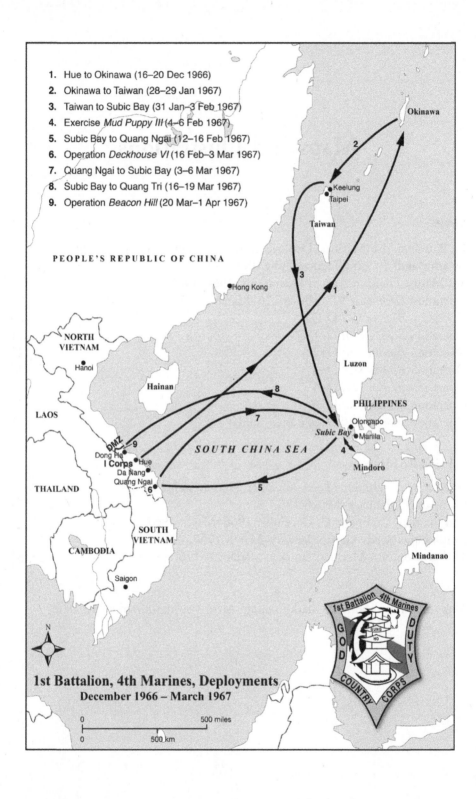

1. Hue to Okinawa (16–20 Dec 1966)
2. Okinawa to Taiwan (28–29 Jan 1967)
3. Taiwan to Subic Bay (31 Jan–3 Feb 1967)
4. Exercise *Mud Puppy III* (4–6 Feb 1967)
5. Subic Bay to Quang Ngai (12–16 Feb 1967)
6. Operation *Deckhouse VI* (16 Feb–3 Mar 1967)
7. Quang Ngai to Subic Bay (3–6 Mar 1967)
8. Subic Bay to Quang Tri (16–19 Mar 1967)
9. Operation *Beacon Hill* (20 Mar–1 Apr 1967)

PEOPLE'S REPUBLIC OF CHINA

Okinawa

Keelung
Taipei

Taiwan

Hong Kong

NORTH
VIETNAM

Hanoi

Hainan

Luzon

LAOS

PHILIPPINES

Olongapo
Subic Bay • Manila

SOUTH CHINA SEA

DMZ
Dong Ha
I Corps • Hue
Da Nang
Quang Ngai

Mindoro

THAILAND

SOUTH
VIETNAM

CAMBODIA

Mindanao

Saigon

N

1st Battalion, 4th Marines, Deployments
December 1966 – March 1967

0 ——— 500 miles
0 ——— 500 km

No Words

In the summer of 1997, William Dorsey found himself driving down a two-lane country road, through the farmland just west of Rossburg, Ohio. Bill Dorsey had driven through Ohio several times in the past three decades and always thought about the Dickey family—especially Mrs. Dickey.

It was just over 30 years since that Easter Sunday in Vietnam. A day hadn't passed since that afternoon in 1967 that Bill hadn't thought of the Dickeys.

He pulled off the road and up to a farmhouse nestled in a grove of shade trees. The house stood out against acres of corn and soybeans stretching in every direction around it. There was a large barn behind the house where farm equipment was stored. The warm early summer air buzzed. Bill motioned for his wife to stay in the car, and then he got out. He walked toward the front door, but stopped; he hesitated, and then walked around toward the back of the house. He didn't know why he decided to walk around to the back of the house.

It was just past noon. The back door was open and he could hear the sounds of someone working in the kitchen. He looked through the screen door and saw a slender little woman wearing an apron. She was moving around in the kitchen preparing lunch. Bill stopped and watched her. He just stood there—watching Mrs. Dickey through the screen door. He had thought about this moment for years, but he still didn't know what to do. He thought to himself again, "What do you say to the mother whose son gave his life to save you?"

Those seconds in the banana grove were never far from Bill Dorsey. He was lying on his back. Shrapnel from an enemy grenade had torn up his leg. "Doc" Long, the platoon's corpsman, was leaning over him, cutting his bloody trousers away so he could bandage the wounds. North Vietnamese bullets cracked in the air around them, making everybody duck their heads. Lieutenant Dickerson was hunkered down next to them, talking on the radio. Doug Dickey had just gotten there to take over as the radio operator from Dorsey and was fumbling with the radio.

Bill Dorsey remembered watching the Chinese "potato masher" grenade bounce onto the dirt a few feet from him with a dull thump. He rolled onto his side away from the grenade—put his arm up over his face ... and waited to die.

In the seconds after he rolled onto his side, another grenade landed near the first one. In the following handful of seconds, Douglas Dickey, a quiet, good-natured farm-boy from Ohio, threw himself on one grenade and then reached out and pulled the other one under him.

Instead of feeling his body shredded by the grenades, Bill Dorsey heard a muffled blast. He couldn't understand how he was still alive. But, when he rolled back over, Doug Dickey was lying next to him—dead.

Later, Dorsey saw in a newspaper that Doug's mother and father had gone to Washington, D.C., to accept their son's posthumous Medal of Honor. The award citation printed in the paper described how Doug had saved a number of his comrades by diving on a grenade.

Bill Dorsey had been trying to figure out what to say to Doug's mom for 30 years. In those years, he had raised a family of his own. He couldn't imagine losing one of his children.

He still couldn't find any words for her. He watched the little woman through the screen door and again asked himself the question that had haunted him for so long: "What do you say to the woman whose son died to save your life?"

Bill Dorsey still had no words.[1]

PART I

THE BEST OF THEIR GENERATION

CHAPTER I

An American Family

"I guess you can say it's kind of a patriotic bunch around here. You're raised up being patriotic ... love of country and that kind of thing."

TIM BARGA, ANSONIA HIGH SCHOOL CLASS OF 1965

Doug Dickey was from a family and a community that made him love his country. Darke County is farm country on the far western edge of Ohio. The area was settled after the Civil War. Its biggest town is Greenville. For miles around Greenville, country roads spread out in a grid, dotted with modest farmhouses and acres and acres of crops—corn and soybeans mostly.

The people of Darke County have a distinctive pride in their community. It was a petite young girl named Phoebe Ann Moses who first drew attention to Darke County. The world came to know her as Annie Oakley. Darke County was Annie Oakley's home. In sharp contrast to the crude and loudmouthed image of Annie Oakley created in Hollywood, the real Annie Oakley took tremendous pride in being a well-mannered lady. Her almost supernatural skill with firearms, beginning when she was eight years old, eventually earned her worldwide fame. Although she toured the world with the Wild West Show, Annie always returned to her home in Darke County. She loved Darke County and the people of Darke County loved her back. Although she could have lived anywhere when she retired from performing, she decided to live out her days in Darke County. "After traveling through fourteen countries and appearing before all the royalty and nobility," she said, "I have only one wish today. That is that when my eyes are closed in death that they will bury me back in that quiet little farm land where I was born."[1] Annie Oakley returned to Darke County. She died there in 1926 among her family, friends, and loved ones. She was buried in the Brock Cemetery north of Greenville with the simple epitaph, "At Rest," etched on her headstone.

For people who work the earth, patriotism comes naturally. The United States of America isn't an abstract idea. It's their home. Farm families understand community, because they have to depend on their neighbors. The often-harsh climate makes hard work and being a member of the community a matter of survival.

The people in Darke County use few words; but the few they say are important. A man who isn't trusted or respected gets little mention—he is damned by silence and the absence of the quiet endorsement, "He's a good man" when his name comes up in conversation. Loving and serving America is bred into the people of Darke County. The VFW and American Legion halls are some of the largest and busiest buildings in the area.

The Dickey men had served America in uniform since the Civil War—usually when the country was at war. After the Japanese attacked Pearl Harbor, Harold Dickey decided he would join the Marines. Before enlisting, he married Vera Horner. Vera was expecting by the time Harold left for training.

Harold was in the middle of training when he was told Vera had died while giving birth to their daughter. The Marine Corps told him he would have to wait to go home. Harold's mother and father, Ray and Verla Dickey, brought the baby girl home from the hospital. They named her Vera after her mother. Ray and Verla Dickey raised Vera for the three years her father was away at war.

Vera actually fit in well at Ray and Verla's house. They had five children, and had spaced them apart by several years each. This created the unusual situation where Harold Dickey's youngest brother, Paul, was 22 years younger. Vera was about the same age as her father's youngest brother.

Harold was given a short leave so he could go home to see his baby daughter just before he left for the Pacific. During that visit, he ran into Leona Schlecty. Leona had known Harold in school and, like everyone in the tightly knit community, was heartbroken about Vera's death. Leona was from a large, established family in Darke County. Her father used to go hunting with Annie Oakley. Leona was the fifth of nine children. "I always thought Harold was a fine man," she said, "back to when we were in school."

Harold and Leona began exchanging letters while Harold was overseas. Slowly, a long-distance romance blossomed while he was fighting in the Pacific.[2]

Harold Dickey was in the 2nd Marine Division during the war. He fought on Saipan and Tinian, and went ashore in Japan immediately after the Japanese surrender as part of the American occupation forces. He saw firsthand the worst horrors of war, including the atomic devastation of Nagasaki.

For Marines who fought in the Pacific, each island campaign birthed its own unique horror. On Saipan, it was Marpi Point.

The battle to take Saipan had been bloody. American Marines and soldiers had to battle over craggy limestone hills from one cave and bunker complex to another. The Japanese soldiers were told they were defending sacred Japanese soil for the first time in the war. The fighting was brutally close—hand grenades, bayonets, and flamethrowers. As the Americans closed in on the last mile of the island, the Japanese launched some of the largest and bloodiest banzai charges of the war. Hundreds charged right into the muzzles of Marine artillery pieces. The slaughter was ghastly. General Saito and Admiral Nagumo, the Japanese commanders, committed suicide as Marines closed in on their headquarters. In just over three weeks, America suffered 16,525 casualties on Saipan; 12,934 of them Marines.[3]

Marpi Point, at the northernmost tip of the island, was the last objective in the 24-day campaign. The Marines, many of whom were hardened veterans of Guadalcanal and Tarawa, were not prepared for what happened at Marpi Point.

There were more than 20,000 Japanese civilians on Saipan. It was the first island seized by Americans with a large population of Japanese civilians. In the last days of the battle, the remaining Japanese soldiers herded the civilians together and read them a message from the Emperor. To Emperor Hirohito, Saipan was sacred Japanese soil. In his message, he told the people on Saipan not to dishonor him and their country by surrendering to the American soldiers and Marines. The civilians were told the Americans would torture them and their children. They were told it was their duty to commit suicide rather than submit to the Americans.

When the Marines finally worked their way along the coast to Marpi Point; they were horrified by what they found. Women were stepping to the edge of the 150-foot cliff, some with their tiny babies in their arms, and leaping to their death.

The Marines yelled for them to stop and brought a captured Japanese soldier up to talk to them with a loudspeaker. He told them to stop killing themselves and their children. American units tried to make it to the cliffs but were held off by some of the last remaining Japanese soldiers. The nightmare continued along the cliffs at Marpi Point. U.S. Navy patrol boats tried to work their way to the rocky beach, to pull survivors from the water. They were slowed because they had to work their way through the hundreds of corpses floating in the water. Looking down from above, Marines could see babies crawling on the beach below, over the bodies of their dead parents. Before the Marines managed to secure Marpi Point and end the carnage, thousands had killed themselves, right before the eyes of horrified young Marines. The Marine Corps' official history of the Saipan campaign called Marpi Point, "the very zenith of horror."[4]

Audie Murphy summed up the sentiments of young men like Harold Dickey who were preparing to return home after years of war: "We have been so intent on death that we have forgotten life. And now suddenly life faces us. I swear to myself that I will measure up to it. I may be branded by war, but I will not be defeated by it." Murphy had earned a battlefield commission and had become the most decorated American in the war—all by the age of twenty. He echoed the vows of millions of other young men who had fought in the war and were now heading home to America. "Gradually it becomes clear," he said. "I will go back. I will find the kind of girl of whom I once dreamed. I will learn to look at life through uncynical eyes, to have faith, to know love. I will learn to work in peace as in war. And finally—finally, like countless others—I will learn to live again."[5]

Like most of the returning combat veterans, Harold Dickey wanted to celebrate life when he came home to Darke County after three years of war. He asked Leona to marry him shortly after he got home. They married and settled down on a little farm in Rossburg, 12 miles north of Greenville. Farming can be fickle. In addition to farming their little spread, Harold also took a job working the second shift at the General Motors Delco Moraine plant in Dayton. The job with GM made sure his family had money even if the crops were poor.

As soon as they had their place, Harold and Leona went to his parents and picked up three-year-old Vera and brought her to their new home. At bedtime, the little girl became hysterical and pleaded to go home to her grandparents. She was adamant that Ray and Verla's house was her home. Harold and Leona Dickey couldn't calm Vera. They eventually relented and drove her back to her grandparents' house. They tried for weeks to get Vera to stay, but the result was always the same—they would have to drive her back to Ray and Verla Dickeys' house at bedtime. Vera had bonded to Ray and Verla while her father was away. The little girl panicked if she was away from her grandparents too long. She just couldn't handle any more changes in her life. Harold and Leona accepted the situation. Vera grew up splitting her time between the two homes. She would often spend all day with Leona but then had to be taken home to her grandparents' house in the evening.

Harold Dickey was a man of few words. "He was reserved and quiet," Leona Dickey said. "He was not very outspoken, but if he said something, you knew he meant it." Harold Dickey never talked much about his time in the Marines, although he was clearly very proud of his service. Later, when his boys would ask him about being in the war, he would deflect their questions by reminding them they had chores to do. Every once in a while, when he was talking with other veterans at a VFW or American Legion barbeque, his sons would overhear little bits of information about his time in the Pacific. "He never talked about the war," Dennis Dickey said of his father, "That was just something you couldn't get out of him."[6]

Douglas Eugene Dickey was born on Christmas Eve, 1946. He arrived early and was just over five pounds. Doug was the oldest of Leona and Harold Dickey's four sons. "Doug was a sweet little guy," Leona Dickey said of her first baby.

Harold and Leona had four boys within seven years. Norman was born a year and a half after Doug. He was followed by Dennis in 1950, and then Steven in 1953. "Just one little kid right after another," Leona Dickey said with a smile. "But that's the way I wanted it. That way, it kept them all close. Each one had to help the other one, and it forms a little bond between them. That's the way I felt," she said.

Harold and Leona made a happy home on their little farm. Harold Dickey showed how much his family meant to him, not with words, but through his hard work. He would farm his land in the morning and then drive 50 miles to the factory in Dayton in the afternoon. He worked at the plant until midnight, then drove home. After getting a few hours of sleep, he would get up and do it all over again. Leona looked after Vera and the boys and also tended to a couple of animals they raised on their farm. The commercial value of the animals on the farm was undermined, however, because Leona Dickey kept getting attached to the calves she raised. "I kept turning them into pets," she said. "Well, those big brown eyes looking at you …" she said with a laugh.

The biggest building in Rossburg is the Methodist church. Faith was central in the Dickey home. Sundays were spent attending services and events at the Rossburg Methodist Church.

All of the Dickey boys were raised as outdoorsmen. Harold taught them to hunt; their mother taught them how to fish and how to gather wild mushrooms. The Dickey boys were routinely dispatched to the other farms to help their neighbors bring in crops and they earned reputations as hard workers.

Tim Barga grew up near the Dickeys and had been Doug's friend since they were in grade school. "He was a pretty mild-mannered guy and a loyal friend," said Barga. "Everybody liked Doug." Doug wasn't a natural athlete, but he loved being part of the school's sports teams. He made the football team, although he didn't get to play much. When he didn't make the cut for the basketball team during his junior year, he volunteered to be their trainer. "He just liked to be part of the team," Barga said. "He liked the camaraderie."[7]

Roger Young also grew up with Doug. Young was one of the football team's star players. "Doug would always be like the second-string guy," he said, "but he'd never give up." Young remembered Doug Dickey as someone who could be counted on. "He was always there … ready to go." Young echoed a statement said again and again by those who knew Doug Dickey: "Doug was always there for you."[8]

All those who knew Doug remembered him as a very gentle person. In addition to sports, he also enjoyed being a member of the school and county chorus groups. He had a beautiful bass voice and sang a solo in the school's operetta. He was someone people found comforting to talk to. "He was bashful around girls," Barga said with a laugh, "like most of us at that age."

On the weekends, Doug and his friends would go into Greenville. The scene was very much like the movie, *American Graffiti*, according to Roger Young. They hung out, trying to look cool. "We'd cruise up and down the main street … pull into the Frisch's Big Boy at the edge of town, have Cokes and hamburgers," Young said. They would stop at the Maid-Rite sandwich shop and add their gum to the mosaic of discarded gum on the wall of the shop's drive-thru. Doug and the other boys made a point of wearing their distinctive black and red Ansonia High School letterman jackets. Each had a large red "A" sewn on the front. "Sometimes, on Saturday night, we'd go to a dance at the Armory." Occasionally there would be a drag race between a couple of souped-up cars out at the edge of town.

It was a good time to be young.

CHAPTER 2

A Distant War

"When you have a son in Vietnam, and he gets killed, you don't want a smiling general with flowers around his neck as the leader at that point,"

BRIGADIER GENERAL FREDERICK J. KARCH, USMC

America in the spring of 1965 was sunny, confident, and optimistic. Americans were flocking to the movies to watch Julie Andrews glide down lush Austrian slopes in *The Sound of Music*. Families gathered around their television sets to watch *Walt Disney's Wonderful World of Color, Bonanza,* and the gentle humor of Andy Griffith and the folks of Mayberry. The airwaves were filled with fast-talking disc jockeys and the joyous sounds of rock and roll. "My Girl" by the Temptations and "Eight Days a Week" by the Beatles topped the charts. The country had emerged from mourning the death of their handsome young president with a commitment to fulfill his legacy. On the first page of their yearbook, the Ansonia High School Class of 1964 printed a photo of President John Kennedy, and his challenge to: "Ask not what your country will do for you—ask what you can do for your country."

By March 8, 1965, the seniors at Ansonia High School were beginning to count the days until graduation. The Ansonia High School Drama Club was rehearsing *Finders Creepers.* They were scheduled to debut the play that Friday. Mrs. Sutton's drama students were going through their final rehearsals.

The play was a comedy about five teenagers who end up spending a weekend in a mortuary. The five teens are shocked to find out that "Mr. Quigley," the corpse lying in the casket, isn't really dead. It turns out Mr. Quigley faked his death so he could figure out which member of his family had tried to kill him. The teens then decide to help Mr. Quigley, and together they uncover who had tried to bump him off.

While the budding actors were running through their lines in the high school auditorium that day, a battalion of U.S. Marines was sloshing ashore through the surf on a beach near Da Nang. Mrs. Sutton's students were oblivious to the war that was starting on the other side of the world. It was the beginning of a war that would define their generation and change America forever.

Most histories mark the beginning of the Vietnam War from the 9th Marine Expeditionary Brigade's landing on the morning of March 8, 1965. That morning, the landing team from 3rd Battalion, 9th Marines, came ashore on Red Beach 2, just northwest of Da Nang. Delayed by bad weather, they finally hit the beach at 0918. The Marines came ashore in landing craft and charged out of the surf as if making an amphibious assault.[1]

They were met on the beach by a large welcoming committee and a banner that read: "Vietnam Welcomes the U.S. Marine Corps."[2] A group of Vietnamese schoolgirls, dressed in the long traditional silk Ao Dai dresses, stepped forward and draped garlands of red and yellow flowers around the necks of several of the Marines. The Marines, fully decked out in combat gear, being met by elegantly dressed schoolgirls with flowers, made the landing seem absurd to many—including the throngs of reporters, who were also gathered on the beach.

The brigade staff had known for weeks the beach was secure and the landing would be "administrative." However, they decided to come ashore tactically because they didn't want to waste an opportunity to drill the Marines on their amphibious landing techniques and because it was also the fastest way to get the battalion and its equipment ashore.

The 9th Marine Brigade was commanded by Brigadier General Frederick J. Karch. General Karch had been a Marine for almost 25 years and was a veteran of the Saipan, Tinian, and Iwo Jima campaigns 20 years earlier. Karch had seen a lot of war. The welcoming committee singled Karch out as the senior Marine on the beach that morning and greeted him warmly while photographers snapped pictures of the landing.

Regardless of the silly spectacle unfolding around him, Fred Karch knew the landing of his Marines marked the beginning of a very difficult and bloody war for America. The decision to send the 9th Marine Brigade ashore that morning was the latest step in America's reluctant 20-year involvement in Vietnam. General Karch, like most senior Marines, had been watching the situation in Vietnam deteriorate for years. He had been reading intelligence reports detailing the growing power and influence of the Viet Cong in the area around Da Nang. He knew the South Vietnamese government was weak and its forces were spread too thin. He, like most officers, had read *Street Without Joy*, Bernard Fall's excruciating depiction of

France's tragic war against the communists in Indochina. Fred Karch had studied the British campaign against communist guerrillas in Malaya. He knew trying to defeat a communist insurgency was going to be a difficult and bloody business. Standing on the beach that morning, Fred Karch knew the landing was the beginning of "a long, hard struggle."

Karch stood out that morning because he maintained a stoic attitude throughout the landing and the accompanying ceremonies. Others were more light-hearted. He remained stoic even after one of the Vietnamese girls draped a garland of flowers around his neck. The press widely distributed the photograph of Fred Karch looking somewhat sour with the red and yellow flowers around his neck.[3] Many interpreted the photo as proof that senior Marine officers were a humorless and even arrogant bunch. The reporters clearly had fun painting Fred Karch as a party-pooper amid the festive, somewhat farcical, atmosphere on the beach that day.

Fred Karch actually had a bright sense of humor and was usually easy-going. He explained later why he decided to remain sober-faced that morning—despite his usually affable manner. The landing of his brigade meant America was going to war; and he knew what that meant for Marines. Fred Karch remained stoic that morning because he was thinking of the young Marines trudging up the beach around him, loaded down with weapons and ammunition. He knew at least one of those Marines would be killed in the next week or two.

Fred Karch knew the photos from that morning would circulate in newspapers and magazines back in the States for weeks. They would still be on the newsstands long after the silliness on the beach was over and the grim reality of war had begun to take its toll. Those photos would still be on the newsstands when a Marine officer went to a home somewhere in the United States and notified a mother and father that their son had been killed in Vietnam. Fred Karch refused to smile that morning because he was thinking of that family. "When you have a son in Vietnam," he explained later, "and he gets killed," he said, "you don't want a smiling general with flowers around his neck as the leader at that point."

Over the years, Fred Karch endured a lot of grief because he refused to smile for the cameras that morning. "That picture has been the source of a lot of trouble for me," he said when he was interviewed years later. "People say, 'why couldn't you have been smiling?'" Karch once found a copy of the photo pinned to a bulletin board in the Marine Corps' Headquarters in Washington, D.C. Someone had written "Semper hilarious" beneath it.

Sadly, Fred Karch's darkest fears about America's entrance into Vietnam were exceeded in the five years following his landing at Da Nang. Despite all the ridicule he endured over the years, Fred Karch never regretted refusing to mug for the cameras that day. "If I had it to do over, that picture would still be the same," he said. "I still think I'd do it the same way, even though I've taken a lot of abuse over it."[4]

The headline on the front page of the *Greenville Advocate* the afternoon following the landing was: "Combat-Ready U.S. Marines Land Near North Vietnam." The short article beneath the headline didn't mention Fred Karch or even have any photos of the landing.[5] For Harold and Leona Dickey, and the other parents, the headline that day was vaguely ominous. War wasn't an abstract concept for men like Harold Dickey. He had lived through it and knew it was unimaginable horror and suffering. As with all men who have been to war, Harold Dickey's greatest hope had been that his generation's service and sacrifices had made the world a safer place for his children. He had always prayed he wouldn't ever have to watch his sons go off to war. That hope faded in the following months as more and more U.S. troops were dispatched to Vietnam.

CHAPTER 3

The Buddy Program

"Some of the guys had gotten draft notices. We knew the writing was on the wall. So, we went ahead and enlisted."

BOB BIRT, ANSONIA HIGH SCHOOL CLASS OF 1965

On Sunday evening, May 23, the 64 members of the Ansonia High School Class of 1965 picked up their diplomas. The ceremony was held in the school's gym. The proud parents posed with their sons and daughters for snapshots wearing their graduation gowns and mortarboards, and holding their new diplomas. It was a big day for the Dickeys. Leona had Doug pose for a photo with his diploma. Of the new graduates, 40 were boys.

The war in Vietnam was 77 days old. Fred Karch's Marines in and around Da Nang had tangled with the Viet Cong several times. Since the 9th Marine Brigade landed, President Johnson had decided to dramatically increase the American commitment.[1] More and more Marine battalions and helicopter squadrons were deploying every week to bolster the security around Da Nang. By the end of May 1965, the number of U.S. Marines in Vietnam had almost quadrupled from 4,612 to 17,558.[2] To meet the growing need for more Marines and soldiers in Vietnam, President Johnson ordered the Selective Service Administration to double the number of young men being drafted.

Military service was considered a normal rite of passage for young men in Darke County. None of the boys from the Ansonia High School Class of 1965 were surprised when draft notices began to arrive shortly after graduation. Most of the boys in the graduating class figured they would serve in the military sooner or later, as their fathers had. "I guess you can say it's kind of a patriotic bunch around here. You're raised up being patriotic ... love of country and that kind of thing," said Tim Barga.

Rather than wait to be drafted, Doug and four of his friends decided they would go ahead and enlist in the Marine Corps under the "Buddy Program." The Buddy Program was an enlistment incentive which guaranteed that friends who enlisted together would get to go through boot camp together. Doug Dickey, Tim Barga, Roger Young, Bob Birt, and David Thornhill, went into Piqua and enlisted together shortly after graduating.

Doug was one of the boys who initiated the plan to enlist together. Some were surprised Doug Dickey was intent on becoming a Marine. He was a quiet and unassuming soul; he didn't seem to fit the traditional image of a tough, hard-charging leatherneck. He told his mother one of the reasons he enlisted was to spare his younger brothers. "He didn't want his other brothers to go. He thought if he enlisted, then the others might not have to go—that's what he thought," said Leona Dickey.[3]

One of the attractive aspects of enlisting, rather than waiting for a draft notice, was that it gave the boys some control over their lives. If they were drafted, they wouldn't have any say in how or when they served. "We didn't want to go in the army," Roger Young said, "so we all enlisted in the Marine Corps." One of the other benefits of volunteering was that they could delay their induction for a few months. As part of their enlistment, they contracted to delay going to boot camp until April 1966. It gave them some time to enjoy life away from high school before going into the military.

The five boys had known each other most of their lives. They each had different strengths. David Thornhill was a clean-cut all-American boy. He got good grades and was popular with the girls. Tim Barga and Roger Young were good athletes and had a running rivalry with each other. They had both been officers in the high school's "Varsity A" club. Doug was the outdoorsman and was active in the school's Future Farmers of America chapter. Bob Birt, like Doug, had also been a member of the school's chorus and was a "real loyal friend" according to Tim Barga.

"We were really close friends—especially in high school," Roger Young said. "We played football together—you know—did all the things that you do in high school together, classes … and a lot of dumb things too," he said with a laugh. "Doug was always the cool-headed guy most of the time."

"Some of the guys had gotten draft notices," said Bob Birt. "We knew the writing was on the wall," he said. "So, we went ahead and enlisted." The Marine Corps had begun offering two-year enlistments in order to quickly fill the ranks in Vietnam. "The Marine Corps was always four years, but they needed people so they dropped it down to two years," said Birt. "So, we signed up for two-year enlistments."[4]

"Quite truthfully," Bob Birt said, "as I think about it," he said, "Vietnam was the farthest thing from my mind." Enlisting in the Marines meant going to Southern California, a dreamland they only knew through movies, television shows, and Beach Boys songs. "We were more enthused about going to Disneyland," he added with a chuckle.

In the seven months between finishing high school and leaving for boot camp, the five boys got jobs to earn some spending money. Doug worked at Lambert's, a small factory in Ansonia that made garden equipment. At night, they would meet in an old empty farmhouse on Tim Barga's father's land. It served as somewhat of a clubhouse for them. They played cards and drank some beer for a few hours before they went home.

Their decision to enlist together strengthened the bonds between them. "We were all a different mix of personalities, but we all were still the best of friends," Roger Young said. "I think that's what it takes to be friends."

CHAPTER 4

Platoon 394

"It made me feel real good to be called a Marine."

PRIVATE DOUGLAS E. DICKEY, USMC

Those who go through Marine recruit training quickly learn the U.S. Marine Corps is much more than branch of the military. It is a tribe. The Marine Corps is a clan of warriors whose membership is jealously restricted. Graduating from Marine Corps boot camp means a lifetime membership in one of the world's most fierce fraternities.

The journey that eventually took the five friends from Ansonia High School to Vietnam began on April 11, 1966. That morning, Doug, Tim Barga, Bob Birt, David Thornhill, and Roger Young, met at the Marine recruiting office in Piqua. The recruiter double-checked their paperwork and put them on a bus to take them to the airport in Cincinnati. Once there, they joined a growing group of recruiters and enlistees gathering from other cities and towns in western Ohio. The young men, each of them carrying nothing more than a small overnight bag, were all bound for the Marine Corps Recruit Depot in San Diego (MCRD).

A recruiter picked one of the boys from the group and handed him a thick manila envelope. The envelope contained the recruiting contracts and medical records for everyone in the group. The recruiters led them to the departure gate, handed them their tickets, and watched them board the plane. Once they were on board the plane, the recruiters could count the group as "shipped." The flight left in the evening and had a lot of empty seats. For Doug and the others, it was the beginning of an adventure. "It was the first time any of us had been on an airplane," said Bob Birt.

It was almost midnight when the plane landed in San Diego. The boys wandered off the plane into the terminal. A Marine was waiting for them. "We were just busy billy-bopping through the airport in our civvies," said Birt, "... and then, all of a sudden, the yelling starts—and the screaming." Birt laughed remembering the spectacle, "... and it was right there in a civilian airport!" The Marine in the terminal ordered them to line up against the wall. He took the manila envelope and called off the names written on the outside of it, checking them off as each man answered. He pointed to a Marine Corps bus parked outside the terminal and told them to get on it. They were told to keep their mouths shut for the short ride to the recruit depot.

When Doug Dickey and his friends arrived at MCRD San Diego in April 1966, there were 12,344 recruits going through training.[1] The Recruit Depot was running at white-hot speed. It was undeniable that America was in an escalating war.

Drill instructors immediately swarmed the bus after it lurched to a stop in front of the Receiving Barracks. The DIs yelled for them to get off the bus and run over to a set of yellow footprints painted on the asphalt. They were told to cover the yellow footprints with their feet and keep their mouths shut. After falling in on the yellow footprints, Doug and the rest of the young men from Ohio were herded into the Receiving Barracks. "Even though it was after midnight, they took us straight in and cut our hair," Bob Birt said. "We got issued utilities, put all of our civvies in a box and shipped them home."

That night, the five boys from Ansonia High School began the hard process that would make them Marines.

Of the five, Doug Dickey would have the hardest time.

By the spring of 1966, the situation in Vietnam had changed dramatically. In the year since Frederick Karch brought his brigade ashore at Da Nang, Hanoi had begun sending their army into South Vietnam. President Johnson responded with a massive escalation—doubling the number of American troops headed for Vietnam. It was undeniable that America was at war. For the Marines, that meant a massive expansion to meet the demands in Vietnam.

Initially, America's strategy and troop levels in Vietnam were developed to help the South Vietnamese fight the Viet Cong guerrillas. It was hoped that a limited American commitment would be enough to stabilize the situation against the lightly armed guerrillas. At the end of 1965, there were about 181,000 American troops in Vietnam, 39,000 of them U.S. Marines.[2]

America's commitment, however, changed sharply in November 1965. From November 14 to 17, the U.S. Seventh Cavalry fought and narrowly won a bloody victory against three North Vietnamese Army (NVA) regiments in the Central Highlands of South Vietnam. It became famous as the "Battle of the Ia Drang Valley." The battle confirmed suspicions that Hanoi was sending its army into South Vietnam. The NVA units were not like the lightly armed Viet

Cong guerrillas. They were large conventional infantry battalions and regiments, complete with heavy weapons and modern communication equipment. Now, in addition to fighting the Viet Cong guerrillas, the South Vietnamese government was also facing an invasion by the North Vietnamese Army. Hanoi infiltrated 36,000 NVA troops into South Vietnam in 1965—three times the number that had been sent the year before.[3]

The entry of large NVA units into South Vietnam demanded an immediate reevaluation of American strategy. The United States and South Vietnam were now also fighting the military might of North Vietnam. North Vietnam was heavily supported by both the Soviet Union and the People's Republic of China, and was sending units that were much more powerful than any forces ever fielded by the Viet Cong.

To meet the growing NVA threat, President Johnson decided to increase the American commitment. He ordered the Pentagon to double the number of American troops in Vietnam by the end of 1966. Furthermore, President Johnson ordered troop levels in Vietnam to continue increasing toward a total of 425,000 by the middle of 1967.[4] To meet this overall troop increase, Secretary of Defense Robert McNamara ordered the Marine Corps to double the number of Marines in Vietnam to a total of 70,000 by the end of 1966.

Traditionally, U.S. national defense policy called for the activation of America's military reservists to quickly provide the troops needed at the beginning of a war. The military had been able to rapidly expand by activating the reserves at the beginning of both World War II and the Korean War. However, President Johnson decided not to activate the reservists at the beginning of the Vietnam War. He feared a political backlash if tens of thousands of middle-class men were pulled away from their families and jobs to fight in Vietnam.[5] Johnson and McNamara decided to rely on the draft to fill the ranks in Vietnam.

Having to double the number of Marines in Vietnam without being able to call up its reservists created a severe manpower problem for the Marine Corps. Despite its tradition as a force composed of volunteers, the Marine Corps had used the draft to fill its ranks before. Unable to recruit men fast enough to meet McNamara's manpower goals in Vietnam, the Marine Corps again resorted to taking draftees.[6] By May 1966, the Marine Corps had inducted 19,573 men through the Selective Service Administration.[7]

Recruiting and drafting thousands of young men only solved half of the problem. The Marine Corps found itself again faced with the wartime challenge of training a flood of recruits while trying to maintain its high standards. These young men—most of them teenagers—had to be turned into Marines. Waves of new recruits flooded into the Marine Corps' recruit depots at Parris Island and San Diego. Almost 9,000 new recruits reported to MCRD San Diego in January 1966 alone.[8]

When the war started, recruit training lasted 12 weeks. By April 1966, it had been shortened to eight weeks—as it had been in World War II and the Korean War. Also, the shortage of trained drill instructors made it necessary to increase the size of recruit platoons, from 76 to over a hundred.

The 130 Quonset huts along the southern side of the parade deck at MCRD San Diego had been more than adequate to house all the recruits at the depot until the end of 1965. However, these quickly overflowed as waves of new recruits began arriving. The depot then emptied out storage buildings, and turned them into barracks. When they ran out of storage buildings, they began pitching tents behind the Quonset huts.[9]

While the duration of recruit training has fluctuated over the years, the process has remained largely unchanged since World War I. New recruits arriving at the depots were shuttled into the Receiving Barracks where they spent two or three days being issued their uniforms and being administratively processed. When a platoon had been formed in the Receiving Barracks, they were turned over to the team of drill instructors who would train them until graduation. The platoon's training was divided into three phases. During the first phase, the recruits were taught discipline and basic skills. The second phase was marksmanship training; the recruits went to the rifle range and were taught how to fire their rifles, and fired for their qualification scores. In the third and final phase of boot camp, the recruits went through advanced training, final inspections, and prepared for graduation.

As soon as the new recruits were marched into the Receiving Barracks, they were lined up along a series of tables and told to stand behind one of the numbers painted on the table.[10] A drill instructor at the front of the room barked: "This is your first step in becoming a member of the World's Finest Fighting Organization—The United States Marine Corps," he told them. "You will do what you are told to do—when you are told to do it!" He concluded his introduction with: "Being privates in the Marine Corps, you are the lowest of the low and you will conduct yourselves accordingly—affording all military superiors proper military courtesy at all times. You will speak only when spoken to—always using the word, 'sir!'"[11]

Recruits usually spent about two days being processed through the Receiving Barracks. The mission of the Receiving Barracks was to get the new recruits ready to train. They were issued green utilities and black combat boots. The clothes they were wearing when they arrived were packaged and mailed home. A drill instructor gave them a lecture explaining that they were now subject to the Uniform Code of Military Justice. The recruits went through a medical examination, a dental check-up, psychological screening, and filled out forms needed to open their Service Record Books. They had their photos taken, and were given their I.D. cards and a set of dog tags. They took a battery of written examinations that were used to classify them according to their education and mental aptitude.

When 76 men were processed and outfitted, they were told to put everything they'd been issued into their green sea bags and fall in on the yellow footprints again. This time, they were met by the three drill instructors who would train them for the next eight weeks. This was called "the pick-up" by drill instructors. In their rumpled new utilities and shaved heads, the young men in the platoon looked pathetic.

Since the Marine Corps' boot camps were established in 1911, enlisted drill instructors, often called "DIs," have been responsible for training new recruits. Since then, drill instructors have made boot camp as tough as possible. The mission has been to increase the recruits' physical, mental, and emotional endurance in order to prepare them for the stresses and horrors of combat. Drill instructors are reminded of this responsibility by the words posted on the wall at the drill instructor school: "Let's be damn sure that no man's ghost will ever say, 'If your training program had only done its job.'"[12]

The atmosphere at the recruit depots was different in the midst of a war. Actor R. Lee Ermey served as a drill instructor at MCRD San Diego from 1965 to 1967. He voiced the sentiments of the drill instructors at that time:

> We were keenly aware that every private we trained was on his way to Vietnam as soon as we finished with him, and that weighed very heavily on our minds, considering now that we only had eight weeks to train them. They were no longer being filtered into the peacetime Marine Corps. They were headed for war, pure and simple, so it was very important that they be trained properly. And if it meant being sometimes a bit inhumane, then that's what we had to do. We were acutely conscious that some of them would not be coming back. The first thing we would do as soon as we hit our table at the mess hall was to open up *Stars and Stripes* and find out if any of our privates were there in the obits.[13]

Boot camp began in earnest when the new platoon met its drill instructors at pick-up. The recruits immediately realized their time in the Receiving Barracks had been the calm before the storm. The three drill instructors who met them were more demanding, louder, and more profane than the ones who had herded them through the initial processing at the Receiving Barracks. One of the drill instructors was usually a staff sergeant and was the platoon's senior drill instructor. The other two were usually corporals or sergeants and were the platoon's assistant drill instructors. As soon as they were picked up from the Receiving Barracks, the platoon was marched to the armory and issued their M14 rifles. From the armory, they were marched to the recruit barracks. At MCRD San Diego, they were marched to the Quonset huts in the recruit area on the other side of the parade deck.

Each platoon was given a unique number and issued a red guidon flag with the number sewn onto it in gold. This number became the platoon's identity for the next eight weeks. If the platoon did well in drill or marksmanship, it would be awarded streamers to attach to their guidon. If the platoon performed poorly, the drill instructor might remove the guidon flag from its pole altogether, while screaming, "You idiots are nothing but a mob! You don't even deserve to be called a 'platoon!'" He would then march them around in front of the other platoons with just the naked pole—looking ridiculous.

Doug Dickey, Tim Barga, Bob Birt, David Thornhill, and Roger Young all became members of Platoon 394. The senior drill instructor for Platoon 394 was Staff Sergeant William L. Moore. His two assistants were Staff Sergeant K. B. Fedrick, and Sergeant J. E. Baughman. There were 76 men in the platoon.

The Dickeys were a very close family. Doug wrote home regularly throughout his time in the Marines. Even after he deployed to Vietnam, it was rare that a week would pass without Harold and Leona Dickey finding at least one letter from Doug in their mailbox. He addressed each letter, "Dear Mom & Dad." Doug wrote his first letter home after he and his friends had finished going through the Receiving Barracks and had been formed into Platoon 394. He started his letter cheerfully, "I am doing fine ... It really isn't so bad as I heard so." He was candid about most of his experiences, even passing along some of the saltier expressions he picked up along the way. He closed each letter, "Your Loving son, Doug." While in boot camp, Doug regularly attended church services on Sundays and even mailed the chaplain's bulletins home to his parents.[14]

During his initial investigation of abuses at Parris Island after six recruits drowned in Ribbon Creek, Wallace Greene found 10 recruits in the base hospital with broken jaws—a result of beatings by drill instructors.[15] This kind of physical abuse was largely eliminated after 1956. During the Vietnam War, however, it was still common for drill instructors to "thump" recruits. This was usually a backhand to a man's chest.[16]

Doug reported some thumping with amusement in his first letter home. "Tim, Puff [Roger Young], Dave, Bob and I are doing fine. We have all got punched in the guts and slapped in the throat and around the head," he said. "A few of the Drill Instructor favorite words they call you are: Sweet Meat, Bucket of Puke, 4 eyes and other various things." He closed his first letter home cheerfully: "I must go now so be good and I will be OK."[17]

Bob Birt clearly remembered their platoon's drill instructors, particularly Staff Sergeant Moore. "He was pretty hard to get along with ... Sometimes they'd play the good-guy, bad-guy routine, and Moore was always the bad cop." However, Birt remembered the drill instructors as usually even-handed. "Don't get me wrong; if you didn't straighten out, I mean, they'd straighten your ass up pretty fast," he said. "But it wasn't anything I would consider 'abuse' as far as I'm concerned."

After moving into the Quonset huts, Platoon 394 began the first phase of their training. Officially, the main objective of the first phase of recruit training was to instill discipline. Others have described the first phase of boot camp as "the shock treatment." Throughout the first phase, the recruits are kept off balance. "It is the time we separate the men from the boys," according to one drill instructor. Another drill instructor summed up the process: "We completely break down their ego. Then we motivate them, very slowly building them back up into what we want them to be,

Marines," he said. "If they build up too fast or too much, then we break them back down. We lower the boom." If the platoon begins to gain too much confidence or the DIs see signs of too much cockiness too soon, then they will initiate a readjustment. "As far as I'm concerned," a DI said, "tomorrow they ain't gonna do nothin' right."[18]

Reveille for the recruits was at 0430. The drill instructors often signaled reveille by screaming and rattling a nightstick around the inside of a galvanized metal trashcan. The recruits were given 10 minutes to get dressed and assemble outside. They were immediately taken on a half-mile run and then formed for calisthenics in the sand-filled exercise area that was often called "The Pit." They were sweating and screaming cadences before the sun had risen. They went through a circuit of pull-ups, bends-and-thrusts, sit-ups, and push-ups—lots of push-ups. Few could do the last repetitions and withered under the drill instructors' screams. Exhausted and panting, they were run back to the huts and told they had minutes to shower, shave, dress, and fall out for chow. By the end of the first three hours of boot camp, most of the recruits couldn't imagine surviving the next eight weeks.

Doug had always been a powerful guy with broad shoulders. At home, he could work in the fields for hours. However, he usually carried extra weight around his waist. He had always been "husky." The drill instructors immediately flagged Doug as a "fat-body" and told him they were determined to sweat and starve the extra weight off him. They forbade him from eating most of the food in the chow hall at meals and assigned him more calisthenics and longer runs than the others.

Bob Birt felt so bad for Doug that he smuggled a hamburger patty out of the mess hall and brought it to him after lights-out one night. Birt shook his head remembering the scene: "He was so hungry. He ate the meat and the greasy napkin it was wrapped in," he said. "He was literally starving."[19] Doug didn't tell his parents about this, but he did write in one letter that he was "lucky" to pass the first physical training test.[20]

Doug wryly reported on some of the deliberate absurdity orchestrated by the DIs. There was nothing but sandy dirt around the Quonset huts. However, the drill instructors had arbitrarily designated certain patches of the sand as "grass." They decreed that these dirt patches be raked and even watered twice a day.[21] "Each morning we get up we make our beds and scrub and mop the floors and rake the area outside," Doug reported. "The ground around our Billets is nothing but sand, but the Drill Instructors call it grass, and you do not walk on the grass."

The recruits spent most of their first days exercising and marching. The physical training, "PT," as it was universally called, got progressively tougher during boot camp. The recruits would PT every day until they graduated. The days were filled with runs and hours of calisthenics in the sandpit.

The only activity that absorbed more time than PT was close order drill. Drill has been the centerpiece of military training for professional armies since the Spartans began marching into battle formed as phalanxes around 500 B.C. Marine recruits spent countless hours on the 20-acre asphalt parade deck at the center of the depot practicing close order drill. Drill taught teamwork because each man in the platoon had to constantly synchronize his movements with the men around him. Those who hesitated or bungled a move disrupted the platoon's formation. It taught discipline because, as a team, they had to immediately and precisely execute the orders of the drill instructors. The recruits spent hours every day marching back and forth on the "grinder" under the hot sun following the hypnotic guttural cadences and commands of the drill instructors. Every day, their movements became sharper. Soon the platoon moved in unison, not as a group of individuals—but as a single confident body.

In the late mornings and afternoons, the recruits attended classes taught by members of the special instructor team. Forty special instructors augmented the drill instructor staff. The instructors often infused their classes with profane anecdotes and always stressed the high standards recruits had to meet before they would be called Marines. An instructor might begin a class on Marine Corps history with a slap at the army or navy. "The doggies don't have any history classes in basic training because they don't have any history…" he would say with a sneer.[22]

The special instructor staff also taught the "drown-proofing" training at the swimming pool, as well as bayonet and hand-to-hand combat instruction. Several of the NCOs who taught the hand-to-hand combat course were first-degree black belts in judo or karate.[23] "We also had a couple of classes on bayonet training which is kind of fun," Doug wrote.[24] "The other day we had our 5th and 6th class of hand to hand combat. In the class we really worked each other over. We used flips and choking holds on our opponent. It was really fun."[25]

The reality of the war in Vietnam was impressed upon the recruits during the weekly parades. The recruits stood in formation while awards were presented to Marines who had just returned from Vietnam. Doug's platoon was in the formation for an award ceremony on May 5. Major General Bruno A. Hochmuth, the Depot's Commanding General, presented 15 combat awards to Marines who had recently returned from Vietnam. Three of the men were awarded Bronze Star Medals for heroics on the battlefield.

Corporal Frank Garcia was one of the men who received a Bronze Star Medal with Combat "V" that day. Garcia had been assigned to the 9th Marines in December 1965. He was a member of a patrol that came under "intense and deadly accurate enemy small arms and automatic weapons fire." According to the citation: "Garcia ran to the aid of a wounded comrade and calmly used his web belt as a tourniquet to stop the profuse bleeding from the Marine's severed leg artery. He then threw himself across the wounded man's chest, shielding him from hostile fire until a corpsman arrived and the wounded Marine could be moved to safety." General Hochmuth also presented four Purple Heart medals to men who had been wounded in Vietnam. For Private First Class Isidoro H. Lopez, it was his second Purple Heart.[26]

"Thursday our Series was in a parade on the parade deck in which 15 medals were presented to a few people for bravery in action and other things," Doug wrote home.

The ceremony had a sobering effect on him. "I was wondering whether you paid my Life Insurance up yet or not, so if you haven't you had better do so right away."[27]

Before leaving for Edson Range, Platoon 394 had another PT test. "Monday of this week we took our X-1 test, but unfortunately, I did not pass this test…" Doug wrote. "I seem to be losing weight because of the running and because I am on a diet."[28]

Platoon 394 was trucked up to Edson Range in the second week of May to start their marksmanship and weapons training. Located on Camp Pendleton, 40 miles north of San Diego, the range was named after "Red Mike" Edson, one of the most famous Marines of World War II. Among his many accomplishments, Edson commanded one of the elite Marine Raider battalions and earned the Medal of Honor while holding "Bloody Ridge" on Guadalcanal against fanatical Japanese assaults. The enormous range complex was a fitting tribute to Edson's memory. Edson had also been one of the Marine Corps' top competitive riflemen.

Camp Pendleton is very different from the recruit depot. The recruit depot is located in the middle of San Diego, wedged between the international airport and the interstate highway. It is surrounded by buildings and concrete. Airliners taking off from Lindbergh Field fly directly over the depot every ten minutes and drown out any other sound. A small section of the base is exposed to San Diego Bay, but it's just a boat marina. There's no beach.

Camp Pendleton, on the other hand, is 200 square miles of undeveloped rolling hills. The land has remained largely untouched since Junipero Serra traveled through it in the 18th Century. The base is teeming with all kinds of wildlife: tarantulas, rattlesnakes, mountain lions, mule deer, and even bald eagles. Camp Pendleton's rolling hills meet the Pacific Ocean along 17 miles of the most beautiful and pristine sand beaches in California.

While many of the facilities at Camp Pendleton are located miles inland, Edson Range was one of the few located on the coast. The barracks buildings at Edson Range looked out across the highway to the beaches and the sparkling blue Pacific Ocean. Doug was immediately enchanted by the Pacific. "Where we are right here," he wrote to his parents after getting to Edson Range, "we can see the ocean from our windows. Highway 101 runs right by Camp Pendleton and the ocean is on the other side of the highway. You ought to see the surfers out there in the morning, and all of the sailboats," he said, "it sure looks nice.[29]

Rifle marksmanship has been the cultural hallmark of the Marine Corps since before World War I. "Every Marine is a rifleman" isn't just a slogan. It's a core principle that has driven Marine Corps doctrine and training. Marines qualify with their weapons every year and all Marines, from private to general, proudly wear their marksmanship qualification badges on their service dress uniforms.

Much of the classroom instruction during the first phase of boot camp was preparing them for their time on the rifle range. They learned to recite the characteristics of the M14 rifle and to disassemble and reassemble their rifles in seconds—even blindfolded. They had to memorize "My Rifle—The Creed of a United States Marine." Written by Brigadier General William H. Rupertus during World War II, the creed poignantly establishes the relationship between a Marine and his rifle: "Before God, I swear this creed. My rifle and myself are the defenders of my country. We are the masters of our enemy. We are the saviors of my life."

Rifle marksmanship is taught as an almost Zen-like art in the Marine Corps. Consequently, the atmosphere at Edson Range was much more subdued than at the recruit depot. The rifle range was run and staffed by top shooters. These Marines, officially known as Primary Marksmanship Instructors, or "PMIs," controlled the range and coached the recruits through the marksmanship training.[30] The PMIs strove to coach the highest scores from every recruit on the range and among the PMIs, there was a running competition as to whom among them got the most recruits qualified as experts on each range detail.

Doug and Platoon 394 spent three weeks at Edson Range. They were assigned as the "maintenance" platoon for the first week, responsible for cleaning the buildings, assembling targets, and doing the laundry for the other platoons.

Military service is a broadening experience for most young men. Among other things, it's the first time most of them meet people from other parts of the country. "That's one thing about the service," Doug wrote home, "you meet a lot of people from different places. We have a guy from Virginia, two guys from Arkansas, two from Louisiana and that is all of the guys from the South. There are a lot of guys from Oregon and Ohio out here. The two guys from Dayton are real nice ... we have a couple of married guys that were going to be drafted so they enlisted in the Marine Corps. We also have a couple of guys with 2 or 3 years of college and they are here for one reason or another."[31]

The first week of marksmanship training was known as "grass week." It was called grass week because the recruits spent it on the grassy area adjacent to the range practicing their shooting positions and "dry-firing" their rifles. This stage of marksmanship training was known as "snapping in." At no point during the week did the recruits touch any ammunition.

The week began with classes explaining the geometry, ballistics, and physiology behind effective marksmanship. These were followed by classes explaining how rifle sights work and how to adjust them for range and windage.

The PMIs then taught the recruits how to assume the four positions they would use to qualify: the standing, kneeling, sitting, and prone positions. Each of the positions required stretching muscles and twisting limbs into unaccustomed places. From each position, the recruits then practiced methodically breathing and squeezing their triggers, "dry-firing," at miniature targets painted on 55-gallon drums. They spent hours and hours practicing their positions and dry-firing at the drums.

Doug enjoyed the platoon's first week. "Well this week is really packed full of goodies," he wrote home. "We started snapping in with our rifle and my muscles really hurt from some of the positions."[32]

Staff Sergeant Moore continued the regimen of PT and inspections when the platoon wasn't actually on the range. Running up and down the hills on Camp Pendleton was tougher than running on the flat recruit depot. "Speaking of running," Doug wrote, "the other night we went on a little 4 mile run through a few hills. This was quite taxing on me but I made it. We saw a few rattlesnakes and tarantulas on our way also. The other night on guard duty one of the guys killed a rattlesnake and was scaring some of the guys with the rattles."[33]

Platoon 394 fired their rifles for the first time on May 19. Raised in the country, Doug and his friends had all fired rifles before. "It is a lot of fun to fire the M-14 rifle and it doesn't kick any, in fact I didn't feel a thing," Doug wrote. "Of course the barrel will tend to rise, but it always comes back down. We fired 15 rounds, five were slow and ten rapid fire from the sitting position, and like I said it was a lot of fun. Saturday we are supposed to fire the .45 cal. Pistol to get familiar with it." Harold Dickey probably smiled a bit when he read his son's letter. He had gone through the same routine 23 years earlier on the rifle range at Parris Island.

Doug discovered the hard way that the Marines running Edson Range were severe whenever any safety precaution wasn't followed. "Well Wednesday I goofed up on the school range. I left one of my magazines in my rifle and the instructors gave me one hundred squat thrusts. I haven't left a magazine in a rifle since then."

The platoon did something to irritate Staff Sergeant Moore one day. Doug didn't mention the details of their transgression but Moore had all 75 men in the platoon jam into a 10-foot by 14-foot area in the Edson Range sandpit and start doing PT. "… boy did we get dirty. It was filled with water also and it was cold."[34]

Doug wrote home the night before their qualification day: "First of all we are going to have qualification day tomorrow and I am pretty excited about that," he wrote. "I have been shooting pretty good all week and hope I will shoot expert tomorrow." Doug was still enchanted by the Pacific Ocean. "I just got up and looked out the window and saw two sailboats," he added.[35]

The recruits started qualification at the 200-yard line. The first 10 rounds were "slow-fire" from the standing position at a 12-inch-diameter bull's-eye target. They were given 10 minutes to fire the 10 rounds, allowing them to carefully aim each shot. The next 10 rounds were "rapid-fire" at a silhouette target. In the rapid-fire string, each shooter had to get down into the sitting position from the standing position; fire five rounds; reload with a fresh magazine; and fire another five rounds. They had one minute to fire all 10 rounds.[36]

At the 300-yard line, they fired 10 more rounds slow-fire, this time from the kneeling position. Then, they fired another 10 rounds rapid-fire from the prone position.

The last string of fire for qualification was 10 rounds of slow-fire from the prone position at the 500-yard line.[37] The shooters had 10 minutes to fire the 10 rounds. From 500 yards, the 20-inch bull's-eye target looked like a tiny speck dancing above the rifle's front sight post. A man had to know what he was doing to hit the target from the 500-yard line. His breathing, his body position, and the way he placed the sling on his arm, had to be correct. Luck played no part in hitting the target from 500 yards. Improper breathing or the slightest flinch would throw the shot completely off the target and into the dirt.

Those who qualified on the rifle range were classified either as experts, sharpshooters, or marksmen, depending on their scores. Expert was the highest qualification followed by sharpshooter; marksman was the minimum qualification. Failing to qualify on the rifle range was a serious problem for a recruit.

"Well, Happy day has come," Doug wrote at the end of Platoon 394's qualification day. "I qualified with my rifle. I scored 215 points out of a possible 250 and I will get a Sharpshooter badge." It was the highest score he had shot all week. "In fact all five of us qualified today," Doug said. "Tim made expert and Puff, Dave and I made sharpshooter, while Bob got marksman. We are all proud of ourselves." Doug was rightfully proud of his shooting at the 500-yard line. "I got 47 points out of 50 from the 500 yard line."

The platoons were in competition with each other on the rifle range. The platoon with the highest scores was rewarded with the marksmanship pennant, which they hung on their guidon. In addition to being pleased with his own performance on the range, Doug was able to boast that Platoon 394 also won the range competition. "Getting back to the range, we got the pennant for taking the range." Despite the rough time he was having in boot camp, Doug was proud to be part of Platoon 394. "We have a pretty good platoon."[38]

Bob Birt remembered being relieved when their platoon won the marksmanship pennant. "There is a lot of competition between the drill instructors," he said. "It was the only one [pennant] we won. But it's the one they [the drill instructors] wanted the most." Staff Sergeant Moore seemed somewhat mollified by the victory. "It would have been a lot harder after the range if we hadn't won," Birt said with a laugh, "so that was good."

Platoon 394 was scheduled to graduate on June 14. With their rifle qualification done, the recruits in Platoon 394 cleaned up their barracks and prepared to head back to San Diego to finish their last phase of training. Doug was looking forward to it. The drill instructors had continued to single him out and push him. He usually did more exercises and was still on a restricted diet. He was harangued when he fell behind on the runs. Bob Birt remembered Doug struggling: "He kept doing his best," he said. "But, you expect a guy to do all that PT and you're feeding him nothing but lettuce. It just didn't sound right."

Although he was usually upbeat, Doug revealed a little bit of his suffering in one of his letters home toward the end of his time at Edson Range. "We only have three weeks of this hell to go through as of Tuesday and I will be glad to get out of it. I wouldn't go through what I went through up to now for nothing."[39]

The recruits were trucked back to San Diego for the last phase of their training. The last two weeks of boot camp revolved around final tests, inspections, and preparing for graduation. "Well we haven't too much time left in this Hell and it is getting pretty rough…" Doug wrote home. Platoon 394 posed for their platoon photo on May 31. Doug was standing in the front row, just behind the guidon flag.

Platoon 394 took their last physical fitness test a few days after returning from Edson Range. Unfortunately, Doug didn't pass the test.

Staff Sergeant Moore called Doug into his office and told him to pack his gear. He told Doug he wouldn't be graduating with Platoon 394. He was being dropped from Platoon 394 and "rolled back" to the Physical Conditioning Platoon at the Special Training Branch (STB). Doug quickly packed his sea bag and double-timed over to the Special Training Branch. He didn't have a chance to say goodbye to his friends or the other guys in the platoon. When the platoon came back from training that day, they saw that Doug's bunk was bare and his footlocker was empty. "We were just told he had been dropped," said Bob Birt.

The Special Training Branch was the collection point for those who were unable to meet graduation requirements for a wide variety of reasons. There were two outcomes for the recruits who ended up in the Special Training Branch. If they improved and met the standards to graduate, they were transferred back into a regular recruit platoon and graduated and they became Marines. If they failed to meet the standards, they were processed for discharge and sent home.

Being sent to the STB was the greatest fear for recruits. Life for recruits in the Special Training Branch platoons was significantly more horrible than it was for the regular recruits. Part of the philosophy of the STB was that the low-performing recruits needed additional "motivation." This motivation was provided by a team of the depot's most unyielding drill instructors. Their training schedule was stripped down to a series of punishing mental and physical tasks. To the other recruits, it seemed like the STB platoons never went to bed or ate. It seemed like they were always somewhere in the background running, doing squat-thrusts, or suffering some type of indignity, accompanied by the constant screaming of their drill instructors.

Tim Barga got a glimpse of Doug one afternoon after he had been transferred into the Physical Conditioning Platoon. Barga and the rest of Platoon 394 were marching on the huge parade deck and passed a cluster of drill instructors. The DIs were tearing into a lone recruit. The recruit was struggling to maintain his composure but was clearly starting to crumble under the intense abuse. As they marched by, Tim realized it was Doug. "He was surrounded by DIs and they were all screaming at him. He was being humiliated," Barga said. "I just felt so bad for him. He was my friend. And I hated to see that."

Harold and Leona Dickey hadn't received a letter from Doug in almost three weeks, which was very unusual. Finally, a letter arrived. "I imagine you were wondering why you didn't hear from me for a while," Doug wrote. "Well I was pretty ashamed to write and tell you about being dropped." He explained that he had failed his physical fitness test and had been rolled back. Platoon 394 had graduated while he was in the Special Training Branch. "I did not see any of the guys on graduation day but I just know they looked real sharp," he said. "I am just fine and doing OK right now. I have been in the sand pit quite a lot but aside from that I am doing fine."[40] By the time Doug wrote, he had managed to pass the physical fitness test. After passing the test, he was transferred into Platoon 3007 to complete his training.

Doug graduated with Platoon 3007 on June 25. It happened to be his father's birthday and he called home for the first time since he'd left. He talked to his parents for almost half an hour.

Doug found out his younger brother, Norman, had enlisted in the Marines while he was in boot camp. He wrote a letter to Norman shortly after he graduated, giving him some advice. He explained about the drill instructors and warned him about all the vaccination shots he would be getting. While his letters to his parents were more cheerful, his letter to his younger brother was more candid. "Boot Camp is a lot of hell," he told Norman. "You are being harassed constantly. No matter how good you may do something it will not be good enough for their standards … Your first two weeks are the worst because they affect you mentally and it really gets you down." Doug's closing advice reflected his broader view on life. He was both optimistic and realistic: "Boot Camp is a real bitch, but you have to make the best of it. In other words, it is what you make it. If you want it to be rough it will be, so don't goof off too much or you will pay for it."[41]

Watching Doug endure boot camp gave Roger Young even greater respect for his friend. "It was really hard on him," Young said, "but his personality came through—I mean, he didn't quit—and he came out of it, I think, a stronger person."

A Marine on his way to Europe during World War I explained to his mother the transformation he underwent in Marine boot camp. His words have resonated with generations of men who have gone through the Marine Corps' recruit depots. Reflecting on his training at Parris Island in 1917, he told his mother: "The first day I was at camp," he told her, "I was afraid I was going to die." Then he said, "The next two weeks my sole fear was that I wasn't going to die. And after that I knew I'd never die because I'd become so hard that nothing could kill me."[42]

After graduating, Doug was sent to the Infantry Training Regiment (ITR) at Camp Pendleton. ITR was the six-week school where new Marines were trained to be infantrymen. "It is kind of funny," he wrote during his first week at Camp Pendleton, "back at M.C.R.D., they called us slime, pukes, turds, maggots, and other little goodies. But here the first thing they call you is 'Marine.' I got a haircut today and he said, 'there is two quarters change Marine!' and it made me feel real good to be called a Marine for a change."[43]

In the same letter, he explained his reason for going to Camp Pendleton: "The reason I have 6 weeks of I.T.R. is that I am going to Viet Nam in October for about 13 months so I have to be prepared as best as possible. I hope this doesn't come as too much of a shock to you, it didn't me. So don't worry about it. But I thought I should tell you because I think you should know."[44]

Doug had a pleasant surprise during his first day at ITR. "I walked into morning chow and saw some of the other guys from 394 and then I saw Tim and he saw me at the same time and then I saw Dave and then Bob came from the other side of the mess hall and we ate chow together. I tell you, I was never so glad to see anyone in my life as I was to see those guys and they were glad to see me too." The other guys from Platoon 394 were in the ITR class ahead of Doug. "It was kind of hard for me to talk to them … because I had a big lump in my throat," Doug said. "I was so excited about seeing them." While they were eating breakfast, the five friends started making plans to explore Southern California together—including a trip to Disneyland. "Well Tim, Rog, Dave, Bob and I are all going to Viet Nam in October so we will be together once again."[45]

Over July and August, Doug was assigned to the 2nd Infantry Training Regiment, located at Camp San Onofre at the northern end of Camp Pendleton. While there was none of the harassment that characterized boot camp, the course at ITR was in many ways much tougher than boot camp. The days started at 0430 and often went until long after dark. There were classes on camouflage, land navigation, small unit tactics, and a long list of weapons. However, most of the days and nights were spent hiking up and down the steep hills, loaded with all the weapons and gear they would carry in combat. The first four weeks focused on basic weapons and tactics. The last two weeks taught more advanced topics, specifically the unique aspects of fighting in Vietnam. A lot of the field training was done at night.

Life for the new Marines was good despite the exhausting days. They usually had the weekends off and were able to explore Southern California. For boys who had grown up in rural Ohio, the world they discovered outside the gate was a dizzying and exotic place. It was full of hot rod cars, pretty girls, and beautiful beaches. It was a world they had only heard about in Beach Boys songs. It was a shock to discover the people and the places in the songs actually existed.

Doug apologized for neglecting to write for a while in one of his letters. "I can't give any excuses, but I did have a lot of fun," he wrote. "I caught up with the rest of the guys and we went down to the Beach Club and had a lot of fun together. All 5 of us were together again and did we have fun. Next weekend Tim Bob Rog and I are planning to go to Los Angeles to see a football game between the Rams and the Browns. We can get in for nothing if we are in uniform."[46]

Most of the instructors at ITR had just returned from Vietnam. They did everything they could to prepare the new Marines for combat. Doug tried to reassure his mother and father: "That is why I said we are better trained than the Marines who are just coming back, because we have samples of most of the weapons used by the VC today and our instructors are helping us out greatly."[47]

The Marine Corps was integrating the hard lessons being learned in Vietnam into the curriculum at ITR. The students had to patrol through a mock-up of a Vietnamese village, complete with actors playing villagers and Viet Cong soldiers. The village was also full of booby traps. "You should see a punji stake," Doug wrote, "it is unbelievable how bad you could get hurt by stepping on them. It is also clever how simple the devices they use against us are, just things a normal 6 year old kid could think of, but they are getting us with them."

Doug had been captivated by the Pacific Ocean since he first saw it while he was at Edson Range. He finally made it into the ocean for the first time during one of their weekend trips to San Clemente. "We had a real good time while we were in San Clemente last weekend. We went down to the beach on Sunday and went for a swim. I didn't think the ocean water was so salty, but you can really taste it." The ocean was a highpoint for him. "You should of seen the beach the other day! It was really nice, the water was warm and I got a bit of a tan."[48]

Doug finished ITR in the third week of August and got leave to go home. "If you could," he wrote to his mother in his last letter before he went home, "when I get home I want you to take a pair of trousers in about 4 inches around the waist for me. It is the first pair of trousers I was issued and they are quite big for me, so can you do that for me."[49]

One of the best days of Doug's life was his first Sunday home after boot camp.

Marines graduating from boot camp were only issued the forest-green service dress uniform. Those who wanted a set of the distinctive dress blues with the high collar and red piping had to go to the base tailor shop and order a set and pay for it with their own money. As soon as he could, Doug had gone to the tailor shop and spent more than a month's pay to buy himself a set of tailored dress blues.

On his first Sunday home, Doug and his family walked into the Rossburg Methodist Church, as they had just about every Sunday. However, when Doug walked in that morning, he was wearing his new dress blues. There were approving smiles and nods from the members of the congregation as the Dickeys took their place in the pews.

Doug had left their little town four months earlier. Those had been the toughest months of his life. An experience that would have embittered many young men, only made Doug more proud to be a Marine. He had met the challenge and had returned home successful—he was now a United States Marine. Leona Dickey smiled remembering that morning. "He was so proud to be a Marine."

PART II

WARRIORS

CHAPTER 5

I Corps: "Marineland"

"The terrain is rugged, the climate is often disagreeable by any standards, and the enemy is a tough, capable fighter."

A Marine's Guide to the Republic of Vietnam.[1]

By the time Doug Dickey and his friends arrived in the fall of 1966, Vietnam had become one of America's biggest and toughest wars.

More Marine units had quickly followed General Karch and the 9th Brigade into Vietnam. When the five boys from Darke County arrived in October 1966, there were 60,000 Marines in Vietnam. In the 18 months since Fred Karch came ashore on Red Beach, 1,700 Marines had been killed and more than 9,000 wounded.[2] At the same time, U.S. Army units had been arriving and building bases to the south.

The Marines were assigned responsibility for the I Corps Tactical Zone at the northernmost end of the country. The area was simply referred to as "I Corps," which the Americans usually pronounced as "eye corps." The five northern provinces in the country had been officially designated as I Corps at the end of 1964, three months before Karch and his brigade landed at Da Nang.[3] Among other things, the I Corps zone was significant because it included the border with North Vietnam along the Demilitarized Zone (DMZ).

Those coming from the southern part of the country could tell when they had entered the I Corps area. The jaunty *esprit* of the Marines was unmistakable. With their attitude, appearance, and terminology, the Marines created an atmosphere in I Corps that was distinct from the other military commands in Vietnam. All the signs in front of the buildings or tents were painted bright red with yellow lettering. Visitors found themselves immersed in nautical terminology. There were no latrines; they were "heads." Doors were called "hatches," floors were "decks," and ceilings were "overheads." Bristling at the Marines' confidence and unique traditions, some army officers in Saigon began snidely referring to I Corps as "Marineland."[4]

Giving the Marine Corps responsibility for the northern provinces wasn't an arbitrary decision. The planners assigned the northern region to the Marines because the Marine Corps' amphibious assault capabilities suited the geography.[5] The coastline in that area of Vietnam is dominated by broad, sandy beaches which were ideal for amphibious operations. The Marines could land almost anywhere along the coast and control the major cities and harbors without having to control the coastal highway that ran the length of the country. It was this operational reasoning that caused the Pentagon and General Westmoreland to assign General Karch and the 9th Marine Brigade to Da Nang in March 1965.[6]

On May 6, 1965, the III Marine Amphibious Force (III MAF) was established at Da Nang as the headquarters for all of the Marine units in Vietnam. III MAF was usually pronounced "three maf." The command had originally been named the Marine Expeditionary Force per the doctrine at the time; however, the word "expeditionary" was changed because it was feared it might evoke memories of the French Expeditionary Corps with the local Vietnamese. Anything that might raise a comparison to the French colonial era was strenuously avoided.

The man chosen to command all of the Marines in Vietnam was Major General Lewis W. Walt. Raised on a Kansas farm and orphaned early in life, "Big Lew" Walt worked his way through school and ended up at Colorado State College, where he earned a degree in chemistry. He was also captain of the football team. Walt joined the Marines in 1936 and served in China before war broke out with Japan. At the beginning of the war, he was leading a company in "Red Mike" Edson's famous 1st Raider Battalion. Walt earned a Silver Star leading his company during the assault on Tulagi.

Lew Walt was awarded the Navy Cross twice during the war. His first was at Cape Gloucester, New Guinea. Nine months later, he earned his second on Peleliu. Despite being seriously wounded at Cape Gloucester, Lew Walt had an unusually charmed life on the battlefield. On at least three occasions during his time in the Pacific, he emerged unscathed from firefights where men on either side of him were cut down. His luck stayed with him in Vietnam. He often directed his personal helicopter fly just over the treetops so he could spot enemy soldiers below. His helo was hit several times by enemy fire and twice he was hit with rounds. However, the slugs lost momentum penetrating the hull of the helicopter and left him with nothing more than a few scratches.

Among other things, Lew Walt was known for his volcanic temper, which he regularly unleashed on the officers around him. His light blue eyes seemed to make him even more menacing to those officers who became the objects of his wrath. His staff joked to each other about being "caught in the twin blues." However, Walt was not one to hold a grudge and quickly cooled off after his first reaction to bad news or unsatisfactory results. Those who were the focus of one of his upbraidings often found Walt's arm around their shoulder later while he told them he had faith in them.

While Walt was a severe taskmaster, particularly with his subordinate commanders and the officers on his staff, he was a different man with the young enlisted Marines. He made it a point to visit his wounded Marines in the hospitals around I Corps several times a week. Those who went along with him on those tours were struck by his humility and could see he was genuinely awed by the young Marines. He actually seemed a bit shy around the wounded Marines. While on his tours, Walt would present Purple Hearts and other awards to the men. Lew Walt said of those visits:

> Those who think a commander's function is confined to the exercise of authority should accompany one to a field hospital. I know of no combat commander who does not do this, often daily, not as a duty but as an obligation to the men whose broken bodies are the price of battle. With few exceptions the spirit of the men, even the most grievously wounded, is a moving and humbling experience. Their first questions are about their buddies and their units. They retain the winning spirit they had in battle even as the plasma drips into their open veins. Most commonly, their next concern is not for themselves, but for the anguish their being wounded may bring to their loved ones at home.[7]

Lew Walt had his staff use a Polaroid camera to photograph the impromptu bedside award ceremonies. He decided to use the Polaroid camera because he wanted to hand the photo to the Marine right then and there. It was the only way to ensure the man had a photograph to show to his family. Walt knew from experience that the chances of getting official photos to wounded Marines after they went into the medical pipeline and were evacuated back to the States was almost nil. When Walt was talking to a grievously wounded young Marine, it was common for him to come away solemn and teary-eyed. Lew Walt's relentless demands on his officers were fueled by his determination to ensure young Marines were not being killed and wounded because of unnecessary blunders by higher headquarters.[8]

Like many Americans, Lew Walt was surprised by the viciousness of the Viet Cong. To maintain control over the population, they carried out an unremitting reign of terror in the cities and villages. Assassinations, kidnappings, and bombings were a daily occurrence. "I had seen a lot of war before Vietnam, but never such war directed at unarmed civilians or projected by the random slaughter of innocents. It was war untempered by any mercy; worse, the good, the kind, the most helpless, were primary targets in this war."[9]

Reflecting on the early months of the war, General Walt said: "We had much to learn. The enemy was everywhere and nowhere. He was not uniformed, unidentifiable until he shot at you, unhampered by the laws of land warfare recognized by the formal states."[10]

Lew Walt commanded the most sophisticated force the Marine Corps had ever sent to war. Eventually, III MAF grew to be the largest force the Marine Corps ever deployed in combat. In addition to the infantrymen, artillerymen, and tankers of the

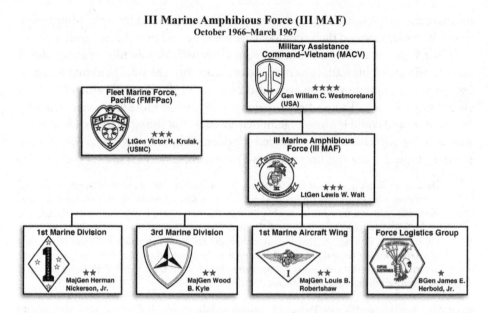

III Marine Amphibious Force (III MAF)
October 1966–March 1967

1st and 3rd Marine Divisions, Lew Walt also commanded the 1st Marine Aircraft Wing (1st MAW). Composed of dozens of Marine helicopter, fighter-bomber, reconnaissance, and transport squadrons, the 1st Marine Aircraft Wing gave Walt his own air force. To maintain and support this massive force, Walt also commanded an extensive Marine logistics force through the Force Logistics Group.

For the first five months after they arrived, American combat units were only allowed to conduct defensive operations around their bases or, in some specific circumstances, they were authorized to deploy to support South Vietnamese forces. These were basically rescue missions to bail out South Vietnamese units who found themselves in dire trouble on the battlefield. Wallace Greene, the Commandant of the Marine Corps, had referred to this defensive posture derisively as "sitting on your ditty box" after a visit to Vietnam in April 1965.[11]

However, in the five months following Fred Karch's landing, the situation for the South Vietnamese had continued to deteriorate. Furthermore, intelligence had detected increasing evidence that Viet Cong units were now massing for attacks against U.S. units—especially the Marine bases in I Corps.

In response, President Johnson decided to significantly escalate the American commitment to Vietnam. On July 28, 1965, at a noonday press conference, he announced both his decision to deploy 50,000 more troops to Vietnam and his decision to allow American combat units to begin initiating independent offensive operations against communist forces in South Vietnam.

With his announcement, President Johnson fundamentally changed the war in Vietnam: America was taking over.

General Walt and the other commanders in Vietnam had been anticipating the policy change for months. General Westmoreland quickly implemented the new policy. On August 6, he issued orders for Lew Walt to take the fight to the communist forces that had been building up around Chu Lai.[12]

On August 18, 1965, Walt launched Operation *Starlite* against the 1st Viet Cong Regiment. The six-day operation involved more than four Marine battalions and included amphibious landings, helicopterborne assaults, and massive artillery and air support. The Marines suffered 51 killed and 203 wounded. Operation *Starlite* was a disaster for the 1st VC Regiment. The U.S. force inflicted at least 623 casualties on the communist force.[13] Evidence suggested much heavier losses. Three weeks after the battle, a Vietnamese agent reported to American intelligence sources that the VC had eventually suffered 1,430 killed in the battle.[14]

Both the Marines and the Viet Cong left the battlefield after *Starlite* with a new and genuine respect for each other's fighting ability. Operation *Starlite* made one thing very clear: Fred Karch had been right. It was going to be a long and bloody war for America.

The war changed dramatically for the Marines in the summer of 1966. Until the Spring of 1966, General Walt and his Marines had been fighting Viet Cong guerrillas around the cities and villages along the coast. Most of the fighting took place in Quang Nam Province at the center of the I Corps zone. However, in 1966, Ho Chi Minh decided to invade South Vietnam and began sending his army directly through the DMZ into Quang Tri Province at the northern end of the Marines' zone. By the end of the summer, the Marines found themselves fighting a full-scale invasion by large, heavily-armed North Vietnamese Army divisions along the DMZ.

The Demilitarized Zone had been established to mark the border between North and South Vietnam as part of the 1954 Geneva ceasefire agreements that ended the fighting between the French and Ho Chi Minh. It was a five-mile-wide strip of land that roughly followed the Ben Hai River. It ran for 36 miles from the Gulf of Tonkin to the Laotian boarder. From 1956 until 1965, the International Control Commission (ICC), composed of representatives from Poland, India, and Canada, patrolled the DMZ to ensure neither country used the area for military purposes. In April 1965, North Vietnamese guards began refusing to allow the ICC members passage into the DMZ.[15]

Before 1966, North Vietnam had infiltrated its soldiers into South Vietnam by sending them down the Ho Chi Minh Trail—skirting just outside South Vietnam's western border. Hanoi had generally respected the treaty agreements regarding the DMZ. Using the Ho Chi Minh Trail allowed Hanoi to infiltrate their troops into South Vietnam and send them into battle posing as Viet Cong units. This supported Hanoi's claim that they were not directly involved in the war and that the war was being fought by South Vietnamese communists against their own government in Saigon.

However, Ho Chi Minh was forced to make a major strategic change in 1966. American-led operations in 1965 and early 1966 had devastated the communist forces in South Vietnam. Ho decided to abandon the façade that North Vietnam wasn't directly involved in the war and began sending the North Vietnamese Army straight through the DMZ to attack the American and South Vietnamese units. At the same time, North Vietnamese soldiers were told their military commitment was now "indefinite."[16]

In May 1966, American photo-reconnaissance missions began finding evidence of troop movement through the DMZ. The aircraft were using infrared heat-sensitive cameras. A smattering of white dots began to appear on the heat-sensitive film. The dots indicated campfires used by the NVA to cook. Within months, the film wasn't showing individual dots anymore, but rather large whited-out areas where hundreds of dots had fused into large white masses. Tens of thousands of NVA soldiers were moving through the DMZ.[17] Ho Chi Minh was sending large NVA units directly through the Demilitarized Zone into Quang Tri and Thua Thien provinces. The North Vietnamese Army was invading the two northern provinces in Lew Walt's zone. From July 1966 to January 1967, Hanoi more than doubled the number of NVA infantry battalions in I Corps from 14 to 32.[18]

General Westmoreland responded by shifting more and more Marine units to Quang Tri, the province adjacent to the DMZ. Intelligence assets were shifted to scour the DMZ for evidence of NVA divisions and regiments moving south.

In July 1966, General Walt launched Operation *Hastings* against the 324B NVA Division. It was the largest American operation of the war up to that point. Lasting from July 15 to August 3, 1966, *Hastings* eventually involved more than 8,000 Marines.

Fighting the NVA was very different than fighting the Viet Cong. "We found them well equipped, well trained, and aggressive to the point of fanaticism," Walt said of the NVA soldiers they fought during Operation *Hastings*. "They attacked in mass formations and died by the hundreds," he added, "They fought bravely and they fought well, and very few of them surrendered. Their men and ours slashed at each other by platoon and company, battalion and regiment, in dune and paddy and hill."[19] The Marines suffered 126 killed and 448 wounded in the bitter fighting. The NVA's 324B Division lost over 700 killed. The Marines managed to capture 17 NVA soldiers.[20] Lew Walt summed up the new situation for the Marines in Quang Tri: "Now we were in a situation similar to that in Korea in 1950—an army coming down from the north to seize and hold ground."[21]

After Operation *Hastings*, it was clear the Marines were fighting two distinct campaigns in I Corps. The 3rd Marine Division was fighting an invasion by NVA regulars in the two northern provinces, while the 1st Marine Division spent most of their time fighting the elusive Viet Cong in the more populated three southern provinces.

Despite the rapidly escalating fighting, President Johnson was still optimistic about the war in Vietnam. Speaking at a parliamentary luncheon in Canberra, Australia, on October 21, 1966, Johnson told the Australian leaders: "I believe there is light at the end of what has been a long and lonely tunnel. I say this not just because our men are proving successful on yonder battlefield. I believe it for this reason: there is a widening community of people who are beginning to feel responsible for what is happening in Vietnam."[22]

I Corps eventually became one of the most storied battlefields in Marine Corps history. Before the war in Vietnam ended, III MAF and its subordinate units in I Corps became the largest combat command in Marine Corps history. At its peak strength in 1968, there were 85,755 Marines fighting in Vietnam, exceeding the number of Marines ashore on either Iwo Jima or Okinawa.[23] By the end of the war, the Marine Corps had suffered almost as many casualties fighting in I Corps as it had fighting the Japanese in the Pacific during World War II.[24]

Some of the battles in I Corps became famous. Hue City, Con Thien, and Khe Sanh became legendary and took their rightful place alongside Iwo Jima, Belleau Wood, and the Chosin Reservoir in Marine Corps history. However, most of the Marines in I Corps fought over nondescript bits of land. They fought over hills that only had numbers to distinguish them from other hills. They fought over patches of jungle or paddies that could only be distinguished by their six-digit map coordinates. Casualty notices sent home to parents and wives during the war usually cited vague locations where loved ones were killed or wounded: "… the vicinity of Gio Linh."

Brigadier General Edwin Simmons was a veteran of some of the most brutal fighting in World War II and the Korean War. He took command of the 9th Marine Regiment on February 16, 1966 while the regiment was fighting the Viet Cong in the area south of Da Nang. Years later, he contrasted fighting in Vietnam with his previous combat experience. "I lost one or two or three killed every day [in Vietnam], five or six or eight or ten wounded every day. In the five or six months that I had the regiment, my total casualties would have been as great as the regiment had in a big fight at Bougainville or Guam." Then he added somberly, "The degree of satisfaction however, was considerably less."[25]

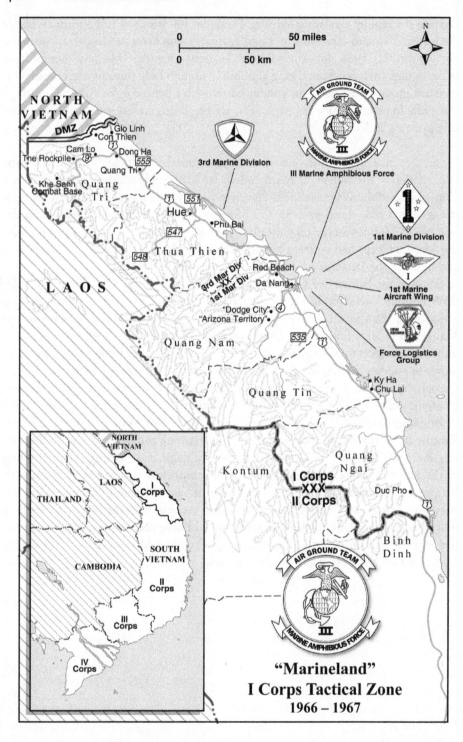

"Marineland"
I Corps Tactical Zone
1966 – 1967

CHAPTER 6

1st Battalion, 4th Marines: God, Country, Duty, Corps

"I am with a pretty good group of men."

PRIVATE FIRST CLASS DOUGLAS E. DICKEY

Doug Dickey reported to 1st Battalion, 4th Marines, on October 10, 1966. The battalion was headquartered at Dong Ha, just below the Demilitarized Zone. Dong Ha had become one of the key locations in Vietnam. It was only 12 miles from the DMZ, making it the northernmost city in South Vietnam. Furthermore, three major lines of communication intersected at Dong Ha, making it the hub of military operations in Quang Tri. In October 1966, most of the rifle companies in the battalion were patrolling in the surrounding hills and paddies as part of Operation *Prairie*.

1st Battalion, 4th Marines, was one of the oldest and most storied infantry battalions in the Marine Corps. Initially activated in 1911, it quickly saw overseas service. As part of the 4th Marine Regiment, it was deployed to the Dominican Republic in June 1916. The battalion had its baptism of fire and suffered its first casualties on June 27, 1916, at Las Trencheras during the regiment's campaign to rout rebel forces from their stronghold in Santiago.[1] After quickly defeating the rebels, the Marines spent most of the next seven years battling the vicious and well-organized bandits who terrorized the countryside. The battalion didn't return to the United States until August 1924, after more than eight years in the Caribbean.

Between October 1926 and February 1927, the battalion was called upon for a unique mission within the United States. U.S. Mail shipments, which often included several bags of cash, were increasingly targeted by heavily armed and violent criminals in the 1920s. On October 14, 1926, eight bandits, wielding shotguns and machine guns, attacked a convoy in Elizabeth, New Jersey. Before leaving with $150,000 in cash, they murdered the truck's driver, and wounded a guard, a police officer, and an innocent bystander in a hail of gunfire.

In response to the increasing violence, the Postmaster General asked the Secretary of the Navy to send Marines to help guard the U.S. Mail. As part of the force, 1st Battalion, 4th Marines, was assigned responsibility for guarding mail shipments in California and Nevada. Their orders were clear: "When our men go in as guards over the mail, that mail must be delivered or there must be a Marine dead at the post of duty."[2] The presence of the flinty leatherneck veterans of the Caribbean, armed with Thompson submachine guns and 12-gauge shotguns, ended the mail robberies.[3]

In February 1927, immediately after finishing their duty guarding the mail, 1st Battalion, 4th Marines, together with the rest of the 4th Marine Regiment, deployed to Shanghai, China, as part of the U.S. military force charged with protecting the American sector within the International Settlement there. The battalion remained in China for more than 14 years and became known as "China Marines." Proud of their exotic reputation and unique ties to the Far East, the battalion adopted a crest that featured a dragon wrapped around an Asian pagoda.

It was clear by the fall of 1941 that war with Imperial Japan was inevitable. Surrounded by thousands of Japanese troops since 1937, the International Settlement in Shanghai was deemed untenable and the order was given to evacuate the American citizens and U.S. military troops from China. Together with the rest of the American military forces, the Marines left Shanghai in November 1941 and sailed to Manila, where they joined General Douglas MacArthur's forces on Luzon.

The Japanese attack on Pearl Harbor on December 7, 1941, crippled the Pacific Fleet. With the fleet out of action, the American forces in the Philippines were isolated with no hope of resupply or reinforcement. Two weeks after the attack on Pearl Harbor, the Japanese landed more than 43,000 soldiers in the Lingayen Gulf and began pushing the American and Filipino defenders steadily back toward Manila. Outnumbered and isolated, the Allied force retreated to Corregidor, the fortified island at the mouth of Manila Bay.

General MacArthur mounted his final defense on Corregidor. On the evening of May 5, 1942, the Japanese began landing troops on the island. The beach was defended by 1st Battalion, 4th Marines. Battling under moonlight, the battalion's Marines inflicted devastating losses on the Japanese landing force, effectively destroying the first two battalions that tried to land.[4] However, by dawn, the Marines had committed their last reserves, and were steadily losing ground against the swarming Japanese landing force which, by then, was bringing tanks ashore. Despite their valiant efforts and bitter fighting, the Marines fell back to their final trench line in front of the Malinta Tunnel.

The defense of Corregidor was clearly doomed. Hoping to avoid the slaughter of more than a thousand wounded Americans and Filipinos lying in the Malinta

Tunnel at the center of the island, Major General Jonathan Wainwright surrendered the remaining Allied forces to the Japanese at just after noon on May 6, 1942.

Colonel Samuel L. Howard, the commanding officer of the 4th Marine Regiment, ordered all of the regiment's colors burned to prevent them from falling into Japanese hands. Then, along with more than 10,000 other American and Filipino soldiers, Colonel Howard and his Marines were marched away as prisoners of war.

The darkest chapter of the battalion's history was written during the next 40 months. Starvation, disease, and senseless murder by Japanese guards badly thinned their ranks over the next three years.

While the original members of the 4th Marine Regiment were struggling to survive as prisoners of the Japanese, the Marine Corps decided to reconstitute the 4th Marine Regiment from the disbanded Raider battalions. The "new" 4th Marine Regiment was established on February 1, 1944, on Guadalcanal. To show their allegiance to the men who were still held as prisoners, the new 4th Marines adopted the motto "Hold High the Torch." Additionally, the men of the newly formed regiment decided they would keep their regimental and battalion colors cased. They vowed not to unfurl them until they had liberated the Marines who were being held by the Japanese. The reconstituted 4th Marine Regiment saw action quickly and played major roles in the campaign to liberate Guam and in the bloody battle for Okinawa.

To punctuate the American victory after Japan surrendered in August 1945, the 4th Marine Regiment was chosen to be the first American combat unit to go ashore on mainland Japan.[5] After establishing their headquarters at Yokosuka, the 4th Marines held a formal parade to honor the regiment's recently liberated veterans of Corregidor. The liberated Marines were seated as the guests of honor at the parade. Although still gaunt and emaciated, they were proudly wearing crisp new Marine uniforms again. The men of the new regiment saluted sharply as they marched past the veterans of the "old" regiment. At the end of the parade, the regiment's colors were finally unfurled. For the first time since Colonel Howard had burned the regiment's colors in May 1942, the 4th Marine Regiment's colors were uncased. A thunderous cheer erupted as they broke loose and flapped in the breeze. Among those cheering that afternoon, the China Marines cheered the loudest. Many of them wept openly. After the ceremony, many of the recently liberated China Marines approached the officers in the regiment and said they wanted to reenlist.

Like most American military units, the battalion went through periods of activation and deactivation after World War II. In 1955, 1st Battalion, 4th Marines, was reactivated and stationed at Kaneohe Bay in Hawaii. The battalion was one of the first units deployed to Vietnam and had been in continuous combat since May 1965.[6]

When Doug Dickey arrived, 1st Battalion, 4th Marines, was commanded by Lieutenant Colonel Jack Westerman. "Blackjack" Westerman was a legend in the

Marine Corps. He enlisted in the Marines after the attack on Pearl Harbor and had fought in the Pacific. After the war, he attended Colgate University and then went back in the Marines as an officer. Shortly after being commissioned, he was shipped to Korea where he led a platoon during the vicious fighting to hold the Pusan Perimeter. Even among the hard-bitten Marine veterans of the Pacific island campaigns, and the desperate battles in Korea, Blackjack Westerman was a distinctly fearsome individual. He was a physically imposing man whose shoulders seemed to span the width of his desk—although he rarely sat at a desk.

One of Westerman's distinguishing marks was a gruesome scar on his left forearm. It ran from his wrist to the inside of his elbow. He had gotten the scar during the Korean War. After days of non-stop fighting on the Pusan Perimeter in 1950, Westerman had crawled under a poncho to take a nap. He awakened suddenly to find a North Korean soldier charging toward him. The North Korean soldier managed to run his bayonet into Westerman's arm, slicing it wide open. Unable to get to his rifle, Westerman grabbed one of the rocks he had been using to anchor his poncho and beat the North Korean soldier to death with it.[7]

Before he left Korea, Jack Westerman had earned the Navy Cross, America's second highest award for bravery. He was a platoon leader in 3rd Battalion, 5th Marines, at the time. When he saw four Marines ambushed ahead of his lines, he collected grenades from his men and ran out to rescue the men who, by then, were badly wounded, and pinned down by intense enemy fire. Westerman moved across 200 yards of fire-swept terrain, rushing forward, then dropping to the ground and throwing grenades; and then rushing forward again. After he reached the Marines, he picked up one of the wounded men and carried him back to his lines. As he made his way back, he had to repeatedly take cover from withering enemy fire. His back was seriously injured from carrying the man to cover.[8] Westerman's heroics were specifically detailed in the Marine Corps' official history of its fighting in Korea—an unusual distinction for a first lieutenant.[9]

Due to his injuries, Westerman was evacuated to a military hospital in Japan. After a brief recuperation, he was sent back to Korea. Three days after returning to his unit in Korea, Westerman was wounded and evacuated again. His buddies joked that his pay should be docked for "unnecessary transportation between Japan and Korea."[10] The back injuries Jack Westerman suffered in 1950 would plague him for the rest of his life. He spent much of his time leading Marine reconnaissance units in the years between the Korean War and his command in Vietnam.

Westerman took command of 1st Battalion, 4th Marines, on June 27, 1966. For the next six months the battalion was in one battle after another. Westerman's Marines were continually fighting the tide of NVA units crossing through the DMZ into South Vietnam.

One of the campaigns launched to stop the invading NVA divisions was dubbed Operation *Prairie*. Westerman's battalion was one of the lead units in the operation in late 1966 and repeatedly clashed with NVA units in the jungle-covered hills just south of the DMZ.

One of Westerman's most notable battles took place over four days in September 1966. On September 15, the battalion began a reinforced patrol north of the "Rockpile," the 700-foot spire of rocks that overlooked Route 9 and the DMZ. Company D was leading the battalion column, followed closely by Company B. The command element followed them, and the two remaining rifle companies brought up the rear of the column. The next day, the lead platoon of Company D ran into a large NVA force. It was later assessed to be an element of the 324B NVA Division.[11] The NVA tried to cut Company D in two but they weren't successful. Company D was soon completely engaged with the NVA in the thick jungle. The Marines found themselves often fighting hand-to-hand against waves of attacking NVA soldiers to keep from being overrun.

Company B managed to move up to reinforce Company D and the two companies formed a defensive perimeter. It quickly became clear the Marines were significantly outnumbered. By nightfall, the two companies were completely encircled by a much larger NVA force—later assessed to be a regiment. Captain Daniel K. McMahon, Jr., the Company D commander, confidently reported to Westerman: "We have 'em right where we want them, they're all the way around us."[12]

For three days and nights, the two surrounded companies fought off wave after wave of NVA soldiers. Their situation was particularly tough during the first 36 hours. The fighting was often hand-to-hand in the dense jungle. Ammunition and supplies ran low and heavy enemy fire drove off helicopters attempting to resupply the companies. At noon on the 17th, a Marine helo attempting to get supplies in and evacuate wounded, was shot down. Luckily, it managed to crash-land within the Marine perimeter.[13]

Although Westerman was confident his Marines would prevail, he prepared for the worst-case situation—that the swarming NVA might be able to overrun the two companies due to their sheer numbers. He planned for Marine artillery to drop a barrage directly on top of the Marine positions. Westerman explained later:

> We did take a few defensive measures. We had every man in Bravo and Delta Company dig in to a depth of five feet. And then, once they dug their holes five feet deep; we had them dig back, so to speak—dig down and back. And the idea of this was that, if they did—or they were overrun—I'd worked it out with the battalion commander of the 3rd Battalion, 12th Marines, Lieutenant Colonel Kirchmann, that he was going to fire 1,000 rounds of 155[-mm] V.T. [variable time][14] right on top of the position. And I feel if he had done so, very few, if any, of our Marines would have been hurt after being dug down and back like they were—with the V.T. fuse. And then I'd move the other rifle companies up where they could counterattack immediately and restore the battle area.[15]

Westerman never came close to ordering the artillery strike on top of the Marine position. Instead, artillery and air support created a "ring of fire" around the companies, hammering the attacking NVA day and night. The ring of fire became one of Westerman's favorite tactical measures and he would use it repeatedly. The artillery fire and bombs from the supporting aircraft often landed within 30 meters of the Marines' perimeter. By the evening of September 18, the NVA had had enough and withdrew.

As Westerman had predicted, the engagement was a disaster for the NVA regiment. The NVA left 259 dead around the Marine perimeter. The weapons and equipment left behind and other grisly evidence indicated another 369 NVA dead had probably been dragged away.[16]

The Marines suffered 23 men killed in the battle. One of those killed was 20-year-old Corporal Benjamin A. Kenison from Jefferson, New Hampshire. In the opening seconds of the battle, one of the Marines in Kenison's squad was badly wounded and ended up trapped in the open. Kenison maneuvered his squad to cover the man with fire. Meanwhile, Kenison crawled up a steep slope under constant enemy fire to get to the Marine. After reaching the man, Kenison picked him up and tried to make a run for the friendly lines. Both men were killed by an enemy hand grenade. Kenison was posthumously awarded the Navy Cross.[17] Of the 47 men wounded in the battle, one of them was Jack Westerman—struck by shrapnel when an NVA mortar barrage hit his command post on September 17.[18]

Jack Westerman loved and respected his young Marines, and was proud that he had come up from the enlisted ranks. Of all of his medals, he was proudest of his Good Conduct Medal; because it is the only medal worn exclusively by enlisted Marines. Wearing it identified him as a "mustang"—an officer who had worked his way up through the ranks from private. "These young Marines today are just as good as any generation of Marines who've ever lived," he said in December 1966. "I look at these 18- and 19-year-olds and some of them are just exactly what I was in World War II." He attributed his battalion's success on the battlefield to the "ingenuity, and common sense, and guts" of his young Marines.[19]

Morale was very high in 1st Battalion, 4th Marines. Westerman's pride and confidence was infectious. "The Marine Corps is a pretty good outfit," Westerman said. "I just don't believe there's a force in the world that can ever give us too much trouble," he said. "I don't want to sound loudmouthed about this thing, or overly confident or something like that, but this is just a feeling that I have—and I think other Marines have the same feeling."

Reflecting on his experience in three wars, Westerman said of the Marine Corps' skill on the battlefield: "You know, we're a real bunch of pros and we've got this thing [fighting] worked out down to a fine science." He attributed success to good leadership on all levels and the fighting spirit of Marines. "We like to go [at the enemy] as Marines, and we've been trained this way all of our lives. We're hard to handle. I don't think any other force in the world can handle us."

Harold and Leona Dickey found a letter in their mailbox from Jack Westerman shortly after Doug reported to the battalion. In the two-page letter, Westerman apologized for having to "resort to a form letter." However, he wrote, "I am sure you can appreciate that the real intent and spirit of this letter is to establish a stronger bond between you and your son and the Marine Corps during this Vietnam crisis." He continued: "You can rest assured that your son's welfare as all his fellow Marines is the concern of his immediate superiors and the Commanding General of the 3rd Marine Division." In the letter, Westerman explained how they would be notified if Doug was wounded and he tried to reassure them: "Our medical care is considered the finest in the world … A casualty here in 3rd Marine Division can be under the emergency care of a surgeon even quicker than if he were at a base in the States." He further said that a chaplain was always present to help with any personal problems; and that religious services of all faiths were regularly and frequently conducted. After giving a brief description of the weather and the mail service, Jack Westerman closed his letter: "If at any time I can answer a question to relieve your anxiety, feel free to write." He then gave detailed instructions regarding how they should address any letters for his personal attention and gave his assurance that any letter he received would be held in confidence. Jack Westerman personally signed the bottom of the letter.[20]

Immediately upon arriving, Doug was issued his rifle, flak jacket, and other field gear, then told to report to 2nd Platoon of Company B. Second Platoon was led by Second Lieutenant Harold "Hedge" Deibert. Thirty-three-year-old Deibert had been a Marine for more than 15 years. He was one of the seasoned staff non-commissioned officers promoted to second lieutenant in 1966. A Korean War veteran who later served as a drill instructor, he was one of the most experienced men leading a platoon.[21]

Doug had his first taste of combat two days after reporting to the battalion. On Wednesday, October 12, 2nd Platoon was dispatched to accompany four tanks from Company A, 3rd Tank Battalion, on a patrol. It was well-worn doctrine that tanks did not operate unless they were accompanied by infantrymen. Despite their formidable armament, tanks were vulnerable—especially in the thick vegetation and broken terrain along the DMZ. The infantrymen served as the eyes and ears of the patrol, looking for mines and tank traps, and screening the tanks from close-in attacks by enemy sappers.

The patrol left the combat base at Dong Ha on the morning of October 12. Doug and the rest of the platoon were riding on the tanks. Just before noon, as the tanks were emerging from a fording site, they were hit with a high volume of fire from their left rear. The NVA soldiers fired several rocket propelled grenades (RPGs), and hit the tanks with a hail of machine-gun and rifle fire. The Marines dove off the tanks and took cover in some holes and brush around the tanks. Three of the tanks were damaged by RPG rockets and the platoon commander for the tanks, First Lieutenant Donald W. Rohleder,[22] was killed. Four of the tank crewmen were wounded.

The tanks deployed into a defensive formation and began returning fire. In their barrage, the tanks blanketed the area with more than 7,000 .30-caliber machine-gun rounds and 700 .50-caliber rounds. They also fired three high-explosive rounds from their 90mm main guns into the suspected NVA ambush positions.

The tankers' most devastating response, however, was the canister fire from their main guns. The canister rounds were like large shotgun shells—each round sending a swarm of more than 1,200 small metal discs tearing through the air. The tankers methodically blasted away at the enemy positions with one round after another. With each blast, the canister fire scythed away swaths of vegetation. Enemy soldiers caught in the pattern were shredded. The tankers had fired 24 canister rounds by the end of the firefight. They counted eight dead enemy soldiers around their position when the smoke cleared. Evidence indicated another 15 had also been killed or seriously wounded.[23]

"We were fighting for about 3 hours then we stopped and the squad I am in went up front along a creek bank and laid down," Doug wrote home the next day. The squad caught some NVA soldiers trying to cross a stream. The soldiers' heads were exposed. "About 5 minutes later someone down the line fired off a couple of shots so we all opened up and then my squad leader shot one in the head and then I shot him also," Doug wrote. "So we got three of them …"

The platoon continued the patrol after the firefight at the creek—the Marines walking behind the tanks for another three miles. The platoon was brought back to the combat base by helicopter that evening. Doug was candid to his parents about his first taste of combat: "I was scared shitless when I got off the tank but after I was called up I calmed down a little bit."[24]

By coincidence, Roger Young was also assigned to Westerman's battalion. Young, however, had been sent through additional schooling at Camp Pendleton before leaving for Vietnam, and arrived weeks after Doug. "I was scared to death," Young said of his reaction to landing in Vietnam. However, some of the shock was softened for Roger when Doug Dickey surprised him by meeting him at the airfield. "I caught a plane up to Dong Ha and when I jumped off the airplane—I'm this scared young kid—and there is Doug waiting on me," Young said. "He was at Dong Ha!" Doug had heard Roger was coming and arranged to meet him at the airstrip. "I jumped off of that C-130, and there he set on one of those mules."[25]

"He was the most excited guy to be there," Young said of Doug. "I was scared to death! And he was just setting there telling me how they had been on patrol … and firing their weapons … and I said, 'Oh my God, what have I gotten into?'" Young could see Doug had changed. "He had come to life," Young said. "You could just tell that he was not the same. He was not the same quiet guy that I left in high school. He really changed over there."

All five of the boys who enlisted together from Ansonia High School saw combat in Vietnam. Roger Young ended up assigned to the Weapons Support Group in the Headquarters and Service (H&S) Company, in 1st Battalion, 4th Marines. "We couldn't see each other a lot, but at least we could if we wanted to at times," Young said. Doug clearly relished the life in a Marine unit. "Oh, he loved it! I mean he loved it! He probably loved it more than the rest of us," Roger said. When asked why he thought Doug Dickey liked being a Marine infantryman, Young said: "He liked being part of a team—the camaraderie."

Tim Barga's memory of landing in Vietnam was echoed by many of the men who fought there. He also arrived in October 1966. Barga was assigned to Company K, 3rd Battalion, 4th Marines. "You think you're pretty invincible at that age," he said. "Then you land there."

The reality of war hit him as soon as he walked off the plane at Dong Ha. "I'll never forget getting there," Barga said. "A chopper came in and they threw a [dead] guy off in a poncho ... then some Marine Corps Recon guys landed and it looked like they'd been chewed up and spit out ... they looked so damn bad ... and then some more wounded came in." Tim was in shock before he had even gotten off the tarmac. "And I'm this little corn-fed boy from Darke County, Ohio, you know. And I'm going: 'Shit! I can really get hurt here!'" War was different than anything he had imagined. "It was scary!" Barga said. "It's all fun and games until you see it ... then the reality sets in." Tim Barga said his immediate reaction upon arriving in Vietnam was: "Oh shit! This is a scary place!"

Bob Birt and David Thornhill also arrived in Vietnam in October. They were both assigned to 1st Battalion, 5th Marines, also as riflemen. Fifth Marines was part of the 1st Marine Division. As such, it operated in the southern half of the Marine Corps' area of responsibility. While Doug, Tim, and Roger faced the NVA up along the DMZ, Bob Birt and Roger Thornhill found themselves chasing the Viet Cong from their base on Hill 54 near Chu Lai. "As far as day-to-day life," Birt said, "it was patrols, and bunker watch, and ambushes." Bob expressed the same frustration most had when fighting the elusive Viet Cong guerrillas: "The enemy would be in front of you one day and behind you the next." Struggling to find the right words to sum up that year of fear, misery, and tedium he spent in Vietnam; he finally said, "It was just—*war*."[26]

Two months after Doug arrived in Vietnam, a second member of the Dickey family landed in Vietnam. On the day after Christmas 1966, Paul Dickey reported to the 1st Marine Aircraft Wing at Da Nang. Paul was Harold Dickey's youngest brother. Two years after he graduated from high school, Paul decided to join the Marines—as his older brother had twenty years earlier. He was trained as a communications specialist and was assigned to the unit that maintained the Aircraft Wing's telephone network. Paul was Doug's uncle, although he was only a few years older.[27]

1st Battalion, 4th Marines, spent October defending the Dong Ha combat base and supporting Operation *Prairie*. For most of the Marine riflemen in Vietnam, life was a series of exhausting hikes into "the bush" hunting the NVA soldiers or Viet Cong guerrillas. "The bush" was the term used by Marines to refer to the rice paddies and jungles outside the barbed-wire perimeters of the combat bases. The only breaks from the patrolling were brief spells when they bivouacked at one of the hilltop combat bases for a night or two before going back out.

Some areas of the bush were worse than others. A dry and bellicose sense of humor is a timeless tradition among combat infantrymen. Just about everybody and everything gets a nickname. Some regions became infamous and picked up nicknames because they were infested with enemy units and were the scenes of repeated battles and bitter firefights. The Marines nicknamed the area north of An Hoa "The Arizona Territory," likening it to the lawless badlands of the Wild West.[28] Likewise, those in the 1st Marine Division nicknamed an area north of the Song Thu Bon River "Dodge City."[29] The area Westerman's Marines fought over most was nicknamed "Leatherneck Square." It was the jungle-covered hills in the quadrangle traced between Gio Linh, Dong Ha, Cam Lo, and Con Thien.

With the monsoon season in full swing, it rained heavily during October 1966. Most of the Marines had never experienced such torrential, seemingly relentless rain. The area around Dong Ha got more than 30 inches of rain in October. Most of it fell in one week between 17 and 24 October. The rivers in the area overflowed their banks into the surrounding paddies; pontoon bridges were damaged.[30] The Cam Lo River flooded, causing one of the platoons defending the bridge to displace to higher ground. The ground became so soggy that units had to build their defensive positions above ground.[31]

In late 1966, the 3rd Marine Division decided to organize a security force to protect the Marine convoys carrying supplies up and down the roads in its area of responsibility. This convoy defense operation became known as the "Rough Rider" force. To man the force, 3rd Marine Division headquarters ordered its subordinate infantry battalions to transfer Marines to their headquarters. In October 1966, Lieutenant Colonel Westerman received orders to detach Company C from his battalion and send it to the division headquarters to become part of the Rough Rider security force. On October 14, Captain D. M. Atkinson and the rest of Company C transferred to the 3rd Marine Division headquarters. Westerman was now left with only three rifle companies and was told there would be no replacements to reconstitute the lost company.

At the end of October, Westerman was ordered to move his battalion 60 miles south from Dong Ha to Phu Bai. His mission was to take over responsibility for defending the Marine base at Phu Bai. Phu Bai, which was about eight miles southeast of Hue, was a critical base in the Marine Corps' network of bases. Among other things, Phu Bai was built around a busy runway and was the logistical hub for the 3rd Marine Division. Westerman's mission was to secure the base, as well as the area north of it up to the southern edge of Hue. Westerman's battalion was dispatched to relieve Lieutenant Colonel Arnold Bench's, 2nd Battalion, 4th Marines.

The battalion began their move to Phu Bai on the morning of November 2. Some platoons flew down to Phu Bai by helicopter while the rest of the battalion rode down in trucks.

Doug and 2nd Platoon made the trip from Dong Ha in trucks, rumbling down Highway 1. Due to decades of bloody fighting along its route, Highway 1 was dubbed the "Street Without Joy" by French journalist Bernard Fall in his landmark 1961 book. One of the advantages of making the trip in trucks was that they got to see Hue City.

War had bypassed Hue, for the most part. An ancient imperial city, Hue had served as the capital of Vietnam for centuries and was considered the heart of Vietnam's cultural and intellectual life. Out of respect for Hue's historic value, both the communists and the South Vietnamese government had avoided military activity in the city.

Hue was a beautiful city. Unlike the primitive villages the Marines had seen since arriving in Vietnam, Hue was a city with elegant buildings built centuries ago. The architecture was a combination of classical Chinese and imperial French. The broad avenues were paved with stone and lined with huge trees. The Perfume River ran through the middle of Hue. The area north of the river was called "The Citadel." It was built as a fortress and was surrounded by stone walls 15 feet thick and 20 feet high. It even had a system of moats, adding to its exotic and mysterious allure. The ancient Imperial Palace sat in the center of the Citadel. The area south of the Perfume River was generally referred to as the "New City." The New City was the center of much of Hue's modern life. The city's modern hospital, Hue University, and a small MACV compound were all located there.

Doug was impressed by Hue. "You wouldn't believe how beautiful that city is," he wrote home. "It really has some beautiful buildings, comparable maybe to Greenville but only more pretty, because it is still influenced by France."[32]

Doug and his friends were some of the last Americans to see Hue in its pristine condition. Fifteen months after they drove through the city, two North Vietnamese Army regiments invaded the city as part of the 1968 "Tet Offensive." The battle for Hue became one of the bloodiest and most destructive battles of the war. U.S. and Vietnamese units retook Hue after weeks of brutal house-to-house fighting. By the end of the battle, much of the ancient city was in ruins.

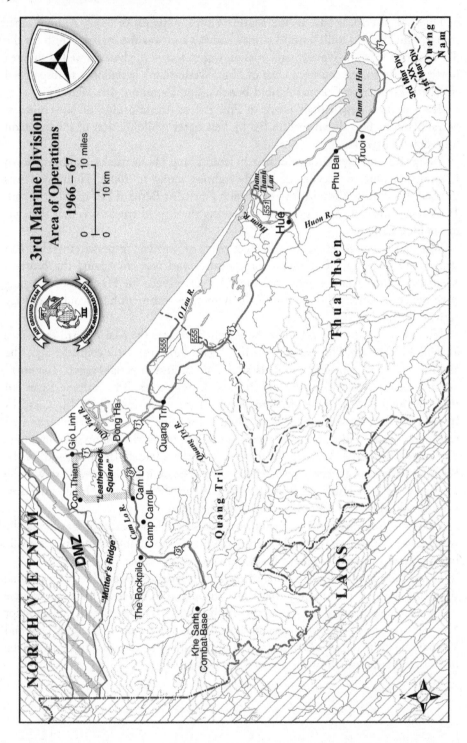

3rd Marine Division
Area of Operations
1966 – 67

CHAPTER 7

Norman

"I let them know that he [Doug] was over there and it was my intention to go over there and take his place."

NORMAN DICKEY

A third member of the Dickey family was beginning his journey to Vietnam while Doug was adjusting to life in 1st Battalion, 4th Marines. At the recruit depot in San Diego, Doug's younger brother, Norman, was going through boot camp.

Norman Dickey was the polar opposite of his older brother in many ways. Norman excelled in several sports and was considered one of the toughest guys in his class. He lettered in most of the sports offered at Ansonia High School. He was almost a head taller than Doug and was lean and muscular. Seeing the two brothers together, one could easily mistake Norman as the older of the two.

Norman's temperament was also very different from Doug's. Doug's enlisting in the Marines was a surprise to many who knew him. However, no one was surprised when Norman enlisted. Tim Barga was also a friend of Norman's. "He was a hard ass!" Barga said with a laugh, "Norman wasn't afraid of nothing. Norman wasn't afraid of the devil!"

As soon as Norman graduated from Ansonia High School in 1966, he went straight to the Marine recruiter and enlisted. Unlike Doug, Norman didn't want any delay. He wanted to head for boot camp as soon as possible. He left for San Diego almost before the ink was dry on his enlistment papers. Furthermore, he was enlisting specifically to go to Vietnam. "Norman was 'gung ho!'" according to Paul Dickey.

However, as Norman was getting ready to graduate from boot camp, the staff at the recruit depot brought him in and told him he wasn't eligible for orders to Vietnam. Norman had run up against the "Sullivan Brothers" regulations.

The regulations were a result of the Sullivan Brothers' tragedy in World War II. The five Sullivan brothers from Waterloo, Iowa, enlisted together in January 1942. As part of their enlistment, they stipulated that they wanted to serve on the same ship together. Consequently, they were all assigned to the USS *Juneau*, a light cruiser. In November 1942, the *Juneau* was torpedoed in the seas off Guadalcanal. The Japanese torpedo hit the ship's ammunition magazine, touching off a massive explosion. The ship sank within minutes, taking most of her crew with her to the bottom.

Ship losses were classified at the time. The boys' parents, Thomas and Alleta Sullivan, weren't informed they had lost all of their sons until months later. The Sullivan brothers became an inspiration to the country. Americans rallied around Thomas and Alleta Sullivan. Their unfathomable loss became a symbol of sacrifice and patriotism. The grieving parents helped promote war bonds in their sons' memory.

However, the loss of the Sullivan brothers was also seen as a cautionary tale. The War Department enacted policies to prevent other parents from suffering the same loss as Thomas and Alleta Sullivan. Each of the services instituted regulations to prevent family members from serving in combat at the same time. It was this set of regulations that brought Norman Dickey into the admin offices at the recruit depot in the fall of 1966. The staff at the recruit depot told Norman that Marine Corps policy prohibited two brothers from serving in Vietnam at the same time. Consequently, they told Norman he was ineligible for combat service in Vietnam because Doug was already there.

Norman was adamant that he had to go to Vietnam. "That was the reason I enlisted!" he said. "I let them know that he [Doug] was over there and it was my intention to go over there and take his place." The Marines told Norman there was only one way he could get orders to Vietnam: He would have to sign a series of waivers and agreements; and the Marine Corps would have to transfer Doug out of Vietnam. Norman Dickey recalled the scene in the admin office later: "I signed a lot of paperwork, and they agreed to let me go and he was supposed to come back." In the end, the admin officer approved Norman's orders for a combat assignment in Vietnam. At the same time, the admin officer initiated the process to bring Doug home early.[1]

Doug was in Quang Tri with Company B participating in Operation *Prairie* while all this was happening and had no idea Norman had managed to get orders to Vietnam, or that his younger brother had volunteered to take his place.

CHAPTER 8

Company C

"I got good men—really great Marines. All of them."

CAPTAIN ROBERT D. KELLEY

After getting settled in Phu Bai, Westerman decided to reconstitute Company C. He told Captain Robert D. Kelley he would be given command of Company C when it was reconstituted. Kelley was thrilled. Bob Kelley was a career Marine officer from St. Louis, Missouri. He was commissioned in 1957 after graduating from St. Louis University. In the years before Vietnam, he had a succession of assignments including commanding a rifle company in 1st Battalion, 6th Marines, at Camp Lejeune.

The chance to command Marines in combat was a tremendous honor for Bob Kelley. Like most Marine officers, Kelley, considered commanding a rifle company in combat to be the defining experience of a Marine officer's career. The opportunity was unexpected because he had already been selected for promotion to major and had been told he, therefore, was too senior to get a company command in Vietnam. Furthermore, he had already served as a company commander at Camp Lejeune. Getting command of Company C was a dream-come-true for Bob Kelley.

The new opportunity came with some concern though. The only way Westerman could rebuild Company C was by transferring Marines from the battalion's other three rifle companies. Kelley was leery that his reconstituted company was going to be formed by taking men from the other companies. It was common for unit commanders to use personnel transfers as an opportunity to get rid of their troublemakers and non-performers. He was worried that his new company would be made up of cast-offs and misfits from the other companies.

Jack Westerman fully understood Kelley's concern because he had been a victim of this practice during his career. Westerman prevented the wholesale dumping of low-performers and short-timers on Kelley by ordering that each company commander send an entire, intact platoon to Kelley. "He said he would relieve any man who sent me shitbirds," Kelley said.

The company commanders heeded Westerman's order and did as they were told. Bob Kelley ended up getting good solid platoons from the other companies. "I thought I was going to get a bunch of the problem cases, but Westerman made sure that didn't happen," he said. "I got good men—really great Marines. All of them." Kelley officially took command of the reconstituted Company C on November 7, 1966.[1]

Captain May, the commander of Company B, transferred 53 Marines from his company to Bob Kelley, including Hedge Deibert and 2nd Platoon. Doug Dickey and the rest of his platoon became Bob Kelley's 2nd Platoon.

On November 10, 1966, Westerman and his Marines took a break from their routine to celebrate the Marine Corps' 191st birthday. Celebrating its birthday is a central ritual in the Marine Corps. On November 10, Marines around the world pause to celebrate the birth of their Corps. No matter where they are, Marines mark the date with some sort of ceremony. The ceremonies range from lavish formal balls in Washington, D.C., to short gatherings between firefights by units in the field.

At Phu Bai, the battalion held a formation that included the traditional cake-cutting ceremony.[2] The ceremony started with the reading of Article 38 from the Marine Corps Manual. The article, written by John Lejeune, was incorporated into the ceremony in 1921. If a unit can do nothing else to commemorate the birthday, it will ensure Lejeune's message is read. Lejeune's words were as relevant to the Marines gathered in Phu Bai that day as they had been to the Marines of the "Old Corps" of 1921.

In his message to the Corps, Lejeune recounted the founding of the Marine Corps on November 10, 1775, by the Continental Congress. He traced the battle history of the Marine Corps and its distinguished service to the country throughout its existence, "… generation after generation of Marines have grown gray in war …" he wrote. Lejeune then spoke of the "eternal spirit which has animated our Corps…" His message closes with a timeless challenge that resonated with those standing in formation on the combat base at Phu Bai: "So long as that spirit continues to flourish Marines will be found equal to every emergency in the future as they have been in the past, and the men of our Nation will regard us as worthy successors to the long line of illustrious men who have served as 'Soldiers of the Sea' since the founding of the Corps."[3]

The reading of General Lejeune's birthday greeting was followed by the cake-cutting ceremony. The cake-cutting ceremony reminds Marines that the future of the Corps is passed from one generation of warriors to the next. While the reading of Lejeune's message is done with formality and reverence, the cake-cutting ceremony is more jovial.

During the cake-cutting ceremony, the oldest and youngest Marines in the command come forward and post themselves in front of the formation. The Adjutant then reads the birth dates of the two men and the dates that they entered the Marine Corps. Both men are subjected to good-natured ribbing as their particulars are read. Typically, when the youngest Marine's age is read, someone will yell from the back, "Damn, I've got socks older than that!" The oldest Marine will often hear someone shout, "Holy cow! His enlistment papers must have been signed by George Washington himself!" A detail of Marines then brings the birthday cake forward. A Marine Corps NCO sword is used to cut the first two slices. The first slice is handed to the oldest Marine. He passes that slice to the youngest Marine beside him. The oldest Marine then takes the second slice of cake. The two Marines then take a bite of their pieces of cake together, to the applause and cheers of the assembled command. The rest of the Marines in the formation then line up for a piece of the cake.

Doug Dickey wrote home about the celebration. "Thursday was the 191st birthday of the Corps and we had a big celebration over the whole thing. It was really nice. Afterwards we all got 2 beers and a soda free from the company. All in all it was quite a thing."[4]

Bob Kelley's first mission as commander of Company C was to take his men to the Truoi operating area four miles south of Phu Bai and set up a patrol base overlooking the roads that led to Phu Bai.[5] One of his primary responsibilities was protecting the bridge over the Truoi River from Viet Cong sappers. By then, it was the peak of the monsoon season. It seemed to rain constantly and the rivers and paddies in the area would suddenly overflow and flood Marine positions. After a few flash-floods, Kelley started to worry more about his Marines drowning than getting killed in firefights.

The perpetually wet environment made immersion foot a constant curse for infantrymen in Vietnam. It afflicted as many as three-quarters of the men in infantry units during the wet season and often put more Marines out of action than any other medical problem, including combat. It occurred when men went days without being able to take their boots off to let their feet dry. As the skin absorbed more and more water, their feet began to swell. Walking became painful. Their feet began to tingle, then burn, and felt as if they were "walking on rope." After a couple of days, the skin began to break down and ulcers opened, which quickly became infected. At this point, men would spike fevers and had to be evacuated to a medical facility. Although some seemed more susceptible to immersion foot, just about everyone ended up getting it to some degree.

The treatment was simple. Men with a bad case of immersion foot were sent to the rear; where they were put in a dry tent and given antibiotics. After a few days spent lying on a cot with their bare feet elevated, the skin usually dried out and their feet would shrink back to normal size. Most men could return to duty in a week or so. Unfortunately, once a man had gotten a case of immersion foot, his feet seemed to be more susceptible to it in the future.[6]

Doug got a bad case of immersion foot after a five-day patrol through the soaked area. His feet became infected and he was sent back to Phu Bai to let his feet dry out and get antibiotics for the infection. "I am feeling fine except one of my toes is swollen," he assured his grandmother in a letter. He explained that they often walked 10 or 15 miles a day on patrol. "We would walk through creeks & rivers and over hills and after a while your feet naturally get sore." Doug told Grandma Nellie he was looking forward to rejoining the company in a day or two. "Well now I am just going to have to stop on this letter as I have to go to chow and then write about 4 more letters." He closed his letter, "Goodbye for now, Your grandson."[7]

Two weeks later, Doug wrote to his grandmother again. Given a break from patrolling, 2nd Platoon was assigned as part of the security force for the combat base. "Well I am just sitting out here in a foxhole. I thought I would write you a few lines. I just got your letters & cards today so I brought my writing gear out to the lines. My platoon is standing the lines back at Phu Bai now. We man them 24 hours a day."

Life back at Phu Bai was better than down in the Truoi area. "We sleep in our tents that we set up and everything is pretty good as I have an air mattress and a blanket to sleep on. The rain has slacked off quite a bit since a couple of weeks ago, but it still rains some every day," Doug wrote. "You asked about the meal I had for Thanksgiving. We had turkey, ham, mashed potatoes, sweet potatoes, and bread. It was a pretty good meal and I liked it very much." He ended with: "Well it must be around noon now and my relief will be coming soon so I will have to close up for now, but I will write later so goodbye. Love, Doug."[8]

Steve Pruitt got to Vietnam and was assigned to 1st Battalion, 4th Marines, at the same time Doug Dickey arrived. They both ended up in Walter Smith's 3rd Squad in 2nd Platoon. Pruitt was from Wilmington, Delaware—a rough rust-belt city. Steve was the 10th of 12 kids in a poor, but unapologetically proud family. As soon as he was old enough, he dropped out of high school and joined the Marine Corps. Steve's brother, Richard, had been in the Marines and Steve saw the Corps as his way out of Wilmington. Also, by the time he enlisted in 1966, the war in Vietnam was raging and Steve wanted to go to war to prove his mettle. "I *wanted* to go to Vietnam," he said later.

Pruitt remembered meeting Doug Dickey in late 1966. "I was a street-wise kid compared to him. He was … a country boy," Pruitt said. "He was the same age, but he was like from a different world than I was. He was just a nice kid—off the farm and, you know. He just liked everybody." Pruitt remembered thinking to himself, "What the hell is he doing here? He shouldn't be here … especially if they're killing people. He's too nice a guy to be doing something like that."[9]

In addition to deploying his battalion to make sure the sprawling base around the airfield at Phu Bai was secure, Westerman was also responsible for supporting the Combined Action Program (CAP), in the area.

When the Marines landed in Vietnam in 1965, they arrived with a definite philosophy regarding how the war in Vietnam should be fought. Marine leaders were convinced the war was principally a counterinsurgency. Senior officers, like General Walt and General Krulak, drew from their experiences while quelling uprisings in the Caribbean and Latin America before World War II. The Marines in those conflicts learned that to be successful they had to gain the support of the local population. If they could gain the trust and support of the local villagers, they could isolate and defeat the guerrillas. The Marine Corps distilled the lessons it learned while fighting these "banana wars" in its *Small Wars Manual*, published in 1940. It became a pivotal work on fighting a guerrilla war. The younger generation of Marine officers in Vietnam generally came to the same conclusions, but also drew their lessons from Britain's successful counterinsurgency campaign against communist guerrillas in Malaya in the 1950s.

Consequently, shortly after landing, the Marine Corps began implementing a number of operations and programs designed to isolate the Viet Cong guerrillas from the villagers. These operations and programs made up what was broadly known as the "pacification" campaign because they were intended to demilitarize and pacify the local villages.

The mainstay of the Marine Corps' pacification campaign was the Combined Action Program. The Marine Corps, under the guidance of Lieutenant General Victor "Brute" Krulak, developed the Combined Action Program in 1965 as a tailored method to combat the Viet Cong insurgency in South Vietnam.

To survive, the Viet Cong had to extort support from the local villagers. They depended on the local villages for food, shelter, and manpower. The Viet Cong guerrillas routinely came into the villages at night and terrorized the villagers to ensure they furnished support. They hauled away rice, meat, and even the young men. Those villagers who didn't cooperate were often tortured or killed. The Viet Cong couldn't survive without access to the villages.

The villagers, who just wanted to be left alone to raise their families and farm their land, found themselves in an untenable position. U.S. and allied forces arrived during the day and searched the village, often finding evidence that communist guerrillas had been there. This made the villagers suspects and subjected the village to more searches and other disruptions. Then, the Viet Cong would return that night and punish the villagers for cooperating with the American and South Vietnamese troops.

The Combined Action Program was designed to remedy this situation. The concept was simple. The program was built on trust. A 15-man Marine squad was assigned to live in a village. The village became their home. During the day, the Marines organized and trained the village militia, known as the Provisional Force (PF), to defend their village. The Marine squad was too small to defend the village by itself and its survival depended on the bonds the Marines forged with the villagers and the readiness of their Vietnamese PF counterparts. The Marines found that, with the proper training, their PF comrades were fierce and loyal fighters.

The CAP Marines earned an unprecedented level of trust and confidence from the villagers because they became part of the village; they didn't abandon the villagers at night and return to the safety of an American combat base. If the Viet Cong came into the village at night, the small band of Marines would share the fate of those in the village.

The CAP Marines also supported development programs, sometimes teaching school and helping with rice harvesting. Each of the Marine squads had a navy corpsman assigned. The corpsman spent the daylight hours providing medical assistance to the villagers, routinely giving immunizations to the children and treating a spectrum of illnesses and injuries.

The Combined Action Program was a success wherever it was instituted. The CAP units galvanized the local villagers to fight off the Viet Cong guerrillas. At the same time, the trust and confidence the CAP Marines earned from the local Vietnamese made them privy to intelligence that often eluded other commands in the area.

The last Marine to earn the Medal of Honor in Vietnam was a member of a combined action platoon. On May 8, 1970, about 150 NVA and Viet Cong soldiers attacked An Diem village in Quang Ngai, intent on punishing the villagers for cooperating with the South Vietnamese government. In the course of the battle, Lance Corporal Miguel Keith, an 18-year-old from Omaha, repeatedly charged into onrushing enemy assaults with his M60 machine gun. While Keith was killed in the three-hour battle, the small band of Marines and villagers defeated the attack and kept the villagers safe. No CAP village was ever lost to the enemy during the war.

The Combined Action Program in the Phu Bai area was the responsibility of Combined Action Company (CAC) A. The CAC was divided into 10 Combined Action Teams spread over more than 92 square miles running from the outskirts of Hue, south along Route 1, fourteen miles to the Truoi River.[10] These teams lived in the villages and often ended up in battles.

Just after midnight on November 15, a Viet Cong force of between 70 and 80 guerrillas attacked the CAC Team 10 position guarding the Truoi bridge. The guerrillas assaulted the position from three sides, hammering the defenders with automatic weapons, mortar fire, and grenades. The Marines and five local PF soldiers defending the bridge held off the Viet Cong with grenades and barrages of rifle and machine-gun fire. The CAC Marines also called in artillery fire from the nearby Marine batteries. The battle raged for more than two hours, but the Viet Cong were never able to get closer than 100 yards to the bridge.

The VC eventually broke off their attack and headed back toward the mountains. The bridge was still firmly in friendly hands the next morning and, surprisingly, hadn't been damaged in the battle. Four Marines, one PF, and nine civilians had been wounded. There was no estimate of Viet Cong losses; however, at around 0900 that morning, a VC guerrilla, still holding his rifle, walked up to the CAC position and turned himself in. He had had enough.[11]

The attack on the bridge, combined with other incidents in the area, indicated the Viet Cong around Phu Bai were becoming more active. Lieutenant Colonel Westerman decided to increase support to the CAC teams. He directed his rifle platoons spend some of their nights inside the villages to reinforce the CAC teams. The time together went a long way toward easing the mutual suspicion that existed between the Marines and the villagers. Doug was charmed by the villagers he stayed with one night in late November:

> The people are very hospitable and we are always welcome in their homes. Last night we went into a home and stayed. And the people were extremely nice & friendly. They gave us their beds and we didn't want to take their beds, but they insisted that we do, so we did. We ate some of their bananas and they were really good. The people were very nice. About 02:30 or 03:00 AM they got up and I was on radio watch and we had some tea. It was hot and it wasn't too bad. One thing, you never refuse anything as they might take it as an offense and feel hurt by it so I drank this hot tea.
>
> The kids were really great. One was 17 and was in the eighth grade & then they had another boy and a couple of young girls.
>
> The kids are really smart, as they are going to school. I was looking at their books and the eighth grader was studying French & English he was beginning to break words down into syllables.
>
> This 17 year old was studying Geometry and he had worked out some very good problems. One of them was studying Biology & Algebra. All in all it was very interesting as we could understand some things that they said & wrote. We gave them some money for letting us stay there, we also gave the kids candy & gum & other things. You would be surprised at how much they understand.
>
> They had a baby with a sore on his wrist and Papasan asked me if I had a band aid so I checked & I didn't have any in my kit so I told him so & he said OK.[12]

Doug bought a three-band transistor radio at the Phu Bai Post Exchange in the middle of November. One of the few entertainments the men had out in the field was listening to American Forces Vietnam Network (AFVN) radio broadcasts.[13] Doug got a charge out of the AFVN "Dawn Buster" radio program that kicked off after the news broadcast at 0600 every morning. The program became famous after Robin Williams depicted the program's disc jockey, Adrian Cronauer, in the 1987 movie *Good Morning, Vietnam*. "I am listening to the Armed Forces Radio and it is pretty good. The announcer comes on every morning and says 'Goooooooooooooooooooood morning Viet Nam!' and it is pretty good."[14]

In December 1966, Jack Westerman received orders designating his battalion to be the next Battalion Landing Team (BLT). It was welcome news. Being selected was both an honor and vote of confidence. As the Battalion Landing Team, 1st Battalion, 4th Marines, would form the core of the Special Landing Force (SLF). The SLF was the Marine Corps' amphibious assault force that prowled the waters off Vietnam on board the ships of the Amphibious Ready Group (ARG).

Amphibious operations, however, are extremely complicated and difficult, and require special training and skills. When Westerman received word that his battalion was to become the BLT, he was also told they would be deploying to Okinawa to go through more than a month of special training to prepare them for the assignment.

Being designated to be the BLT was good news to the Marines in the battalion. It meant escaping from the punishing routine in northern Quang Tri—at least for a while. Okinawa would be paradise compared to the bush and combat bases along the DMZ. Likewise, living on board the ships would be luxurious; they would be sleeping in clean beds, taking hot showers, and eating three hot meals every day.

On December 13, Blackjack Westerman and his Marines turned over their responsibilities in the Hue–Phu Bai area to 2nd Battalion, 9th Marines, and prepared to leave for Okinawa. On December 15, most of the battalion boarded the USS *Lenawee* (APA-195) at Coco Beach near Hue. The *Lenawee* was a massive "Victory Ship" troop transport from World War II. This was *Lenawee's* last deployment before being decommissioned. They sailed for Okinawa the following day. The remainder of the battalion left the next day on board the USS *Comstock* (LSD-19) and the USS *Washburn* (AKA-108).

CHAPTER 9

Okinawa

"Second Platoon really had a good thing going among themselves."

CAPTAIN BOB KELLEY.

Jack Westerman and his battalion reached Okinawa on December 20. They disembarked the ships at White Beach and were trucked up to Camp Schwab. Camp Schwab became their home for the next six weeks.

U.S. Marines had been on Okinawa since the morning of April 1, 1945. That was the first day of the 82-day battle to seize the island. The battle for Okinawa was one of the most brutal and bloody campaigns of World War II. The island was considered part of Imperial Japan and the Japanese soldiers fought for every foot of it. By the end of the campaign, more than 14,000 Americans had died. More than 77,000 Japanese soldiers were killed.

America retained the island after the war and used it to garrison a forward-deployed Marine division in the Pacific. Until 1965, Okinawa had been a sleepy backwater for Marines. That changed with the decision to land American troops in Vietnam. The island became the major staging area for Marines on their way to and from Vietnam. The camps were crowded and convoys were constantly moving up and down the highway that ran through the middle of the island. Okinawa became a crossroads. Wide-eyed new Marines, fresh from boot camp, on their way to Vietnam, crossed paths with battle-scared, war-weary veterans on their way home.

The Marine Corps named its six main bases on Okinawa after Marines who earned the Medal of Honor posthumously during the battle to take the island.[1] Camp Schwab was named for Private First Class Albert E. Schwab. Schwab was a flamethrower operator with 1st Battalion, 5th Marines, during the battle. On May 7, 1945, the 24-year-old scaled a steep ridge to attack a Japanese machine-gun position that had his company pinned down in the narrow canyon below. Schwab destroyed the enemy position with his flamethrower, enabling his comrades to seize the ridge. A second enemy machine gun opened up, raking the Marines with fire, and killing several of them. Schwab immediately attacked that enemy position. During his "one-man assault" Albert Schwab destroyed two more enemy positions despite being badly wounded in the course of the action. He was killed making his final assault. Admiral Clark presented the Medal of Honor to Albert Schwab's three-year-old son, Steven Albert, a year later.

Okinawa was paradise compared to Vietnam. The men of 1st Battalion, 4th Marines, got to live in barracks and sleep in real beds with crisp clean sheets. They took hot showers every day, ate steaks in the chow hall, and had liberty in the town outside the camp in the evenings. The break from Vietnam also gave the doctors and corpsmen a chance to get ahead of some of the rampant health problems caused by months in the field. Those suffering from immersion foot were able to dry out their feet. Infected leech bites and the oozing ulcers known as "gook sores" were finally able to heal in the clean, dry environment.

One of the main tasks for the battalion while on Okinawa was to bring replacements on board. One of the new men was First Lieutenant Dave Rumsey. Kelley assigned him to be his new executive officer. A graduate of Brown University, Rumsey had been commissioned through the school's NROTC program two years earlier. Rumsey brought some unique experience with him. He had spent the past year as one of the officers in charge of the Basic School's "Demonstration Unit." The Demonstration Unit was a group of Marines assigned to the Basic School to help teach infantry skills to new lieutenants. The unit also acted as an enemy "aggressor force" during field exercises. A collegiate track and field runner, Rumsey had also been assigned to the Marine Corps' track team while at Quantico.

Another replacement who reported to the battalion on Okinawa was a freshly minted 23-year-old second lieutenant from Delaware named Larry Dickerson. Dickerson had just graduated from West Virginia University, where he had been a star baseball player. Westerman sent Dickerson to Bob Kelley's company. Kelley had shifted Hedge Deibert over to his Weapons Platoon and assigned Dickerson to take over 2nd Platoon.

Dickerson was in a tough spot with the Marines in his platoon. He was following in the footsteps of a number of "mustang" officers—older, more experienced men who had been commissioned after spending years as enlisted men. The last platoon leader for 2nd Platoon had been Hedge Deibert, one of the most experienced Marines in the battalion.

After Kelley sent Deibert to take over the Weapons Platoon, Staff Sergeant John Szymanski had led 2nd Platoon. Szymanski, like Deibert, had years of experience as an infantryman. Szymanski had also been recently selected for an officer's commission and was waiting for his orders to Quantico. In addition to their experience, both Deibert and Szymanski were noticeably older than the Marines in the platoon, giving them a natural mantle of authority.

Dickerson, on the other hand, had been in the Marine Corps less than a year—all of it spent in school, and he was about the same age as many of the Marines in his platoon. He looked boyish next to the two hardened vets who had led the platoon. Bob Kelley knew Larry Dickerson was in a tough spot. "I sat the older guys down and told them to take Dickerson under their wing and help him get started." Kelley also decided to assign John Szymanski as Dickerson's platoon sergeant. Kelley believed Szymanski was one of the best SNCOs he had and was confident he would be a supportive and patient mentor to Dickerson.

Getting a new platoon leader could be a cause for anxiety among the Marines in a rifle platoon. A platoon leader has more direct impact on the lives of his men than any other officer in the Marine Corps. If a platoon leader is good; his men will thrive. If he's incompetent or arrogant; the Marines will pay for it with their blood.

Additionally, Vietnam was a "platoon leader's war." The young lieutenants in Vietnam shouldered a disproportionate amount of responsibility. In World War II and in the Korean War, platoon leaders usually operated within larger units. Their company and battalion commanders guided them closely and made most of the tactical decisions. However, in Vietnam, due to the terrain and the nature of the enemy, platoons were often patrolling independently in the countryside, isolated from higher headquarters. The young lieutenants often had to make decisions that would have been made by men with more experience and seniority in previous wars. Additionally, platoon leaders were fighting an unconventional enemy who often didn't wear a uniform. Trying to distinguish the enemy from the civilians, while conforming to complicated rules of engagement, was a problem that hadn't been faced by young officers ever before. The majority of young platoon leaders in Vietnam performed superbly. They were technically competent and worked hard to be good leaders. They tried to lead by example and paid the price for it. Of the 920 Marine officers killed in Vietnam, 593 of them were lieutenants.[2]

Larry Dickerson, however, earned the trust of his Marines during his first formation with 2nd Platoon. Charlie Runnels was one of the Marines standing in the formation and recalled how Dickerson impressed them that day:

> He introduced himself and told us who he was. And then he said, "OK, I want every man in this unit who has actually been in combat to put his hand up." And, of course, all of us did.
>
> And then he said, "Now, everybody here who has never been in combat—put their hand up." And he put his hand up—the only one.
>
> And he turned to Sergeant Szymanski, our platoon sergeant, and says, "Sergeant 'Ski," he said, "I want you to continue to run this platoon and I'm going back here and follow you guys until I've learned what I'm doing."

Dickerson's candid admission that he had a lot to learn, and that he was willing to learn it from them, put the men at ease. They immediately trusted him. He quickly learned to lead his men in combat and proved to be both smart and brave. Charlie Runnels ended up spending more than 22 years in the military. "He was probably the best 'straight-out-of-school' second lieutenant I ever saw," Runnels said. "He read people well. He understood the right things to say—and he was an extremely courageous individual himself."[3]

Leona Dickey remembered hearing about Larry Dickerson in a letter she got from Doug at the beginning of 1967. "Doug wrote home: 'Don't worry about me, mom. At Christmas, the lieutenant got me ice cream for my birthday!'" It was Dickerson's little gestures, like trying to do something special for his Marines on their birthdays, that initially earned him the respect and trust of his platoon.

Bob Kelley had been concerned about 2nd Platoon. However, he saw that Dickerson and Szymanski seemed to really get along and the personalities in the platoon seemed to mesh. "Second Platoon really had a good thing going among themselves," he said.

The rifle platoon is the building block of the Marine infantry battalion. According to the regulations in 1967, a fully manned rifle platoon had one officer and 45 enlisted Marines. A platoon was divided into a headquarters section and three squads. The headquarters section was composed of the platoon leader, usually a second lieutenant; a platoon sergeant, who was a staff sergeant; the platoon guide, who was a sergeant; and a radio operator.

The remaining 42 Marines were divided into three squads. Of the 14 men in each squad, one was designated as the squad leader. One was the squad's grenadier and was armed with an M79 grenade launcher. The remaining 12 men in the squad were divided into three fireteams.

Each of the four men in a fireteam had a distinct role. One man was designated as the fireteam's leader. He coordinated the team's actions; he carried an M14 and also served as a rifleman. One man was the team's automatic rifleman; he was armed with an M14 configured to fire in the fully automatic mode like a machine gun and used his rifle to lay down a base of fire for the team. The remaining two Marines in the team were riflemen—armed with M14s. They formed the maneuver element for the fireteam.

In Vietnam, however, infantry leaders rarely had anything close to the number of Marines called for in the regulations. After time in the field, illnesses, injuries, and battle casualties often thinned units down to half the numbers they were supposed to have.

Each rifle platoon in Company C was also augmented with machine-gun teams and 3.5-inch rocket launcher teams from the company's Weapons Platoon. The machine-gun and rocket teams gave the platoons increased firepower.

A machine-gun team was usually two men. One man, the "gunner," carried the 23-pound M60 machine gun. The other man was the assistant gunner, or "A-gunner." In addition to carrying several hundred rounds of belted ammunition and spare barrels, the A-gunner helped direct the gun's fire.

The rocket teams were also two-man teams. Each team employed a 3.5-inch rocket launcher, often called a "bazooka." Like the machine-gun teams, one man carried the launcher, while the other man carried the ammunition.

It was customary to assign the same machine-gun and rocket teams to the same platoon. For all intents and purposes, these teams became part of the platoon. Although it varied depending on missions, 2nd Platoon usually went into the field with machine-gun teams led by Private First Class Ed Gutloff and rocket teams led by Corporal Larry Normand.

Normand was from Baton Rouge and was attending Louisiana State University in 1966. He had a draft deferment as a cadet in the school's ROTC unit. However, the routine in the ROTC unit quickly grated on him. "I got tired of it … It was so petty … LSU was one of those schools that they shaved your head and everything else—and you had to wear khakis and march around. I just got tired of it." Larry decided to drop out of school. "I knew as soon as I dropped out of college, I was going to be drafted. So, I went down and enlisted in the Marine Corps for two years," he said. "And the next day I got my draft notice."[4]

One of the other rocket men assigned to Dickerson's platoon was Private First Class Gary L. Hudson, an 18-year-old from Louisville, Colorado. Hudson had enlisted in large part because he felt it was his duty. His father had flown 51 missions as a ball-turret gunner in a B-17 in the Fifteenth Air Force during World War II. Chuck Hudson had been officially credited with shooting down a German fighter plane—a rare achievement for a machine-gunner on a Flying Fortress. Gary enlisted in the Marines for two years immediately after he graduated from high school. Gary was an adventurer. "He seemed to love doing dangerous things," Isabelle Hudson said of her son.

It's probably safe to say Gary Hudson was the only member of Westerman's battalion who had ever actually wrestled a bear. His mother remembered the afternoon during his senior year in high school when Gary and a couple of his buddies showed up at the Hudsons' home laughing and hooting. Gary's clothes were shredded and he was covered in the most putrid grease and slime Isabelle Hudson had ever smelled in her life. It was so bad she refused to let him in the house. When she asked what had happened, the boys proudly told her Gary had just wrestled a bear. She thought they were kidding. "I said, 'Oh—he did not! You're just trying to get me upset.'"

The boys said, "No! He wrestled a bear!" They told her they had gone up to Boulder where you could pay a guy to wrestle his bear.

Isabelle Hudson said she still didn't believe them: "And they brought out a picture of Gary and the bear!" she said. "The bear, of course, had been declawed and had been muzzled," Isabelle Hudson said. "He was always doing things like that." Remembering what a battered mess Gary was that afternoon, she said with a laugh, "I think the bear won."[5]

Each infantry platoon was also augmented with navy corpsmen. The specially trained corpsmen served as the medics for the Marines. The U.S. Navy has provided medical support to the Marine Corps since the Revolutionary War and navy corpsmen have been fully integrated into Marine infantry battalions since World War I. Since then, navy corpsmen have always gone into battle beside Marines.[6]

The term "corpsman" was coined before World War I to refer to the enlisted medical specialists because they were members of the navy's Medical Corps. Although the official rank designations have changed over the years, the title "corpsman" has endured and remains the term most often used. Officially, they were designated as "Pharmacists Mates" during World War II. During the Vietnam War, they were officially designated as "Hospitalmen."

There were two navy corpsmen assigned to Dickerson's platoon: Hospitalman Third Class Greg Long; and Hospitalman Greg Nichols. Greg Long was the senior corpsman in 2nd Platoon. Long had enlisted in the navy from Idaho. In boot camp, he was told he could choose between being a corpsman or a dental assistant. He chose to become a corpsman: "I figured I'd rather work in a hospital than mess around watching somebody work in somebody's mouth," he said.

Greg Nichols grew up in Anderson, Indiana, but his family moved to San Diego before his senior year in high school. He got his draft notice after graduating. Military service was a tradition in his family. His father had been a rifleman in Patton's Third Army during World War II. "I knew about Vietnam and figured I'd be going and I wanted to earn my rite of passage like so many people in my family had done," he said. "That's what made me end up going." Nichols originally considered enlisting in the Marines, but he also had an interest in medicine. The recruiter told him navy corpsmen served as the medics for the Marines. "I said, 'Well, I want to be with the Marines and I'd rather be a corpsman—in that capacity.' So, I decided to sign up as a hospitalman recruit; and I joined the navy."[7]

During the Vietnam War, the path to becoming a combat corpsman with the Marine Corps started when a sailor graduated from one of the navy's boot camps. Those sailors designated to become hospitalmen were sent to the "Corps School." Most hospitalmen were destined to work as orderlies in hospitals or in sick bays on board ships. Consequently, the curriculum at the Corps School was a broad introduction to medical care. Among other things, the new corpsmen were taught basic physiology; and learned how to draw blood, give injections, read vital signs, and how to maintain medical records. After graduating from the Corps School, most of the new corpsmen were sent to work in hospitals.

However, a number of corpsmen in every class were designated to serve with the Marines. Many of them volunteered for the duty. The hospitalmen who were bound for duty with the Marine Corps were sent to the Field Medical Service School (FMSS) at Camp Pendleton for additional training.

It was at the Field Medical Service School that hospitalmen were turned into combat corpsmen. The mission of the Field Medical Service School was to teach hospitalmen how to be battlefield medics. If they graduated from the FMSS, they were designated Fleet Marine Force (FMF) Corpsmen. Most were then sent to infantry battalions in Vietnam.

Field Medical Service School was a dramatic departure from any of the other training the sailors had received. The five-week school was located on the Marine base at Camp Pendleton and was staffed with both veteran corpsmen and Marine infantrymen. At the Field Medical Service School, the new corpsmen learned how to live and work in Marine units. It was an eye-opening experience for most of the sailors. "Our biggest job is trying to convince these sailors that they are going to spend their tour of duty as Marines," said Harold Donovan, the navy medical officer who commanded the school.[8]

When the corpsmen arrived at the school, they were issued Marine utility uniforms, helmets, flak jackets, and packs. For the first two weeks, they learned about the Marine Corps. They attended classes on the history and organization of the Marines, followed by classes on weaponry, land navigation, and offensive and defensive infantry tactics. They went to the rifle range and fired the M14 rifle and the .45 automatic pistol. As corpsmen, they would carry a .45 as their standard weapon. Following the classroom instruction, they went into the field and learned to live like infantrymen. They practiced basic patrolling and small unit tactics, lived in tents, and learned to dig fighting holes.[9]

After learning to live in the field, the corpsmen began the medical phase of their training. Each man was issued a "Unit One," the battlefield first aid kit carried by corpsmen. A Unit One contained an assortment of surgical instruments in addition to bandages and first aid equipment.

They received advanced instruction on battlefield first aid. The corpsmen teaching the classes were combat veterans. The training focused on "the golden hour." A wounded man had a good chance of surviving if the corpsman could keep him alive through the first 60 minutes immediately after he was wounded. The new corpsmen were taught how to treat an array of severe injuries. They were drilled on the treatment of gunshot wounds, burns, traumatic amputations, and shock. They learned how to triage wounded, and coordinate their evacuation from the battlefield.[10] The instructors impressed on the students again and again that they would have to rapidly make life-and-death decisions miles from any doctors or hospitals.

The physical training was the toughest part of the school for most of the new corpsmen. The sailors had to get in shape so they could keep up with Marine riflemen on the battlefield. Marine SNCOs led the corpsmen through daily PT sessions, including calisthenics and unit runs. They began a grueling regimen of conditioning hikes loaded with the equipment and gear they would have to carry in the field. The hikes got longer and longer until they were making 20-mile treks up and down the hills of Camp Pendleton. "It was the toughest thing I had ever done to that point," Greg Nichols said of his time at the Field Medical Service School.

Corpsmen occupy a unique place in the Marine Corps. It's traditional for Marines to call their corpsman "Doc," regardless of his age or rank. It's a sign of acceptance and respect. Every Marine knows his life may depend on a corpsman one day. Navy corpsmen serving with the Marines are authorized to wear Marine Corps service dress uniforms, complete with the Marine Corps' eagle, globe, and anchor devices. The only difference between the uniforms is that the FMF corpsmen wear their U.S. Navy rank insignia on the sleeve rather than Marine Corps chevrons. Marines jealously guard their symbols and traditions. Allowing corpsmen to wear Marine Corps uniforms was done to acknowledge and honor the special and critical role they play in the Marine Corps.

It became clear to the new corpsmen going through the Field Medical Service School that a lot was expected of them. Every day, when they walked into the school's building, they walked past more than a dozen photos of corpsmen who had earned the Medal of Honor while serving in Marine units. Most of those corpsmen had died earning the award. By the end of the Vietnam War, four more navy corpsmen had earned the Medal of Honor while serving with Marines. Two of those men, Petty Officer Wayne M. Caron, and Petty Officer David R. Ray, were killed saving their Marine comrades.

In the months since they had been the platoon's corpsmen, Long and Nichols had treated every imaginable injury and illness, from bullet and blast wounds, to immersion foot, and malaria. It also fell upon the corpsmen to monitor the mental health of the men in the platoon. They would keep an eye on men who were starting to show the symptoms of battle fatigue or who were dealing with bad news from home. A man who had gotten a *Dear John* letter from a wife or girlfriend often found Long or Nichols taking a seat next to him during chow and casually striking up a conversation.

Keith Wheeler was a war correspondent who was saved by a navy corpsman after he was hit in the neck by shrapnel on Iwo Jima. He said of the corpsmen, "They are the men who are in battle but not of it. Their mission is to not to kill, but to save… They are not fighting men, although they share every hardship and danger equally with the fighting men… They are entirely devoted to the idea of killing the enemy and they regard the enemy dead with as little pity as do the men who kill them."[11]

"The difference between a fighting man and a corpsman," Wheeler said, "appears when there are wounded to deal with. The quality of mercy knows no creed or nationality. I have seen them expose themselves to danger to save the lives of wounded Japanese." Wheeler summed up the role of navy corpsmen: "Samaritans in hell."[12]

The personnel assignments in the battalion were completed by the end of the year. Larry Dickerson got his new platoon together on New Year's Day, 1967, and had a group photo taken. There were 35 men in the photo. A few of the platoon members were absent because they were on leave or had been sent to school. As the platoon leader, Larry Dickerson, stood in the front and center position of the group, flanked on his left by Staff Sergeant John Szymanski, his platoon sergeant; and on his right by Sergeant Larry Wilson, his platoon guide. 1st Squad was led by Sergeant Colin McClelland, 2nd Squad by Corporal Lionel Lawson, and 3rd Squad was led by Corporal Walter Smith.

With the manning of the platoon largely resolved, Dickerson and Szymanski began their training. The company was sent through the jungle warfare course up at the Northern Training Area (NTA). Although most of the men had already spent plenty of time fighting in jungles, the days spent at NTA were still worthwhile. Building rope bridges and practicing patrolling gave Dickerson and his men a chance to get to know each other and build the bonds that turn a group of men into a team.

After the jungle warfare course, Company C began training for the battalion's amphibious assault mission.

Westerman assigned Kelley's company to be the battalion's "surface assault" company for the battalion. This meant Company C would make most of their landings in amphibious tractors, "amtracs," while the other companies trained principally to make their assaults riding in helicopters. The amtrac's official designation was: Landing Vehicle, Tracked, Personnel (LVTP-5). The amtracs were 43-ton armored vehicles that could launch from a ship at sea and then "swim" to the beach using their specially configured tracks to propel them through the water. They were basically large armored boxes with treads on the bottom. Once ashore, the amtracs functioned as armored personnel carriers. They could carry up to 34 combat-equipped Marines.[13]

For Kelley and his Marines, however, the pride of being trusted with the traditional Marine mission of actually "hitting the beach" was somewhat tempered by the fact that riding in an amtrac was a universally unpleasant experience. The Marines inside were usually packed in so tightly it was hard to move more than an inch or two. Once the door-ramp was closed, there was no escape for the Marines in the troop compartment. It was torture for anyone who might be claustrophobic. The air in the troop compartment became stuffy and thick almost immediately, and the exhaust from the engine usually found its way into the troop space, making the situation worse. The amtracs were very slow in the water and rolled constantly. Seasickness was a certainty for the Marines packed in the hot, stuffy compartment. A man who got sick had no choice but to vomit into his own helmet. By the time the amtrac climbed out of the surf, the Marines would rather face a beachhead full of enemy than spend another second trapped in the miserable metal box.

1st Battalion, 4th Marines, trained on Okinawa through January 1967. It was a busy schedule. The break from operations in Vietnam also gave Westerman an opportunity to pull his battalion together—to give the veterans and the replacements a chance to get to know each other and to bond. They had sports competitions, beach parties, and barbeques. Westerman had some of the Marines put together a cruise book before they left Okinawa. The cruise book was similar to a high school yearbook. It had photos of all the Marines in the battalion, organized by company. Part of the book featured photos of significant events.

While on Okinawa, Westerman had an official crest designed for the battalion. Until then, a number of crests had been used. Tracing its heritage to the "China Marines" before World War II, the new crest featured a dragon wound around an Asian pagoda. The words, "gung ho" were written on the pagoda, reflecting the battalion's lineage to Evan Carlson's Raider Battalion. The crest was framed by the battalion's new moto: "God, Country, Duty, Corps." The new crest was featured on the cover of the cruise book. In the following months, the battalion proudly put the new crest on its official reports and on the signs in front of their buildings. The crest Westerman instituted was used by 1st Battalion, 4th Marines, for decades.

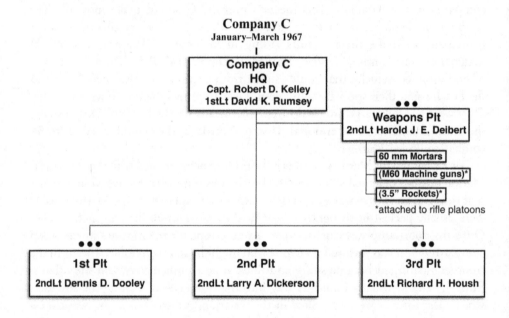

Company C
January–March 1967

2nd Platoon, Company C
December 1966–March 1967

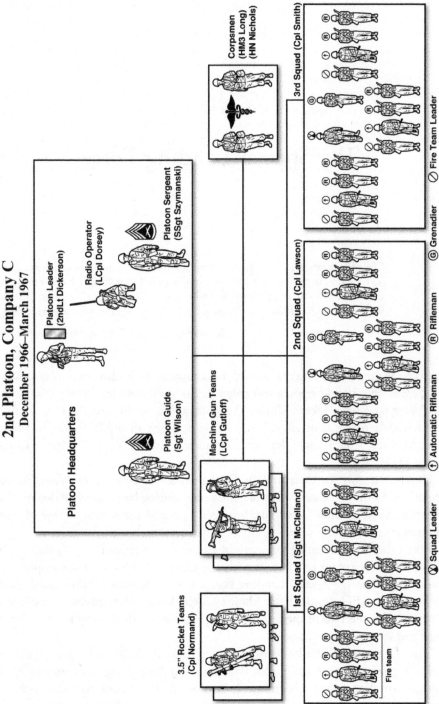

Platoon Headquarters

Platoon Leader
(2ndLt Dickerson)

Radio Operator
(LCpl Dorsey)

Platoon Sergeant
(SSgt Szymanski)

Platoon Guide
(Sgt Wilson)

Corpsmen
(HM3 Long)
(HN Nichols)

Machine Gun Teams
(LCpl Gutloff)

3.5" Rocket Teams
(Cpl Normand)

3rd Squad (Cpl Smith)

2nd Squad (Cpl Lawson)

1st Squad (Sgt McClelland)

Fire team

Ⓧ Squad Leader   Ⓡ Rifleman   ⊘ Fire Team Leader

⊕ Automatic Rifleman   Ⓖ Grenadier

CHAPTER 10

The Special Landing Force

"To effect a landing ... in the face of enemy resistance requires careful training and preparations, to say the least; and this along Marine Corps lines. It is not enough that the troops be skilled infantry men or artillery men of high morale: They must be skilled water men and jungle men who know it can be done—Marines with Marine training."

MAJOR EARL H. ELLIS, U.S. MARINE CORPS, 712 H OPERATIONAL PLAN, 1921[1]

The U.S. Marine Corps had made amphibious assault its fundamental mission since the 1930s. The island-hopping campaign in the Pacific during World War II and the daring landing at Inchon during the Korean War established the U.S. Marines as the world's preeminent amphibious warriors. Many in the Pentagon, including most Marines, would argue that amphibious assault was the U.S. Marine Corps' reason for existence.

However, during the Vietnam War, few Marines were ever part of an amphibious operation. As the war escalated, more and more Marine battalions had deployed to Vietnam. Most of these battalions, however, operated miles inland. Few of these Marines ever saw a ship or even glimpsed the coastline.

When the U.S. Seventh Fleet established the Amphibious Ready Group in the the waters off Vietnam in 1965, the Marine Corps got back into the amphibious assault business. The Special Landing Force, the 2,000-man Marine assault force on board the ARG, brought the Marine Corps' legacy of amphibious warfare to Vietnam. The Marines in the SLF were amphibious warriors. They lived on board ships and struck from the sea.

The SLF consisted of a Battalion Landing Team, a Marine helicopter squadron, and a logistic support unit. The Battalion Landing Team was essentially an infantry battalion that had been heavily reinforced. Those reinforcements included detachments of tanks, amtracs, artillery, engineers, and medical personnel.

The Special Landing Force gave General Westmoreland a unique capability. The chain of command in Vietnam was complex and convoluted. Technically, as a naval task force, the ARG was under the command of the Pacific Fleet, headquartered in Pearl Harbor. In practice, however, the Marines and the landing ships in the South China Sea functioned as part of William Westmoreland's reserve and were generally at his beck and call. He could order them to land anywhere along the coast with very little notice.

Also, the SLF was one of the few American forces in Vietnam that could still surprise the enemy. Viet Cong operatives stayed close to all the U.S. bases in Vietnam and reported any activity indicating American forces were preparing for battle. It was almost impossible for U.S. units in Vietnam to keep their operations secret. However, the SLF did its preparation at sea. There were no enemy operatives on board to betray their plans. Consequently, the amphibious task force could surprise communist forces by appearing off a beach and land without warning.

In keeping with naval tradition and doctrine, amphibious task forces were commanded by U.S. Navy officers during the Vietnam War. An ARG was usually commanded by a U.S. Navy captain. As the task force commander, he had overall command of both the ships in the group, and the Marines in the landing force. When Westerman's battalion became the BLT in January 1967, the ARG was commanded by Captain John D. Westervelt. Westervelt had joined the navy before World War II and had risen quickly through the ranks. He had spent most of his career at sea, most often in command of ships.

The ships in the ARG were designed specifically to transport Marines and launch them in amphibious assault operations. There were usually at least three ships in the ARG. The flagship of the group was usually a "big deck" amphibious assault ship (LPH). The amphibious assault ships were designed to accommodate a Marine helicopter squadron and were distinctive because they looked like small aircraft carriers. Usually, the other two ships in the ARG included an amphibious transport dock (LPD), and a dock landing ship (LSD). These two ships were unique because they had well decks that could be flooded to launch and recover landing craft or amtracs. The ships in the Amphibious Ready Group usually spent six months or more in the seas off Vietnam before returning to their home ports on the West Coast.

Directly below Westervelt in the chain of command was Colonel Harry D. Wortman as the commander of the Special Landing Force. Wortman had been in command of the SLF since August 31, 1966. As such, he commanded all the Marines embarked on board the ARG shipping, including Westerman's battalion, Kenneth Huntington's helicopter squadron, and the supporting logistics unit.

Harry Wortman was a 1941 graduate of Beloit College and had joined the Marines in July 1942. He had fought with the 2nd Raider Battalion during World

War II and was wounded during the Bougainville campaign.[2] In the desperate first days of the Korean War, Wortman earned a Bronze Star Medal while serving with the 7th Marines. He graduated with honors from the Naval War College in 1964 and then was sent to the Western Pacific shortly after being promoted to colonel.[3]

Since taking command of the SLF, Wortman had led it through two amphibious operations. In Operation *Deckhouse IV*, from September 15–18, 1966, the SLF landed just south of the DMZ and engaged NVA units infiltrating through the DMZ just north of Dong Ha.[4] During the second week of January 1967, Wortman commanded the SLF through Operation *Deckhouse V*. During that operation, the BLT, commanded by Lieutenant Colonel James L. Day, landed in the Mekong River Delta as part of a joint operation with Vietnamese Marines.

With 1st Battalion, 4th Marines, ready to deploy, the SLF began assembling again in the second week of January 1967. Marine units from Vietnam and Okinawa began boarding the three ARG ships that would be their home and base of operations. The three ships were: the USS *Iwo Jima* (LPH-2), the USS *Vancouver* (LPD-2), and the USS *Point Defiance* (LSD-31). The *Iwo Jima* was the largest of the three and served as the flagship and home for most of the command and headquarters staff. It also served as the base of operations for the helicopter squadron. The *Vancouver*, the *Point Defiance*, and the *Iwo Jima* had all been serving in Vietnamese waters for more than six months and were due to rotate back to California soon.

Blackjack Westerman assumed the BLT mission from Lieutenant Colonel Day's 1st Battalion, 9th Marines. Day's Marines had been serving as the BLT since

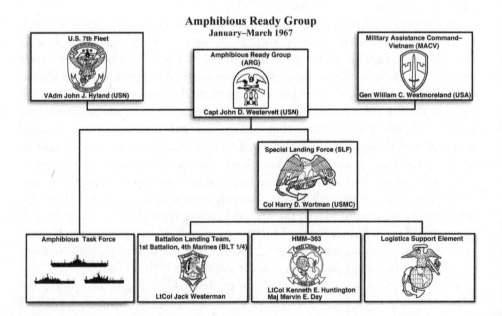

Amphibious Ready Group
January–March 1967

December 1966. Day and his battalion had executed Operation *Deckhouse V* in January—a landing against the Viet Cong in Kien Hoa Province south of Saigon. Due to the shallow offshore sandbars and mud flats in the area, Day's Marines had endured 23-mile trips on board landing craft in rough seas to get from the ships to the landing beaches.[5] It had been an ordeal. When they got back to Okinawa, Day's battalion disembarked and flew back to Phu Bai.

On January 16, 1967, Jack Westerman received orders officially designating 1st Battalion, 4th Marines, as the Battalion Landing Team for the SLF. Westerman and his Marines began packing their equipment at Camp Schwab and prepared to board the ARG ships anchored in the harbor down at White Beach.

CHAPTER 11

HMM-363: "The Lucky Red Lions"

"I took care of the job in the cockpit and got scared later."

FIRST LIEUTENANT TIM O'TOOLE

At about the same time Jack Westerman was getting ready to move his battalion on board the Amphibious Ready Group ships, Lieutenant Colonel Kenneth E. Huntington, the commanding officer of Marine Medium Helicopter Squadron 363 (HMM-363), received orders assigning his squadron to be helicopter support for the Special Landing Force. At the time, HMM-363 was flying from Ky Ha, the helicopter air base adjacent to the fixed-wing runway at Chu Lai.

HMM-363 called themselves "The Lucky Red Lions." Their squadron patch featured a red lion emblazoned over a four-leaf clover. The squadron was established in 1952 and was one of the first helicopter squadrons deployed to Vietnam in 1965. Its pilots and crewmen had flown combat missions almost every day since. Lieutenant Colonel Huntington had commanded the Lucky Red Lions since October 1966. Bill Collier, one of the young HMM-363 pilots, described him: "Colonel Huntington was older, very much a father figure in his gray crewcut and calm demeanor. We trusted his word."[1]

HMM-363 was one of nine medium-lift helicopter squadrons in Vietnam at the end of 1966. The squadron began 1967 with 23 UH-34D helicopters[2] and a total of 242 men, including a navy flight surgeon. The first 18 days of January were typical for the squadron. It flew 2,951 sorties; 311 of them medevacs. Squadron helicopters were fired upon 53 times and were hit by enemy fire 15 times, wounding two pilots, two crewmen, and one of the squadron's corpsmen.

January 11 was a particularly bad day for the squadron. First Lieutenant Robert Schena and First Lieutenant Gary Shields were piloting a routine mission ferrying six Marines from the 1st Shore Party Battalion to Quang Ngai. One of the pilots radioed they had suddenly lost their engine and were ditching in the water just offshore from Chu Lai. The weather was stormy and the surf was running high. Tragically, the four-man crew, as well as the six Marines in the troop compartment, all drowned in the surf before rescue teams could get to them.[3]

At the Ky Ha air facility, Huntington began making arrangements to get his squadron on board the ARG ships. The plan was to fly the squadron onto the USS *Iwo Jima* when it steamed by on its way to Okinawa.[4] The plan worked well. At 0830, on January 19, the squadron began lifting its men and equipment out to the *Iwo Jima*. The squadron was safely on board by 1750. By 2054, the ship had secured from flight operations and began steaming north toward Okinawa with HMM-363 on board.[5]

Helicopters had become an essential part of Marine Corps operations by 1966. Marine helicopters first saw combat during the Korean War. At that time, the small aircraft didn't have the power to lift more than a few hundred pounds. However, they were integrated into the reconnaissance and observation squadrons and were able to fly along the battlefield and give commanders timely intelligence and often served as messengers.

The role of the helicopter grew in the years following the Korean War. It was an airframe developed by Russian-born engineer Igor Sikorsky in 1954 that made the Marine Corps a helicopterborne force. The aircraft was initially designated the HUS-1. Its powerful nine-cylinder reciprocating engine and large cargo capacity made it appealing to the Marine Corps. By June 1961, the Marine Corps had bought 233 HUS-1s. Eventually the Corps had 540 in its inventory.[6] In September 1962, the official designation of the Sikorsky HUS-1 was changed to UH-34. That year, HMM-362, commanded by Lieutenant Colonel Archie Clapp, was sent to Vietnam to help transport South Vietnamese Army units as part of Operation *ShuFly*. Clapp's squadron, flying UH-34Ds, became the first Marine helicopter squadron to fly combat missions in Vietnam.

Despite its awkward appearance, the UH-34 could do incredibly complicated maneuvers. "The UH-34 was a very nimble aircraft," said Tim O'Toole, one of the pilots in HMM-363. "You could control that thing!" he said. "You could write your name with it if you stuck a big pen on the end of it. The controls were really, really good." That maneuverability was possible because Sikorsky had incorporated a number of fine adjustment controls in addition to the standard controls found in most other helicopters. Among the unique controls was a twist throttle as part of the collective. The twist throttle was actually designed by Harley-Davidson and was similar to the throttles found on the handlebars of a motorcycle. The myriad of controls that made the UH-34 so agile also made it a challenge to fly, even for seasoned pilots. It demanded the utmost skill and attention. "You literally couldn't scratch your nose if you were maneuvering the aircraft," O'Toole said. Those who flew the UH-34, earned a lot of respect in the aviation community. "One thing about the '34," O'Toole said, "it was the hardest aircraft anyone has ever flown."[7]

Bill Collier later said of flying the UH-34D: "We did not drive these H-34 helicopters. We did not fly them. We put them on. They became an extension of our bodies. We became one with them."[8]

Helicopter squadrons in Vietnam had a unique warrior culture—a result of their distinct mission. In many ways, they served as a cultural link between the fixed-wing fighter-bomber pilots who zoomed over the battlefield dropping bombs, and the Marine infantrymen slogging along in the rice paddies and jungles below. The helicopter pilots had the traditional élan and devil-may-care attitude of naval aviators, yet they also displayed the grim determination of the infantrymen they carried into battle and medevac'd back to hospitals.

War is a bit different for helicopter pilots. In addition to the enemy on the ground, the pilots must constantly work to thwart the force of gravity. From the moment they take off, gravity is trying to pull them back to earth. They temporarily overcome gravity's pull with the complex contraption wrapped around them. It takes an internal combustion engine, transmissions, gear boxes, hydraulic pumps, and blades whirling at hundreds of RPMs to keep them from crashing to earth. Any interruption in the carefully synchronized mechanical process will immediately surrender them to the force of gravity. If that happens, then there is only one question of value: "How far is it to the ground?"

When an infantryman describes a harrowing battle, he is likely to describe geography. He will reference folds in the earth—hills, ravines, and deadly flat spaces where there was no cover. Life or death for infantrymen is often dependent on topography.

When a helicopter pilot describes a near-deadly mission, he will often talk about readings on his control panel. He will talk about temperatures increasing; RPMs dropping; and needles creeping toward red lines on gauges. His life, and the lives of the others on board his aircraft, are dependent on the health of the flying machine. It wasn't uncommon for a pilot to be oblivious to bullets cutting through the aircraft inches from him because he was so intensely focused on keeping the machine in the air.

"I took care of the job in the cockpit and got scared later," O'Toole said of combat flying. "I never really got to trembling until I got back and set on the edge of my cot—and then started thinking about it," he said. "Then you'd sit here and start shakin', you know." He laughed and added, "Because, if you didn't, you weren't normal."

The pilots formed close bonds with the enlisted Marines in their squadron. In helicopter squadrons, half of the men in the air at any one time were the squadron's enlisted aircrewmen. The aircrewmen performed a number of critical tasks. They served as the pilots' eyes below and to the rear of the aircraft—talking to them constantly over the aircraft's intercom system, guiding them around obstacles and fine-tuning the aircraft's positioning when landing, or when they were hovering to pick up loads with the helicopter's winch. The crewmen also served as the aircraft's damage control team—putting out fires, making emergency repairs, or jettisoning cargo when necessary. One of their most critical jobs was to coordinate all of the activities in the cargo compartment. This often included leaving the aircraft to organize the situation in the landing zone. Lastly, the helicopter crewmen manned the machine guns mounted in the doors of the helicopter, using them to strafe enemy positions and return fire when the aircraft was flying into or out of hot landing zones.

Like the infantry units they carried into battle, the helicopter squadrons fought and bled on a daily basis. The blackened wreckage of helicopters in the hills and paddies around Vietnam were mute monuments to the sacrifices of the helicopter pilots and crewmen.

It was not uncommon to see a UH-34D limp toward the airfield at Dong Ha or Phu Bai, riddled with bullet holes and trailing smoke. When the ground crew got to the aircraft, they would often find one of the pilots unconscious and slumped forward against his harness; and one of the crewmen lying on the deck of the cargo compartment in a pool of blood and expended machine-gun casings.

Marine helicopter squadrons quickly built a proud legacy in Vietnam. It's impossible to calculate the number of lives saved because helicopter pilots and their crews braved enemy fire to evacuate badly wounded men. That dedication, however, came at a price. By the end of April 1967, 37 helicopter pilots had been killed in action and 229 had been wounded. Fifty-two aircrewmen were killed in action during the same period, and 311 wounded.[9] By the end of 1970, 252 Marine helicopters had been lost in combat.[10]

By the end of the war, two Marine aviators had earned the Medal of Honor. Captain Stephen W. Pless earned the award on August 19, 1967, when he landed in the middle of a large Viet Cong unit that was overrunning a stranded group of U.S. soldiers from a downed helicopter. Two years later, on January 31, 1970, Private First Class Raymond M. Clausen, a 22-year-old aircrewman, earned the nation's highest award by repeatedly leaving his helicopter and racing through enemy fire to recover wounded Marines pinned down in a minefield.

For Marine infantrymen in Vietnam, the helicopter was a lifesaver. General Walt credited helicopter crews with saving the lives of countless Marines in Vietnam. "The combat troops were not given to superlatives, but they unabashedly call the helicopters and the men who fly them 'Angels of Mercy,'" Walt wrote. "There is hardly a place they have not gone or risks they have not taken to get the wounded out of battle and back to emergency care."[11]

CHAPTER 12

Two Brothers

"We went into town and had a few beers and got our picture taken together. That was the last time I saw him."

NORMAN DICKEY

On January 26, a convoy of trucks carrying Westerman's Marines began rolling through the gate of Camp Schwab and rumbled down the narrow highway toward White Beach, the U.S. Navy's port facility in Buckner Bay, 31 miles south. For the next two days, convoys of jeeps and trucks brought the battalion down to the piers.

Company C was one of the first companies to roll through the gate. At the port, Bob Kelley and his Marines were directed to the USS *Vancouver,* a 522-foot amphibious warfare ship. The *Vancouver* was one of the newer ships serving off the coast of Vietnam. In addition to a flight deck for helicopters, it had a well deck in the stern that flooded so amtracs and landing craft could launch from inside the ship.

The *Vancouver* and the rest of the ARG ships were riding at anchor in Buckner Bay, just offshore from the navy's piers at White Beach.[1] The Marines hauled their packs, weapons, and sea bags off the trucks and clambered on board landing craft for the ride out to the *Vancouver.* Once on board, a team of Marines directed them to their berthing areas, where they were assigned bunks and lockers. Doug and the rest of the platoon stowed their gear and started to get settled in.

That evening, while he was eating chow, Doug was summoned to the quarterdeck. When he got to the quarterdeck, he was surprised to find Norman standing there. Doug knew Norman was in the Marines and hoped they would get a chance to meet up somewhere, but he didn't expect to see him on Okinawa. He certainly never expected to find him standing on the quarterdeck of the *Vancouver.*

Norman had gotten the orders to Vietnam he wanted. After finishing his infantry training in California, he was issued orders to 3rd Battalion, 4th Marines, which was operating west of Dong Ha at the time. On his way to Vietnam, Norman happened to get a short layover in Okinawa. He knew Doug was on Okinawa and was determined to see him. He asked around and quickly found out Doug's battalion had embarked on the ships and was getting ready to sail. "The day I got there, I went U.A." Norman said later, "and I went out to the boat that he was on and looked him up."

Doug took Norman down to the berthing area and introduced him to the guys in his platoon. After meeting the platoon, they sat down and started getting caught up on the news from home.

After some chit-chat, Norman told Doug about what had happened in boot camp when he asked for orders to Vietnam. He told Doug about the regulations that prohibited family members from serving in combat at the same time. He told Doug about all the papers he had signed so he could go to Vietnam. He explained that the Marine Corps wasn't going to let both of them serve in Vietnam at the same time. Finally, Norman explained that he would be taking Doug's place in Vietnam; and that Doug was going to be transferred to a non-combat assignment or sent home early.

Doug was shocked. He never imagined his younger brother would end up taking his place in Vietnam—and that he would end up going home early. One of the reasons he had enlisted in the first place was so his younger brothers wouldn't have to go to Vietnam. Doug was angry at first and told Norman he shouldn't have done it. Norman just told Doug there wasn't anything he could do about it at that point. The paperwork for Doug's transfer had started when Norman was in boot camp and was already working its way through the system.

Doug calmed down when he realized there wasn't much he could do about the situation. And he agreed that it wasn't fair to put their parents through the ordeal of having both of them in Vietnam at the same time. He knew his mother was already really worried.

"When I found Doug on his ship I don't think he could believe I was there," Norman said later. "I think he was happy to see me and maybe a little upset but we really didn't have a heated argument. It was just two brothers that hadn't seen each other for a while having a quick visit. I couldn't stay long because I was afraid of missing a [unit] movement."[2]

By then it was getting late and Doug decided to see if he could get permission to take Norman back to Camp Hansen. Liberty for the Marines and the crews of the ships was restricted because they were getting ready to sail. Doug found Lieutenant Dickerson and asked if he could get a Special Liberty pass so he could take Norman back to Camp Hansen. Dickerson went to Bob Kelley with the unusual request. Both men had brothers and knew this was a time when the rules had to be bent.

Kelley signed a special pass. On their way back to Camp Hansen, Doug and Norman stopped in town and had a couple of beers together.

"Last evening I had a pleasant surprise while I was on the ship as Norman just happened to show up while I was eating chow," Doug wrote home the next day. "Well, we talked for a while and then I talked to my Lieutenant and he talked to the Captain and he gave me Special Liberty and I went back to Camp Hansen with him and we went and had a good time," Doug wrote. "I talked to him until about 11:00 PM and then I caught a cab and came back [to the ship]." Doug didn't mention anything to his parents about Norman taking his place in Vietnam or that he might be coming home early.[3]

The two brothers were very close and had really missed each other. Norman wrote home two days later and told his parents about their time together. "I almost cried when I saw him and he almost did the same when we said good-bye."[4]

That evening is a cherished memory for Norman Dickey. "We went into town and had a few beers and got our picture taken together," he said. "That was the last time I saw him."[5]

CHAPTER 13

Exercise *Mud Puppy III*

"Mud Puppy III was terminated and the BLT backloaded aboard ARG shipping and sailed for an up-keep period at Subic Bay. Minor discrepancies in the loading plan were corrected at Subic Bay with little difficulty."

1ST BATTALION, 4TH MARINES, COMMAND CHRONOLOGY[1]

Westerman's battalion was augmented with a number of additional Marine and navy units when it became the Battalion Landing Team. These units began to converge on White Beach from other bases in Okinawa. The reinforcements added nearly 500 men to Westerman's command. His battalion swelled from 1,152 to a total of 1,641 men in a matter of days. Additionally, his complement of navy doctors and corpsmen almost doubled from 56 to 90.

By the evening of January 27, Company A, Company B, and the battalion headquarters had settled in on the *Iwo Jima*, and the ARG was ready to sail. The task force was scheduled to sail to the Philippines for Exercise *Mud Puppy III*, a large-scale amphibious exercise on the island of Mindoro. Although the battalion had been training for more than a month, it still needed to train with HMM-363 and the three ships. The purpose of the *Mud Puppy* exercise was for the battalion to actually rehearse an amphibious landing before it went back to Vietnam.

Captain Westervelt, however, scheduled a port call in Taiwan on their way to the Philippines. The *Iwo Jima* and the other ARG ships had been heavily engaged off the coast of Vietnam for months, often operating around the clock for weeks at a time. The sailors had earned a break. To reward the crews, Captain Westervelt scheduled a liberty stop in Keelung. Taiwan was considered one the best liberty ports in the Far East, and the crews were looking forward to a few days there.

At 0803 on January 28, the USS *Vancouver* weighed anchor and got underway from Buckner Bay, following the USS *Iwo Jima* out to sea. The USS *Point Defiance* took station astern of the *Vancouver* and the three ships steamed southward at 16 knots. The ships arrived in Keelung harbor on Sunday morning, 29 January and dropped anchor.

Unfortunately for the Marines and sailors on the *Vancouver*, their dreams of liberty in Taiwan were dashed shortly after dropping anchor. The captain was told there was no berthing available for his ship. Therefore, it was decided that the *Vancouver* would continue on to the Philippines. That afternoon, the *Vancouver* weighed anchor again and headed for Subic Bay. It arrived in Subic on Tuesday morning, 31 January, and was anchored by 0830.

The *Point Defiance* arrived two days later. However after it got to Subic, the *Point Defiance* was given short-notice orders to return to Vietnam to conduct independent operations in the Vung Tau area and then to continue to Thailand. The USS *Thomaston* (LSD-28) took its place in the ARG and the Marines on the *Point Defiance* were transferred to the *Thomaston*.

The USS *Iwo Jima* arrived in Subic on the morning of February 3, and joined the other two ships. The three ships got underway that afternoon and headed south to Mindoro, a small island about 130 miles south of Subic. American units regularly used the northern coast of Mindoro to practice amphibious operations. In addition to being away from the crowded air and sea traffic around Subic Bay, the northern coast of Mindoro had a number of river deltas that resembled the terrain of Vietnam, particularly the Mekong Delta.

Amphibious landings are the most complex and dangerous military operations. To be successful, they must be meticulously planned, rehearsed, and executed. Amphibious landings require the precise synchronization of ships, aircraft, and troops. Every man and every piece of equipment is assigned a specific place in the landing plan. Poor planning results in chaos: waterborne traffic jams form as too many amtracs or landing craft try to use the same beach; units land in the wrong place; and supplies get lost. Communication networks have to be coordinated or no one will be able to talk to each other.

Since they left Okinawa, Westerman and his officers, together with the officers from the ships, and the staff of HMM-363, had spent most of their time drafting the landing plan they would use in Vietnam. The plan they produced was 150 pages of schedules and tables. It spelled out the exact timing and composition of each wave of amtracs and landing craft to hit the beach. The tables detailed the men assigned to each helicopter or amtrac. Every radio frequency was carefully coordinated with organizational diagrams. The routes for the helicopters to fly into and out of the landing zones were clearly defined and laid out like highways in the sky.[2]

The plan called for the Amphibious Ready Group to use a combination of methods to get the Battalion Landing Team ashore. Each method had its advantages and disadvantages.

In the surface assault waves, a company of Marines would go ashore using LVTP-5 amphibian tractors. Amtracs had been an integral part of every amphibious task force since they had proven to be so critical during the near-disastrous landing at Tarawa in 1943. The lumbering armored vehicles afforded the Marines in the assault waves some protection while they approached the beach, and then served as armored personnel carriers to move the Marines inland. Amtracs, however, were very slow in the water and could only carry a fraction of the BLT's men and equipment.

In addition to the surface assault, two companies would use helicopters from HMM-363 to get ashore. The advantage of using helicopters was that it was the fastest way to get an assault force ashore. The helicopters also allowed the Marines to fly over the beach and land miles inland, avoiding bloody fights at the water's edge. Helicopters, however, could only transport small groups and were restricted by weather. Helicopterborne assault forces were also vulnerable to antiaircraft fire and could be decimated if the enemy had even rudimentary antiaircraft weapons.

Lastly, heavy equipment and supporting units were brought ashore using the navy's landing craft. Developed during World War II, landing craft were flat-bottom boats that ran themselves up to the beach and then dropped their bow ramps to offload their cargo. Although the landing craft were slow, they could carry very heavy equipment and vehicles ashore. The BLT's platoon of M48 tanks, for example, could only be brought ashore in the ARG's 119-foot "utility boats."

1st Battalion, 4th Marines, began its practice landing on the afternoon of February 4. Bob Kelley and his company, riding in amtracs, landed at 1302 and were the

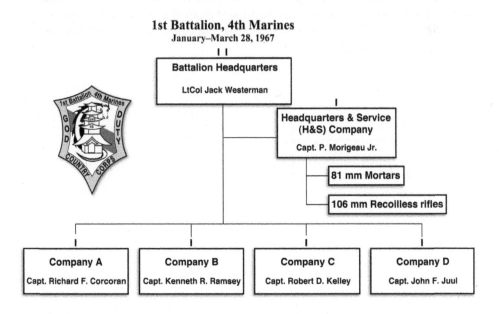

first ashore. At the same time the amtracs were climbing out of the surf on Green Beach, 14 of Lieutenant Colonel Huntington's helicopters, carrying Company A, landed at LZ Eagle, just inland from the beach.

For the next three hours, the bay was a flurry of activity. Amtracs and landing craft went back and forth between the beaches and the three ships offshore. Wave after wave of helicopters ferried men and equipment from the ships to landing zones. Most of the battalion was ashore by 1600.

For the next two days, the battalion simulated patrolling and calling in artillery and air support. In addition to working with the amtracs, Kelley and Company C practiced using small boats in one of the nearby rivers.

On the morning of the 6th, the battalion began the most difficult phase of the exercise: returning to the ships. Rendezvousing with ships bouncing around in the ocean is more difficult and dangerous than going ashore.

Kelley's company was the last unit to withdraw from the beach. After the other companies were on their way back to the ships, Kelley and Company C got the order to climb into their amtracs and return to the ships. After he and his Marines had jammed themselves into the vehicles, the amtracs clattered into the surf and churned across the bay back out to the ships. All of the men from the battalion were back on the ships and stowing their gear just as the sun was setting. A few minutes later, the ships got underway and sailed back to Subic Bay. The exercise was a success. The SLF's landing plan had worked.

The ARG was back in Subic on the afternoon of February 7. The next three days were spent making final preparations for their return to Vietnam. After inspections and making sure all of their gear had been cleaned and stowed properly, Jack Westerman granted liberty and the Marines and sailors of the BLT headed into Olongapo for a short break.

CHAPTER 14

Operation *Deckhouse VI*

"Everything you touched blew up. Everything was full of punji stakes."

LANCE CORPORAL CHARLIE RUNNELS

The Special Landing Force received orders for their first operation on February 11, 1967. The ARG sailed for Vietnam the next day. The operation was named *Deckhouse VI*. Their mission was to help clear the Viet Cong from the southern end of Quang Ngai Province.

Operation *Deckhouse VI* was part of the 1st Marine Division's campaign to eliminate the Viet Cong from Quang Ngai Province. Quang Ngai had gotten little attention from the American and South Vietnamese military until early 1967. Until then, the priority had been to secure the more vital areas around Da Nang and Chu Lai to the north. In the absence of significant South Vietnamese or American forces, the Viet Cong had taken over most of Quang Ngai.

Major General Herman Nickerson, the commanding general of the 1st Marine Division, together with the local South Vietnamese military leaders, decided the time had come to start clearing the communists out of Quang Ngai. They decided to begin the campaign in Duc Pho, the southernmost district of Quang Ngai. Duc Pho was a communist stronghold. The Marine Corps' history of the war summed up the situation in Duc Pho at the beginning of 1967: "Astonishing as it may seem, the Communist control of the area was so complete that many of the inhabitants had never come in contact with military forces other than the Viet Cong."[1]

Fighting in Duc Pho was going to be different for Westerman and his Marines. They had spent 1966 in northern Quang Tri Province fighting the North Vietnamese Army in the hills and jungles just south of the DMZ. Duc Pho was 196 miles south of the DMZ at the extreme southern end of the Marine Corps' area of responsibility.

Not only was the weather and terrain different in Duc Pho, but Westerman and his Marines would be fighting a different kind of enemy in the Viet Cong.

Duc Pho was a 12-mile-long, wedge-shaped region with its point to the south where the Annamite Mountains cut across the coastal plain and met the South China Sea. The district expanded northward to a seven-mile-wide marshy plain of rice paddies and swamps at its northern border with Mo Duc, the adjoining district. Most of the 144 square miles of Duc Pho were covered with water: rivers, estuaries, paddies, swamps, and salt flats. The areas that weren't soggy, were covered with farming and fishing villages. The northern half of the district was dominated by the Tra Cao River and its tributaries. The area was mostly flat except for Nui Dang—a cone-shaped hill that rose from the coastal plain and overlooked the Tra Cau River delta. The district headquarters for Duc Pho was located at the base of Nui Dang. The southern half of Duc Pho was dominated by two large inland estuaries, overshadowed by the tail of the Annamite Mountains. Sa Huynh was the principal settlement at the southern end of the district, located on the coast where the Nuoc Man estuary met the sea.[2]

Duc Pho was a critical region for the Viet Cong. They had to control the area because it was one of the most fertile farming and salt-producing regions in Vietnam. They needed the steady supply of rice, meat, fish, and salt to feed their guerrillas. Also, the Viet Cong needed manpower—and Duc Pho was home to thousands of villagers. The Viet Cong relentlessly recruited and extorted the villagers to join their ranks as guerrilla soldiers, or forced them to serve as laborers to haul supplies and build fortifications.

The geography of Duc Pho also made it important to the Viet Cong. The Annamite Mountains cut across South Vietnam along the southern end of Duc Pho. The spine of the mountain range was covered with thick forest and jungle, making it an invaluable infiltration route to the coast from the Ho Chi Minh Trail in Laos. The Viet Cong also used the bays and river deltas along the coast of Duc Pho to infiltrate men and supplies from the sea.

The Viet Cong in Duc Pho presented a different threat to Blackjack Westerman and his Marines. The NVA regulars they had faced up in Quang Tri had fought as conventional soldiers. The NVA wore uniforms and fought as battalions and regiments.

However, most of the enemy in Duc Pho were "Local Force" Viet Cong guerrillas, who didn't wear uniforms. They usually wore loose-fitting black shirts and pants, which the Americans nicknamed "black pajamas." They used hit-and-run tactics and rarely engaged in protracted battles. They ambushed small patrols but usually vanished after the initial volley. They sniped at American and South Vietnamese units from the treelines, then disappeared.

The Viet Cong's most effective weapon was the booby trap; which they planted by the hundreds around the villages and trails of Duc Pho. The devices ranged from simple pits filled with sharpened bamboo "punji" stakes, to large antitank mines packed with several pounds of explosive.

The Viet Cong were cunning and shrewd. They studied American behavior and planted booby traps just about anywhere an American soldier or Marine might step. They would even booby-trap the shady area under a tree where a man might stop to get out of the heat for a few minutes. The booby traps were often made from captured or discarded American hand grenades, mortar, or artillery rounds. They even turned American trash into booby traps, stuffing discarded C-Ration and Coca-Cola cans with explosives.[3]

While many of the mines and booby traps didn't actually kill; they were very effective. Booby traps and mines eventually wounded more Marines than any other weapon in Vietnam, even edging out the percentage of wounds caused by enemy bullets. For Marines on patrol, the most haunting aspect of booby traps was that they were responsible for the vast majority of amputations suffered in Vietnam. While a man might survive a booby trap, he was often maimed for the rest of his life.[4]

General Nickerson planned two operations to start clearing the Viet Cong out of Duc Pho. The campaign would begin with Operation *Desoto*. During Operation *Desoto,* a reinforced battalion, dubbed "Task Force X-Ray," would helicopter into the northern end of the district near Nui Dang and start sweeping the villages in the northern half of Duc Pho. The second part of the campaign to clear the Viet Cong out of Duc Pho would begin with Operation *Deckhouse VI*. During Operaiton *Deckhouse VI,* Westerman and his Marines would land at the southern end of Duc Pho near Sa Huynh and sweep northward; eventually, the two Marine forces would meet.

Operation *Desoto* began on January 27 when companies from 3rd Battalion, 7th Marines, the lead units of Task Force X-Ray, helicoptered into landing zones northwest of Nui Dang and began sweeping the villages to the north and west. The region was a Viet Cong stronghold. Over the next three days, the Marines hit increasing resistance. The villages were ringed with trench lines and bunkers, and the rice paddies were full of hidden machine-gun nests and booby traps.

In one incident, Marines were receiving fire from a thatched hut. A recoilless rifle team was brought up and directed to fire a round into the hut. When the smoke cleared, they were surprised to see a large cylindrical concrete bunker standing where the thatched hut had been. A second round destroyed the bunker.[5]

On January 30, Company I hit a large Viet Cong force near Hai Mon village. These were "Regular Force" Viet Cong. They were full-time soldiers who used conventional tactics and heavy weapons. The Marine company was pinned down in deep rice paddies all day long, taking heavy machine-gun fire from three sides. They weren't able to extricate themselves until well after dark; after elements of Company M managed to battle their way to their position.

On January 31, two companies from 3rd Battalion, 5th Marines, joined the battle and began working their way toward the Tra Cau River. On February 5, they assaulted through Hai Mon village and enveloped Hill 26. The Marines surprised the Viet Cong on the hill by assaulting from the west. About 30 Viet Cong tried to escape across the Tra Cau River by boat, but were raked with fire from Marines on the hill and the attack helicopters circling overhead.

When the Marines searched Hill 26, they found an elaborate tunnel, bunker, and cave network dug into the hill. Combat engineers used more than 3,600 pounds of explosives to collapse the fortifications.[6] For the next two weeks, Marine companies from Task Force X-Ray continued to sweep the area. There were daily firefights, but no protracted battles.

Operation *Deckhouse VI* was launched three weeks after the beginning of Operation *Desoto*. It was planned to take place in two phases. In the first phase, Westerman's battalion would land at Sa Huynh, 14 miles south of the Task Force X-Ray units conducting Operation *Desoto*. During this phase, Westerman's battalion would spend about 10 days clearing the Viet Cong out of the coastal villages around Sa Huynh.

An imposing figure. LtCol "Blackjack" Westerman (middle) on the beach near Sa Huynh on February 17, 1967 during Operation *Deckhouse VI*. Westerman is briefing VAdm John J. Hyland (second from right) on the progress of the operation. Hyland was the commander of the Seventh Fleet. In the photo are (left to right): BGen Louis Metzger (commander of the 9th Marine Brigade), Col Joseph LoPrete, LtCol Westerman, VAdm Hyland, and Capt John D. Westervelt (commander of the Amphibious Ready Group). (U.S. Navy, JOC Jim Falk)

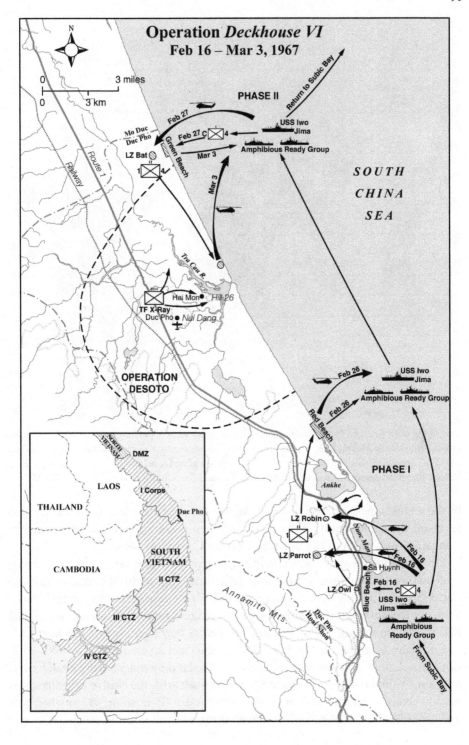

Operation *Deckhouse VI*
Feb 16 – Mar 3, 1967

One of the objectives of Operation *Deckhouse VI* was to intercept Viet Cong boats bringing men and supplies into the Sa Huynh area. Marines from 2nd Platoon search a Vietnamese boat during the first day of the operation. The Marines in the photo are (left to right): Lionel Lawson, Kent Hansen, Dennis Heider, Ray Baer (leaning into boat), and Charlie Runnels (back to camera). (USMC A188494)

In the second phase of *Deckhouse VI*, Westerman and his Marines would go back on board the ships; steam up the coast, and then make another landing in the Nui Dang area, just north of the units conducting Operation *Desoto*.

Operation *Deckhouse VI* began on February 16. Jack Westerman had sent a message to all his company commanders two days earlier and directed that it be read to all hands just prior to launching from the ships. It read: "If we receive fire, let's draw blood. I don't like reports that state: Quote: Negative results: Unquote. Blackjack sends." Bob Kelley read the message to his Marines just before they climbed into the amtracs.[7]

Company C landed across Blue Beach, near Sa Huynh village at 1000, while Company A and Company B were helicoptered to landing zones northwest of Kelley's position.[8] While the Marines made fleeting contact with the elusive guerrillas, they quickly became aware of the Viet Cong's booby traps. "Everything you touched blew up," according to Charlie Runnels. "Everything was full of punji stakes."

Jim G. Lucas, a 52-year-old war correspondent with Scripps-Howard, accompanied Westerman's Marines during Operation *Deckhouse VI*. Lucas was one of the most distinguished journalists in Vietnam and had seen the worst of war. He had been a Marine combat correspondent during World War II and had been decorated in seven island campaigns, including Tarawa, where he was mistakenly reported as killed in action. Lucas personally witnessed the horrifying carnage at Marpi Point on Saipan.[9] After leaving the Marines, he went back to being a newspaper reporter and spent more than two years covering combat in Korea. Among his many honors, Jim Lucas was awarded the Pulitzer Prize in 1954 for his reporting on the Korean War.

Jim Lucas was as close as any reporter in Vietnam got to embodying the spirit of Ernie Pyle.[10] Like Pyle, Lucas eschewed the press cliques that camped out in the bars around Saigon and mobbed the brass at press conferences. He had spent most of his time between January 1964 and the Marine landing in 1965 trudging through jungles and rice paddies with American advisors, covering a war that many in America didn't even realize was happening. He stayed in Vietnam after the war escalated in March 1965, and spent most of his time with American combat units, often tagging along on combat patrols. Jim Lucas liked the young American soldiers, sailors, airmen, and Marines he met. He made it a point to put their names and their hometowns in his stories—refusing to let them become anonymous statistics.[11]

Viet Cong snipers were generally poor shots and most Marines considered them more of an annoyance than a serious threat. However, it became painfully clear that the Viet Cong snipers in Duc Pho were an exception to this rule. They were extraordinarily accurate and deadly, often hitting Marines from over 500 yards. The snipers in Duc Pho had been very well trained and were equipped with state-of-the-art weapons.

To counter the Viet Cong snipers, additional Marine scout-sniper teams were attached to the rifle companies during *Deckhouse VI*. A sniper team from the 26th Marines was attached to Bob Kelley's company. That afternoon, one of the snipers, Corporal Kenneth T. Russell, stepped on a mine and was killed. Russell became the battalion's first casualty of the operation.

Kenneth Russell was a native of San Angelo, Texas, and had been a football star in high school. He had been briefly married and left behind a daughter. Jim Lucas was with Kelley's company and described Russell's death:

> A kid named Russell—that was his last name—got it first. Russell was a scout-sniper and a good one. Like Frank [Alaniz], he was 20 years old. Walking a few yards off the road, weapon at the ready, eyes searching the hamlets and the treelines, he'd stepped on a land mine.
>
> It had to be a big one. It blew off a leg and an arm. He died on the spot.
>
> Vietnamese Popular Forces who'd come down off their hill when the Marines came ashore shouted a warning to him in Vietnamese. No one understood, of course. Frank swore loudly. He helped wrap what was left of the kid named Russell in a rubber poncho for the trip back to the beach.[12]

Over the next week, Westerman's Marines patrolled the coastal area and chased the Viet Cong around the villages. Every day, small groups of Viet Cong fired at them and then would vanish. Usually, the guerrillas didn't hit anybody. The Marines usually didn't know if they hit anybody when they returned fire. It was frustrating and unnerving.

Grisly evidence was often the only way the Marines knew they had hit any of the Viet Cong after a firefight. On March 20, Marines from Company A followed a blood trail after a firefight. Along the trail, they found a severed hand, approximately 25 feet of intestines, a thumb, and several portions of bones "believed to be ribs," and "extensive entrails and portions of scalp and hair."[13]

Jack Westerman also sent the platoon of M48 tanks ashore and attached them to Bob Kelley's company. Kelley welcomed the big steel beasts. The tanks gave him a lot more firepower—which was good for his Marines. If one of his platoons took fire from an enemy position, Kelley would have them hold their position rather than assault. He would then bring one of the tanks up to the position. Kelley would pick up the phone on the rear of the tank and direct the tank commander to use its 90mm gun to blast the enemy positions with canister, high explosive, or white phosphorus rounds.

Jim Lucas watched Kelley one day when one of his platoons hit a Viet Cong "suicide squad" in front of Na Diem, a deserted village near Sa Huynh. "Na Diem was a typical Viet Cong village, deeply entrenched with Ponji traps, bunkers and trenches," Lucas wrote. "Capt. Bob Kelley of Sikeston, Mo. brought up tanks and leveled it," Lucas said. "Na Diem burned briskly. The people long ago had fled." Jim Lucas had spent more time in Vietnam than most military officers and knew the Viet Cong well, concluding: "The Viet Cong defenders slipped back into their holes and tunnels and got away."[14]

Sergeant Larry Wilson and Doc Long had a close call with one of the Viet Cong snipers during *Deckhouse VI*. Wilson had taken to wearing his wristwatch suspended from a bootlace around his neck. He did this because, like many men in Vietnam, he found that the tropical heat and grime often caused a rash or infection to develop where the watchband rubbed against his wrist.

Wilson and Long were walking along when one of the snipers opened fire. The first round hit well in front of them. They weren't terribly concerned at first.

The sniper's next round was a one-in-a-million shot for Larry Wilson. Wilson happened to turn sideways just as the sniper fired his shot. The bullet came in through the right sleeve of his flak jacket and slid under the fabric of the jacket and exited through the unzipped opening in the jacket. As the bullet came out the opening, it hit the wristwatch hanging around his neck with full force. The watch exploded and pieces of it flew into Wilson's chest. Standing next to him, Greg Long also felt sharp impacts to his face and arm.

Both men thought they had been hit by a bullet and dove into a nearby ditch. Once in the ditch, they started frantically examining their wounds expecting to find bullet holes. They were both bloody messes.

To their surprise, they discovered all their wounds were caused by pieces of the wristwatch. "I had blood all over my chest—and it was all from the bezel ring on that watch," Wilson said, "and I had about a dozen pieces stuck in my chest; I was bleeding like a stuck pig." Doc Long had a long gash on his jaw. It turned out that it had also been caused by a piece of the watch. Larry Wilson laughed remembering the scene with both of them lying in the ditch, picking pieces of the wristwatch out of each other. "Doc Long found the second hand or minute hand from the watch sticking out of his elbow," Wilson said with a laugh.[15]

Much of their time during *Deckhouse VI* was spent slogging through the countryside. Lionel Lawson remembered hearing Doug Dickey, Roger Cain, and Gordy Cardinal break the monotony by imitating "Froggy the Gremlin" from the kids' show *Andy's Gang*. They would imitate Froggy's trademark, "Hiya Kids! Hiya! Hiya! Hiya!" Most of the guys in the platoon had grown up with Andy Devine and Froggy. "Those guys would do that back and forth all the time," Lawson said. "Doug was a fun-loving guy. He liked to clown around—have a lot of fun, he really did."

Bill Dorsey was the platoon radio operator and had trained Doug Dickey to be a back-up radio operator. Dorsey liked Doug. "He was kind of a big guy—muscular, more so than me," he said. "Because I was very small. I weighed 125 pounds when I was in the jungle," Dorsey said. "But he was pretty good size. He was kind of a Midwestern farm boy—just laid back. I'd never seen him get angry. He was just an easy-going type person … just a hard worker, I guess you'd say. He would always pack his load and more," he said. "I mean, he was a really nice person—just one heck of a nice guy."

The battalion was also tasked with supporting the more benign "pacification" aspects of the war. The pacification programs were intended to generate goodwill with the villagers. One program sent medical and dental teams to treat the villagers. Most of the villagers had never had professional medical care in their lives. The American medical teams could cure a host of ailments with basic medicines and treatments. Helping sick children, in particular, quickly earned the villagers' appreciation.

Kelley and his Marines would ring the village to make sure the Viet Cong couldn't disrupt the program while the medical teams were treating the villagers. The Marines and local villagers usually viewed each other with suspicion at first. Most of the villagers in the Sa Huynh area hadn't ever seen U.S. Marines before Westerman's battalion came ashore. The local Viet Cong had told them the Americans and South Vietnamese soldiers were vicious and corrupt. For the Americans, the incessant sniper fire and booby traps cast an ominous pall over the seemingly sullen people they met in the villages.

On the third day of the operation, Company C was assigned to provide security for a medical outreach in Sa Huynh. Not long after Kelley and his Marines had set up their security, curious children from the village started to approach the Marines. The kids quickly realized the Marines were friendly and liked to give stuff to children.

That day, Gunnery Sergeant Ralph Grant's brief friendship with one of the little boys in the village was captured by Marine photographer T. W. Bland, Jr.

Grant was a tough career Marine. From Racine, Wisconsin, he was the youngest of 10 children. He dropped out of high school to enlist in the Marines so he could fight in Korea. He returned from Korea a decorated teenage combat veteran. Among his assignments in the decade after returning from Korea was a tour as a drill instructor. Westerman assigned Ralph Grant to be Bob Kelley's company gunnery sergeant when Company C was reestablished. Kelley and Grant worked well together. "Skipper Kelley was a great leader and made sure I looked out for the troops," Grant said. Gunny Grant was conspicuous in the field for two things: he had taken to wearing a red bandana around his neck; and he carried a shotgun in addition to the standard-issue .45 automatic. When asked about the bandana, Grant would say defiantly, "It gives the Cong something to shoot at." The shotgun served a more practical purpose. "I wanted something for close quarters," he said.[16]

On the morning of February 19, Gunny Grant looked over to find a cheerful little Vietnamese boy sitting next to him. "He came to me and just sat down," Grant said. By then Ralph Grant had a family of his own waiting for him back in the States and he couldn't help but think of his own sons.

He offered the little boy some of his C-Rations and ended up showing him how to use the plastic spoon that came with the rations to dig the food out of the cans. The boy was fascinated with the spoon and seemed to like saying the word "spoon." Grant and the other Marines nicknamed the boy "Spoon" because he was the only boy in the area who could pronounce the word. By the time Staff Sergeant Bland arrived with his camera, "Spoon" had made himself at home in the middle of the Marines and was happily munching away on C-Rations while wrapped in a Marine poncho.[17]

Second Platoon suffered its first casualty during Operation *Deckhouse VI*. On Tuesday, February 21, the platoon was crossing a field when Viet Cong guerrillas opened fire. In the exchange with the Viet Cong, four Marines were wounded and Private First Class Marvin Cole was killed. Cole was picking up a rifle grenade he had dropped and a sniper's bullet hit him in the leg.

Cole was a well-liked and cheerful 19-year-old rifleman from Fort Smith, Arkansas. He was the youngest of 14 children. Oscar and Voyle Cole had raised their children to be patriotic Americans and were proud that all eight of their boys had volunteered to serve in the military.[18] Cole, like Dickey, had enlisted in the Marines with two high-school friends using the Buddy Program after he graduated from Lincoln High School.

Initially, the wound didn't seem that serious. However, he was bleeding badly by the time the corpsmen got to him. It appeared the bullet had torn open an artery. Doc Long and Doc Nichols quickly bandaged his leg and cinched it with a tourniquet while Lieutenant Dickerson radioed for a medevac helicopter. Despite everyone's best efforts, Marvin Cole died during the flight to the *Iwo Jima*. He had lost too much blood and had gone into shock. His loss was a blow to the platoon. "I never saw that guy without a smile on his face," Lionel Lawson said of him. "He had a smile all the time. Great personality. Great kid to be around."[19]

Jim Lucas summed up the impact of a loss like Marvin Cole. "It seems to me that death is a much more personal matter in a little war like Viet Nam. In bigger wars, such as World War II and Korea, it was a constant thing. Men died in bunches, and the shock was somehow muted. In Viet Nam, it happens often, but it usually involves one or two men, and it always is unexpected. It's a lot like losing a member of the family."[20]

In addition to the threat posed by the enemy, American soldiers and Marines were also in danger of being killed by other Americans. The "friendly fire" casualties were the unavoidable consequence of extremely lethal weapons in the hands of scared, tired, and fallible young men. Despite the safeguards and procedures put in place to prevent these tragedies, they still happened. Sometimes, an artillery battery mistakenly dropped rounds on an American unit; or a plane released its bombs too late—or too early; or two patrols stumbling through the jungle in the middle of the night opened fire on each other. Americans killed by other Americans due to mistakes or blunders caused an unfathomable bitterness.

Doug Dickey almost became a friendly fire casualty on February 22. "Well I must tell you that I almost got greased by a helicopter…" Doug wrote in a letter home.[21] The squad was deployed in a sugarcane field. He and Ray Baer were lying in the field about four feet apart. A Huey helicopter was receiving some sniper fire from a treeline to their right. "Well, after the Huey had fired about 6 rockets and a good many machine gun rounds he made another pass over and opened up on my squad," Doug wrote. "Well, my buddy and I were only about 4 feet apart and he put 3 rounds in between us … rounds were going all around me. So he went to make another circle and I got up and ran into the sugar cane. That was the closest I have come to death over here."[22]

On February 25, Lieutenant Colonel Huntington was leading a 12-aircraft lift to pick up Company A to take them back to the *Iwo Jima*. The helicopters were hit by enemy fire in the landing zone and both Huntington and his copilot were wounded. With Huntington out of action, Major M. E. "Lucky" Day took command of HMM-363.[23]

The first phase of *Deckhouse VI* ended on February 26. By then, the battalion had moved five and a half miles north of their original landing points south of Sa Huynh. The companies began flying out to the ships from Red Beach, just north of Sa Huynh. Kelley's company ringed the beach while the rest of the battalion either flew back to the ships or boarded landing craft. Once the rest of the battalion had gotten safely back to the ships, Company C packed into their amtracs and headed back out to the ships. The Amphibious Ready Group began steaming north as soon as all the Marines were back on board. The Marines and sailors spent all night cleaning weapons, reorganizing supplies, and refueling helicopters, amtracs, and landing craft.

The second phase of *Deckhouse VI* began at 0830 on the morning of February 27. Westerman's battalion began landing on Green Beach, 18 miles north of Sa Huynh, fourteen and a half hours after pulling off Red Beach. Westerman's mission was to complement and reinforce the Task Force X-Ray units executing Operation *Desoto* in the area around Nui Dang.

It was immediately clear the battalion was facing a different enemy in the Operation *Desoto* area. Captain Richard F. Corcoran's Company A was assigned to fly into LZ Bat just inland from where Bob Kelley was landing on Green Beach. Before Corcoran and his Marines arrived, the LZ had been hammered with naval gunfire; then sorties of fighter-bombers had swooped in and pounded the LZ with bombs.

Despite the heavy preparation, the helicopters hit a barrage of antiaircraft fire as soon as they began their approach into the landing zone. Eight of the 14 helicopters were hit. The door gunners in the helicopters fired thousands of rounds of machine-gun fire into the area surrounding the landing zone. Two UH-1E Huey gunships circled the LZ, strafing the enemy positions with machine-gun fire and rockets. One helo was hit so badly, three of the Marines on board were wounded before the helicopter had a chance to land. The helicopter immediately became its own medevac and had to return to the *Iwo Jima* without landing in the LZ.[24]

Captain Corcoran only managed to get into the LZ with his 1st Platoon. They quickly organized a defensive perimeter. The helicopters carrying the rest of his company were rerouted to the beach and began landing near Bob Kelley's men. The remaining platoons from Company A quickly moved from the beach to LZ Bat and linked up with Corcoran and 1st Platoon.

By noon, the battalion's headquarters and three of the rifle companies were ashore and had begun to move out. All afternoon, the Marines hit pockets of Viet Cong soldiers. At one point, the Viet Cong managed to hit one of the Huey gunships circling over the rifle companies and it was forced to make an emergency landing back at the beach. It was quickly confirmed that they were fighting Main Force Viet Cong units. All day long, the Marines ran into enemy soldiers wearing green or tan uniforms and outfitted with packs, ponchos, and helmets.

In the late afternoon, Bob Kelley sent a patrol to check an area where he had called in an airstrike. The patrol ran across six soldiers in tan uniforms and unloaded at the escaping VC soldiers.[25] Intelligence later identified the enemy as members of the 19th Main Force Battalion, a force of about 400 full-time soldiers.[26]

Westerman and his battalion moved through the area in a broad search-and-destroy mission until the morning of March 3. Contact was constant over the four days. In addition to the firefights and ambushes, Westerman's battalion uncovered large Viet Cong fortifications and supply caches.

Operation *Deckhouse VI* ended on the morning of March 3, and the battalion began a tactical withdrawal back to the ARG ships. As before, Kelley's company provided security on Green Beach while the rest of the battalion went back to the ships. The battalion was back on board by that evening.

Westerman's battalion inflicted serious damage on the communist forces in the Duc Pho area. They had killed 301 Viet Cong soldiers and destroyed hundreds of Viet Cong fortifications. They captured hundreds of weapons, and a mountain of ammunition, and destroyed 30 tons of enemy supplies.

The Battalion Landing Team suffered seven killed and 127 wounded during the 16-day operation. Eight of the wounded were corpsmen.[27]

Jim Lucas filed his report toward the end of Operation *Deckhouse VI*, after trudging along with 1st Battalion, 4th Marines. In his dispatch, he made a point that resonated with the men who fought the war. Lucas took exception to the standard verbiage often used in military press releases and wire service reports after combat operations. He specifically took exception to an official communiqué from Saigon which had described the American casualties as "extremely light."

In contrast, Lucas highlighted the suffering each of those casualties represented. He described the death of Kenneth Russell on the first day of the operation—blown apart by a landmine. He detailed the serious wounding of Corporal Frank Alaniz. "Frank felt nothing. He stared, uncomprehending, at the red stain on the front of his fatigues, saw the black-red blood pour out onto the sand, unwilling to believe it was his. He dropped to his knees, almost prayerfully, and froze there."

Lucas flew out to the *Iwo Jima* and watched the efforts by Dr. Ronald Bouterie and his surgical team to keep Frank Alaniz alive. Bouterie emerged exhausted from surgery at 1:30 a.m. He and his team had spent more than six hours working on Frank. It was touch and go for a while. Frank almost bled out on them and they had to give him 10 transfusions of whole blood in the course of the surgery. Bouterie came out of the operation room and reported to Lucas that Frank Alaniz was going to live. He would be shipped back to a hospital in the States in a few days for further treatment.

Frank Alaniz probably would have died of his wounds in World War II or Korea. One of the helicopters from HMM-363 had whisked him from the battlefield to the *Iwo Jima* 20 minutes after he was hit. Frank was wheeled into surgery minutes later. In World War II or Korea, he would have waited more than six hours before evacuation to a hospital. Frank Alaniz was a tough kid. He was sitting up in his bed the next day, chatting.[28] Blackjack Westerman was one of the first to visit him.

"There is hardly a place they have not gone or risks they have not taken to get the wounded out of battle and back to emergency care," General Walt said of the helicopter pilots and crews. A UH-34D from HMM-363, "The Lucky Red Lions," evacuates a Marine who was wounded by sniper fire on February 23, 1967, during Operation *Deckhouse VI*. The wounded Marine was flown to the medical facilities on board the USS *Iwo Jima*. (USMC A188499)

In his article for Scripps-Howard at the end of Operation *Deckhouse VI*, Jim Lucas took a swipe at the glib reporting on American losses. He wryly titled his dispatch: "Grim Side of Rice Paddy War: Casualties 'Light'—For Some." His title highlighted a sad aspect of the Vietnam War. The military command and the American people were becoming numb to the human price being paid in Vietnam. Unlike World War II, where casualties were suffered in ghastly numbers, tied to distinct campaigns and battles; casualties in Vietnam were suffered in a steady, day-to-day bleeding by units in incomprehensible small-unit actions.

To the American people, the dead and wounded were becoming statistics. The politicians in Washington tried to minimize the impact of casualties to avoid difficult discussions about the war's progress. In his report, Jim Lucas emphasized that each one of those casualties represented enormous loss and suffering for the men who fought the war and their families. Most of them, like Marvin Cole, and Kenneth Russell, died on days when the official reports classified casualties as "light." Jim Lucas considered Frank Alaniz lucky. He survived his wounds and was headed home. "He has walked through his last Viet Cong Village," Lucas wrote, "worried about his last mine, seen his last buddy die."[29]

The battalion had completed Operation *Deckhouse VI* by the evening of March 3 and the ships began sailing back to Subic Bay.

Father Stephen Almasy, the battalion chaplain, led the battalion in a memorial service on board the USS *Vancouver*. Almasy had been with the battalion since June 1966 and was very well regarded by the Marines. He made it a point to be near the front lines while the battalion was in contact and often went in with the first wave. Led by Almasy, the battalion sang a number of hymns and then recited the 23rd Psalm. Bob Kelley and John Juul then read the names of the men from their companies who had been killed in the operation. Father Almasy closed the service by leading the battalion in singing the hymn, "Eternal Father Strong to Save."[30]

The *Iwo Jima*, the *Thomaston*, and the *Vancouver* had been away from California for more than eight months. Operation *Deckhouse VI* marked the end of their deployment to the Western Pacific and they were due to go home. With their deployment complete, they first had go back to Subic to offload the SLF before preparing to sail for California. The *Iwo Jima* and the other two ships arrived in Subic on the morning of March 5.

Jack Westerman was proud of his battalion's performance. He was particularly proud of their ability to disengage from operations in the Sa Huynh area and then make another amphibious assault into the *Desoto* area. "The BLT probably executed the quickest backloading and assault landing in Marine Corps History," he wrote. "A bare fourteen and ½ hours lapsed from the completion of the tactical withdrawal in Phase I until the assault waves touched down on the beach in Phase II. In a matter of less than 36 hours all assault elements were disengaged, backloaded and were relanded over an opposed beach with an entirely new mission and concept of operations."[31]

CHAPTER 15

Subic

"The morale was excellent throughout the reporting period. The maximum liberty possible was enjoyed by all hands during the Battalion Landing Team's stay at the SLF Base Camp in the Philippines."

LIEUTENANT COLONEL "BLACKJACK" WESTERMAN

The Amphibious Ready Group anchored in Subic Bay on Sunday morning, March 5, 1967. Westerman's Marines disembarked and moved up to the SLF Base Camp in the Cubi Point area of the base. The camp was a cluster of Quonset huts on the hill overlooking the airstrip. The SLF Base Camp was specifically established so Marine units could bivouac there while training or waiting for ships. The following day, the *Iwo Jima* and the other ships began their trip back to the United States. They made a port call in Hong Kong for a few days before heading back to San Diego.

The Special Landing Force had no serious training obligations for more than a week while they waited for the USS *Princeton* and the other ships that were taking over the ARG mission from the *Iwo Jima*, the *Thomaston*, and the *Vancouver*. The stopover in the Philippines was a chance for the Marines to get some liberty.

Subic Bay was considered one of the best liberty ports in the world. The town of Olongapo, outside the U.S. Navy base at Subic Bay, had one industry: separating servicemen from their money. It did this by giving young sailors and Marines whatever their hearts desired—for a reasonable price. Olongapo was a sprawling maze of bars; there were hundreds of them within walking distance of the front gate. The bars offered cold beer, loud music, and lots of pretty girls.

Most of the bar owners in Olongapo tried to come up with gimmicks to distinguish themselves from their competitors. There were country-western bars, jazz bars, "soul" bars, and bars named after cities and states. The quest to come up with an original name often yielded comical results. One place was named the "Dance Your Ass Off Bar." Another was an uncanny reproduction of Hugh Hefner's Playboy Club, complete with plush leather booths and girls dressed in the distinctive "bunny" outfits. One bar featured a pool filled with live alligators.

The crowd in Olongapo was very young. The mixture of cheap beer, lively girls, and young men who were at war, made Olongapo the wildest town on earth. It wasn't unusual to see a drunken sailor chasing an alligator down the unpaved street—followed by a screaming Filipino bar owner; followed by a local policeman with his pistol drawn; followed by a crowd of sailors and Marines—who were all cheering for the alligator.

Jack Westerman believed Marines who fight hard should also get to play hard. He and his Marines had done plenty of hard fighting since he took command. His young warriors had done everything he had asked—and more. He couldn't have been more proud of them. As far as Jack Westerman was concerned, the battalion's layover in Subic Bay was the time for his Marines to play hard.

The U.S. Navy, however, administered the base at Subic and maintained a number of restrictions on liberty in Olongapo. One restriction was that no Marine or sailor was allowed to leave the base without a liberty card. A liberty card was a wallet-sized pass with the man's name on it. The cards were issued to the men by their commands and had to be presented to the gate guards before they were allowed to leave the base.

Furthermore, everybody had to be back on the base by midnight every night—a policy known as "Cinderella Liberty." A man who failed to make it back to the gate before the midnight curfew had his liberty card confiscated and was reported to his command. To punish those who missed the curfew, the base MPs would hold the confiscated liberty card for a week. This restricted the man to the base for a week. Because it was rare for a ship or a unit to spend more than a week in Subic, a man who lost his liberty card effectively lost any chance to enjoy the town. To add to the misery, those without liberty ended up pulling work details while their buddies headed into town every night. Being restricted to the base was a particular torture for rowdy young Marines and sailors. They could hear the music and revelry from the bars in town while they were on the work details.

Blackjack Westerman viewed the navy's regulations as petty and silly. He also bridled at having some faceless navy officer or gate guard dictate whether men under his command got liberty or not. As far as he was concerned, he and his officers alone would discipline his Marines—no one else.

Jack Westerman felt his men deserved the best liberty possible while in Subic. The stop in the Philippines was only a short reprieve from the misery of sweltering jungles and fetid rice paddies. He knew that some of the young faces he saw every morning at the battalion formation wouldn't be there in a month. He knew some of those young men would be dead or lying in a hospital within days or weeks.

Westerman wasn't going to let silly regulations cheat those young men out of their last chance to drink a cold beer—or feel a woman's touch.

To circumvent the rules he saw as stupid, Westerman directed his company commanders to type up seven liberty cards for every Marine. If a gate guard confiscated a man's card, the Marine could stop by his company office and pick up a new one and head back out through the gate the next day—in direct defiance of the well-known base policy. This made it possible for the Marines to leave the base even if they had failed to meet the curfew the day before.

Blackjack's Marines hit the town like a typhoon for 10 days. Westerman required his Marines be back at the camp for a morning muster, followed by calisthenics and a unit run. He didn't care how long they spent in town as long as they were there for the morning muster. Many of the battalion's Marines came staggering through the gate just before sunrise. The gate guards quickly amassed a growing pile of liberty cards—many with the same names on them, and realized they were fighting a losing battle trying to restrict Westerman's men. "We finally reached the point, where we'd throw our Liberty Cards in the guard shack and they'd just throw them back at us," Charlie Runnels said with a laugh.

Bob Kelley remembered the layover in the Philippines, "You'd get reports from the Shore Patrol and we'd just tear them up. It was a lot of fun and games."

By the time they got to the Philippines, 2nd Platoon was a tightly knit group. For most of them, liberty in Olongapo was like nothing they could have imagined. Many of the bars were air-conditioned; their juke boxes were filled with the latest records from the States, and the San Miguel beer was ice-cold. In every bar, beautiful young girls mobbed them as soon as they walked through the door. The local police knew the city relied on the American servicemen for business and rarely interfered with the ribald partying. Controlling the sailors and Marines and breaking up fistfights between the Americans was left to the roving teams of shore patrolmen from the base.

Second Platoon decided to make the "White House" bar their base of operations while in Subic. The bar was on the second floor—above another bar. They took the place over. Lionel Lawson remembered starting to walk up the stairs and having to dodge a sailor who came tumbling down from above. After watching the sailor go past him, he stepped out and started to go up the stairs again, only to hear a yelp. He jumped out of the way again as another sailor came tumbling down the stairs. "I looked up at the top of stairs and there was Ray Baer—and he had another sailor in a headlock—and was about to toss him down the stairs too."

Ray Baer was one of the platoon's true rowdies. He was a big guy from Kansasville, Wisconsin. Baer had grown up as an outdoorsman and loved to scrap. He had already demonstrated genuine bravery on the battlefield against NVA soldiers and Viet Cong guerrillas. When a firefight started, you were sure to see Ray Baer in the middle of it somewhere. One Marine summed up Ray Baer's reputation: "He was a good man to have around when the shit hit the fan." For Ray Baer, fighting with sailors was just good fun.

The scene on the stairs is one of Lawson's most vivid memories from the two weeks in Subic. "I yelled up to Ray, 'Hold on a second, at least let me get to the top of the stairs.'" Baer just smiled, and told Lionel to come on up. After he got to the top of the stairs, Lawson heard cussing and swearing as the third sailor went rolling down the stairs. "That was Ray," he said with a laugh.

Greg Long and Doug Dickey had been in Company B together and became friends. "He was always in a good mood. You could go talk to Doug and he'd cheer you up one way or the other," Long said. "He always had something nice or funny to say."[1] Long recounted an incident in Olongapo with Doug Dickey: "I'll never forget … we had him in this bar. And we told Doug we were going to get him 'lucky,'" Long said. "We paid the best-looking girl to come over and sit on his lap and rub his leg…" Long said with a laugh. The girl played along, teasing Doug and offering to show him "a good time." The other guys all encouraged him to take the girl to one of the hotels in town and spend the night with her. But Doug wouldn't do it. He gently lifted the girl off his lap and set her on another chair. "He just said, 'No, no, no. I can't do that. I can't do that,'" Long recalled. "He had been raised with strong values and they stayed with him. He was just an awesome young man," Greg Long said. "For as young as we were—and as stupid as we were—he stayed true to his beliefs. You couldn't have asked for a better person than Doug Dickey."

While in the Philippines, Doug got the official notification that he was going to be transferred out of 1st Battalion, 4th Marines—and out of Vietnam, as soon as they completed their next operation. The paperwork Norman had started in boot camp had finally worked its way through the system. Greg Long remembered borrowing money from Doug while they were in Subic. "And he told me when we left the Philippines, he said, 'Doc, you make sure you pay me this back,' he says, 'because I'm saving my money because I'm going home.'"

John Szymanski also got his orders to the Officer Candidates School while the battalion was in the Philippines. He was nearing the end of his year-long assignment to Vietnam and was scheduled to leave for the States at the beginning of April. The Marines in 2nd Platoon threw him a going-away party. They also got together and bought a Zodiac Olympos wristwatch and had it engraved on the back: "J.S.S. Good Luck, 2nd Plt, "C" Co." Szymanski was speechless when they presented the watch to him. They also gave him a large carved wooden eagle, globe, and anchor with an engraved brass plate on the bottom. The engraving read: "John Stephen Szymanski. In Appreciation, 2nd Platoon, C Company, 1st Battalion, 4th Marines." Szymanski told his wife the two gifts were the greatest honor he could have received—because they came from his Marines.

Blackjack Westerman further destroyed his relationship with the navy officers who commanded the base at Subic one night in the officers' club at Cubi Point.

Westerman decided to get his officers together for an evening and passed the word for all of them to meet at the officers' club. The club catered mostly to the navy pilots stationed at the nearby airstrip. The Marines were using it because it was the only officers' club near their camp.

Captain John F. Juul, the Company D commander, was one of the officers there. "We were all in the bar, having a beer. And everybody was gathered around Blackjack and we were all having a beer and he was telling us sea stories—we were having a good time. We weren't necessarily being rowdy. We were just talking loud and laughing and cutting up there, you know, what Marines do when they gather around the bar—nothing serious."

In keeping with the protocol of the officers' club, Westerman and his officers were wearing their summer service khakis—a short-sleeve service dress uniform. "I remember that because Blackjack was wearing his Navy Cross," Juul said.

As it approached midnight, the manager came and told Westerman the club was going to close soon and he would have to take their party elsewhere. According to Bob Kelley, Westerman told the manager they wanted to stay a while longer, and assured the manager that they would take care of locking up when they left.

The manager realized Westerman and his Marines had no intention of moving on any time soon and called the base duty officer. The duty officer was a navy commander. John Juul remembered him: "He came up and kind of muscled his way through the captains and lieutenants who were all gathered around Westerman," Juul said. "And he starts getting after Blackjack on why we're making so much noise and said, 'Why do you Marines have to come in and disrupt the club?'"

Bob Kelley also remembered the scene when the duty officer arrived: "He shows up and challenges Westerman," Kelley said, "and tells him to take his 'ungentlemanly conduct' elsewhere, or words to that effect."

All of a sudden, the navy officer was lying on the floor. "Jack really cold-cocked him," Kelley said with a laugh.

"I didn't actually see 'the connection,'" Juul said, remembering the scene. "I just heard something like a 'splat,'" he said with a laugh. "He just laid this guy out!"

The evening was definitely over at that point. Juul remembered one of the Marines saying, "It's time to get out of here." And they all hustled Westerman out the door.

The story about Westerman slugging the navy officer had spread through the battalion by breakfast the next morning. Blackjack was summoned to the admiral's office early that morning. "They had a little discussion about his conduct," Bob Kelley later surmised.

After breakfast, the officers were told they had to meet in the chow hall at 10 o'clock for an all-officers' meeting. They all figured it had to do with the incident at the club the night before. No one had seen Westerman all morning.

They mustered at 10 o'clock; but Westerman wasn't there.

Ten o'clock came and went. Westerman still hadn't been seen. Juul remembered waiting in the chow hall. "Everybody's saying, 'Where the hell is he? What's going on?'"

Then, all of a sudden, the sergeant major came in and called everybody to attention. The officers all snapped to attention. "And Blackjack walks up to the front of the mess hall, where everybody was sitting," Juul said. "I don't think he even gave the order to sit down."

Westerman was clearly agitated. Juul remembered the scene: "He just turned to us and said: 'I don't want to hear about anymore goddamn fighting in the O' Club!'" Then Jack Westerman spun on his heels and marched out. "And we were kind of stunned at first. But we knew what had happened," Juul said. There was a long pause after Westerman stormed out. "Then the whole group just burst out laughing."[2]

No one knows exactly what was said at the meeting between the admiral and Jack Westerman, or how serious the repercussions were from his conflict with the navy brass at Subic. It has been speculated that it probably damaged, if not totally ruined, his chances for promotion to colonel. Regardless, those who knew Jack Westerman are confident he didn't care. By that point, Jack Westerman would have thrown away a dozen promotions for his Marines.

The navy officer who got belted by Jack Westerman that evening probably never really understood why Westerman slugged him. Westerman wasn't that upset about being told the club was closing for the evening. The issue was deeper.

Jack Westerman had commanded a Marine infantry battalion during one of the bloodiest periods of the Vietnam War. More than 45 of his men had been killed since he had assumed command. He had seen every one of those bodies. He had seen them on makeshift litters, being lugged back to a combat base by their buddies after a night patrol. He had seen them wrapped in ponchos and lined up along the edges of helicopter landing zones, their exposed combat boots a stark reminder that young men were wrapped in the rubberized cloth. He had seen them covered with bloody sheets in the battalion aid station.

Several hundred more of his Marines had been wounded. The corpsmen and surgeons had managed to keep those men alive—men who had been torn apart by bullets and shrapnel. Those men survived; but sometimes there wasn't much left. Many of those shattered young men had been star athletes in their high schools just a year earlier. They would go home, but Jack Westerman knew their lives would never be the same.

The duty officer's pompous and insulting attitude probably uncorked a volcano of frustration that had been churning in Jack Westerman for a long time. That night, Jack Westerman just wanted to laugh and drink beer and tell stories with his young officers. He knew this would be the last time he would ever see some of those young men. In fact, by the end of the month, two of those officers would be dead, another six would be badly wounded.[3] When the duty officer barged into the middle of their gathering that night, he didn't realize he was disrupting a cherished ritual for Jack Westerman.

Needless to say, decking the command duty officer in front of a crowd at the officers' club was a serious breach of discipline for any officer, much less a battalion commander. In other circumstances, Westerman would have been relieved of command and court-martialed.

But, in March 1967, America was in a rapidly expanding war—and Jack Westerman was a proven combat leader. With the NVA flooding across the DMZ every week, America needed men like Blackjack Westerman leading Marines on the battlefield. The admiral, having no doubt commanded men in war himself, might have sympathized with the battle-weary Marine lieutenant colonel standing in front of his desk that morning. He seems to have decided that a scrap at the officers' club just wasn't that big of a deal. The admiral chewed out Jack Westerman and then sent him back to lead his battalion.

The incident in the officers' club only enhanced Blackjack Westerman's reputation with the Marines in his battalion. They knew Blackjack Westerman was more than their commanding officer. He was one of them.

The USS *Princeton* (LPH-5), the USS *Ogden* (LPD-5), and the USS *Monticello* (LSD-35) left California a month earlier to take over as the Amphibious Ready Group. The ships arrived in Subic on March 6. Westerman and his Marines started boarding the ships on the morning of March 15, and had all of their equipment, vehicles, and supplies stowed by that evening.

On March 16, the three ships, with 1st Battalion, 4th Marines, on board, left Subic Bay and sailed toward Vietnam. As they stood on the fantail of the ships and watched the Philippines slip over the horizon, there were no regrets. Jack Westerman considered the stay in Subic Bay a success. He wrote in the battalion's monthly report: "The morale was excellent throughout the reporting period. The maximum liberty possible was enjoyed by all hands during the Battalion Landing Team's stay at the SLF Base Camp in the Philippines."[4]

CHAPTER 16

A Purple Heart

"I just knew that something was wrong in the world."

LEONA DICKEY

By February 1967, there were three members of the Dickey family serving as Marines in Vietnam. Doug had been with 1st Battalion, 4th Marines, since October 1966. Paul Dickey, Harold's youngest brother, arrived in December 1966, and was stationed at Da Nang with the 1st Marine Aircraft Wing. Norman Dickey arrived in January 1967. After meeting with Doug in Okinawa, Norman flew to Dong Ha and joined 3rd Battalion, 4th Marines, and was assigned to Company K. The battalion was headquartered in the northern end of Quang Tri, conducting search-and-destroy patrols in the area between Dong Ha and Cam Lo.

"I spent a lot of sleepless nights, I'll tell you," Leona Dickey said, reflecting on the first months of 1967. "A mother can't hardly have two kids in combat, and a brother-in-law, and not have some sleepless nights there," she said. "It was pretty hard on me too."

Norman Dickey joined one of the most legendary companies in one of the most legendary battalions in Vietnam. The battalion became famous in the last week of September 1966 for its assault to take Nui Cay Tre, the ridgeline overlooking the Rockpile and Route 9. The set of hills had been fortified by the NVA 324B Division and Lieutenant Colonel William J. Masterpool and his Marines had to battle for every inch.

Larry Burrows, one of the most respected photojournalists in Vietnam, and Arnaud de Borchgrave, a *Newsweek* editor, followed Masterpool and his Marines into the battle. Both men filed harrowing reports of the assault. One of Burrows's photos was featured on the cover of *Life* magazine the next month. It was a color photo of one of Masterpool's Marines cradling a badly wounded comrade in his arms.[1] During the battle, 3rd Battalion, 4th Marines, had been assigned the radio call sign "Mutter." To honor Masterpool and his Marines, Nui Cay Tre became known as "Mutter's Ridge"—a designation that endured until the Americans left Vietnam.

Within 3rd Battalion, 4th Marines, Company K carried a number of distinctions. Two Marines from the company had earned the Medal of Honor during Operation *Hastings* in July 1966. Captain Robert J. Modrzejewski, the company commander; and Staff Sergeant John J. McGinty III, leading the 1st Platoon. Both earned the award on July 18, 1966.

Captain James J. Carroll, took command of the company after Modrzejewski. Carroll earned the Navy Cross leading the company during the assault to take Mutter's Ridge but was killed during the battle. The Marines named the combat base south of the battlefield "Camp Carroll" in his honor.

When Norman Dickey arrived, Company K was commanded by Captain J. M. Mahoney. On St. Patrick's Day, March 17, 1967, a platoon from Company L ran into an NVA company northwest of Dong Ha. The platoon was quickly outnumbered and surrounded. Late that afternoon, Mahoney and Company K were helicoptered out to reinforce the besieged platoon. Company K battled its way to the platoon and then fought off assaults against its perimeter around the landing zone. The battle was extremely violent and lasted well into the night. Eight Marines were killed and 27 were wounded.[2]

Norman Dickey was among those badly wounded. An enemy bullet tore through his leg, passing through his femur and knee and left his leg a twisted mess of shattered bone and torn muscle.

Tim Barga was also in Company K and tracked down the platoon corpsman after he heard Norman had been wounded. The corpsman gave Barga an earful about treating Norman Dickey. "That crazy bastard got hit and he was still shooting," Barga said, "and the corpsman was trying to get him rolled over to take care of him and he's still screaming and cussing and saying, 'I'll kill you, you sons-of-bitches!'" Barga said, "And he was still firing as fast as he could!" Tim Barga wasn't surprised. "That's Norman," he said with a laugh.

"I had a strange feeling all that day," Leona Dickey said. "I knew that something had happened all day long. I just knew that something was wrong in the world. I don't know how mothers have this, but they do—like an intuition—something's going to happen." She recalled:

> I had braces on Dennis and Steven's teeth. I had taken them to the orthodontist that day and when we came home—I had a funny feeling all that day. And I had left my dinner dishes so I could take the kids to the orthodontist and I just knew something was going to happen. I just knew something was wrong in the world.

So, it was just dark, and I was there at the sink washing the dishes …

And I saw that car pull in and I saw that [Marine Corps] sign on the door of the car.

Well, they slowly got out of the car and I went to the door. I didn't wait for them to come to the door. I went to the door and I yelled out, "Which one is it and how bad is it?"

They just stood there and looked at each other—you know—these two guys.

And I'll bet he thought, "Boy, I wonder about her …"

Well, he just stood there and his hands were shakin' and he had the paper.

I said, "Give me the paper, I'll look for myself." So, he handed me the paper and I saw that it was Norman, and he had a leg wound, it said.

Those two fellahs were so shook up.

The two Marines, Captain Robert E. Johnson, and First Sergeant William M. Turner, were from the Marine Corps Reserve Center in Dayton. It was the first casualty notification they had done. Leona Dickey invited Johnson and Turner in for coffee. When the Marines left, the neighbors began to arrive. They had seen the Marine Corps sedan drive through town to the Dickeys' and were concerned. By that time, many of the boys from the area were in uniform somewhere. Dennis and Steven were there when the Marines came to the house. Leona Dickey reassured them: "I told the other kids, I said, 'Now, he'll be alright. You know how Norman is—he'll be just fine. He'll get better.'"

Norman's wounds were serious. He was medevac'd to the USS *Repose* (AH-16), one of the hospital ships in Vietnam. They managed to save his leg and then he was quickly flown back to the United States. The policy was to send badly wounded men to the military hospital closest to their home. Norman was sent to the hospital at Naval Station Great Lakes, Illinois, 40 miles north of Chicago. The Dickeys made plans to drive up to see him as soon as he was able to receive visitors.

While he was commanding the Marines in Vietnam, General Walt made it a regular practice to visit the hospitals in I Corps and present Purple Hearts to wounded men who were on their way home. Walt happened to be touring the *Repose* while Norman was being stabilized. Norman Dickey got his Purple Heart from Lew Walt that day. He also got a Polaroid photo of Walt giving him the medal. "I still have that photo," Norman said.

CHAPTER 17

Operation *Beacon Hill*

"The art of war is simple enough. Find out where your enemy is. Get at him as soon as you can. Strike at him as hard as you can and as often as you can, and keep moving on."

ULYSSES S. GRANT

"... and now we are going to go on Operation Beacon Hill. We are going to land about 5,000 meters south of the DMZ ... and after that we don't just know what is going to happen."

PRIVATE FIRST CLASS DOUGLAS E. DICKEY[1]

The North Vietnamese invasion of Quang Tri through the Demilitarized Zone, which began in May 1966, continued through the first months of 1967. Despite Hanoi's wholesale military occupation of the DMZ, the American command in Saigon had continued to abide by the provisions of the 1954 Geneva agreements and strictly limited any military operations in the five-mile-wide buffer area. By 1967, however, that restraint appeared more and more absurd.

The Tet holiday fell during the second week of February in 1967. As the most celebrated and revered holiday in Vietnam, both sides had agreed to a ceasefire. However, almost immediately, U.S. reconnaissance aircraft began detecting large North Vietnamese troop concentrations moving through the DMZ. It was undeniable that Hanoi was exploiting the holiday ceasefire to stage their forces for attacks against the U.S. bases in Quang Tri.

As a result of the blatant enemy movements in the DMZ during the Tet ceasefire, the restriction against firing artillery into the DMZ was finally lifted.[2] On February 25, 1967, American artillery in Quang Tri began pounding North Vietnamese troop concentrations in the DMZ and northward. The artillery offensive against the NVA units infiltrating through the DMZ was named Operation *Highrise*.[3]

As part of Operation *Highrise*, the Marines decided to move artillery onto a small hilltop at Gio Linh, just 2,100 meters south of the DMZ.[4] From Gio Linh, the American artillery could not only hit targets in the DMZ, but also strike targets inside North Vietnam. Led by Lieutenant Colonel Bill Rice, the 12th Marines established a firebase at Gio Linh on February 26 and began targeting NVA concentrations in the DMZ.[5]

The effectiveness of Rice's artillerymen was clear from the enemy's reaction. Two days after Rice and his men began firing from Gio Linh, the NVA pummeled the base with more than 400 mortar, artillery, and rocket rounds in a 17-minute period. Initially Rice and his batteries were only supposed to be at Gio Linh for four days. However, the four-day "artillery raid" was extended indefinitely because the artillery was so effective from that position. Eventually, Gio Linh became a permanent firebase for the Marines.

While moving the artillery to Gio Linh made it possible to hit NVA units in the DMZ and northward, the firebase was a source of anxiety from the start. No other American firebase was that close to the DMZ. In fact, the Marines at Gio Linh were closer to the enemy regiments staging in the DMZ than they were to their own reinforcements at Dong Ha. Gio Linh was also a tiny outpost; the entire camp only covered two acres and had almost no natural barriers between it and the thousands of NVA soldiers staging in the DMZ. Marine leaders were haunted by nightmares of Gio Linh being overrun by waves of NVA soldiers.

General Walt had been uneasy about the small firebase at Gio Linh for some time. After an inspection trip to the base in early March, he had considered pulling the artillery out of the area altogether.[6] Hanoi clearly wanted to eliminate Gio Linh. Among other things, four U.S. Army self-propelled 175-mm howitzers had begun operating from the base.[7] The 175-mm guns could lob 150-lb shells 21 miles and were pounding targets well inside North Vietnam.[8]

Shortly after his visit to Gio Linh, Lew Walt began receiving reports that enemy units were massing north of the firebase. He had already been getting reports about NVA buildups farther west. To counter the growing threat, Walt proposed using the Special Landing Force to hit enemy units coming through the DMZ. Using the SLF was an attractive option because Westerman's battalion could come ashore north of the Cua Viet River and attack westward into the enemy's left flank with almost no warning. General Westmoreland and Vice Admiral John J. Hyland, commander of the Seventh Fleet, endorsed Walt's plan and dispatched the SLF to Quang Tri. The operation was named *Beacon Hill*.

Westerman and the SLF received their tasking for Operation *Beacon Hill* just before sailing from the Philippines. The scheme of maneuver was fairly simple. It called for the SLF to land just below the DMZ and attack westward.[9] The Special Landing Force was going to hit the NVA units south of the DMZ before they could mass on Gio Linh. Once they secured the area around Gio Linh, Westerman and his battalion would continue westward and link up with the Marine units conducting Operation *Prairie III* around Con Thien. Con Thien, like Gio Linh, was a Marine base close to the DMZ, and it sat astride one the main infiltration routes used by the NVA. Con Thien had also been the scene of escalating enemy activity.

Beacon Hill was scheduled to take place from March 19 to April 1. Westerman and his staff had finished their detailed planning by the time the Amphibious Ready Group was off the coast of Vietnam.

As with Operation *Deckhouse VI* a month earlier, Bob Kelley's company was assigned to make the beach landing in amtracs. The other three rifle companies would fly farther inland and land by helicopter. Kelley reduced the thick operation order to: "Bad guys crossing the DMZ—and since we were landing; we would be able to hit their flank."

By then it had been ascertained that Westerman and his Marines would be facing the 812th, 90th, and 31st regiments of the 324B NVA Division.[10] These were not the part-time Viet Cong guerrillas infamous for harassing units around the villages farther south. The NVA soldiers crossing the DMZ were professionals by every definition. Most of them had been drafted as teenagers. They were told they would serve in the army until the war ended, or until they were too badly crippled to fight. They underwent months of initial military training at their "School of the Soldier." This was similar to American boot camp. Then, they went through more formal training on weapons and tactics. Finally, they were marched south—either down to the DMZ or down the Ho Chi Minh Trail. The grueling march south, while enduring U.S. airstrikes, further hardened the communist soldiers.

The NVA soldiers were organized into platoons, companies, battalions, and regiments; and wore uniforms complete with rank devices. They often wore a distinctive green or tan pith helmet with a red star device on the front. Their tactics were the same as those used by every other modern army. The NVA used artillery and mortars to support their attacks and covered advancing troops with heavy machine-gun and rocket fire. They used modern wire and radio communications to coordinate their movements. The only significant difference between the NVA and their American opponents was that the NVA didn't have significant air power.

The NVA units were led by intelligent, shrewd, and professional officers. And the soldiers of the 324B Division were extremely disciplined and tough. The North Vietnamese soldiers left almost nothing behind on the battlefield. This made it difficult for allied commanders to identify enemy units or assess losses after a battle.

While the Viet Cong tended to avoid prolonged battles, the NVA maintained contact and often fought to the death. While the VC preferred to snipe at U.S. forces from long range; the NVA favored fighting American units up close. The NVA referred to this tactic as "grabbing them by the belt." The NVA leaders had devised this tactic to neutralize American air and artillery support. The NVA soldiers tried to get as close as possible to the American units when they attacked. They did this so the Americans couldn't call in air or artillery support against the NVA soldiers without risking hitting themselves.

It was rare that NVA soldiers were captured. Those who were captured by American forces were usually badly wounded. Nguyen Van Hung, an NVA private interviewed after the war, gave some rare insight into the world of the NVA soldier:

> When I got my draft notice I knew I was destined to go south. And I knew the chances of coming back were very slim. About a hundred guys from my village had gone, starting in 1962, and none had returned ... The government was very explicit about it. They said, "The trip has no deadline for return. When your mission is accomplished you'll come back." Uncle Ho had declared, "Your duty is to fight for five years or even ten or twenty years." So it was clear to me that the whole business was going to be long and dangerous. I was really agitated when I left for the army.[11]

Any Marine who fought the NVA respected them as dangerous and tenacious adversaries. A common tattoo worn by veteran NVA soldiers testified to an extraordinary dedication that was tinged with fatalism. The tattoo read like an epitaph: "Born in the North—to die in the South." When the NVA and the Marines clashed, both knew there would be no quarter asked—and no quarter given. A Marine officer later summed up his experience fighting the NVA: "But the NVA were absolutely the toughest, most dedicated sons of bitches you'd ever want to fight."[12]

On March 18, while still on board the USS *Ogden*, Doug wrote letters to most of his family. His older sister, Vera, had married George Moore after high school. George was a career soldier and they were living in Germany. Doug wrote to her and said he enjoyed the time he spent in the Philippines and that he had met a nice girl named Rosa. "Maybe some day I will go back there and see her again," he wrote. He explained that his unit had been on Operation *Deckhouse VI* and Operation *Desoto* earlier and they were now going back to Vietnam for Operation *Beacon Hill*. "Well we have been messing around with the VC for the past couple of months and now will be going back for another crack at it." He told her he was looking forward to getting back to Dong Ha because he would be able to get together with Tim Barga, Norman, and a couple of his other buddies. Doug closed his letter by gently prodding Vera to write home more often, although he understood she was busy. Vera was raising a family of her own now, "... so keep trying to write anyway and she [mom] will understand."[13] Doug also wrote a letter to Norman that day. He didn't know Norman had been seriously wounded the previous day and was going through emergency surgery on the USS *Repose*.

D-Day: Monday, March 20, 1967

The beginning of Operation *Beacon Hill* was delayed for a day because rain and fog obscured the helicopter landing zones. The operation was launched when the

Capt Robert D. Kelley's Company C, loaded in amtracs, heads for Blue Beach, just north of the Cua Viet River, on the first day of Operation *Beacon Hill*. "Since we were landing; we would be able to hit their flank," Kelley said of their mission. The USS *Monticello* (LSD-35) is in the background. (USN 1121212)

weather improved the following afternoon, on Monday, March 20. The operation began with Company A, commanded by Captain Richard F. Corcoran, flying into LZ Bluebird, next to Gio Linh, at 1336. Company A's mission was to augment the Marines and soldiers defending the firebase—and also stand by as the battalion's reserve. The battalion command element also landed at that time and moved into the firebase at Gio Linh.

An hour later, the helicopters from HMM-363 flared into LZ Sparrow about a mile southwest of Gio Linh and dropped off Company B, commanded by Captain Kenneth R. Ramsey. Twenty minutes after Company B landed, Bob Kelley and his Marines came ashore at Blue Beach just north of the mouth of the Cua Viet River.

The last unit of the battalion arrived at 1600, when Company D, commanded by Captain John F. Juul, landed at LZ Bluebird, and joined the battalion command element and Company A.

As soon as they were ashore, Company C climbed out of the amtracs and started hiking toward their first objective, which was four and a half miles inland. The weather was hot and humid—over 95° with humidity over 80 percent. The beach north of the Cua Viet River stretched for miles inland and was a seemingly endless expanse of blindingly white sand dunes.

Kent Hansen, one of the riflemen in 2nd Platoon, remembered trudging through the soft white sand for miles in the heat. "It was so hot that officers were carrying equipment for guys who were really hurting, so we lost a few crossing the beach."[14]

Kent Hansen had ended up in the Marine Corps because he decided to take a break from his studies at U.C. Berkeley to go skiing. "I got to thinking, 'You know, I've been going to school for a long time—I need a vacation.'"

Kent figured he would take a short skiing trip and then return to Berkeley for the next term. He packed his skis and drove to Colorado. However, when he phoned home after a month up on the slopes, his father told him there was a letter from the Selective Service Administration waiting for him. The university's registrar had notified the Selective Service Administration when Kent didn't register for the next term. "I could not understand how this could happen in such a short time," he said with a laugh. The letter said he no longer had a draft deferment and his status had been changed to 1-A. It furthermore directed him to report for induction screening.

Kent was still determined to be back at Berkeley for the next term despite the draft notice. He went down to the military recruiting offices and asked if he could join the reserves. The recruiters told him it was too late because he'd already received his induction notice.

However, a Marine recruiter intercepted Kent while he was wandering around the offices. "He was an old Marine gunnery sergeant—sucking on a cigar," Kent remembered. The crusty old gunny got his attention by telling him the Marines were offering the shortest enlistment available. The Marine Corps was offering two-year enlistments specifically to meet its ballooning requirements for riflemen in Vietnam. The other branches required at least a four-year enlistment. The recruiter sweetened the deal by telling Kent he wouldn't have to report to boot camp for 120 days. The Marine Corps' offer seemed like the best solution. Kent figured he could continue skiing for a couple of months; then serve his enlistment; and be back at Berkeley within two years. "So, I said, 'Outstanding! I can go back skiing!'" He enlisted that afternoon.

"I felt pretty good about the decision until I was driving home," Hansen said later. "And then it dawned on me," he said, "I said to myself, 'What have I done? I've joined the Marine Corps!'" Kent knew one of his father's friends had been a navy officer in the Pacific during World War II. He'd heard the man mention working with Marines during the war. "I stopped at his house and told him what I had done." Kent was surprised by the man's reaction. "He laughed at me!" It started to dawn on Kent Hansen that a two-year enlistment in the Marines might not be such a sweet deal after all. "I just went back to skiing," he said, "and at the end of the season, I showed up and went in."

After he got to boot camp, the Marines offered him an opportunity to go into one of their officer programs due to his college background and high test scores. He declined the offer. Then they tried to convince him to go into one of the more

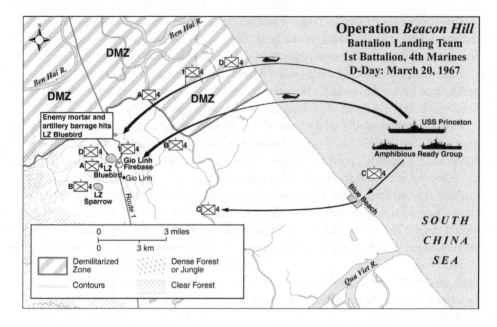

intellectually demanding fields, like intelligence, or avionics. He rejected all the offers because they all came with a four-year obligation—and Kent Hansen was determined to be a civilian again in 24 months. Sticking with his two-year enlistment, however, meant he was going to Vietnam as a rifleman. "And that's how I ended up being an 0311 [rifleman]," he said with a chuckle 40 years later.

Private First Class Hansen arrived in Vietnam in September 1966. The day he arrived, he was quickly issued a rifle and field gear and put on a helicopter and flown up to Company B's position near the Rockpile. The company had suffered a lot of casualties during Operation *Prairie* and was critically short of men. As soon as he got off the helicopter, he was hustled over to the platoon area and assigned to a patrol that was getting ready to leave the perimeter. He found himself following a Marine through the barbed-wire perimeter into the jungle that evening. "Here it is … I haven't been in-country for 24 hours and I'm going out for an ambush."

In the months that followed, Kent Hansen realized he liked being a Marine. He had always liked challenges and adventures—and Vietnam was turning out to be the adventure of a lifetime. But most of all, he liked the men he was serving with. "They were all really good men," he said. "Just really good guys."

Beyond the beach stretched miles and miles of rice paddies and marshland. By the end of the first day, Company C had moved about four miles inland and had reached their objective for the night. As they always did, they began digging their fighting holes as soon as they stopped.

The battalion suffered its first casualties just after sunset that day. For an hour, beginning at 1915, the command element and the two companies at LZ Bluebird, came under a concentrated barrage of mortar and artillery fire. More than 300 rounds blasted their position in an hour. Three Marines were killed and 12 were wounded in the barrage.

D+1: Tuesday, March 21, 1967

On Tuesday, Company A remained at Gio Linh while the other three companies moved westward in a broad sweeping formation: Company D to the north; Company C in the middle; and Company B to the south. As they moved westward, both Ramsey's and Juul's Marines began to run across evidence of recent enemy activity in the area. Ramsey reported finding a small collection of enemy equipment and ammunition, including a bloody backpack. Juul's men came across more enemy ammunition, gear, and some medical supplies. Juul noted the stash also included bags of rice originating from an American charity.

As the companies moved forward, aircraft in the area reported seeing NVA units digging in ahead of them. Captain Ramsey's Marines were ahead of the other companies and made the first contact with the NVA on Tuesday afternoon. Ramsey's 3rd Platoon ran into an 80-man NVA unit and engaged in a fierce firefight. In the course of the battle, the Marines called in several airstrikes on the enemy positions, with devastating effects.

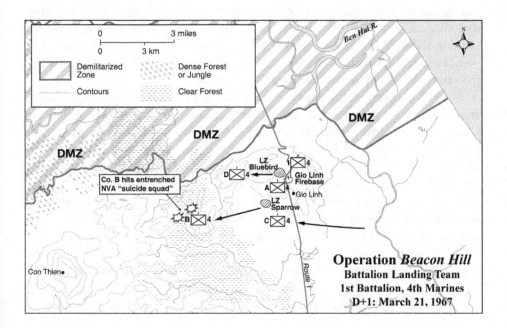

Operation *Beacon Hill*
Battalion Landing Team
1st Battalion, 4th Marines
D+1: March 21, 1967

Company B was in a running battle with the NVA unit until after sunset that day. At one point, 1st Platoon managed to surprise an NVA unit that was preparing an ambush. The Marines cut them to pieces. By the end of the day, Ramsey had suffered eight wounded. His Marines counted 18 enemy bodies in their path and saw evidence that another 25 dead had been dragged away.

Corporal James M. Couch II was one of the Marines in the lead squad when Company B initially made contact that day. As they came up a trail, an NVA machine gun dug into a bank opened fire, raking the Marines coming up the trail. There were other NVA soldiers dug in along the flanks of the trail. "They had us pinned down—this machine gun. We couldn't go back and we couldn't go forward either, so we just waited—kept returning fire and throwing grenades and trying to get this one guy out of this trench." Ramsey maneuvered the rest of the company up and directed air and artillery strikes. "We killed quite a few of them," said Couch, "[but] some of them got away."

As they were going through the enemy trenches, they discovered the reason some of the NVA soldiers had fought so stubbornly. "These men—these North Vietnamese regulars, had sandbagged—they had their positions sandbagged in. Plus, these men—themselves—had sandbags on their feet. They were sandbagged into the positions," said Couch. "It was more like a suicide squad."[15]

D+2: Wednesday, March 22, 1967

The pace of the battalion slowed on Wednesday as all three companies started to run up against more enemy. At 1215, Company D suffered seven wounded when they were hit with a mortar barrage. Juul's 3rd Platoon spotted the enemy mortar position and called in air and artillery strikes, saturating the enemy positions with bombs and artillery shells. Juul's men saw secondary explosions following the strikes, indicating the enemy mortar positions had been hit.

At 1315, between 15 and twenty 82-mm mortar rounds hit Company B. Shortly after the barrage, they spotted two enemy platoons just north of their position. Company B assaulted toward the enemy platoons and quickly ended up in a pitched battle with a larger NVA force. At times, the fighting was extremely close and the Marines and NVA soldiers were throwing grenades back and forth at each other. Eventually, Ramsey had his men pull back and he called in mortar and artillery strikes on the enemy positions. In the short but violent battle, five Marines were killed and 14 wounded. When Ramsey's men surveyed the battlefield later, they counted 46 enemy dead and suspected another six had been dragged away.

A couple hours later, Ramsey's Marines ran into another NVA unit. The battle began at 1600 and lasted until almost midnight. In the opening exchange, one of the fire teams from the lead platoon got pinned down on the opposite side of a hill, and was separated from the rest of the company. The enemy was too close to call in

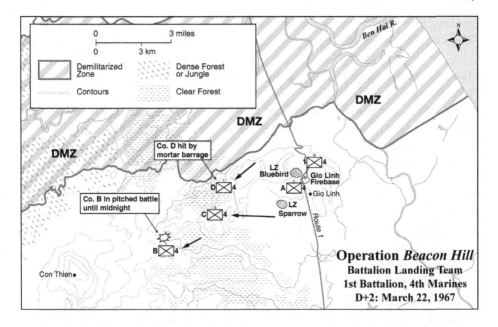

Operation *Beacon Hill*
Battalion Landing Team
1st Battalion, 4th Marines
D+2: March 22, 1967

artillery or air strikes without hitting the pinned-down platoon. The Marines ended up slugging it out at close range.

At one point, Ramsey's men caught an NVA unit trying to maneuver around the flank of the pinned-down Marines. Ramsey' men ambushed the enemy before they could get into position and mowed them down. After repeated attempts, the trapped fire team was eventually rescued. By the time the battle was over, another eight Company B Marines had been wounded. They counted 18 dead NVA around their lines and reported seeing evidence that probably another 30 had been killed.[16]

According to Sergeant Salvador Martinez, who was the acting platoon leader for Ramsey's 1st Platoon at the time, it was clear Company B was surrounded. "That night, after pulling back into a more stable position, we received heavy mortar fire—81 and 82s from this reinforced North Vietnamese company. During this time, Charlie Company came down to support us and help us to break out."[17]

D+3: Thursday, March 23, 1967

On Thursday, March 23, Bob Kelley moved his company up to Company B's right flank. By that morning, Company C had moved about 11 miles inland from their landing beach. They had been moving through terrain that was more heavily wooded for the past day. The area was mostly dry rice paddies, separated by thick hedgerows. As they moved forward, Kelley reported seeing a number of civilians leaving from one of the few villages in the area. An hour after seeing the exodus of civilians, Company C began taking sniper fire. It appeared that Kelley and his men were running into elements of the same NVA unit that Company B had been fighting. With the platoons spread out in tactical formations, Company C continued westward.

The Marines in 2nd Platoon remember "Holy Thursday" because it was the day John Szymanski was killed.

At 1225, the platoon was moving through some fields near one of the small villages in the area. As they came up a path, the Marine walking point spotted an NVA soldier digging in the field ahead. The NVA soldier kept digging as the Marines walked toward him. He seemed to be oblivious to the American Marines who were walking right toward him. The Marines held their fire because they were afraid he might be a lost South Vietnamese soldier or just a villager. When they yelled to him, he suddenly realized what was happening and grabbed his rifle off the ground next to him and started firing at them. The Marines returned fire. By that time, the soldier was sprinting for the treeline. As soon as the Marines opened fire, a number of NVA soldiers in a nearby system of trenches returned fire. It quickly turned into a fierce firefight.

The standard procedure in 2nd Platoon when they hit an enemy unit was for Dickerson to move forward with the main body to provide a base of fire, while John Szymanski, as the platoon sergeant, led a smaller maneuver element around the enemy's flank. That afternoon, Szymanski, along with one squad, began moving from the left flank of the platoon. They carefully moved through an open area between two hedgerows.

The squad with Szymanski was led by Sergeant Colin "Mac" McClelland. McClelland represented a little-known phenomenon of the Vietnam War. He was one of more than 12,000 Canadians who enlisted in the American military to fight in Vietnam.[18] From Paris, Ontario, McClelland had been raised in the shadow of Canadian soldiers who had fought in World War II and Korea. He had grown up hearing about the men who stormed Juno Beach on D-Day, and had pushed the Communist Chinese and North Koreans back to the 38th Parallel during the Korean War. Communism was on the march against the free world and Colin McClelland felt it was his duty to actively fight it just as the generation before him had fought the Nazis, the Imperial Japanese, and the communists in Korea.

After serving in the Canadian militia for a while, McClelland decided he wanted more action. He decided to join the U.S. Marines. "I went with the Marines because I figured they were the first in," he said. "Wherever America is going to be in trouble, the Marines have got to go in. So, that's why I enlisted." It took him a year to complete all the paperwork required to enlist in the U.S. Marine Corps while still a Canadian citizen. After completing the paperwork, he went to Buffalo, New York, and enlisted. By a spectacular coincidence, John Szymanski, his future platoon sergeant, was the recruiter in upstate New York in 1964 and processed Mac's paperwork and put him on the bus to Parris Island.

From their position on the platoon's left flank, Szymanski and McClelland could hear the escalating rifle and machine-gun fire to their right. They knew Dickerson and the rest of the platoon had hit a significant NVA position. At the head of the squad, along with McClelland, were Kent Hansen, Jim Ver Helst, and Michael Whitt. As Szymanski and the squad moved forward, they slipped around the side of a hedgerow—figuring it was a likely enemy position. Once they got around the hedgerow, they began moving back toward the main body of the platoon.

As they were crossing an abandoned rice paddy, they hit an NVA position. "When we were three quarters of the way across the rice paddy, they opened up," Hansen said. "They had dug in on the other side of the dike, using the dike as the front part of their trench." The enemy had a machine gun in their position and it quickly had Szymanski and his men pinned down. The NVA threw a volley of grenades among the Marines and several men were wounded. At that point, John Szymanski, armed with just his .45 automatic and some grenades, charged the enemy machine gun and destroyed it.[19]

McClelland was about 50 yards away. He saw Szymanski crawl up to the edge of the enemy position and fire his pistol. "He just stuck it up over the trench and fired down into it," McClelland said, "but then it jammed on him, and he turned to fix the jam and all of a sudden, this NVA popped up and—'Bam!'" McClelland remembered the feeling of helplessness as an NVA soldier suddenly appeared and fired. "I couldn't do anything because it was so fast!" he said. "Before I could bring my weapon around—anything. And it was just so fast." Szymanski was killed instantly. The other Marines gunned down the NVA soldier. "Ver Helst crawled over to check him [Szymanski] and found he was dead," McClelland said.[20]

John Szymanski's death marked the beginning of a firefight that lasted more than two hours. Michael Whitt was badly wounded at about the same time Szymanski was hit. Four more Marines were wounded in the running gun battle that afternoon. It turned out they had hit a dug-in NVA platoon. Second Platoon eventually cleared the enemy trenches and the company continued to move forward. The NVA left five of their dead when they withdrew, evidence suggested at least another 10 had been dragged away.

Losing John Szymanski was a hard blow to the men in 2nd Platoon. He had been their rock. Although he was just 26 years old, the career-Marine had seemed old and wise to the younger Marines in the platoon. He shouldered responsibility with quiet confidence. "He was a real nice guy," Steve Pruitt said. "He was intelligent ... he'd speak to you and tell you, 'Here's what I want you to do...'" They all liked him. "Szymanski was a hell of a guy," Pruitt said. John Szymanski's death hit Larry Dickerson particularly hard. The two men had forged a close partnership and friendship in the months since Dickerson had arrived in Okinawa.

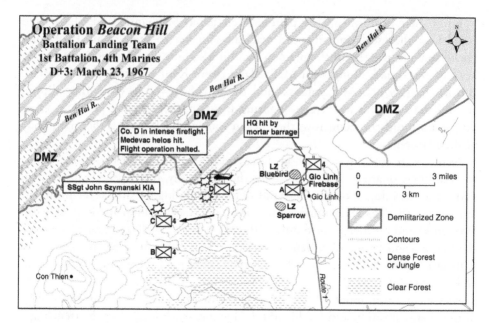

Operation *Beacon Hill*
Battalion Landing Team
1st Battalion, 4th Marines
D+3: March 23, 1967

Bob Kelley had lost one of his best leaders. "He was a real fine gentleman. He was exceptionally well liked by his troops," he said. "They all thought he had his stuff together."

John Szymanski was married. His wife, Loretta, and their two children were waiting for him in Nevada. Szymanski was scheduled to leave for Quantico to begin his officer training at the end of the operation and Loretta was preparing for the cross-country move. Their son, Jim, was three, and Stephanie was almost two. John Szymanski was posthumously awarded a Silver Star for his actions that day.

1st Battalion, 4th Marines, was hitting the outer security of a larger NVA unit as it moved westward. At about the same time that Company C was seeing action, Company B was also involved in a brief firefight. The battalion continued to meet stiffer and stiffer resistance as it approached Con Thien.

After sunset, Company D's position was bracketed by a barrage of 82-mm mortar rounds, followed by an enemy probe that turned into a brief firefight. Captain Juul had his men clear a landing zone while he radioed for medevac helicopters to lift out the wounded. When he radioed for the medevac, Juul had stressed that several of the wounded were "Alpha-Zulus," meaning they were in critical condition and would probably die soon if they didn't get to an aid station.

The Marine helicopter pilots from the Lucky Red Lions earned John Juul's enduring respect that night. As they made their approach, the pilots asked how "hot" the area was. Juul told them they had been taking fire in the last 10 to 15 minutes. This usually would have caused the helicopter pilots to reconsider the mission. "And they came in anyway," Juul said. "Phenomenal flying. Unbelievable!" he said. "They flew in—at night—with just a couple of strobes on the ground to bring them in."

As the helicopters neared the landing zone, Juul's Marines laid down covering fire to suppress the NVA who were in the thick brush around their position. The enemy unleashed a storm of fire at the aircraft just as the wounded were being loaded on the helicopters. "You could see the green tracers going right through these helicopters—coming from two or three different directions," Juul said. "There were these '34s, and they were getting pieces shot off of them as they tried to lift out of the LZ."

The helicopters managed to get airborne with the most critically wounded on board. While they were lifting off, the pilots reported seeing two heavy machine-gun positions 200 yards north of Juul's position and called in an artillery barrage on them. Two of the three helicopters made it all the way back to Dong Ha. One of the UH-34s was so badly shot up it could barely stay in the air and had to make an emergency landing at LZ Bluebird, near Gio Linh. Miraculously, none of the pilots or crewmen were wounded during the medevac flight. However, all three aircraft were riddled with bullet holes, including 12.7-mm holes from Soviet-made antiaircraft guns.

Due to the heavy antiaircraft fire and the amount of damage the helicopters had taken during the mission to get Juul's men out, the division air liaison officer halted helicopter operations in the area. Of his 21 wounded Marines, the HMM-363 helicopters had managed to lift out the 10 most seriously wounded before flight operations were stopped. "It was just heroic flying," John Juul said, still praising the pilots and their crews 46 years later. "I have had a tremendous amount of respect for combat helicopter pilots ever since—and I've told that to many people. These pilots are very special people."

D+4: Friday, March 24, 1967

Good Friday started with a battle for Bob Kelley and his Marines. Kelley had ordered Second Lieutenant Dennis Dooley, the leader of 1st Platoon, to send an ambush patrol out the night before as part of the security for the company. Dooley tasked Sergeant Carl H. Martin to take his squad out. Martin had taken his squad out as an ambush patrol Thursday night and set up a position forward of the Company C perimeter. All night long they heard NVA soldiers moving around them.

Carl Martin had enlisted in the Marines in 1963 after graduating from high school in Orlando. After graduating, Martin went looking for a job. Everywhere he went, the first question employers asked was whether he had completed his military service. Businesses were reluctant to hire young men right out of high school because they often lost a new employee to the army after he got his draft notice. Martin had always considered joining the Marines. He had been raised hearing about his uncle who had been a Marine in World War I. Also, his half-brother had served in the Marines after World War II. After being turned away by another employer, he decided he might as well enlist. "Darn, I might as well go and get that out of the way," he said. "And, of course—to me—there was never any question about which way to go. It was to be a Marine." Carl Martin arrived in Vietnam in May 1966 and was sent to Westerman's battalion in November 1966, as one of the replacements that helped Bob Kelley reestablish Company C.[21]

That Friday morning, Sergeant Martin was leading his squad back toward the company lines. It was still dark but dawn was approaching. Private First Class Robert Alvarez, a 20-year-old from Clint, Texas, was walking point. As they neared the road that ran just outside the company perimeter, Alvarez gave the hand signal for the squad to stop and go to ground.

Martin came up to see what was going on. Alvarez pointed to the road and whispered for Martin to watch. A moment later, dim silhouettes of heavily armed men scurried across the road toward the Company C perimeter. Then more shadowy figures trotted across in front of them. Martin's first thought was that they were seeing another Marine patrol returning to the company.

Martin radioed the company command post and asked if they had another squad out on ambush. It was unusual to have more than one squad out on ambush at the same time. It was generally not done specifically to avoid situations where two Marine patrols might accidentally fire on each other. The reply from the company CP was unequivocal, "No. You're it."

Barely speaking in a whisper into the handset, Martin replied, "You better not be bullshitting me because, if you're wrong, I'm getting ready to kill some Marines." The CP reiterated to Martin that he was the only friendly patrol outside the perimeter. It became clear to Martin that an enemy unit was staging to assault the company perimeter. "And so, the next guys that run across the road, me and Roberto, and Doug Lee, just shot them—killed them right there," said Martin, who quickly realized they had taken on a much larger force. "I mean all hell broke loose." Martin said. "They just threw everything at us; and we had a firefight that probably lasted two or three hours."

Martin and his men were still shooting it out with the NVA when the sun rose. Shortly after dawn, he was ordered to get his men back inside the company perimeter as soon as possible. "They told me, 'You've got to come in off the road with your men because we're getting ready to have air power come in.' So we went in."

Martin lost three Marines that morning. Robert Alvarez had distinguished himself throughout the fight. "He was fighting like crazy," said Martin. Alvarez was wounded in the course of the battle, but kept fighting. While they were making their way back to the company perimeter, Alvarez took up a position to provide cover so the other men in the squad could cross into the company perimeter. Unfortunately, just as a corpsman was about to go to his aid, the enemy fired a volley of RPGs at Alvarez.

Shrapnel from one of the rockets killed him. He was posthumously awarded the Silver Star Medal for his actions that morning.

In addition to Alvarez, 18-year-old Private First Class Antonio Velasquez, from Santa Maria, California, was killed by a mortar blast.

Also, Private First Class Edward Conway, a 19-year-old from Fenton, Minnesota, was trying to recover Velasquez when he was killed by a sniper.

Martin had his men back within the Company C perimeter shortly after dawn.

Second Lieutenant Dick Housh, the platoon leader for Kelley's 3rd Platoon, was also killed that day. Thirty-three-year-old Housh was another of the older veterans in the company. He had earned a battlefield commission after spending more than a decade as an enlisted man. He was a tall man who towered over most of the Marines in the company and had the reputation of being both very professional and very friendly. Mac McClelland had gotten to know Housh. "If you were going to get shit from him, you probably deserved it," he said with a laugh. McClelland had seen Housh in action during an earlier firefight: "He was a brave, brave man. I watched him take out a machine gun once—I was so frickin' impressed. I couldn't believe it," McClelland said. "It was like something out of a movie. It was amazing."

At one point during the day, Company C began receiving sniper fire across their perimeter. Bob Kelley told Housh to take 3rd Platoon forward of the company perimeter and sweep the sector where they figured the enemy fire was coming from.

Dave Rumsey and Dick Housh had gotten to be friends while in Okinawa and had ended up going on liberty in the Philippines together. "He was the most outgoing of those three or four platoon leaders," Rumsey said. "He was always offering advice and, of course, I was more than willing to listen because—I may have been kind of wet–behind-the-ears as far as being in combat, but I figured I'm at least smart enough to learn from some of the guys that had been there and done that."[22]

Shortly after Housh and his platoon left the perimeter, a firefight erupted. A few minutes later, Sergeant Hill, Housh's platoon sergeant, radioed back to the company CP and reported they had killed the sniper, but that Lieutenant Housh had been killed in the fight. When Kelley told Hill to return to the perimeter, it became clear the platoon had become disoriented in the thick jungle.

Bob Kelley called Dave Rumsey over and told him Housh was dead and that he was now the platoon leader for 3rd Platoon. Kelley then told Rumsey his first mission was to take a patrol out to bring the 3rd Platoon men back to the company position. Kelley wanted to bring the platoon back before it could be ambushed by a larger enemy force, or worse, before it ended up being fired on by one of the company's other units while trying to find its way back to the company perimeter.

Kelley told Larry Dickerson to send one of his squads with Rumsey to accompany him when he went out to find 3rd Platoon. After talking to Sergeant Hill on the radio, Rumsey went to a high spot overlooking the jungle in front of the company and told Hill to "pop a smoke." When Hill triggered the smoke grenade, Rumsey was surprised to see how close the platoon was. "I actually heard the pin pop on his grenade," he said. "I was expecting them to be some distance away, but he was close. So, we wandered on down there." 3rd Platoon was soon back in the company lines. Dick Housh was laid down with the other Marines who had been killed that day. Bob Kelley arranged for them to be flown out when a helicopter became available.

Rumsey pieced together what had happened after talking to Hill and the other Marines in the platoon. "They had located the sniper that had been shooting. He was in a hedgerow." Housh, who had taken to carrying a shotgun in addition to his .45, set up part of the platoon as a base of fire. "So, they had located where the sniper was and kind of laid down a base of fire," Rumsey said, "and then Housh charged forward with the shotgun and put a shotgun blast in the hedgerow where this sniper was, and then kind of jumped into the hedgerow." Unfortunately, the enemy soldier was slightly off to the side of where Housh had gone in. The NVA soldier fired and hit Dick Housh as he came into the hedgerow. "So, I'm sure he died while airborne, jumping into this hedgerow," Dave Rumsey said, "you know, point blank."

"I just know that everybody I talked to—that had been with the 3rd Platoon— really loved him," Rumsey said, "because he wouldn't ask them to do anything he wouldn't do himself," he said, "and frankly, he got killed because he was leading by example." Richard Housh left behind a wife and three young children.

Within two days, 3rd Platoon would also lose Dave Rumsey. While he and one of the platoon's sergeants were scouting a new position, there was an explosion. The sergeant took the brunt of the blast. They were never able to figure out exactly what the device was. It could have been a grenade tossed at them, an unexploded mortar round that detonated when the sergeant accidentally stepped on it, or, most likely, it was a booby trap. Rumsey figured it was probably a booby trap tripped by the sergeant. Initially, Dave Rumsey didn't think he was too badly hurt and figured he could stay in the field with the company. However, as Doc Long was looking him over, he kept finding more and more shrapnel wounds. Captain Kelley ordered Rumsey to take the next medevac out to the *Princeton* to get patched up.

By the end of Good Friday, Bob Kelley's company had been assaulted by an NVA company. Six of his men were killed and 17 were wounded that day. The NVA left 38 of their dead scattered around Kelley's lines before withdrawing into the jungle. They also left behind several weapons and more than a dozen full backpacks. Looking for anything of intelligence value, the Marines dug through the packs, finding letters from home and other personal items—in many ways, the NVA packs were the mirror images of their own.

At 0750 on Friday morning, at about the same time Sergeant Martin was getting his patrol back inside Kelley's perimeter, Lieutenant Colonel Westerman sent out new

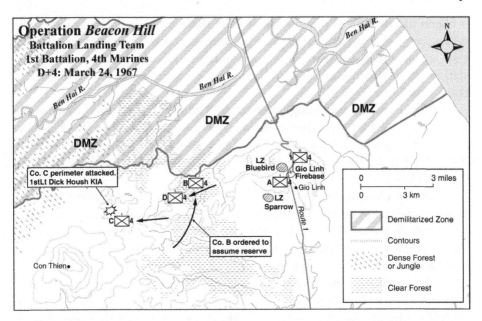

Operation *Beacon Hill*
Battalion Landing Team
1st Battalion, 4th Marines
D+4: March 24, 1967

orders from his command post at Gio Linh, directing Juul and Kelley to continue attacking westward toward Con Thien. He ordered Captain Ramsey, however, to start marching his company back to the battalion CP at Gio Linh.

Shortly after receiving the orders to continue westward, Marines from Juul's 3rd Platoon surprised a team of four NVA soldiers trying to wheel a Soviet machine gun into position ahead of them. One of the NVA soldiers was killed while the other three managed to escape, leaving the gun and their backpacks behind.

In response to the new orders, Captain Ramsey was turning his company back toward Gio Linh, and had his men on the move by 0850. Four hours later, as they were moving through some thick vegetation, they ran into another NVA unit. The enemy broke contact after a 15-minute firefight, heading south, away from the Marine lines. Ramsey called in artillery. When his Marines moved through the enemy position, they found 10 dead. His company suffered no casualties.

The rest of Good Friday passed without significant contact. All three rifle companies, however, continued to run across abandoned enemy campsites, and discarded equipment, catching glimpses of enemy soldiers moving in the distance. At one point, Company D came across 23 enemy dead scattered over an area they had targeted with artillery the day before.

By Friday, it was clear that Westerman and his men had found the fight they were looking for. As intended, the battalion had hit the main body of a significant NVA force infiltrating through the DMZ. It appeared they were hitting the flank of an NVA unit moving south toward the Marine base at Con Thien.

Hanoi had designated the low hill at Con Thien a principal objective and was sending most of a division against it. Con Thien was important to Hanoi because it sat astride one of the main infiltration routes into South Vietnam. As long as Marines controlled the hill at Con Thien, the communists would have a much harder time in the area.

Con Thien, which ominously translates as "Hill of Angels," would become one of the Marine Corps' legendary battlefields of the Vietnam War. The American people didn't become familiar with Con Thien until it was featured on the cover of the October 27, 1967, issue of *Life* magazine. That cover featured one of David Douglas Duncan's stark black and white photos.

By the time Duncan went to Con Thien and took his photos, the hillock had been the scene of dozens of pitched battles and had been pounded by so much firepower it was nothing but a muddy moonscape. Night after night, NVA units charged the Marine perimeter. The fighting was often hand-to-hand. Men beat each other to death in the mud under the indifferent light of illumination flares.

Yet, despite ghastly losses, the Marines still owned the hill when the sun rose every morning. NVA artillery blanketed the hill during the day, forcing the Marines to live below ground. The Marines had to make daring forays into the open between barrages to repair the damage from the night before and prepare for the assault that was sure to come when darkness fell again.

Duncan's haunting photo on the cover of *Life* captured the "thousand-yard-stare" in the eyes of one of the defenders. The young Marine is looking into the camera with an eerie, vacant gaze. It's the look of a man who's fought too hard—for too long. Next to the photo were the words: "Inside the Cone of Fire at Con Thien."

D+5: Saturday, March 25, 1967

Kelley's and Juul's companies were hit repeatedly with enemy mortar fire early on Saturday morning between midnight and dawn. Kelley's company position was on a small hill surrounded by jungle.

Marines often referred to an area full of enemy troops as "Indian country," a reference to the westerns they had grown up watching as kids. Kent Hansen remembered thinking it was obvious they were deep in Indian country. "You could see movement of the NVA. You'd see them dart from tree to tree," he said. "We dug in that night and we dug in deep."

The NVA hit the company position with a mortar barrage that night. "They worked us over good. I mean we really got nailed," Hansen said. Greg Nichols remembered sticking his head up at the end of the barrage and finding a half a dozen fresh craters within 10 feet of his fighting hole.

Company B made it all the way back to LZ Bluebird and became the battalion's reserve, thus relieving Company A. Company B was spared any mortar barrage that

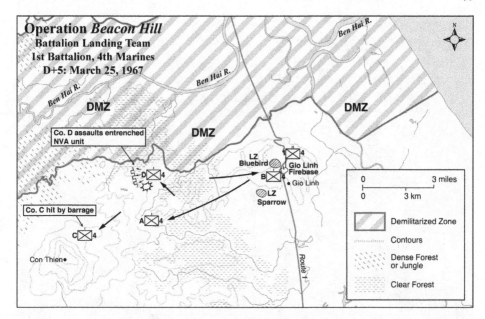

Operation *Beacon Hill*
Battalion Landing Team
1st Battalion, 4th Marines
D+5: March 25, 1967

night. However, their perimeter was repeatedly probed by the NVA. The enemy soldiers would crawl in close to their lines and try to pitch grenades into their fighting holes.

Company A marched westward and moved to a position south of Company D.

Both Company C and Company D continued their westward advance after dawn on Saturday morning. At 1415, Captain Juul's 3rd Platoon, led by Second Lieutenant Clyde Baker, tangled with an NVA unit and quickly found themselves taking fire from their front and both flanks.

One of the men who found himself in the center of the action was Sergeant Jimmie L. Blick, a combat photographer from the 3rd Marine Division Headquarters, who had been dispatched to photograph Operation *Beacon Hill.* Blick and Lance Corporal Wells, a motion picture photographer, had waited on the airfield at Dong Ha for two days before they could hitch a ride on a resupply helicopter out to film and photograph Westerman's battalion in action. They finally got a ride out just before sunset on March 24. Blick had been in the Marines for five years and in Vietnam for four months. In those four months, he had been on several operations.

He and Wells were dropped off in Company D's perimeter that evening. After he introduced himself to Captain Juul, Blick and Wells went and dug their fighting holes and got situated for the evening. As was the standard practice, the men slept on the ground next to their fighting holes. "We heard the rounds leaving the tube," Blick said of the mortar attack that started just after two in the morning. "I was sleeping outside my hole and—after a while I guess you develop an ear for the

PFC D. R. Goodwin (center), a rifleman in Clyde Baker's platoon, has his arm bandaged by a corpsman after being wounded on March 25, 1967, the sixth day of Operation *Beacon Hill*. The photo was taken by Sgt Jimmie Blick. (USMC A188534)

sounds and everything—I was asleep but as soon as my mind registered that sound I knew what it was and I just rolled over into my hole."

The company went to full alert and opened fire into the darkness, suspecting the mortar barrage was part of a ground assault. The Marine fire slackened quickly except in one section of the perimeter, where an NVA unit was trying to breach the line. However, the NVA soldiers had been caught right in the sights of one of Juul's machine-gun teams. "I think the gooks walked right into a machine gun emplacement. I think that's what stopped them," Blick said later.

Juul called in artillery on his preplanned targets, blanketing the area around his company perimeter. "The next morning, we went out there and there was blood all over the area," Blick said. The NVA soldiers had policed up the battlefield. "There weren't any weapons dropped or anything; there was just a lot of blood—no bodies, just blood trails leading off."

Company D moved out at 0830 the next morning. Second Lieutenant Clyde Baker's 3rd Platoon was at the head of the column. Blick usually tried to take up a position behind the leading squad in the column—just behind the first machine-gun team. He believed this put him in position to be close to the action while not being a nuisance. "This way, you're not in the way of any firepower that is needed at the front." Blick was armed with his Nikon 35-mm camera and a .45 automatic pistol.

"From that time on, Delta 1-4 was my favorite outfit … they were real professionals." Sgt Jimmie L. Blick, waits to be evacuated after being wounded by an enemy mortar round. A combat photographer, Blick was dispatched to photograph Operation *Beacon Hill* and ended up leading squad rushes against enemy positions. (USMC 188536)

The column moved about 800 meters before climbing a small hill. The side of the hill was terraced with rice paddies that were dry and it appeared they hadn't been tended in a long time. The edge of each terrace was lined with a row of banana trees. The Marines worked their way up the side to the top of the hill. The top of the hill was largely clear except for thigh-high underbrush.

"The point man started across and that's when the gooks hit us," recalled Blick. An NVA .50-caliber machine gun cut down the first four men in the platoon. A corpsmen ran forward to get to the wounded and he was also hit. "Then they started hitting us from a 45-degree angle toward the flanks with two other machine guns," Blick said. "They were throwing a lot of stuff at us, like they had it to waste."

Part of the platoon fell back to one of the lines of banana trees at the edge of the paddy. As soon as they fell back, the enemy began a mortar barrage, and walked the rounds right along the line of banana trees. "They got us good," Blick said. "They more or less planned that the Americans would drop back to that row—and they got some people."

Despite his assignment as a combat cameraman, Jimmie Blick soon found himself leading assaults against enemy positions. One of the bedrock principles in the Marine Corps is that every Marine is first and foremost a rifleman. All Marines, regardless of their specialty or rank, are required to qualify on the rifle range every year and are expected to stay sharp on basic infantry knowledge. Jimmie Blick was no exception.

After the ambush of the lead squad and the mortar barrage, the platoon was trying to get itself organized. Lieutenant Baker turned to Blick and ordered him to take over as squad leader. "He said, 'You rush one side, and I'll give you covering fire. Then you hit the deck and give me fire and I'll rush the other side,'" recalled Blick.

Setting aside his Nikon, Blick picked up a discarded M14 rifle and collected a bunch of magazines from some of the wounded men. "And that's what we did," Blick said. He and Baker made repeated rushes against the NVA positions. "They were dug in bunkers and everything," Blick said. "Just before we went for the final charge, the platoon commander had us throw Willie-Peter [white phosphorus] grenades—about six of them—right along the line. We throwed them as far as we could," said Blick. "And I think that did the trick, because we got up and started running when they were still in the air—and they exploded and everything—and they gave us covering smoke." Blick and Baker made it to the enemy line. "We killed a few in their bunkers—throwing grenades in them. I guess the rest of them just *didi'd* [retreated] on down the hill."

Sergeant Blick was hit in the back and neck with shrapnel in the course of the assault and was medevac'd out that evening. Although he went on to spend another eight months in Vietnam and participated in several more combat operations, he considered *Beacon Hill* his most noteworthy experience. "I guess you might say—from that time on, Delta One-Four was my favorite outfit. During those two days, I got to know the people real well and have nothing but praise for them. They were real professionals." Jimmie Blick was later awarded the Bronze Star Medal for his actions that day. Lieutenant Baker earned a Silver Star.[23]

Captain Juul brought the rest of the company up to Baker's position. Within an hour, Company D was in a violent firefight with an NVA battalion. The NVA battalion was in a set of fortified trench lines and bunkers stretching several hundred yards across Juul's front. Juul and his men assaulted the position and the battle raged into the evening. "And as we probed it, we realized it was something much bigger than we thought and we tried to maneuver to both sides of it and still ran into resistance on the flanks, and that's when one of my platoon commanders was killed," Juul said. It turned out Company D had hit the outer security around an NVA regimental command post.

Juul, like Kelley, had a mixture of platoon leaders that included salty old hands with decades in the Corps, and young lieutenants fresh out of college. One of Juul's most promising officers was 25-year-old Jack Cox. Cox, who had been a football star at the University of Georgia, was a very well-liked and respected officer.

Jack Cox was commanding Juul's 1st Platoon. With Clyde Baker's 3rd Platoon already engaged, Juul was discussing the situation on the radio with Cox, weighing possible options. "He was telling me the fire wasn't too heavy over on the right and he was going to go ahead and move in further," Juul said. "And it was during that conversation that he abruptly dropped off the line," he said. "Then the radio operator picked up the handset and told me that he was seriously hit."

An enemy bullet had hit Cox in the head while he was talking to Juul. "I told them to bring him back so we could get him medevac'd right away," Juul said. "But by the time they brought him back, he was dead." John Juul helped carry Jack Cox's body to the helicopter. "He was just an outstanding individual, one of the best platoon commanders I had," Juul said.

A few minutes later, he was told he had also lost Corporal Charles Clanton. Clanton's skill on the battlefield had earned him a set of corporal's chevrons despite having been in the Marine Corps for just over a year. Juul remembered the 19-year-old from Alabama as "one of my best squad leaders."

With nightfall approaching, Juul decided to have his men pull back so he could use artillery and air support to pound the enemy fortifications. Eventually he directed napalm strikes on the enemy positions. By the end of the day, Juul had lost five Marines killed and six wounded. He spent the night calling in fire support on the enemy positions and preparing to make an assault the next day.

Company C spent Saturday night dug in just north of Con Thien.

PART III

THE BATTLE

CHAPTER 18

Easter Sunday

"I'll never forget the Easter of '67. I never want to see anything like that again ... A lot of my friends are dead."

PRIVATE FIRST CLASS GARY L. HUDSON

Easter Sunday was on the 26th of March in 1967. Most American units in Vietnam were planning church services and, if possible, some kind of a special meal to mark the holiday. The chaplains at Phu Bai held a sunrise service to celebrate the holy day and the cooks on the base prepared a special Easter meal for the Marines.[1]

There was little recognition of the holiday for the men in Company C. Easter Sunday started out hot and humid. Bob Kelley and his Marines were up before dawn, tightening up their packs and gear, and cleaning and checking their weapons.

Kelley had received orders to take his company from their position just north of Con Thien and march toward a spot about a thousand yards south of the DMZ. They were going to make a thrust right into the NVA unit north of Con Thien. Bob Kelley knew he and his Marines were going about as far into Indian country as they could without actually invading North Vietnam.

On Kelley's orders, boxes of ammunition and grenades were brought up and the men were told to load up with the ammo. Kelley believed his men needed two things to survive on this type of combat patrol. They needed water; and they needed ammunition. Everything else—even food—could wait until they were out of enemy territory.

Each man draped additional bandoleers of ammunition over his flak jacket and put as many hand grenades as he could fit into his pockets. Additionally, machine-gun belts were spread-loaded among the Marines in the company. Larry Normand and the other men in the rocket teams were told to leave the heavy, cumbersome 3.5-inch bazooka tubes behind because the rocket launchers would be almost useless in the thick vegetation. Normand and his men went out that day as additional riflemen, armed with M14s. The amount of ammunition delivered seemed excessive to Mac McClelland at the time. "We were trying to figure out how to carry it all," McClelland said. "We didn't know, by the end of the day—we would have shot it all."

The day was extremely hot, even by Vietnam standards, and the vegetation got thicker and thicker as they moved north. The jungle canopy trapped the heat and turned the jungle floor into a sweltering oven. The Marines tried to stay away from the few established trails that crisscrossed the area. Trails were obvious spots for enemy ambushes and booby traps. However, the jungle got so thick their progress slowed to a crawl as they hacked against the wall of undergrowth in front of them. They ended up having to alternate between using the trail network and pushing their way through the jungle to keep moving toward their objective. They would hack their way through the jungle for a while; then pop out onto a trail and follow it for a hundred yards or so. After following the trail for a while, they would head back into the jungle and start chopping their way forward again.

A couple of hours into the patrol, Company C reached its objective—a point close to the southern edge of Demilitarized Zone. Following procedure, the company began to move back toward Con Thien using an alternate route. On the way back, they came across a water point, probably built by the French. It was a pagoda built into the side of the mountain around a natural spring. Inside the little structure there were a number of ceramic pipes coming out of the hillside and emptying into a small pool. The cool, fresh spring water was a blessing. The Marines filled their canteens and ran their heads under the water before moving on.

Second Platoon was leading the company as they began to move back toward Con Thien. Bill Dorsey was Lieutenant Dickerson's radio operator. Dorsey had the distinction of being one of the few men in history to be drafted into the Marine Corps. When he reported to the local draft board in Cleveland, Georgia, in 1966, he was told he was going into the Marines. The Marine Corps had been forced to use the Selective Service to get enough men to fill the skyrocketing demands for Marines in Vietnam. "There were 19 of us who went down for the draft and they put us all in the Marines," Dorsey said with a laugh years later. "It was one of the few times in the Marine Corps that they ever had a draft."

The young men who were drafted into the Marine Corps during the Vietnam War performed superbly. By the time they graduated from boot camp, most of the draftees were as proud to be Marines as those who had volunteered. In March 1969, a young Marine from Nebraska named Ronald L. Coker earned the Medal of Honor trying to rescue his squad leader. Coker had been drafted. By the end of the war, 42,655 men had been drafted into the Marine Corps.[2]

As Dickerson's radio operator, it was Dorsey's job to carry the 24-pound PRC-25 radio on his back and relay communications back and forth for Dickerson. Dorsey, like all radio operators in Vietnam, knew he was a marked man. The enemy viewed his radio as the most dangerous piece of equipment carried by American infantrymen. Using their radio, small American units could initiate and direct devastating artillery barrages, or summon swarms of fighter-bombers loaded with napalm. A pinned-down American patrol could call for reinforcements—dozens of helicopters loaded with more infantrymen. Consequently, NVA and Viet Cong soldiers scoured the battlefield looking for the telltale tape antennae. Once they found the radio, they targeted it with everything they had. While the life expectancy of a Marine rifleman along the DMZ had gotten much shorter since 1965, radio operators always had it worse. "I didn't realize that I'd reduced my life span from eleven seconds to three," Dorsey said. Dickerson, as the platoon's officer, was also a marked man. He would tease Dorsey about the danger that came with carrying the radio. "He would say: 'Get away from me with that thing. You're going to get me shot.'"

Contact

After leaving the pagoda, the platoon resumed their tactical formation. Just as they got back on the narrow trail, mortar rounds started dropping just to their rear. Knowing the enemy was sure to start "walking" the mortar rounds toward them, the Marines started double-timing up the trail. Bill Dorsey remembered trotting up the trail. "All of a sudden, I looked down and there was a blue-coated communication wire running along beside the trail." It was an NVA field phone line. It meant they were in the midst of a substantial enemy force. "I had a pair of dykes to cut wire, so every time I got a second, I'd stop and cut it," Dorsey said.

After getting safely beyond the mortar fire, the platoon stopped and quickly reorganized back into its tactical patrol formation. The Marines from Lionel Lawson's 2nd Squad were at the head of the platoon. After going about 25 meters up the trail, they came to an open area. As the first men moved into the area, they were engulfed by a roar of explosions and machine-gun fire. The men at the front of the column were raked by fire and bracketed with a series of jarring blasts—either from command-detonated mines or hand grenades.

Private First Class Larry Larson had taken over as the platoon's point man just minutes before. As the point man, he was the Marine at the very front of the formation. Twenty-year-old Larson was killed in the first burst of fire.

Larry Larson had spent most of his life preparing to become a priest. He was from Carmel, California, and had attended the Carmel Mission School and then had gone on to Holy Redeemer Seminary High School in Oakland. He shocked his family by enlisting in the Marines after he graduated from high school. He told his parents later that he didn't feel he could justify going directly into the seminary while other young men—many with wives and children—were being drafted and sent to Vietnam. He wasn't comfortable with the idea that a married man with a family might be drafted and sent to Vietnam to fill his spot while he was in the seminary. Larry decided he had to enlist before he could faithfully enter the seminary to become a priest.

The other Marines nicknamed him "Pack Rat." He had earned the name because he was habitually stashing extra stuff in his backpack, pockets, and pouches. He would then produce all kinds of unusual things when people needed them. His other trait was that he never used profanity—a truly rare accomplishment after months as an infantryman.

McClelland's squad was on the left flank just behind the point element and also came under a hail of fire. Nineteen-year-old Lance Corporal Jim Ver Helst, one of McClelland's men, was near Lawson's men and crawled up to help them. He got up the trail but was cut down in a hail of enemy fire. Jim Ver Helst had enlisted in the Marines after graduating from high school in Mason City, Iowa. He was known in Mason City for building things, and was a particularly good welder. He was looking forward to getting home and driving the brand-new burgundy Ford Mustang he had bought just before enlisting.

Private First Class Victor H. Van Vactor was also killed in the first moments of the battle. Van Vactor was a tall, rail-thin 19-year-old from Louisville, Kentucky. He was the youngest of four boys. His oldest brother had been a Marine. Victor had tried to join the Marines right after he graduated from Trinity High School in Louisville in 1965. The Marine recruiters turned him away because he had a history of asthma. He then tried to enlist in the army, but was also turned away because of his asthma. He went back a year later. This time, the Marines took him. There were few men who have been as proud to wear a Marine Corps uniform as Victor Van Vactor.[3]

Corporal Bob Bryson was hit the same time as Larry Larson. One of the few married men in the platoon, he had become a father in January when his daughter, Lisa, was born. Bryson's wife, Jo-Ann, was the daughter of a career navy man. When Bob was sent to Vietnam, Jo-Ann went to stay with her folks in Spain, where her father was stationed. Bob Bryson was overjoyed at having a daughter and kept talking to the other men in the platoon about his new baby girl.

Jerry Idziak and Lionel Lawson crawled through the dust and machine-gun fire to Bob Bryson. A bullet or chunk of shrapnel had hit him in the neck and blood was spurting from his carotid artery. They told him to "hang on" as they tried to stanch the bleeding. But the blood kept pumping out of his neck. Bob Bryson knew he was dying. He gripped their hands and said, "Tell my wife and daughter I love them! Tell my wife and daughter I love them!" He started to fade. Jerry Idziak was holding Bob Bryson's hand and felt it relax. "Then I knew he was gone," Idziak said.[4]

Private First Class Floyd Larrabee ran forward to check on Ver Helst, and discovered that Jim was dead. While he was checking on Jim, an enemy bullet took off part of his foot.

The NVA were firing from a series of trenches and bunkers dug in along the hedgerows and treelines. The air was filled with the distinctive staccato bursts of communist machine guns. As the platoon moved up and deployed, they realized they had enemy fire coming at them from three sides.

The volume of fire was deafening. North Vietnamese bullets scythed across everything that was more than a foot or two above the ground, chopping the banana trees and scrub to pieces and leaving the ground covered with splintered vegetation. Enemy grenades came flying over the trees in clusters and dropped among the Marines. The Marines cussed and swore as they jumped and rolled away from the grenades that thumped onto the ground next to them. "Every time somebody showed their face, they got shot or a hand grenade came in and blew up," Bill Dorsey said.

An NVA attempt to envelop and overrun the Marines from the left was stopped. "I heard guys running through the woods off to my left," McClelland said, "and I had my guys open up into the woods—and then I heard whatever was in the woods running back."

While clearing a jam in his rifle, McClelland was hit. "My shoulder was facing the enemy and a round hit me just behind the top of my shoulder, smashed my collarbone and went across and went up into my neck." Larrabee, although himself wounded, crawled out and dragged McClelland from the line of fire and back toward Doc Nichols. "After that, everything got a little weird for me, because I was kind of in and out," McClelland said. "I remember just being dragged around a lot."

Mac McClelland was dragged back to Greg Nichols, who, as one of the corpsmen, had moved up to get closer to the wounded at the head of the platoon. Unfortunately, Doc Nichols quickly became another casualty. He had pulled McClelland down behind a small berm and was working on him. "I was laying on my side and as I was patching him up, my right arm came up," Nichols said. "I saw the guy raise up and fire at me—and he caught me in the right shoulder." The NVA bullet tore through Nichols's shoulder, his ribs, and into one of his lungs. The other members of the platoon remembered seeing Nichols and McClelland trying to bandage each other up. With Nichols badly wounded, Greg Long was now the only corpsman for the platoon.

The Marines in 2nd Platoon were pinned down and taking fire from three sides. It was clear to everyone in the platoon they were caught in a well-planned and well-executed ambush. It was the worst situation for infantrymen. The NVA had dug in along the edges of the clearing in front of the banana grove and had pinned down the leading section of the platoon in a "kill zone," the area where an ambushing force can methodically rake the pinned-down men with gunfire and hand grenades until they're killed off one by one. The Marines caught in a kill zone also served as bait. Anyone who tried to move up to help them was also shot down.

For men to survive an ambush, they must override many of their natural instincts. For this reason, Marines constantly practiced "immediate action drills" to sharpen their counter-ambush techniques. The natural reaction for a man caught in an ambush is to hug the ground. While this may seem to be the safest thing to do, it actually plays directly into the hands of the ambushing force. As long as the men stay on the ground, they can't effectively return fire and they become stationary targets. Every minute spent on the ground means more casualties and decreases their chances of survival. Eventually, the ambushing force will advance and overrun those trapped in the kill zone, killing or capturing any survivors.

An immediate assault against the ambushing force is the only way to survive. Instead of hugging the ground, those caught in the ambush must rise and charge directly at their ambushers. Charging right into the guns of the ambushing force is the only chance to "break" the ambush and force the enemy to withdraw.[5] An aggressive counter-ambush assault can quickly turn the tables and send the shocked ambushing force running for their lives. This demands the utmost in discipline and courage. The counter-ambush assault has a much better chance of success if the two forces are close to each other. That afternoon, the Marines from 2nd Platoon and the NVA were within 50 yards of each other.

Lionel Lawson was leader of 2nd Squad. He and his squad were pinned down in the kill zone. Lawson had enlisted from Tamaqua, Pennsylvania, after graduating from high school in 1965. The men in the platoon had nicknamed him "Chooch." As with many nicknames, it had a bent logic to it. Someone had associated Lawson's first name with the Lionel toy company that made model trains. Somehow, that became "Choo choo," associating him with trains. That was shortened to "Chooch." To this day, Lionel Lawson is known as "Chooch" to the other men of 2nd Platoon.

"I knew we were in trouble because, usually, when we got in a firefight, we threw more lead back at them than they threw at us," Lawson said, "but, man, they were throwing 30 times more lead back at us. I knew we were in trouble."

Lieutenant Dickerson came forward and saw the situation was bad. Dickerson realized he couldn't envelop the enemy to take the pressure off Lawson's men. The enemy line was too long and entrenched. He told Lawson they had to get organized and make an assault to break the ambush.

As he had been trained, Lawson took action. "So, I stood up and said, 'Let's go! Fix bayonets! We're going!'" The men pulled out their bayonets and snapped them onto the barrels of their M14s, "and away we went," said Lawson. Lionel Lawson and his men charged the initial line of enemy soldiers, firing their weapons, and screaming at the tops of their voices. Their assault forced the NVA back across the open area to a trench line dug along the hedgerow on the far side of the clearing.

Dennis Heider was one of the Marines in Lawson's squad. He remembered hearing Lawson's command to fix bayonets. "I'll always remember that sound—of the bayonets going on the rifles," he said. Heider stood up just as an NVA soldier also stood up, directly in front of him. "He couldn't have been more than ten yards away," he said. "I can still see his face. He was as surprised and scared as I was," he said. "We both went for our rifles—it was like a duel ... I was faster," Dennis Heider then said quietly. "I can still see his face..."[6]

In the course of their assault against the NVA line, an enemy grenade detonated a few feet behind Lawson and shredded his legs with shrapnel. He found himself stuck in no man's land between the main body of the platoon and the enemy trench line. It was a while before anyone realized Lawson hadn't made it back to the platoon's lines. When he heard Lionel yelling, Jerry Idziak ran out and picked him up and carried him back to the perimeter.

With a laugh, Lionel Lawson often refers to the charge he led into the ambush line as "my John Wayne moment." He has also been teased for years about his order to "fix bayonets." It sounded outrageously anachronistic—a relic of the 19th century. No one thought they would ever hear that order given on a modern battlefield. However, Lionel Lawson's assault was a textbook maneuver and it was effective. It took the initiative away from the NVA soldiers long enough for 2nd Platoon to get organized. It established a viable line of defense, and gave them a chance to retrieve their wounded. Lionel Lawson looks back on the assault with some pride, "Hey," he said with a chuckle, "they followed me—and it worked."

Lawson's assault was successful and pushed the NVA back to their secondary lines on the other side of the field. Second Platoon established a perimeter into the clearing, with the center of their line forward of an old bomb crater. The crater was deep enough and wide enough around that it provided some shelter from enemy fire. The crater quickly became the point for collecting the wounded and dead.

The battle raged over the small clearing between the two lines. The Marines were in an abandoned banana grove on one side of the field while the NVA were operating out of a series of trenches and bunkers on the opposite side of the field. The NVA made repeated assaults across the field, trying to overrun the Marines. The Marines counterattacked and pushed them back into the trenches. The Marines tried to flank the enemy's lines and managed to get close and sweep the trenches with fire a couple of times, only to have enemy reinforcements replace the losses in a matter of minutes. The two sides were not more than 100 yards apart most of the afternoon.

Kent Hansen and Private Haywood Swearingen made an assault from the right side of their platoon line into the NVA's left flank. Swearingen was stitched across his body by an enemy machine gun. Bullets hit him in the wrist, left shoulder, and right side. Swearingen remembered Kent Hansen dragging him back to the crater. "I was kind of in and out of it after that," Swearingen said. "There were more dead in the crater every time I woke up." His wounds were so severe that he ended up spending four months in an iron lung.[7]

Jerry Idziak was also part of the assault against the enemy's left flank. Idziak was considered one of the toughest guys in the platoon. He grew up in Grand Rapids, Michigan, the youngest of three brothers. His father had been a professional boxer.

He had played lots of sports in school and was a defensive end on his high school's football team. He had already impressed the guys in the platoon with his consistently gutsy moves in combat.

While most of the platoon got along fine, the noticeable exception was Jerry Idziak and Ed Gutloff. Gutloff was the platoon's machine gunner. Even though Jerry was white and Gutloff was black, everyone who knew the two men agreed that it was not a racial issue. Both men got along with everybody else in the platoon regardless of skin color. They just didn't like each other. "It really wasn't some kind of racial thing," McClelland said. "They just hated each other." Gutloff was a big tough guy from the Bronx. Idziak grew up on the streets of Grand Rapids, another tough place. Jerry Idziak and Ed Gutloff were two genuinely tough guys who just seemed to annoy the hell out of each other. Most in the platoon chalk the animosity up to two big egos that banged into each other all the time.

As they were moving forward, Idziak and Hansen ran into an NVA bunker they hadn't seen. The machine gun in the bunker opened fire and cut Idziak across the waist and legs. A bullet smashed from one hip all the way through to the other. To the men who saw him get hit, it looked like Jerry had been cut in half by the machine gun. Right after he went down, grenades detonated around him, sending chunks of shrapnel into him.

Jerry Idziak immediately knew he was very badly wounded. He screamed for everybody to stay away from him. He yelled that he was a dead man and he didn't want anyone else to get hit trying to get to him. "At that time, I just was screaming for everybody to get the hell out of there," he said later. He was in excruciating pain and pleaded for Hansen and the other Marines to shoot him in the head and leave him. He was sure he was going to die and didn't want them to get killed trying to get to him; and he didn't want to be captured alive. "But Marines don't do that," he said softly, remembering the scene years later. Despite his pleas, his fellow Marines wouldn't abandon him.

Steve Pruitt heard Jerry screaming and started to crawl forward. Just as he was starting to get up to make a run for Jerry, Walter Smith tackled him and pinned him to the ground. Lying on top of him, Smith hissed into Pruitt's ear that he was going to get himself killed and to keep his ass down. Smith growled that he had already lost too many men and didn't want to lose anymore.

Ed Gutloff was the first man to make a run into the hail of enemy fire to try and save Jerry Idziak. Despite the bullets tearing up the ground all around Jerry, Gutloff rose and charged toward him. Ed Gutloff was cut down in a hail of fire. He fell dead a few feet from Jerry. Colin McClelland summed up the whole situation later: "Gutloff just saw a Marine in trouble and did what all Marines do." Ed Gutloff was posthumously awarded the Bronze Star Medal for his actions that day.

More Marines came forward. Jerry remembered seeing them maneuver against the enemy bunker that had shot him. It was only about 20 yards from him. He caught glimpses of Doc Long, Kent Hansen, and Larry Alley moving around. "I don't know how they did it, but they blew that bunker apart," he said.

After they destroyed the bunker, Kent Hansen crawled out to pull Jerry back to the platoon perimeter. There were still plenty of NVA machine guns covering the area and Hansen knew he had to stay below the grazing enemy fire. He crawled out to Jerry, staying just below the enemy fire. When he got to Jerry, he climbed over him and straddled him. He told Jerry to wrap his arms around his neck. Then, pushing with his toes and his elbows, Hansen began dragging Jerry to safety, inch by inch, while enemy bullets cracked in the air just inches above them. Every time Kent pushed forward, the ground pulled at Jerry's wounds. It felt like he was being torn in half. He tried to stifle his screams but couldn't help himself at times. After several minutes, Kent had managed to drag Jerry out of the line of fire and put him down in the crater with the rest of the wounded. Jerry ended up being the most badly wounded man in the platoon who survived.

Ed Gutloff's sacrifice still haunts Jerry Idziak. He never talks about that day without praising Ed Gutloff, often tearfully. The man he had resented so much was killed trying to save his life. "He was a real goddamn hero," Jerry Idziak said. "That guy was a *real* hero."

In the course of the fighting, the lines shifted back and forth. The wounded men in the crater watched as the battle raged around them. Mac McClelland was lying in the crater, unable to move or talk:

> I remember them fighting back and forth over it [the crater] because I remember the grenades going back and forth. You could see their grenades—because they were the old potato-masher style—going over our heads. I remember seeing a group go over our heads. And then I saw a group of our grenades—good old egg-style grenades go back. And then I saw another group of theirs go over and then I saw a group of ours … except that this time, they were mixed with theirs, and then I saw a group of theirs come over and I saw a group of theirs go back. There weren't any of ours … and I thought, "I hope they haven't got us surrounded and are trying to figure out where we are and just throw grenades." It turned out our guys had gotten some of their grenades and were throwing them back at them.

At points, it appeared the men in the crater had ended up between the two lines. "I remember hearing a guy yelling: 'The wounded are out there! The wounded are out there! We've got to drive them back!'" Mac McClelland said. A few moments later, he heard Marines open fire and rush forward. "I remember a machine gunner walking by the edge of the crater—shooting, and then it was a pretty big fight for a while."

Another time, someone got all the Marines who had M79 grenade launchers together and formed them into a skirmish line. They began moving forward while barrage-firing into the enemy lines. It reminded McClelland of Revolutionary War tactics from the 18th century. "It was like old British firing, like, 'Load! Aim! Fire!' and they just kept doing that for at least ten volleys. 'Load! Aim! Fire!' I kept hearing that, 'Thump, thump, thump' [as they fired] and then 'Wham, wham, wham' [the exploding rounds]."

In the course of the battle, Floyd Larrabee was hit again. This time it was much more serious. He was dragged into the crater with a bullet wound in his body. He said he couldn't feel his legs, but actually seemed cheerful. He and Jerry Idziak were propped up, back to back, because they both had wounds that made it hard to breathe if they lay down. Larrabee spent some time loading magazines and tossing them up to the guys who were still up on the line fighting. Mac McClelland was in the crater with Larrabee and Idziak. "Someone asked Larrabee if he was OK and he said, 'Yeah,' but he was really tired," McClelland said. "Eventually, he just said, 'I've got to get some rest ...' and then he never woke up."

"We were talking about our families and stuff and all of a sudden, he wasn't talking anymore," Jerry said. "I knew he had died but I didn't move because he held me in an upright position where I could breathe. That was terrible," he said. "I still have nightmares about that."

Lionel Lawson was sitting next to Larrabee. "Jerry and I were talking to him and all of a sudden he stopped talking and he just slumped over ... and he was gone." It was guessed later that Floyd Larrabee had died from internal bleeding. He was one of the other married men in the platoon. His wife, Evelyn, was waiting for him in their little house back in Olathe, Kansas.

1st Platoon, led by Second Lieutenant Dennis D. Dooley, was situated to the rear of the company near Captain Kelley's command post. The platoon had been rotated back because they had taken a number of casualties on Friday. Dooley was one of Bob Kelley's older mustang platoon leaders. He had enlisted in the Marines in April 1951 and was quickly sent to Korea. While in Korea, he earned a Silver Star for rescuing a Marine who was caught on a barbed-wire obstacle after their patrol was ambushed. Dooley went into the fire-swept area directly in front of an enemy machine gun, got the man free, and helped get him back to the Marine lines. Dennis Dooley got out of the Marines for a spell, but enlisted again in 1956 with the intention of making it his career. He rose through the enlisted ranks and was offered a commission in 1966. Lieutenant Dooley was highly respected in the company.[8]

Bob Kelley knew Larry Dickerson had his hands full and told Dooley to go up and see if he could help him. Dooley could tell 2nd Platoon had been hit hard and decided to take a few men up with him to help. He ended up going forward with three of his grenadiers. One was Corporal Douglas W. Lee, a 20-year-old from Winston-Salem, North Carolina. Lee was a fire team leader in Sergeant Carl Martin's squad. Martin liked Lee and described him as "gung ho." Lee had bright red hair and freckles and wore a set of the heavy-frame regulation glasses. Doug Lee had impressed Martin two days earlier during the firefight while they were returning from the ambush patrol. In addition to being a fire team leader, Doug Lee also carried one of the squad's M79 grenade launchers. "I'll tell you what," Martin said, "he did us proud on that day—Good Friday, the 24th. He was able to drop those darn M79 rounds right where we needed them."

Another of the grenadiers Dooley took with him was Phillip Key. Key grew up in Columbus, Ohio, and enlisted in the Marines right after graduating from high school in 1965. He jokes about how casually he decided to join the Marines. "I wanted something to do and I think the Marines were the first recruiter's door at the post office, that was about it."[9]

The third grenadier that day was Michael Helton. Helton was from Dayton, Ohio, and had enlisted in the Marines in January 1966. Like many others, he had enlisted to avoid being drafted into the army. "I knew damn well within a week or two that I was getting a notification to join the army," he said with a laugh. "And sure enough, I went down and enlisted in the Marine Corps; and about a week later, I got my draft notice."[10]

Phillip Key remembered Dooley shouting for the platoon's grenadiers. "That's when Lieutenant Dooley said, 'M79 men up!'"

Dooley told Martin and the rest of 1st Platoon to stay where they were while he and the other men went up to help 2nd Platoon. Key remembered going forward with Doug Lee and Mike Helton. "We went up—and passed the company CP. They told us where to go and we went further on up the trail and we got to this treeline where 2nd Platoon was." As he and the other men moved forward, they passed the crater. As he passed, he saw Doc Long in the crater patching up the wounded.

Martin remembered Lee coming back to their position a little while later. "He said, 'Lieutenant Dooley sent me back to get as many grenades as I can.'" The 1st Platoon Marines were deployed in a defensive perimeter around Kelley's CP. Lee then went up and down the ranks collecting grenades. "I remember him holding his shirt out—and we all just threw our grenades in there for him," said Martin. "Heck, he must have left out of there with 20 or 30 of them. And he went up—beyond us, to where 2nd Platoon was," Martin said. "And so, my lieutenant and him became a part of 2nd Platoon."[11]

Dennis Dooley earned his second Silver Star that Easter Sunday while helping the Marines in 2nd Platoon. He led assaults against enemy positions and pulled wounded men back to safety. It was Dooley who organized the barrage firing of the M79 grenade launchers McClelland had heard. He was eventually wounded but refused treatment.

Sergeant Larry Wilson, the platoon guide, hadn't had a chance to dump his pack since the fighting started. When he rolled over on his back to get to his ammunition, the pack forced his face up into the line of fire. An NVA bullet hit him in the face, tearing a triangular hole in his cheek.[12] He put a battle dressing on the wound and kept fighting. However, the dressing kept slipping off and his teeth showed through the hole—giving him what looked like a ghoulish sideways grin. "It looked pretty bad," said Dave Rumsey. "I mean, there were guys wounded a lot worse, but, I don't know why, but that just really bothered me for some reason."[13]

Company C had lodged itself into the teeth of a fortified NVA unit that had been staging to attack Con Thien. This was the fight they had been looking for; however, the terrain and the enemy's superior numbers made it impossible to maneuver. Dickerson and 2nd Platoon were at the center of the fray—and were going to have to slug it out with the NVA.

Their mission now was to inflict as many casualties as possible on the NVA and drive them back into the DMZ. Dickerson and Captain Glenn Takabayashi, the battalion's Air Officer, were able to call close air support, and the jets began dropping bombs. Kent Hansen remembered marking the enemy lines by throwing smoke grenades into their positions, "That's how close we were."

Enemy bullets cracked the air inches above their heads so loudly it made their back teeth hurt. They hugged the ground as they crawled through the dust and broken vegetation. To take drinks from thir canteens, they had to turn their heads to the side and suck the water out without raising their heads off the ground. The heat seemed to take the air out of their lungs. The concussion from enemy grenades made them dizzy, and American artillery rounds and bombs impacting less than a hundred yards away sent waves of concussion through the underbrush. In the chaos, the shadowy silhouettes of enemy soldiers darted through the haze and smoke.

Most of the men remember the day in fragments—small, disjointed events that were burned into their memories by adrenaline. Steve Pruitt vividly remembers seeing Gordy Cardinal firing his M14 on full auto into NVA soldiers who were trying to sneak into their position using the banana trees for cover. Cardinal and Pruitt were in the same fire team and were best friends. "He was the craziest son of bitch you ever wanted to meet," Pruitt said with a laugh. "But," he added, "if you wanted somebody beside you with a weapon—he was the man." Cardinal would empty an entire magazine into an enemy soldier. "That day, he put that thing on automatic and he was blasting guys up into the trees," Pruitt said. "He'd push them way up in the air. Dead bodies were going up into the trees. He never let off," Pruitt said. "He didn't let up. Then he'd just laugh. That's the way he was. He'd just smile," Pruitt said. "That's what I remember about that day."[14]

Charlie Runnels remembered crawling forward into a thick hedgerow flanking an NVA trench. Armed with an M79 grenade launcher, he was able to fire into the enemy lines. "I was in a hedge that was so thick, I just stuck my M79 right into it and touched it off," he said. "I finally had a hole there about six inches in diameter and I'm firing through it and they had no idea where this stuff was coming from. I cleared the whole side of the trench out there for a while. Then I ran out of M79 rounds." With no more grenades, Runnels crawled back to the Marine positions.

Later, Runnels would point to another piece of luck that helped the Marines that day. Westerman's Marines were still armed with the trusty M14 rifle. The Marine Corps had resisted adopting the M16 for a number of reasons since deploying to Vietnam. Finally, in 1966, General Westmoreland ordered that they trade in their M14 rifles for the new M16s.[15] Those Marine units initially armed with the new M16 rifle experienced serious problems with the new rifle. The M16s jammed and malfunctioned for a myriad of reasons, and cost men their lives in firefights.[16] Eventually, the problems with the M16s prompted congressional investigations. To make the rifles reliable, the Marines had to refit them with a number of improvements.[17] Luckily, Westerman's battalion had gone ashore in *Beacon Hill* still armed with the M14. If even a handful of the rifles in 2nd Platoon had become inoperable during the battle, Dickerson and his men would have had a much harder time. "A lot of the reason that I'm still alive is because I had an M14," Runnels said.

One of Phillip Key's vivid memories was of the tremendous explosions when the jets came in and started dropping their bombs just forward of the Marine lines. He saw a spotter plane fire a rocket into the enemy positions. A few moments later, a jet thundered overhead and dropped its bombs. "They were right above the treetops," he said. "You could see the plane coming in. And you pretty much knew when all this ordnance was going to hit the deck," he said. "And I remember having my back to this tree ... I'm trying to hide behind this tree, and all these sparks and smoke and everything is going past this tree, you know—past me! I know there was guys from the 2nd Platoon on the other side of that tree somewhere—and how they survived that I don't know."

Marines do not abandon their dead. It's an article of faith between Marines that every man will go home. Larry Normand remembered being part of the team organized to go out and retrieve the bodies of the men killed earlier that day.

They stacked their rifles to the rear, wanting to be as light as possible for their sprint into the enemy line of fire. They figured they would have both hands full and wouldn't be able to use their rifles anyway. Other men were going to cover their rush with fire. The only weapons they had with them were the hand grenades they had on their belts and in their pockets.

"I ran out there and was just about to drag somebody back and one of the NVA soldiers popped out of a spider hole right in front of me," Normand said. "So I hollered and chucked a hand grenade at him." Larry immediately realized he had forgotten to pull the pin on the grenade. "I mean, we were both just staring at each other," he said with a laugh later. "I just grabbed the dead Marine and ran on back."[18]

Most of the platoon killed other young men that day. The fighting was close and they saw the faces of the NVA soldiers they shot with their rifles, and blew apart with grenades; they heard the screams. By the end of the battle, most of them had killed several men that way. Those memories are vivid—and private.

While Lieutenant Dickerson was leading 2nd Platoon, Bob Kelley had his hands full as the company commander. Company C had driven into the heart of a larger NVA force, probably a regiment. Kelley was now, for all intents and purposes, surrounded. With 2nd Platoon holding the center, Kelley coordinated artillery and air support and moved Marines from one place to another—shoring up the thin spots in his perimeter before the NVA could run a unit through them.

Above and Beyond the Call of Duty

As the day went on, Larry Dickerson found a small depression in the ground forward of the crater and was trying to coordinate air and artillery strikes from there. He and Bill Dorsey were lying on the ground, trying to stay below the grazing machine-gun fire. Dorsey was lying next to him relaying his messages over the radio. A grenade exploded near them and Dorsey's leg was shredded with shrapnel. "It was a couple of hours into the fight … and that's when I got hit in the leg," Dorsey said.

Doc Long came up and started cutting away Dorsey's bloody trousers so he could bandage the wounds. Charlie Runnels was trying to do what he could to help with the wounded and had moved up with Long. Runnels was one of the last men left from Lionel Lawson's squad who wasn't dead or wounded. "I didn't have much else to do since my squad was gone," Runnels said.

With Dorsey hit, Dickerson needed another radio operator. Doug Dickey had been trained as a replacement radio operator. "When I got there, Dickerson yelled for me to go get Dickey, because he was our back-up radioman," Runnels said. "So I went and I grabbed Dickey because he was in 3rd Squad. I pulled him out and I told him the lieutenant needed him to take over the radio because Dorsey was hit," Runnels said. "I kind of left him there and I started to leave—and then there were two grenades came flying in."

"Lieutenant Dickerson was hunkered down up close to my head," Bill Dorsey said later. "Doc Long was working on me, and Dickey had took the radio and was standing up near my right foot—and that's when the hand grenades started coming in," he said. "I seen it come in over some of the trees and, of course, somebody yelled, 'Grenade!' And I heard the thump and I just rolled over with my back to it and put my arm up over my head …"

Greg Long had gotten to be pretty good friends with Doug Dickey even though they had very different personalities. Long was one of the platoon's wild men; he was rowdy and gregarious and had a vast repertoire of off-color jokes and stories, which he constantly told to entertain the guys in the platoon. Long's voice could almost always be heard anytime the platoon was together. Doug, on the other hand, was quiet and his humor was self-deprecating, and he didn't usually cuss or swear. But the two men had something in common. They both genuinely liked people

A family of patriots. Harold Dickey after graduating from Parris Island in 1943. (Photo courtesy of Dennis Dickey)

A young widower, Harold Dickey was given a few days of leave to meet Vera, his baby girl, before he deployed to the Pacific. (Dennis Dickey)

"The war was something he never talked about." Harold Dickey beside a destroyed Japanese artillery piece on Saipan in 1944. (Photo courtesy of Dennis Dickey)

The Dickey family: Harold and Leona, Doug, Dennis, Steven, and Norman. Audie Murphy summed up the dreams of men like Harold Dickey after years of war: "I will go back. I will find the kind of girl of whom I once dreamed. I will learn to look at life through uncynical eyes, to have faith, to know love." (Dennis Dickey)

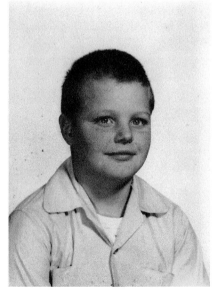

"Each one had to help the other one, and it forms a little bond …" Norman, Doug, and Dennis. All three brothers served as Marines during the Vietnam War. (Dennis Dickey)

"He was just a special little kid. Everybody liked him …" (Photo courtesy of Dennis Dickey)

When he didn't make the cut for the basketball team during his junior year, Doug volunteered to be their trainer (kneeling, left). "He just liked to be part of the team." (*The 1964 Oracle*)

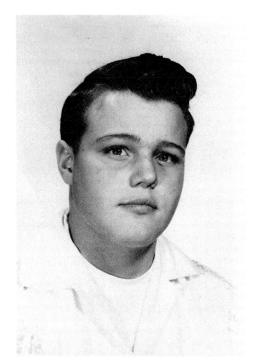

"He was always there ... ready to go." Doug's senior-year football picture. (*The 1965 Oracle*)

"Just the kind of son any mother would cherish. He was so unselfish with everything that he did." (Photo courtesy of Dennis Dickey)

"He had a beautiful bass voice." Doug Dickey (left side back row) in the Darke County Honor Chorus during his senior year. (*The 1965 Oracle*)

Tim Barga	Bob Birt	Doug Dickey	Dave Thornhill	Roger Young

The Buddy Program: "Some of the guys had gotten draft notices. We knew the writing was on the wall. So, we went ahead and enlisted." (*The 1965 Oracle* and *Platoon 394 Graduation Book*)

Of the five friends who enlisted together, Doug had the toughest time in boot camp. "I always think of the ridicule he took and if those guys only knew how brave he was," said Tim Barga. Doug with Sgt Baughman at MCRD San Diego. (*Platoon 394 Graduation Book*)

Platoon 394 with the five buddies from Darke County. Front row: Bob Birt (4th from left), Doug Dickey (3rd from right). Second row: Tim Barga (1st from left), Dave Thornhill (3rd from left). Fourth row: Roger Young (7th from right). By the end of the war, GySgt Moore, the senior Drill Instructor (seated, center), Doug Dickey, and four other members of the platoon had been killed in action. (Photo courtesy of Dennis Dickey)

"He was so proud to be a Marine." Doug and his mother after attending church at the Rossburg Methodist Church on his first Sunday home after boot camp. (Photo courtesy of Leona Dickey)

"That's the best picture of him," Leona Dickey said. Private First Class Douglas E. Dickey official photo. (USMC)

"I am with a pretty good group of men," Doug Dickey told his parents. Second Platoon, Company C, at Camp Schwab, Okinawa, on New Year's Day 1967. (Photo courtesy of Larry Normand)

Greg "Doc" Nichols · Jerry Matthews · Haywood Swearingen · Greg "Doc" Long · Victor VanVactor

Jerry Idziak · Edward Czuba · Tim Wallace · Roger Cain · Bob Bryson · Michael Whitt · Bill Dorsey · Gordy Cardinal

Charlie Runnels · Seales · Floyd Larrabee · Lyle Mahoney · Charlie Burgess · John Ross · Ray Baer

James Tomlin · James VerHelst · Marvin Cole · Doug Dickey · Steve Pruitt · Trahas · Larry Larson · Abston

Jeff Hild · Lionel Lawson · Larry Wilson · Larry Dickerson · John Szymanski · Albert · Walter Smith

"God, Country, Duty, Corps." 2ndLt Dennis Dooley (left) and 2ndLt Dick Housh (right) in the Philippines posing beside the battalion's new crest. (Photo courtesy of Dave Rumsey)

Brothers. Doug and Norman managed to meet in Okinawa on January 26, 1967. "That was the last time I saw him," Norman said later. (Photo courtesy of Norman Dickey)

Norman Dickey was badly wounded on St. Patrick's Day, nine days before his brother, Doug, was killed. After months in the hospital, he was able to come home for a visit. His father, younger brother, Steven, and his sister, Vera, are standing to his right. (Photo courtesy of Norman Dickey)

"The kids were really great," Doug told his parents. Second Platoon members in a village near Sa Huynh during Operation *Deckhouse VI* (left to right): Bob Bryson, Larry Dickerson, Lionel Lawson, Greg Nichols, Walter Smith, Dennis Heider, and Steve Pruitt. (Photo courtesy of Dennis Heider)

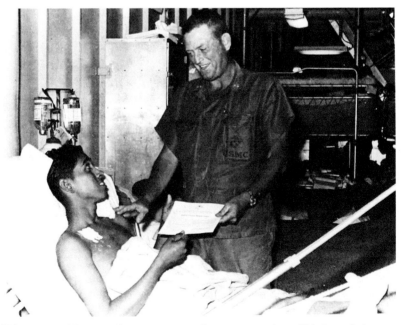

"These young Marines today are just as good as any generation of Marines who've ever lived." LtCol Jack Westerman presented Sgt Frank Alaniz with his promotion warrant while he was recuperating on board the USS *Iwo Jima*. Alaniz was wounded during Operation *Deckhouse VI*. (USMC A650937)

"Now, don't worry about me too much as I can take care of myself," Doug reassured his parents after months at war. In December 1966, he was sent to Phu Bai to recuperate from immersion foot caused by weeks of patrolling in the monsoon-soaked countryside. (Photo courtesy of Dennis Dickey)

"To do something like Doug Dickey did—you can't ever really get over that for the rest of your life." Four of the men Doug Dickey saved in 1967 stand beside his grave in 1997. Bill Dorsey, Charlie Runnels, Larry Dickerson, and Greg Long. (Photo courtesy of Dennis Dickey)

"Some of the 'gungy gang.'" Lionel Lawson's squad in Vietnam. Top row (left to right): PFC Robert Broyles, LCpl Charlie Runnels, Cpl Lionel Lawson, LCpl Timothy Wallace. Bottom row: PFC Jerry Matthews, LCpl Mike Whitt, PFC Mahoney, PFC Jerry Idziak. (Photo courtesy of Robert Larson)

"It was something I had to do." Dennis Dickey (center, sitting on fuel tank) on board the USS *Coral Sea* as a plane captain in VMA-224. Like his two older brothers, Dennis enlisted in the Marines after high school and served in Vietnam. (Photo courtesy of Dennis Dickey)

GySgt Ralph Grant pauses briefly on the trail moments before Company C hit the NVA positions on Easter Sunday. Grant was distinctive in the field by the shotgun he carried and the red bandana he wore around his neck. (Photo courtesy of Larry Normand)

"Tougher than woodpecker lips." A rare photo of a captured NVA soldier from 1969. Although markedly smaller than the average Marine, the NVA soldiers were exceptionally tough and respected foes. (USMC 3D-8-6-082-69)

"He came to me and just sat down." GySgt Ralph Grant makes friends with a local Vietnamese boy during Operation *Deckhouse VI*. The Marines nicknamed the boy "Spoon." (USMC A191129)

Enemy grenades came flying over the trees in clusters. A Chinese Communist "Chi Com" grenade. (USMC A87528)

Movement to contact. Second Platoon maneuvers toward the DMZ minutes before hitting enemy positions on Easter Sunday. (Photo courtesy of Larry Normand)

The fighting was close and savage. An unidentified Marine hurls a grenade toward NVA positions during Operation *Beacon Hill*. (USMC A188457)

"I took care of the job in the cockpit and got scared later." 1stLt Tim O'Toole, pilot of YZ-69, the medevac helicopter shot down on Easter Sunday while trying to evacuate 2nd Platoon's wounded. (Tim O'Toole)

He recited Shakespeare during firefights. Kent Hansen enlisted after dropping out of U.C. Berkeley. He had earned four Purple Hearts by the time he left Vietnam. (*1967 Battalion Cruisebook*)

"… you could see the tracer rounds going through the helicopter …" YZ-69, the medevac helicopter shot down on Easter Sunday. (Photo courtesy of Larry Normand)

The Supreme Sacrifice

Floyd Larrabee

Ed Gutloff

Doug Dickey

Marvin Cole

Bob Bryson

Jim Ver Helst

Victor Van Vactor

John Szymanski

Doug Lee

Larry Larson

(1967 Battalion Cruisebook)

"People called us from all over the United States." Doug's heroism was featured in newspapers across the country. *The Washington Post* published a photograph of Harold and Leona Dickey the day after the award ceremony. (*The Washington Post*)

United Press International

Navy Secretary Paul R. Ignatius, left, presents the Medal of Honor citation to the parents of Marine Pfc. Douglas E. Dickey of Rossburg, Ohio, at the Marine Corps barracks. Dickey was killed in Vietnam when he threw himself on a grenade to protect his colleagues.

Posthumous Award

A Marine Hero Is Honored

Associated Press

A 21-year-old Marine who dived on an enemy hand grenade to save his comrades' lives was awarded posthumously the 31st Medal of Honor of the Vietnam war yesterday.

Pfc. Douglas E. Dickey of Rossberg, Ohio, was honored by top officials of the Navy and Marine Corps in a spe-

cial ceremony at the Marine barracks.

Secretary of the Navy Paul R. Ignatius presented the Nation's highest military decoration to Dickey's parents, Mr. and Mrs. Harold Dickey.

Dickey and five other men were pinned down by enemy gunfire March 26, 1967, during an operation in Quangtri

Province when someone yelled, "Grenade!" Dickey dived on it.

"He must have realized it was too late for us to take cover," recalled one of the others, Hospitalman 3/c Gregory R. Long. "He gave me one short glance and lunged forward, deliberately covering the grenade with his body."

"God gives you strength when you don't have any," Leona Dickey said of getting through the ceremony. Harold and Leona Dickey accepted their son's Medal of Honor during a ceremony at the Washington Navy Yard on April 16, 1968. Secretary of the Navy Paul R. Ignatius is to the Dickeys' right; General Leonard F. Chapman, the Commandant of the Marine Corps, is to their left. (USMC)

"His letters were full of dreams and hopes." Sandy Lee accepts her husband's posthumous Silver Star from Col Louis H. Steman in 1968. (Reprinted from *Leatherneck magazine*)

"He was always so positive." John Szymanski (center) accepts a recruiting award before deploying to Vietnam. (Photo courtesy of Loretta Szymanski)

"We're fighters—our job is to fight." Larry "Packrat" Larson on Okinawa. Larson was preparing to become a priest before he enlisted. (Photo courtesy of Robert Larson)

His humble upbringing in rural Kansas made him sympathize with the Vietnamese villagers. Floyd Larrabee with villagers in Quang Ngai Province. (Photo courtesy of Larry Normand)

"He was really proud of being a Marine." Victor Van Vactor with his mother and father before he deployed to Vietnam. (Photo courtesy of Richard Van Vactor)

"He was a tough guy, but he was a gentleman." Jim Ver Helst (right) standing beside his burgundy 1966 Mustang. Vance Shipman, one of his friends from the wrestling team, is to his right. (Photo courtesy of David Ver Helst)

"Tell my wife and daughter I love them," were Bob Bryson's last words. He graduated from Aquinas Institute in Rochester, New York, in 1962. (*The 1962 Arete*)

Larry Dickerson flanked by Ray and Isabelle Ver Helst (left) and Leona and Harold Dickey (right) during the platoon's reunion in 1997. They are standing in front of the American Legion post that bears Doug's name. (Photo courtesy of Larry Normand)

Brothers forever. Second Platoon reunion in Mason City, Iowa, in 1998. (Photo courtesy of Dave Rumsey)

1. Lionel Lawson
2. Jerry Idziak
3. Dave Rumsey
4. Kent Hanson
5. Greg "Doc" Long
6. Colin McClelland
7. Harold Deibert
8. Steve Pruitt
9. Bob Kelley
10. Dave Jacobs
11. Bob Larson
12. Ray Baer
13. Bill Dorsey
14. Larry Wilson
15. Larry Dickerson
16. Larry Normand
17. Greg "Doc" Nichols
18. Gordy Cardinal

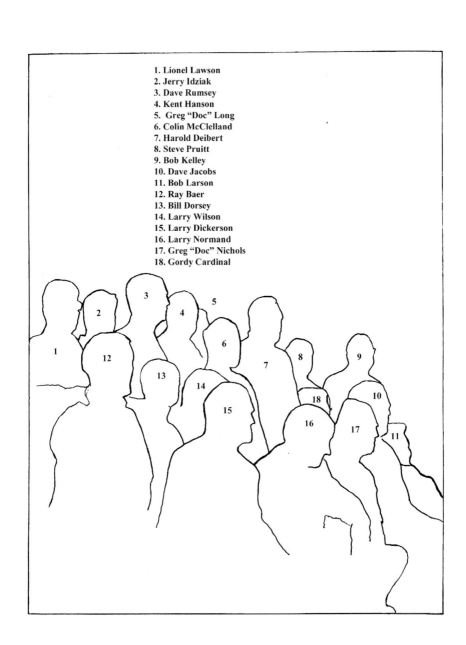

and tried to help them. This made them good friends. "He was always in a good mood," Greg Long said. "You'd go talk to Doug and he'd cheer you up, one way or the other."

"You know, it seemed like forever," Greg Long said of the seconds that passed after the grenades came in. He saw Doug look down at the first grenade. Then he saw Doug look up—and glance into the faces of the men around him who were trapped in the grenade's blast area—they were his friends. "He kind of glanced around before he dove on the grenade," Long said.

"But I don't know," Doc Long said trying to describe those moments, "you couldn't ... you couldn't count the time," he said. "From when the first grenade came in—he fell on top of it," Long said. "He only had one arm in the radio, and he didn't ... it was like he fell on it—and looked up—and here come another," Long said, "and he grabbed that one."

Greg Long couldn't believe what was happening. "I remember him turning his head and looking me right in the face," Long said. "I looked him right square in the face," he said. "I was looking square at him ... And it seemed like forever and we were just looking at each other. I mean, he knew he was going to die," Long said. "And he had this like *pacified* look on his face ... and I was just starting to think, 'Whew! They're duds!'—when they exploded."

Bill Dorsey had rolled over with his back to the grenade and braced for the blast. "But the sound was, like, muffled," he said. "It sounded like a dud, instead of a real hand grenade, and, of course, I didn't know until I rolled back over that Dickey had jumped on top of it. He was lying right beside me. I didn't know what had happened to him until they rolled him over. And he'd taken the complete blow of the grenade into his chest and stomach area—and basically saved four lives."

Shocked by what he had just seen, Charlie Runnels went to Doug to roll him over. "I was going to see how bad he was hit," said Runnels. "I was going to roll him over for Doc—and to see how bad he was hit ... and ... he was limp." Still thinking maybe Dickey was just wounded, he started to roll Doug over. Doc Long stopped him: "Doc said, 'He's dead—just lay him down.'"

Remembering that day, Greg Long said, "He had only three days left. If we'd made it back to Dong Ha, he would have gone home."

Phillip Key was moving along the lines just as the grenades came in toward Lieutenant Dickerson's position. "I was walking around behind them, when somebody yelled, 'Grenade!' and I hit the deck ... and then the grenade went off. I didn't see Dickey or what happened then. I was turned away from the grenade." Key felt his side being peppered with bits of shrapnel. When he looked up at Dickerson and the other men from 2nd Platoon, they were all looking down at Doug. He remembered seeing someone roll Doug over. "And somebody said, 'Oh my God! It's Dickey!'"

Doug Dickey was covered and dragged to the edge of the bomb crater. Most of the men in the platoon didn't know what had happened, only that the platoon had lost another man, and that it was Doug Dickey this time.

The Death of YZ-69

Doc Long told Lieutenant Dickerson a number of wounded men in the crater were in critical condition and had to be medevac'd out as soon as possible. Larrabee's death before they could get him flown out was a stinging loss in Long's mind. All the wounded were steadily losing blood. Long was particularly worried about Jerry Idziak.

It was getting close to sunset and they had to try the medevac before dark. Dickerson got a flight of helos from HMM-363 to come in and attempt a medevac. The Marine pilots and their crews showed impressive guts again.

The helicopters from HMM-363 had been landing and refueling at Dong Ha rather than flying all the way back to the *Princeton*. First Lieutenant Tim O'Toole and his crew were sitting in the ready room at the Dong Ha airstrip after flying some routine resupply missions when the medevac request from Company C came in. The mission was classified as "urgent," meaning the wounded Marine probably wouldn't live unless he was evacuated to a hospital within an hour or so.

The aircraft that was designated as the duty medevac bird was already out on another mission. O'Toole told the duty officer he would fly the mission.

Tim O'Toole had earned his commission and his gold naval aviator wings through the Marine Corps Aviation Cadet "MarCad" program. The MarCad program was established to meet the pressing need for pilots in Vietnam. The program was unique because it expanded the pool of prospective pilots by allowing those without college degrees to earn a commission as a Marine officer. Distinguished enlisted men and those applicants with two years of college, who performed well on a battery of tests and who demonstrated an aptitude for flying, were sent through 18 months of training at the naval flight school at Pensacola. Those who successfully completed the training—including the flight qualifications to become naval aviators—were commissioned. They had to serve three years after they got their wings. MarCad officers didn't have to go through the Officer Candidates School or the Basic School at Quantico.[19] The vast majority ended up flying helicopters in Vietnam. Once commissioned, and flying combat missions, MarCad pilots became indistinguishable from the other Marine Corps pilots.

Tim O'Toole had dropped out of Virginia Tech after completing more than two years of his studies and then applied for the MarCad program. He proved to have an aptitude for flying and did well. Although he was one of the junior officers in the squadron, O'Toole had been in Vietnam since May 1966 and had flown hundreds of combat missions. He had had several helicopters he was flying shot to pieces. The squadron commander had designated him as one of the few pilots in the squadron qualified to fly as a "strike leader." This meant he was responsible for flying the lead helicopter on large squadron operations. While O'Toole is modest about his flying skills, Bill Collier wrote later, "Tim was one of the best helicopter pilots ever, bar none, a natural."[20]

Married shortly after pinning on his wings, O'Toole had a young wife and a five-month-old daughter he had never seen waiting for him back in Pensacola.

Tim O'Toole was flying YZ-69 that day. The helicopter had "Breakfast of Champions" painted on the side. His copilot was Brian Wise. O'Toole told the crew to collect one of the duty corpsmen and head out to the aircraft. It was already approaching twilight and O'Toole wanted to get going as soon as possible so they wouldn't have to try to attempt the medevac in total darkness. Combat missions meant flying without lights either on the helicopter or at the landing zone. Flying at night without lights was extremely dangerous. The pilot had to rely totally on his night vision to maneuver the helicopter into and out of the zone. "Urgent" medevacs were the only combat missions they would attempt in darkness. Resupply and other less critical missions could all wait until morning.

The opening in the jungle canopy above the 2nd Platoon perimeter was just big enough for a single UH-34, "… and when we got to the zone … it was tight. Real, real tight!" Tim O'Toole said later. "We were taking a lot of fire going in. Our gunner told us he thought it was a 37mm—radar-controlled 37mm—'cause of the size and the color of the tracers." With the sun beginning to set, they started into the landing zone. O'Toole couldn't find a spot to land. "I could only hover because it was Marines all under us. There was really no place to land."

Todd Ryan, one of Bob Kelley's radio operators, heard one of the pilots from YZ-69 come over the radio: "Fuck it Charlie, I'm coming down. Get your priority medevacs ready …"[21]

The helicopter set down just beside the crater and the wounded were quickly grabbed up and thrown on board the helicopter. There were seven men tossed in on top of each other inside the helo as it briefly touched down. The North Vietnamese gunners opened fire on the helicopter as soon as it came in. The helo was on the ground only seconds while it was loaded and began to lift off. The aircraft struggled to get airborne.

As it got to about treetop level, maybe 40 feet high, it was raked with fire—including fire from an enemy .50-caliber machine gun. The wounded Marines in the helo heard the bullets punching through the helicopter's magnesium skin. Doc Nichols was one of the wounded who had been thown into the helo. "It was like popcorn. The rounds were hitting like popcorn—just hundreds of them it seemed like—coming into the chopper—very intense fire."[22]

Mike Helton had been wounded and was in the crater and watched the helicopter come in. "I remember the helicopter," he said. "I couldn't believe that. What a bunch of guys with big brass balls those guys are. They brought that damn helicopter down. I remember him coming in and as he was sitting down, you could see the tracer rounds going through the helicopter. He came down and set on the edge of that hole with one wheel on the ground."

Piloting the helicopter, Tim O'Toole recalled, "So, I pulled in all the power until I had over-boosted the engine—which held together—got up to the treetops, shuddered a little bit and started moving out across the treetops, and then we started losing more power. So, what I did was just level it up and settle it down in the trees … probably 50 yards from the platoon. And it tore the rotors up. But we landed on the wheels." Later, O'Toole guessed the enemy fire had damaged the tail section, binding the linkages to the tail rotor. This overloaded the engine, which caused the dramatic loss of power after they got into the landing zone.[23]

In an amazing feat of airmanship, the two pilots managed to keep the helicopter under control enough to crash-land it just outside the Marine perimeter. The fuselage broke in half when it slammed down onto the edge of the banana grove—in the no man's land between the Marine and the NVA lines. As the helicopter was coming down, its rotor blades started hitting the trees. There was a deafening sound as the engine screeched to a stop. The rotor blades smashed into the trees, sending chunks of vegetation flying through the air just above the heads of the Marines below. The Marines hugged the ground and cussed as the helicopter landed heavily just outside their perimeter. The fuselage broke just behind the engine and bent sideways as the helicopter hit the earth.

Marines rushed out from the perimeter and started pulling the wounded men from the wreckage and dragged them back to the crater. Incredibly, none of the wounded were killed in the crash. The aircrew from YZ-69 managed to make it to 2nd Platoon's lines uninjured.

Lionel Lawson was the last one dragged from the wrecked helo. For a second time that day, he found himself wounded and lying forward of the friendly lines. "At first, they got everyone out but me as I was trapped in the tail section. It was dumb luck that [Charlie] Runnels was running past and I yelled to him and he pulled me out and slam-dunked me in the crater with the other wounded."[24]

In one of the odd occurrences of the day, Jerry Idziak had not been loaded on the helicopter—and he was the principal reason it had been requested. It appeared that everybody loading the helo thought somebody else had loaded Jerry. "They forgot me and left me there," he said. It was actually fortunate that he had been left: Jerry was so badly wounded, he probably wouldn't have survived the crash.

One beneficial aspect of the helo crash was that it ended up being a much-needed ammunition resupply for the platoon. By that time, the platoon was running dangerously low on ammunition. The helicopter was armed with two M60 machine guns and was carrying several boxes of ammunition. The Marines made repeated trips to the downed helicopter to retrieve the guns and ammunition.

All of the ammunition in the helicopter was belted and had to be broken up so the individual rounds could be used in the M14s. The wounded men in the crater began pulling the machine-gun belts apart and loaded magazines for the rifles. Then they passed the magazines to the Marines who were still up on the line shooting it out with the NVA. Again, it proved fortunate that Westerman's battalion hadn't been rearmed with the M16 rifle. M16s wouldn't have been able to use the M60 ammunition.

When Bob Kelley was asked what they should do with the two pilots and the two aircrewmen who were now in 2nd Platoon's perimeter, he told Dickerson to turn them into two more machine-gun teams.

Tim O'Toole found himself huddled in one of the shallow trenches inside the 2nd Platoon perimeter. "I was in the trench there, and I pulled out my revolver and checked that I had six bullets—and I had a bandoleer around my waist. I said, 'I don't know what I would do with this thing, but I'm going to fire it until all my bullets are gone.'" He watched as the young riflemen moved around him, coordinating with each other as they rushed forward firing their weapons. "I mean, I was actually prepared to die that night. I sort of made peace with myself." Then he laughed and added, "… and put all six bullets into my .38 revolver." Assuming that pilots probably knew more about current weather forecasts, one of the Marines asked O'Toole if he knew how much moonlight they would have that night. "I couldn't believe how calm they were … all those Marines in that platoon. They were, you know, just calm and talking to me about the moon." Sitting in the trench without his helicopter—with just his revolver, O'Toole said later he felt, "useless."

"But I just remember those guys … that I was so proud of them and so amazed by them. I mean, they'd been through hell; they'd lost all these people and they were going about their business like, 'I'm still alive … I've got to do my job.' I was absolutely blown away by that," Tim O'Toole said later. "I actually wrote letters home about that and talked about it when I got home. That's how amazed I was—that there wasn't any panic."

A Costly Victory

The battle lasted into the evening, but the NVA seemed spent. As the sun set, the Marines organized their defensive perimeter for the night. The NVA were known for staging large assaults after dark, often in the hours after midnight. The word was passed to be prepared for an enemy assault. The Marines dug out and expanded their fighting holes. Bob Kelley ordered everyone to fix bayonets.

Air support and artillery created a "ring of fire" around Company C that evening. "Puff the Magic Dragon," the Air Force C-47 armed with cannons and miniguns, circled overhead all night, firing into the enemy positions when they thought they saw a target. The C-47 and the artillery kept dropping illumination flares over the enemy positions.

For most of the night, it was quiet except for the hissing of the illumination flares floating down on their parachutes. The burning magnesium from the flares coated the area in a harsh silver light. The shadows rocked back and forth as the flares swung under their parachutes. The Marines strained their eyes, trying to penetrate the shadows for any signs of movement. At times, they could hear the NVA talking in hushed tones. They heard men moving through the vegetation; an occasional metallic clank; the sound of digging. No one slept.

The enemy attempted one weak probe that night, but it was easily repulsed.

The Marines relaxed as the sun began to rise. David Gregg later wrote, "...we had never before experienced such pleasure at the sight of sunlight."

Kent Hansen punctuated the dawn by standing and loudly mimicking the Armed Forces Radio disc jockey from Saigon, yelling, "Goooooooooood moooorning, Viet Nam!" Loud bursts of laughter mixed with profanity came from the fighting holes around the perimeter. For the Marines in 2nd Platoon, Hansen's announcement made it official: the battle was over. They had survived. Bob Kelley heard Hansen from his position and let himself laugh and relax for the first time in a day.[25]

Not long after sunrise, Kelley organized a sweep through the enemy positions. When the Marines advanced through the enemy positions, they found that the NVA had pulled out during the night, abandoning their trenches and bunkers. As they swept through the area, they found evidence the NVA had taken a beating. Uncharacteristically, the enemy had left 25 of their dead scattered around the abandoned trenches. The sounds the Marines had heard all night had been the NVA soldiers pulling out of their positions and dragging their dead and wounded away. Grisly evidence and drag marks indicated at least another 15 bodies had been dragged away.

That Monday morning, Carl Martin noticed Doug Lee hadn't returned and assumed he was still up with 2nd Platoon. When Lieutenant Dooley asked him where Lee was, Martin got a bad feeling. He had assumed Lee had been with Dooley the whole time.

Martin remembered a discussion he had had with Doug Lee while they were back at one of the combat bases months earlier. Lee told him about a recurring dream he had been having since he was teenager. Doug said he had wanted be a Marine since he was a kid. "He also said that, on more than one occasion, he had dreamed he was wounded in combat," Martin recalled. "He also conveyed to me that he could see himself lying curled up on his side with a wound to his stomach. He pictured himself lying with his head resting on his forearm." Lee also told Martin that, in the dream, he could hear himself crying out: "Sandy, it hurts so badly." The strange thing about the dream, Lee told Carl Martin, was that he had started having it years before he ever met his wife, Sandy, or joined the Marines.[26]

Right after talking to Lieutenant Dooley, Carl Martin went up to the 2nd Platoon lines, hoping to find Doug Lee sitting in one of the fighting holes, or maybe among the wounded waiting to be evacuated. When he didn't find him, he started checking out the perimeter. It wasn't long before he found Doug's body. "… he was lying in the fetal position with his head on his forearm," Carl Martin said. "When we lifted him up—he was lying in a pool of blood from a stomach wound." Decades later, Martin is still haunted by Doug Lee's death. "He was laying exactly the way he'd told me in his dreams … very eerie."

Carl Martin becomes a bit quiet when he talks about finding Doug that morning. "I remember picking up Lee's glasses … and they were smoked over, just like if you'd had them over a heavy smoke or something." Jim Charles, the 1st Platoon corpsman, had come up with Martin to help him look for Lee. Doc Charles said he would make sure Doug got evacuated with the other casualties. Martin gave the thick military regulation glasses to Jim and told him to make sure they got sent back to Doug's wife with the rest of his effects. He couldn't say why he felt it was important, but he just felt it was.[27]

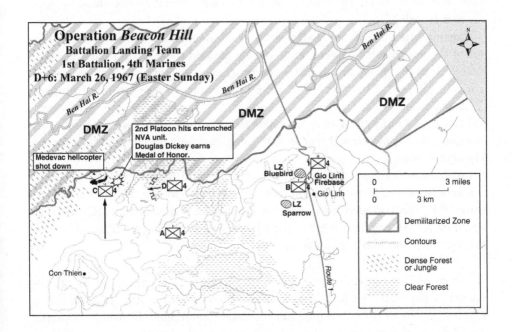

Statements collected after the battle detailed Doug Lee's actions that day. After getting back to the 2nd Platoon position with his load of grenades, Lee had joined the 2nd Platoon Marines in their assaults against the NVA positions. At one point, he forced one of the enemy machine guns to displace. In the course of the battle, an enemy mortar round exploded near Lee, mortally wounding him.[28]

A year after he was killed, Doug Lee's widow, Sandy, accepted his posthumous Silver Star from Colonel Louis H. Steman at a ceremony at the Marine Corps Air

Station in Beaufort, South Carolina.[29] Their baby daughter, Cindy, was with Sandy at the ceremony. Cindy had been born a week after Doug had deployed to Vietnam. Doug Lee had talked constantly about the little girl he had never met.

The Medevacs

Medevac helicopters began landing to evacuate the Marine dead and wounded. Looking down as they flew out, the wounded men got a stark look at their battlefield. It was a blackened, blasted landscape, with a little clear spot in the middle marking the bomb crater they had used. The crater was filled with bloody pieces of uniforms and discarded bandages. Thousands of brass shell casings surrounded the crater and sparkled in the sunlight.

After sweeping the area, Kelley was given orders to move the company back toward Gio Linh. Second Platoon had gone into the battle the day before with more than 40 Marines. There were only 12 men left when they assembled to move out that morning.

A maintenance team from HMM-363 and a team of combat engineers arrived on one of the medevac helicopters. They quickly decided there was no way to salvage YZ-69. After removing all the radios and other valuable gear, the engineers rigged it with explosives. What was left of YZ-69 was blown to pieces before Company C left the area.

Larry Dickerson walked among his men that morning as they were getting ready to move out. He mentioned that he was going to nominate Doug Dickey for the Medal of Honor.

Intelligence analysis later confirmed that Kelley and his men had tangled with at least a battalion. Second Platoon faced at least three-to-one odds in the banana grove. The NVA had planned and executed a very deliberate attack, believing they would be able to trap and overrun the Marine unit that had penetrated their area so deeply. But the Marines had prevailed.

The most serious casualties were flown out to the USS *Princeton*, an Essex-class aircraft carrier from World War II that had been converted into an amphibious assault ship. Under the supervision of Lieutenant Commander Ronald R. Bouterie, the SLF's chief surgeon, the LPH had been turned into an extensive medical evacuation station for the operation. Part of the hangar deck was transformed into a surgical ward, adding more than 200 beds to the ship's usual 37-bed capacity. They ended up using all those beds by the end of the operation. Bouterie and his team of surgeons and corpsmen had become experts in providing medical care to wounded Marines during amphibious operations, and had developed several new procedures while running the aid station on the USS *Iwo Jima* during Operation *Deckhouse VI*.

Bouterie's team had developed a five-stage program for handling battlefield casualties.

When the helicopters landed on the flight deck, they were met by ordnance men and a medical team. Wounded Marines often still had their weapons, ammunition, grenades, and other explosives with them. The ordnance team collected and inventoried all the items to make sure they didn't end up in the treatment facility below decks and create a safety hazard. The medical team quickly assessed the wounds on each man. If he needed emergency neurological or eye surgery, he was immediately put on another helicopter and flown to one of the designated medical facilities ashore in Vietnam where specialists were standing by to provide that care.

After the weapons and explosives had been secured and the men assessed; they were lowered down to the triage area in the hangar deck. In the triage area, their uniforms were cut off and their wounds were closely inspected and evaluated. This stage ended when they were prepared for surgery.

From the triage area, the wounded men were taken into the third stage of treatment: the Shock and Resuscitation Area. During this stage of treatment, blood transfusions were given, chest tubes inserted, and emergency surgery was performed.

The fourth phase of treatment was post-operative care. Wounded men were carefully monitored and taken back into surgery if necessary. Otherwise, their medical treatment proceeded and chest tubes were removed, and wounds progressively closed.

Once a wounded man was stabilized, he was evacuated to one of the large hospitals ashore in Vietnam where his treatment continued. If necessary, he was eventually evacuated back to the United States. Over 75 percent of the wounded treated on the *Princeton* eventually returned to their unit—a tribute to the rapid care.[30]

Colin McClelland remembered arriving on the *Princeton*. Bouterie and his men had built a conveyer to take the wounded from the flight deck down to the hangar deck. It reminded McClelland of riding down a coal chute. "I just remember the blood that was all over the walls—they were covered, just streams of it running down the walls." He was wheeled into surgery. "The next thing I knew, I was waking up—puking—and then, after that, I was OK."

Jerry Idziak had refused morphine the entire time he was lying in the crater. "I was hurting so frickin' bad," he said, "… it was just unbearable. But I didn't take any drugs. No morphine. I think this is what made me survive. I really do," he said. "I said to myself, 'If you take any drugs, you will go into shock.'"

He remembered arriving on the ship. "They dropped me into the ship, and the doctor looked at me and said, 'You're not going to make it. You don't have any blood…'" The medical team looked at his dog tags and summoned a Catholic chaplain. "A priest gave me last rites," Idziak said. "The doctor said, 'I'm sorry, but that's all we can we do for you.'"

Against all odds, the navy doctors decided to roll him into the operating room and see what they could do. Jerry survived. "I woke up and then I started to realize I was alive because I could spot a few of the guys [from the platoon] around me." Jerry explained his survival with a laugh later. "I'm a Polack, you know. We're pretty hard to kill."

Sergeant Larry Wilson, the platoon guide, was also evacuated. Although he had stayed on the battlefield after being hit in the face, the wound had gotten worse. By the time he was flown out to the *Princeton*, he could barely breathe and was having double vision. Bouterie and his team went to work on him, clearing away shattered teeth and stitching up the gaping hole in his cheek. After a couple of days on the *Princeton*, Wilson was able to get out of bed. "I walked into the head and I looked in the mirror; and what I saw looking back at me scared the crap out of me," he said. "My left eye was swollen completely shut and my right eye was about half shut." He had stitches running up the side of his face. "They took real good care of me." Wilson was eventually sent to the naval hospital in the Philippines. After a little more than a month, he was sent back to Vietnam.[31]

The Dead

As the wounded were flown out, the men who had been killed began their journey home. Marines have a unique relationship with their fallen comrades. Keith Wheeler, a war correspondent in the Pacific during World War II, wrote about it while he was reporting on the Marines' campaign on Saipan in 1944:

> Marines do not treat their dead as do civilians nor as so the men of other armies. When a civilian dies, he ceases. His body is washed and painted and dressed into a grotesque imitation of life that emphasizes death and he is marked for dead with flowers and pomp and prayer that were not his habit in life.
>
> In other armies, men accept their dead only with fear or anger or sorrow and—most tragic of all—with disbelief as though it were a monstrous thing that men should actually be killed in action, but Marines are casual about the fact of death and toward their own dead they are companionable.
>
> They do not banish a dead man from them because a shell has torn him in two or a bullet has smashed his head. But they bury his body when there is time for burial. But when there is not, they have no compunction about sleeping beside him. And when there is time, they fashion him a cross for his grave, but even then they do not mark him for pointed segregation. There is a big Marine cemetery in Charan Kanoa, but there are also isolated crosses gleaming whitely in the midst of Marine activity on Saipan.[32]

Marines don't use terms like "body" or "corpse" when referring to the dead who have to be evacuated. They will use the man's name, often including his rank with a tone of deference. A Marine coordinating their evacuation may even refer to a group of casualties as "… the guys." An uninitiated bystander would conclude the men being discussed are still alive. It's not uncommon to see a Marine gently tuck in the edges of a poncho covering a body waiting to be evacuated, as if he's afraid the man will get a chill, or as if he is trying to keep him from being unnecessarily exposed. Killed Marines are never left unattended. Someone is always nearby, watching over them.

A Marine killed in battle is elevated to the highest level of reverence. His death gives him a stature no living Marine can attain. Even men who have achieved the highest awards for valor and have risen to the highest echelons of command in the Marine Corps, will honestly admit they are humbled when they are reminded of their comrades who "paid the full measure" for wearing a Marine uniform. It is a strong combination of sorrow and respect.

David Gregg and Todd Ryan, two men who were part of Bob Kelley's company headquarters, helped load their killed comrades on the helicopters for evacuation that morning. Gregg remembered carrying Doug Dickey to the helicopter that morning. He remembered Dickey's face was "relatively unscarred." He said that Doug's face had, "… a strange tranquility."

Gregg had become friends with Victor Van Vactor. The two had bonded while chasing girls and drinking beer in Olongapo. "We had a great time there," Gregg said. As Gregg and Ryan carried Victor to the helicopter, the poncho covering his face blew open. "I suddenly looked away and decided I wanted to remember Vic's happy face on our final liberty … I reattached the poncho around Vic's head and never again saw my friend," Gregg said. "When Todd and I handed Vic up to the gunner on the helicopter, I had my head turned away from the aircraft, like some people do when they're getting a shot in the arm."[33]

Doug Dickey, Larry Larson, Ed Gutloff, and the other Marines killed in the battle were flown to the USS *Princeton*, where a medical officer examined each of them and issued death certificates. They were then flown to the Graves Registration Unit in Da Nang. The Marines there made sure there was no doubt as to the identity of each man and the casualty messages were sent out. Then they carefully prepared the men for their trip home. After all of the mortuary functions were completed, the Marines were dressed in new service dress uniforms and inspected—ensuring their chevrons and awards were correct.[34] Once they were ready to be transported, each Marine was assigned an escort, who stayed by the side of the fallen Marine until he was finally home to his family. Escorts often stayed until after the burial. Each Marine was buried with an honor guard firing a 21-gun salute over his grave. Until he was finally home, the Marine was still treated as a member of his unit. He would always be a comrade.

Douglas Dickey's sacrifice that afternoon probably saved more than just the lives of the four men who were gathered around the radio that day. The platoon was under heavy pressure from a numerically superior enemy. If Lieutenant Dickerson had been killed, the platoon would have lost its leader at a critical point. John Szymanski, the other man who could have taken Dickerson's place, had been killed three days earlier. Two of the three squad leaders were already badly wounded and were lying in the crater. Through the radio, Dickerson was coordinating critical air and artillery support. If he had been killed and the radio destroyed, the platoon would have lost its most important defensive weapon at a crucial point in the battle. It's very likely their slender defense would have been disrupted sufficiently for the assaulting NVA to crack the platoon's fragile line. Likewise, if Doc Long had been killed, there would have been no one left to provide urgent—often lifesaving—medical care for the wounded. If Douglas Dickey had not saved those men, the battle in the banana grove would have been much tougher for his platoon. His sacrifice may have averted a much greater disaster for the entire platoon.

While Bob Kelley's company was moving north on the morning of Easter Sunday, John Juul's company had moved out to renew their assault on the NVA positions they had been fighting the day before. Juul's men rushed the enemy lines to find the NVA there had also retreated, abandoning their trenches and bunkers. Juul reported finding weapons and ammunition scattered around the trenches, "… plus pieces of bodies and blood and a lot of drag marks."[35]

Operation *Beacon Hill* lasted until the 1st of April, although there was little contact in the last week. By the end of *Beacon Hill*, 1st Battalion, 4th Marines, had suffered 29 killed and 230 wounded.

Roger Young was in the battalion's Weapons Company and heard about the heavy casualties Company C suffered on Easter Sunday. He searched out a member of Doug's company and asked how Doug was. "And he told me he was dead—so I kind of went into shock," Young said. Roger got in touch with Tim Barga. "Tim came over that night and we laid out there all night. We set there and talked about it." To replace the losses from *Beacon Hill*, the Marines from Weapons Company were transferred to the rifle companies to fill in for the lost Marines. Young asked to go to Company C. "I chose Charlie Company—which Doug was part of. And then I got a taste of all that combat myself," he said.

Bob Birt and David Thornhill didn't find out Doug had been killed for weeks. Bob and David were both in 1st Battalion, 5th Marines, stationed on Hill 54, about 132 miles south of Doug's unit. They hadn't seen Doug, Tim, or Roger since they left California. Bob and David had been assigned to different rifle companies in the battalion. They often went weeks without seeing each other because their companies conducted operations at different times. "But we got to see each other every once in a while," Birt said.

David Thornhill had arranged to get their hometown newspaper, the *Greenville Advocate*, mailed to him in Vietnam. He would find Bob and pass the papers along to him when he could. It was comforting to read about what was happening back home when they had a break between patrols or when they got time to sit down and eat a hot meal.

One day in April, Bob was on Hill 54 when he looked up and saw David coming toward him. He looked upset. David handed Bob a copy of the *Advocate* he had just received in the mail. When Bob looked at the paper, he saw that Doug's boot camp photo was on the front page. "County Marine Dies in Action in Vietnam War" was written below Doug's picture. The short article said Doug's parents had been notified their son had been killed in action on March 26, and that funeral arrangements were pending at the Oliver Funeral Home in Ansonia. "That's how I found out that Doug had been killed," Bob Birt said, "because it was in the newspaper. We just couldn't believe it." Almost five decades later, Bob Birt said of that day, "As a young man … going to war, you don't think about dying," he said. "But it happens." Then he added softly, "It's terrible."

The End of an Era

Easter Sunday marked the end of an era for 2nd Platoon, Company C, and 1st Battalion, 4th Marines.

The battalion's heavy combat, culminating with Company C's battle on Easter Sunday, marked the end of Blackjack Westerman's combat command. It was unusual for battalion commanders in Vietnam to hold command for more than six months. Westerman had been on the job for ten months. He was overdue for rotation. He had hurt his back while fighting in Korea and had been suffering bouts of intense pain throughout his tour in Vietnam. In March, he had gotten ill and it had turned into pneumonia. He had argued to stay in command, but it was decided he would turn over command to Lieutenant Colonel Theodore J. Willis. Willis took command on March 28, while the battalion was making its way back to Dong Ha. Jack Westerman was transferred to the regimental headquarters where he became the executive officer for the 4th Marine Regiment. It was a desk job that would allow him to heal up.

Bob Kelley's promotion was waiting for him when he and Company C returned to Dong Ha at the end of *Beacon Hill*. He could no longer dodge the dreaded staff officer assignment. The joy of being promoted to major was dimmed by having to turn over his command. Bob Kelley turned over command of Company C on April 3, and he became the battalion's operations officer.

Most of 2nd Platoon was dead or wounded by the end of the battle on Easter Sunday. Although replacements arrived in the following weeks, 2nd Platoon never had the cohesion again that it had after training together on Okinawa, and going out on liberty together in the Philippines. The individual replacement policy meant men rotated in and out of the platoon at random, making it difficult for them to bond like they had before.

Larry Dickerson remained as the platoon leader for the rest of the year. He led the platoon in more battles and became a battle-hardened veteran and respected combat leader. He ended up earning a Bronze Star Medal and a Purple Heart before he rotated home. John Szymanski would have been proud of his lieutenant and it was probably Szymanski's voice Dickerson heard advising him during those months.

Many of the men who survived the battle on Easter Sunday transferred out of the platoon in the following months. Kent Hansen, the Berkeley dropout, became one of the platoon's most respected fighters. One member of the platoon described him as, "One brave and crazy son of a bitch." To demonstrate that a higher education and being a combat Marine were not mutually exclusive, Hansen once stood up in a firefight and—while laying down covering fire with his M14, recited the soliloquy from Act 5 Scene 5 of Macbeth: "Life's but a walking shadow ... told by an idiot, full of sound and fury, signifying nothing."

Kent Hansen's combat tour was completed after he earned his fourth Purple Heart and he was transferred from 2nd Platoon. It was Defense Department policy that anyone who earned three Purple Hearts had to be transferred to a non-combat assignment. It was considered inhumane to ask more of anyone who had been wounded three times already. Also, no commanding officer wanted to try to explain to a grieving widow or a young man's parents that their loved one had been killed after already narrowly cheating death three times.

Charlie Runnels remembered when Hansen was wounded a third time. "We bundled him onto a helicopter and told him, 'Have a good life—congratulations! You're out of this mess.' And we shipped him out."

About four days later, a resupply helicopter landed and Kent Hansen jumped off. He had decided he didn't like being in the rear and missed his friends. Runnels remembered the scene: "Lieutenant Dickerson runs up to him and says, 'Hansen, what are you doing here!'"

Hansen told the flabbergasted platoon leader, "Well, I told the first sergeant that I didn't see any reason I had to go, and I wanted to stay, so he let me sign some papers and told me I can stay just as long as I want to!" Before Dickerson could straighten out the situation with the company first sergeant, Hansen was in another firefight and was wounded again. This time he was sent all the way back to Da Nang and specifically told to stay off any helicopters unless he had official orders.

Ray Baer, another member of the platoon who had an appetite for firefights, earned his third Purple Heart at about the same time and was sent to Da Nang with Hansen. The two men were good buddies and it was only a matter of time before they got into trouble.

Combat infantrymen, "grunts," are immediately identifiable in a rear area. Even after replacing their rotted utilities and having them turn in their rifles and grenades, they have a particular aura to them. They emanate a combination of boredom and disdain for the formality and routine hustle and bustle in the rear. They have a distinctive gait—a kind of slouching slide, developed from months of carrying weapons and loaded packs. The slide comes from learning to walk without making the load bounce. Combat grunts are treated with high regard in the Marine Corps. Their sun-darkened skin, scars, ragged utilities, and sinewy muscles earn them a unique prestige among Marines.

Hansen and Baer had figured out that they could pin on sergeant chevrons and drink for free at the NCO club while they were stuck in Da Nang. The scheme worked until they were spotted by Gunnery Sergeant Edwin Emanuel, who happened to stop at the club for a beer while he was passing through Da Nang on his way back to Company C from an R&R trip. He immediately knew the two "sergeants" at the end of the bar to be frauds. Emanuel made it clear to Hansen and Baer that their phony sergeant days had ended. He also made it clear that they were not to set foot in the NCO club again. However, he sympathized with his two young Marines and was surprised they were still in-country. He told them he would look into the situation when he got back to the battalion.

A few days later, Baer and Hansen both received orders to Okinawa. They were assigned to the brig staff on Okinawa as "chasers" for the rest of their tour in the Far East. As chasers, they traveled around the area and collected military prisoners and brought them back to Okinawa. It was a suitable assignment for the two men. Few prisoners ever considered giving the two large combat veterans any trouble. But more importantly, the assignment allowed them to operate independently and enjoy some good liberty. Ray and Kent often had to make trips to Thailand and other locations where they could enjoy a few days of liberty as part of the job. When his tour in the Far East was completed, Kent Hansen was sent to Camp Pendleton to be processed for discharge. True to his plan, he was back at Berkeley for the winter session in 1968.

The battalion was still recovering from *Beacon Hill* a month later. It was rare for Marine commanders to admit they were worried about their personnel strength. However, Lieutenant Colonel Willis candidly wrote in the battalion's monthly report for April, "… personnel shortages, caused mainly from heavy casualties during Operation Beacon Hill I, plagued the Battalion."

According to the Marine Corps' *Table of Organization*, a rifle company was supposed to have at least 216 men.[36] Willis wrote that the three rifle companies which had participated in the operation "experienced severe shortages of deployable Marines: field strength averaging 125–135." He further noted: "At one point in time, Company D could muster but 104 men in the field."

The battalion was kept operational by quickly receiving 193 replacements from the 3rd Marine Division. Willis also cannibalized other units within his battalion to find Marines to send to the rifle companies. He transferred most of the Marines from the Recoilless Rifle Platoon to the rifle companies and stripped every man out of the Headquarters and Service Company who wasn't essential. By the end of April, the rifle companies were back to strength—at least on paper. Willis noted that each company had between 20 and 30 men on the company roster who were actually wounded Marines still recovering in the battalion's aid station.[37]

Lieutenant Colonel Willis's tenure as battalion commander was cut much shorter than Westerman's. In late April, 1st Battalion, 4th Marines, was assigned to provide security for the engineers who were scraping out the trace for "McNamara's Wall," the idiotic scheme to build a wall through the jungle just south of the DMZ. The battalion was repeatedly hammered with artillery and mortar fire, and Willis was wounded twice in April.

In May, the battalion was assigned to defend the base at Con Thien. On May 8, the NVA staged a massive attack on the battalion's position, similar to those staged by the Red Chinese in Korea. They attacked in human waves. John Juul's Company D took the brunt of the attack. Hundreds of NVA soldiers emerged from the jungle and swarmed toward Company D's lines. The enemy briefly breached their lines using satchel charges and flamethrowers. Juul and his Marines restored their lines by the next morning, but suffered 32 men killed in the battle. Most of the remaining men in the company were wounded. Among the wounded was John Juul. Despite being severely wounded, Juul had ordered two of his Marines to hold him up in a standing position so he could direct the company's defense. He was later awarded the Silver Star for his leadership in the battle.

Bob Kelley's tour with 1st Battalion, 4th Marines, also ended on May 8. Kelley had been wounded at the end of April when mortar rounds hit the battalion CP. He was also at Con Thien on May 8 when the NVA attacked and wrenched his knee badly while scrambling to get into a fighting hole during one of the rocket attacks that pummeled the battalion's position. He was eventually evacuated to the USS *Repose*, where he underwent surgery to put his knee back together. Bob Kelley was nearing the end of his tour by the time he was discharged from the hospital ship. He finished his Vietnam tour assigned to the 3rd Marine Division staff.

On May 12, during another attack on Con Thien, Lieutenant Colonel Willis was wounded a third time. He was rotated out after having been the battalion commander for 46 days.[38]

The initial survey of the battlefield after *Beacon Hill* showed the NVA had left 334 dead in the wake of Westerman's battalion.[39] A month later, on April 24, Company A was patrolling in the area and discovered a series of graves dug by the NVA when they were retreating from *Beacon Hill*. There were 104 bodies from the 31st Regiment in the graves. Company A's gruesome discovery, together with additional intelligence, caused the NVA losses during *Beacon Hill* to be revised to 455 confirmed killed, with another 515 as probable.[40] The communist Vietnamese government still keeps losses from the war a tightly guarded secret. It will probably be generations before the numbers are revealed. All estimates project that Hanoi lost over a million soldiers during the war against American forces.

Three weeks before Operation *Beacon Hill* was launched, the 812th Regiment of the 324B NVA Division had surrounded and badly mauled a small task force from 2nd Battalion, 3rd Marines. The task force had been sent to rescue a trapped reconnaissance team. The NVA had carefully lured the Marines into an ambush against overwhelming numbers.

In the ensuing battle, parts of the Marine unit were overrun. The battalion commander, Lieutenant Colonel Victor Ohanesian, and the battalion sergeant major were killed.[41] Bob Sheridan, the battalion operations officer, and one of the few officers to survive the battle, described the ordeal as "a complete horror show."[42] A young Marine from Compton, California, James Anderson, Jr., earned the Medal of Honor in the desperate fight. Like Doug Dickey, he smothered a grenade to save his comrades.

The men of 1st Battalion, 4th Marines, had accomplished their mission. Westerman and his Marines had inflicted ghastly casualties on the NVA south of the DMZ during Operation *Beacon Hill.* The NVA had hoped to trap and overrun Company C on Easter Sunday in the same way they had almost wiped out Ohanesian's Marines a month earlier. Instead, the NVA had been badly bloodied and forced to retreat.

To the young men who fought in the banana grove on Easter Sunday, the battle became a defining event in their lives. For Gary Hudson, one of the rocket men who witnessed Doug Dickey's heroism, the day remained a watershed event for the rest of his life. In the course of the battle Hudson was wounded in the hand. Gary, like Doug, wrote home every week. On March 30, four days after the battle, Gary wrote a long letter to his father:

> This last operation startled my whole view of Vietnam. We landed the 20th of March. It was alright the first few days. But then I guess you say our luck run out on the 23rd of March we were hit by 2 reinforced companies of hard core … and then Easter we almost got wiped out. It was hell … I'll never forget the Easter of '67. I never want to see anything like that again. I'm alright so don't worry. I got shot in the meaty part of the left hand by a gook but it's okay! I was lucky. A lot of my friends are dead.[43]

CHAPTER 19

The Gold Star

"The wearing of a small gold star … would be a far more beautiful reminder of the life that has been given as a sacrifice in the struggle to maintain Liberty, Justice and Truth throughout the world."

THE GOLD STAR[1]

In Rossburg, the Dickeys were preparing to make the 300-mile drive up to the hospital at the Great Lakes naval base to see Norman. After being stabilized on board the *Repose*, Norman was routed through the medical facilities in the Far East on his way home. After more than a week, he had finally arrived at the naval hospital north of Chicago. Harold Dickey's brother-in-law, J. D. Weaver, had been stationed at Great Lakes when he was in the navy and had volunteered to drive the family to the base.

It had been nine days since Captain Johnson had come to the Dickeys' farm to tell them Norman had been wounded. Leona Dickey was in the kitchen when she saw the Marine Corps sedan coming down their driveway again. She saw that Captain Johnson was in his dress uniform again. The car rolled to a stop in front of the house. She watched as Captain Johnson got out of the car and began walking toward their front door.

She met the ashen-faced officer at the door. Johnson struggled to speak. "I know what you're going to say," she said before he could say a word.[2]

Leona Dickey remembered the moment vividly. "When that car pulled in and the captain and the first sergeant got out; I knew what was wrong," she said. "I could read it on their faces. They didn't have to tell me a thing. I could see what the score was … and I was devastated."

Doug's two younger brothers, Dennis and Steven, were home when the Marines arrived with the news. "They said, 'We think you better sit down,'" Dennis said, "so we knew right away that something bad happened. And then they told us about Doug."

Harold Dickey had already gone to work at the GM plant. "He was at work at the time," Dennis said, "but they contacted him and he came home." Harold Dickey had always remained thoroughly composed through every family tragedy. He had remained stoic even after his own father's death in 1965. But Harold Dickey broke down and wept openly that day when he was told Doug had been killed. "I think that's the only time I ever seen him shed a tear in his life," Dennis said. "That was the first time and the only time."

Steven Dickey was 14 years old; Doug had always been his "big protector." There was a special bond between the two brothers. "That was the toughest day of my life right there," he said. "It was pretty tough to take—sitting and watching mom and dad crying. We were all crying."[3]

The neighbors began to arrive at the Dickeys' home. The minister from the church came out. The family's doctor spent most of the day at the house. The following weeks were a haze to Leona Dickey. Her neighbors were there every day to help. They brought food and helped with chores.

A few days after getting the news about Doug, the Dickeys drove up to the naval hospital at Great Lakes to tell Norman. For Steven, the hospital was a tremendous shock. "That was a big hospital," Steven said. "I remember going in there and there were just beds and beds and beds and all these guys who had been shot up." They finally found Norman in among the hundreds of wounded men. He was in traction with a cast reaching from just under his arm all the way down to his left foot.

"Norman took it pretty hard because he thought when he got there [Vietnam], Doug should have come home," Dennis said.

George Moore was stationed in Germany and he and Vera were living near Frankfurt. A Red Cross representative from the army base brought them the news about Doug. They immediately flew home.

While Leona Dickey didn't remember many details from those painful weeks after Captain Johnson told her Doug had been killed, those around her, like Diane Birt, were struck by her incredible strength and composure.

Diane remembered going to the Oliver Funeral Home with her parents to pay their respects during the memorial service for Doug. Most of the community was there to show their support for the Dickeys. It was hard for the 19-year-old to fathom that a boy she knew had been killed in a war. "Doug was kind of happy-go-lucky, a bit of a jokester," she said. "He was a nice guy."

Doug's death was particularly upsetting for Diane for another reason. Diane had married Richard Birt shortly after she graduated from high school.[4] Not long after they were married, Richard got his draft notice and went into the army. By the time Richard was leaving for Vietnam, Diane was expecting their first baby. Doug's death while Richard was fighting in Vietnam made Diane's worst nightmares seem all too real.

Diane arrived at the funeral home with her parents and had no idea what to say or do. Thirty-eight years later, Diane was still moved remembering Leona Dickey's compassion and kindness toward her that evening. "I remember Doug's mother, Leona, seeing me come in with my parents," she said, "and there I was pregnant—and my husband in Vietnam also…and she just left the receiving line and came over to me and took me out on the porch at the funeral home—which was closed in—and said: 'How hard it must be for you to come here…'" Leona Dickey sat out on the porch with Diane for some time, trying to comfort the anxious newlywed. Richard made it home safely from Vietnam and he and Diane have been happily married since. Diane has known the Dickeys all her life. "You know, they're nice people," she said.[5]

Doug's funeral was held at the Rossburg Methodist Church on Friday, April 7. It had been just over seven months since Doug had walked into the church proudly wearing his new dress blues. Hundreds of people from all over the county came to show their respect. The crowd overflowed down the steps of the church and out into the field around it. Doug was buried in the Brock Cemetery with full military honors following the service. A Marine honor detail fired a rifle salute over his grave. It was still cool and the volleys from the rifles cracked across the early spring field.

Harold Dickey didn't talk much about Doug's death, but Leona could see it affected her husband deeply. He had seen men die in combat during his time in the Pacific. "He could picture the combat," she said. "He knew what they had been going through. It was very hard for him."

After Norman had been in the hospital for more than a month, a bundle of letters arrived. It was mail forwarded from his battalion in Vietnam. Among the letters was the one Doug had written from the USS *Ogden* the day before Operation *Beacon Hill*.

> Dear Brother:
> Well today we are just off the coast of Viet Nam in a holding area just outside Da Nang I think.
> Tomorrow we are going to land 5,000 meters from the DMZ, and make a sweep covering 20 miles to Dong Ha. So I will probably see you up there. Well I have a letter written to your company commander so he can verify that I have a brother over here, so then he will write my company commander & tell him.
> Well next month I will only have one year left in the Corps and will have been over here 6 months, pretty good huh?
> We are going to take all of our gear off of the ship as we are not coming back on it again.
> Well how have you been doing? Have you been going up north much or not?
> It sounds as though they have been having quite a bit of snow back home.
> Well I am going to get my machete sharpened today and I have another big blade that I am going to take ashore with me too.
> Well I am going to quit now as I have many more letters to write so I will say goodbye & see you soon maybe!
> Your Brother
> Doug[6]

Since she was a little girl, Leona Dickey had chronicled the most important points in her life by writing poems. Her collection of poems served as her journal. She kept her poems hidden away—a practice she adopted after her older brothers found some of her poems and teased her about them. After Doug was killed, Leona Dickey wrote one of her poems:

Rose Garden

Four little Roses were planted
In a garden called Fam-i-ly
And I loved each one with a special love,
For each one was different, you see!

I tended my little rose garden,
With very special care,
And nursed each little hurt, and bruise,
So each one got his share.

And my garden grew from tiny buds,
Almost to a full grown bloom
When angry shadows of war,
Cast a haze of gloom.

For when my garden was ready to bloom
Into full ma-t-urity,
The Lord reached out, and took one bloom
From my garden of fam-i-ly.

He took the happy smiling one,
For all up there to see;
And He must have known it would break my heart
To take just "one" little bloom from me.

And it shattered the beauty of a rose
From my garden of fam-i-lee
For the first to bloom, has faded,
And now, there is only three.

So, I'll cherish what's left of my garden
I know he would want it that way,
And I'll ask the Lord to grant one wish;
That three little roses can stay.

And now from a crimson sunset,
I picture the crystal sea,
And I catch a glimpse of the image,
Of the Rose He took from me.

Leona Dickey, 1967[7]

The war continued for the people in Darke County. Two days after Doug was killed, the local paper reported that five more young men from Darke County had enlisted in the Marine Corps together.[8]

Twenty-five young men from Darke County, including Doug Dickey, eventually made the supreme sacrifice in Vietnam.[9] By the end of the War, 58,178 American servicemen and women had died in Vietnam. Of those, 14,837 were U.S. Marines.[10]

A woman from the American Gold Star Mothers came to the Dickey home a few weeks after Doug was killed. She sat and talked quietly with Leona Dickey. She was one of the few who truly understood her loss and pain. She had also lost a son to war. She gave Leona Dickey a small lapel pin before she left. It was about the size of a dime. It had a gold star set in the center against a purple background, bordered by gold laurel leaves.

The Gold Star Mothers were formed by Grace Seibold after World War I. American doughboys didn't make it into the trenches of the Western Front until the last seven months of the war. However, the American Expeditionary Force suffered more than 53,000 combat deaths in those seven months. The country was traumatized by the losses. Grace Seibold's son, George, was one of soldiers killed in August 1918. She believed that, "grief, if self-contained, is self-destructive."[11] She decided to channel her grief into meeting with, and comforting, other mothers who had lost a son or daughter to war. Eventually, her network became the American Gold Star Mothers. While the organization did charitable work, their principal mission remained comforting grieving mothers. Tragically, their membership grew with each war.

Leona Dickey had become one of the war's Gold Star Mothers. For the next four decades, she also made those quiet visits to comfort other grieving mothers. Over the years, Leona Dickey often wore the Gold Star pin she was given that day in 1967. If someone asked her about the little purple and gold pin, she would touch it lightly and softly say, "My Doug…"

CHAPTER 20

A Marine Hero is Honored

"By that act, he saved the lives of five other Americans. That was the supreme act of love, as expressed by the Apostle John when he said, 'Greater Love hath no man than this, that a man lay down his life for his friends.'"

PAUL IGNATIUS, THE SECRETARY OF THE NAVY

The Medal of Honor had become one of the most revered military decorations in the world by 1967. The small bronze star hanging from a strip of blue ribbon eclipsed even the highest ranks and positions. Generals, admirals, and national leaders often felt diminished in the presence of a man who wore the Medal.

Presenting the Medal of Honor to a young soldier during a ceremony in 1945, President Harry Truman honestly admitted his envy: "I would much rather have that Medal around my neck than be the President of the United States," he said. "It is the greatest honor that can come to a man. It is an honor that all of us strive for, but very few of us ever achieve."

Although the Medal of Honor wasn't created until the Civil War, its roots can be traced back to the dark days of the Revolutionary War. The Founding Fathers initially shunned any notion of military awards or decorations. They deliberately wanted to avoid anything that seemed to echo the trappings of European royalty with its echelons of titles and knighthoods.

Despite these reservations, George Washington was moved to establish an award to recognize the bravery of his young soldiers during the Revolutionary War. Washington understood bravery amidst the horrors of battle. Years before taking command of the Continental Army, he had fought in the savage French and Indian War. As a 23-year-old officer, George Washington had distinguished himself during the Battle of the Monongahela in July 1755. By the end of the battle, Washington had had two horses shot out from under him and at least four bullets had cut through his clothing, barely missing him. A British leader later praised his heroics, saying the young officer, "behaved ... as bravely as if he really loved the whistling of Bullets."[1]

As the Revolutionary War dragged on, George Washington was moved to create a military decoration to officially commend the sacrifices and heroics of his young soldiers. Washington believed a true soldier would not talk about his bravery. Therefore, those who wished to recognize him, must give him something to wear that would attest to his bravery "without words."[2]

To recognize brave Continental soldiers, Washington created the Badge of Military Merit on August 7, 1782. With the Badge of Military Merit, Washington established the bedrock philosophy that would distinguish America's military awards from those of the European monarchies. Washington made it clear the decoration would be awarded without regard to class or rank. "The road to glory in a patriot army and a free country is thus open to all," Washington decreed. Furthermore, he said the award would be given to "cherish virtuous ambition" and "foster and encourage every species of military merit." Washington additionally required that recommendations for the award be accompanied with factual statements and "incontestable proofs" to justify the award.[3]

The actual decoration presented by General Washington to his soldiers was a heart-shaped piece of purple cloth with a wreath embroidered around the edge. The word "Merit" was embroidered in the middle of the heart.

George Washington's philosophy was a dramatic departure from the practices in Europe. In the European monarchies, decorations were usually given to nobility and members of the upper class. The sacrifices of battlefield soldiers were often ignored. Washington turned that system upside down. It was the battlefield soldier who would receive the recognition in the American army, not the officers or gentry. There are three verified cases where Washington awarded the Badge of Military Merit during the Revolutionary War. General Washington awarded all three of them to enlisted men. It was never awarded again. However, Washington's Badge of Military Merit was used as the model for the Purple Heart when it was designed in 1932.

No military decorations were used between the Revolutionary War and the Civil War. Instead of decorations, soldiers and sailors who distinguished themselves in battle were usually given promotions or other career enhancements.

With the outbreak of the Civil War, there was a renewed desire to recognize heroic acts on the battlefield with military decorations. Consequently, the Medal of Honor was created. Abraham Lincoln signed the law creating the "Medal of Honor for enlisted men of the Navy and Marine Corps" on December 21, 1861. Six months later he approved a similar Medal of Honor for soldiers in the Union Army. Echoing Washington's philosophy, initially, the Medal of Honor was intended only to recognize enlisted men. Later, the regulations were modified to make officers also eligible for the award.

The stature of the Medal of Honor grew steadily in the century after it was established by Abraham Lincoln. Joshua Chamberlain, Alvin York, and Audie Murphy became national heroes after receiving the Medal of Honor.

Immediately after the battle on Easter Sunday, Larry Dickerson went to Bob Kelley and told him about Doug Dickey diving on the grenade and saving his life and the lives of the other Marines that afternoon. Kelley told Dave Rumsey to start collecting witness statements and write a nomination for the Medal of Honor. A talented writer, Rumsey had earned a reputation as one of those rare individuals who could get paperwork through the system. After the battalion got back to Dong Ha, Rumsey began collecting witness statements, and assembling the paperwork necessary to nominate Doug for the Medal of Honor.

In keeping with George Washington's philosophy, Doug Dickey's nomination for the Medal of Honor didn't start in the halls of power. It started on a muddy hilltop. Men in filthy battle uniforms, sitting on ammo boxes, wrote statements about what they had seen. Other men, lying in hospital beds, dictated their statements to officers. A clerk, sitting at a plywood field desk in a humid tent, typed out the recommendation on a battered typewriter.

By the middle of April, Rumsey had completed the package. Lieutenant Colonel Theodore J. Willis, the new battalion commander, signed the letter nominating Doug Dickey for the Medal of Honor on April 19, 1967, and forwarded it up the chain of command.[4]

The decision to nominate Doug Dickey for the Medal of Honor was not taken lightly by Bob Kelley, Blackjack Westerman, Lieutenant Colonel Willis, or any other Marine in the chain of command. They knew the letter they wrote would eventually be handed to President Johnson. Only the President has the authority to award the Medal of Honor.

In his statement, Larry Dickerson explained the circumstances that caused the six Marines, including Dickey, to be crowded into the small space:

> As I was strapping the radio on Private First Class Dickey's back someone hollered, "Grenade!," and we flattened on the ground. Apparently the grenade had hit at a distance and bounced before I saw it land no more than three feet from us and right next to the corpsman who was administering first aid. Without regard for his own safety, I saw Private First Class Dickey deliberately throw himself upon the grenade. He gave his life in a conscious effort to save the lives of those Marines around him.

Greg Long, Charlie Runnels, and Bill Dorsey also wrote statements. Dorsey wrote: "After the explosion, I looked around and saw the smoke coming up only a few feet behind me, I didn't see how I kept from getting killed or at least badly wounded. I thought the Platoon Commander, the corpsman who had treated me and Private First Class Dickey were dead. Then someone said, 'Oh God! It blew him all to pieces, and he jumped on it to save our lives!' I crawled back to safety and was later evacuated by chopper to the USS *Princeton* for treatment."

Two other men witnessed the event and wrote statements. Gary Hudson, the rocket man from Colorado, had been nearby and saw the incident. He and Doug Dickey had gotten to be pretty good friends. Hudson had turned 19 a month earlier. Like Larry Normand, he had left his rocket tube behind that day and had spent all day as a rifleman. "I was about eight yards from Private First Class Dickey when he was helped on with the radio by his Platoon Commander," Hudson wrote. "I saw Private First Class Dickey, without regard of his own life, jump on the grenade. He gave his life in order to save at least two men from death and at least four other Marines from serious injury."

The other man who wrote a statement was Corporal Walter B. Smith, Dickey's squad leader. Smith wrote:

> I was about twenty feet from Private First Class Dickey when someone yelled, "Grenade!" The four of them lay flat on the ground, but when the grenade hit the ground, it bounced right into the center of the group, no more than three feet from any of the four Marines. It was then that Private First Class Dickey apparently realized that the grenade was so close that it would surely kill or grievously wound them all, and that it was too late to run. I saw him scramble over and deliberately cover the grenade with his body. The blast killed Private First Class Dickey, but he saved the Platoon Commander, the Corpsman and the wounded radio operator from probable death, and two other Marines from likely injury.

At the time Doug Dickey's award was submitted, the discrepancies between the witness statements were attributed to the inevitable variations that happen when people observe an event from different vantage points. The recommendation was submitted with the understanding there was one grenade. Thirty years later, the members of the platoon were able to compare their recollections. As it turned out, there were two grenades. Doug dove on the first one, and then grabbed a second grenade that landed and pulled that one under him.

Once Lieutenant Colonel Willis signed the recommendation, it was forwarded up the chain of command. The recommendation was reviewed by at least ten different echelons. The priority for those reviewing a recommendation for the Medal of Honor was to "jealously guard" the standards established to earn the nation's highest award. The law governing the Medal of Honor at the time said:

> There must be no margin of doubt or possibility or error in awarding this honor. To justify the decoration, the individual must clearly render himself conspicuously above his comrades by an act so outstanding that it clearly distinguishes his gallantry beyond the call of duty from lesser forms of bravery; and it must not subject him to any justified criticism. The deed must be without detriment to the mission of his command or to the command to which attached.[5]

Harold and Leona Dickey didn't know Doug had died saving his comrades or that he had been nominated for the Medal of Honor. The only information they had at the time was the official telegram brought by the Marines to notify them that Doug had been killed. It said only that Doug had died from "multiple shrapnel wounds in the chest while participating in action with hostile forces in the vicinity of Gio Linh."[6]

A year after Doug's death, Robert Johnson, who had just been promoted to major, and First Sergeant Turner came to the Dickeys' home again. By then, Johnson and Turner had been to the Dickeys' home several times and had become close to the Dickey family. In addition to notifying them when Norman was wounded and Doug had been killed, they had helped coordinate Doug's funeral.

This time, the two Marines came to tell Harold and Leona Dickey that Doug was going to receive the Medal of Honor. Johnson told them the award ceremony was scheduled to take place in Washington, D.C. in mid-April.

Norman was still up at Great Lakes when he was told Doug was going to receive the Medal of Honor. He had been discharged from hospital, but was still going through extensive rehabilitation and was assigned to the Marine barracks near the hospital while the Marine Corps evaluated his fitness for further service.

The Marine Corps took care of all the arrangements to get the Dickey family to Washington for the ceremony. Major Johnson and Marine escorts accompanied the Dickeys from the moment they were picked up at their house until they arrived back home four days later.

The award ceremony took place on Tuesday, April 16, 1968, at the Marine Barracks in Washington, D.C. The barracks is known in the Marine Corps as "Eighth and Eye" because it sits at the corner of 8th Street and I Street in southeast Washington, D.C. The Dickey family was brought from their hotel in downtown Washington to the barracks in a procession of limousines with a police escort.

Before the ceremony, Emily Chapman, the Commandant's wife, gave Leona and Harold a tour of their residence, which overlooked the parade field. Emily Chapman had two boys of her own and her heart ached for any mother who had lost a son. "She took me over there to the Commandant's house," Leona Dickey said. "She was so nice and they had a tea there for us. They were just lovely people."

At just before noon, the Dickeys were escorted out to the grass parade ground at the center of the barracks. Surrounded by red-brick buildings, the parade field has an elegant feel. The other members of the family, Doug's comrades, and other dignitaries filled the chairs running along the side of the field. The Marine Band was formed at the end of the field while two companies of Marines from the barracks were formed along the opposite side of the field. The day was brisk and sunny.

The ceremony began when Harold and Leona Dickey were escorted over to stand beside Paul Ignatius, the Secretary of the Navy, and General Chapman. Ignatius was presenting the award because President Johnson was unavailable.

The color guard marched up and posted itself in front of the group. The Marines snapped to attention and the band filled the air with "The Star-Spangled Banner." Harold and Leona Dickey held their hands over their hearts until the last note had faded.

After the color guard retired, Paul Ignatius stepped to the lectern. Ignatius was called upon to present nine posthumous Medals of Honor during his tenure as Secretary of the Navy. He said later those ceremonies were, "the most profound moments of my time in office."[7] Ignatius looked down briefly at his notes and then began his remarks:

> Mr. and Mrs. Dickey, distinguished members of the Congress, ladies and gentlemen.
> We are here today to speak of a very brave young American who gave his life for us in Vietnam.
> Private First Class Douglas E. Dickey earned his country's highest military honor by a classic act of courage and self-sacrifice. He threw himself across a live grenade that had been tossed among his comrades. By that act, he saved the lives of five other Americans. That was the supreme act of love, as expressed by the Apostle John when he said, "Greater Love hath no man than this, that a man lay down his life for his friends."
> PFC Dickey proved that he was his brother's keeper, even though it cost him his own life. He had the unflinching courage, the unshakable belief, and the unqualified commitment to ideals that made him unhesitatingly perform this noble, heroic, unselfish deed rather than seek refuge for self-protection. He is a shining example to all Americans, to all men who believe that good will—that love—must prevail over the madness of hatred, oppression, and war, if our world is to continue as the abode of man. He was a man of love who sacrificed his own life while opposing those evils. Therefore we honor him today.
> Mr. and Mrs. Dickey, in the name of the Congress, I pass to you the Medal of Honor of the United States, won so deservedly by the hero who was your son.
> I give you this, our country's greatest honor. It is poor compensation for your loss. But be assured that the death of your son will have meaning. For I give you also my solemn pledge that our country will persist and will prevail in the cause for which your boy died.[8]

After Paul Ignatius completed his remarks, General Chapman, the Commandant of the Marine Corps, stepped to the lectern and read the official citation which detailed Doug's actions on Easter Sunday. This was the toughest part of the ceremony for Harold and Leona Dickey. They both fought off tears when Chapman read that Doug "quickly and unhesitatingly threw himself upon the deadly grenade, absorbing with his body the full and complete force of the explosion."

After the Commandant finished reading the citation, a Marine brought the Medal of Honor and the framed citation forward. Paul Ignatius took the Medal and handed it to Harold Dickey. Ignatius then stepped to his right and handed the citation to Leona Dickey. Harold Dickey kept looking down at the Medal in his hands, holding back tears.

"God gives you strength when you don't have any," Leona Dickey said later about getting through the award ceremony.[9]

With the award ceremony completed, General Chapman signaled for the Barracks to pass in review. While the parade spared none of the pageantry, it was done with a solemn and somber tone. The Marine Band led the formation, resplendent in their scarlet tunics and gleaming instruments. The band was followed by the two ceremonial companies from the barracks. Arrayed in their dress blues and shouldering polished rifles with burnished bayonets, each platoon rendered a sharp salute as they marched past Harold and Leona Dickey.

After the last platoon had marched off the field, Secretary Ignatius and General Chapman stood with the Dickey's and greeted the guests.

The Dickeys spent three days and nights in Washington. They were accorded the treatment usually reserved for diplomats and high-ranking dignitaries. They were given tours of the capital and taken to some of the nicest restaurants, and driven everywhere in limousines.

The experience was overwhelming. Vera was living in Monterey, California, while George attended the army's foreign language school there. He was a staff sergeant at the time. "It's kind of hard to believe when all of that attention gets showered on you," she said. "We're country people—little country farmers—and to have ceremonies like this showered upon you; it's staggering. It really was. Because we certainly weren't accustomed to anything like that."[10]

"They were very nice, very nice to us," said Leona Dickey. "But, I was like a fish out of water, because we grew up out here in the country. I had never been to the nation's capital," she said. "It's quite a place."

An NBC news team attended Doug's award ceremony. NBC was producing a 30-minute television show called: *Vietnam: The War This Week*, which featured a wide variety of stories about the war. While filming the award ceremony at the Marine Barracks, Dean Brelis, the show's lead correspondent, became intrigued by the story and wanted to know more about the young Marine who had sacrificed himself to save his friends.

Brelis and his crew followed the Dickeys back to Ohio to get more background information for their story. When NBC's New York office contacted Leona Dickey and asked about a film crew coming out, she told them the family was exhausted and wasn't interested in the project. Despite her objections, Brelis and his crew arrived in Rossburg the day after the family got home. "I told them I didn't want to see anybody," Leona Dickey said. Harold Dickey flatly refused to have anything to do with the journalist and his film crew.

Brelis had originally intended to get some brief footage and head back to New York. However, he was surprised and captivated by what he found when he came to Darke County. He began interviewing people who had known Doug. The crew rode the school bus and interviewed Dennis and Steven, and some of the others who had known Doug.

Tim Barga and Dave Thornhill had just gotten home. They survived their tours in Vietnam and had been discharged. Asked about Doug, Tim told Brelis, "I've never seen him angry. Not once—not really angry ever."

Dave Thornhill told Brelis, "He was a buddy, just a real good friend. We got along real well together."

Herb Schlecty's interview was touching. He had been one of Doug's Sunday school teachers. Filmed sitting in one of the pews in the Rossburg Methodist Church, Schlecty talked softly:

> Well, Doug was a little unusual for a young man in his feelings ever since I've known him, and I've known him since he was born—in his church, in his church affiliations.
>
> He had a little more on the ball for God than probably any other child I was around in this church. I mean, not because he's gone; but because the way he lived.
>
> He had a concern—a deep concern—for religion.
>
> I remember, one time, in our Sunday school class, we brought up the subject … I said, "I want to relate one thing to you boys and girls: That friends are hard to come by, that at time of trial, they don't always add up to what you might think."
>
> I said, "In the bible somewhere it's written: 'A man who gives his life for a friend … greater love no man has shown than to give his life for a friend.'"
>
> Doug says, "I believe I'd do that."
>
> I remember that distinctly.

Before the film crew left, Leona Dickey relented and agreed to be interviewed about Doug. It was filmed in the Dickeys' living room. Leona sat in a chair, wearing a suit. Brelis asked: "Mrs. Dickey, what kind of son was Douglas?"
Leona Dickey spoke softly:

> Well, he's a little hard to describe: very affectionate and always complimentary, thoughtful, considerate, and just the kind of a son any mother would cherish. He was so unselfish with his … everything he did.
>
> And I think he felt a little more responsibly by having three younger brothers.
>
> And he helped me out a great deal.
>
> And of course, you learn to know your first son the best, you have him a little longer you know.

Brelis then said, "This is a tough question, Mrs. Dickey. How do you justify losing Douglas in Vietnam?" He seemed to be fishing for some kind of provocative anti-war statement. A spark of anger or disappointment seemed to flash through Leona Dickey's eyes. There was a long poignant pause. Then she looked directly at Dean Brelis and began to speak:

> That's a very difficult question.
>
> He volunteered for service and he also volunteered to give his life to save his friends—and I can feel no bitterness…
>
> Since he made this choice himself, he sacrificed himself to save his friends…
>
> How could I be bitter about that?
>
> He fully realized what he was doing, I think, and … well, I have word from the boys who were with him; and he actually just gave them a quick glance and dived on that grenade.
>
> It was … I don't know…
>
> It hurt me a great deal to lose him. But I can't feel bitter. There are so many people who die for no reason at all; and this was a definite reason—giving his life in this way.
>
> I couldn't be bitter.

> I still worship the same God I've always believed in and the same God he believed in. And I guess it takes a *very* big man to do this.

Leona Dickey then looked at the journalist, and with emotion starting to sweep over her, said softly, "Does that answer your question?" Brelis made no reply and ended the interview.[11]

A month after the Dickeys returned from Washington, a more intimate ceremony was held to recognize Doug in his hometown. While it couldn't compete with the grandeur of the ceremony in Washington, the ceremony in Rossburg on May 9, 1968, was powerful because all the people there knew him. It was originally planned to be held outside and include a small parade through town, led by the Ansonia High School Band. However, rain forced them to move to the large shed on the town's car lot, the largest structure in the town. Rossburg had a population of about three hundred. Most of them were there.

The ceremony began with the Ansonia High School Band playing the national anthem, followed by an invocation by the Reverend Albert Kuntzman. Marlin Thompson, the Superintendent of the Ansonia schools, then spoke. He talked about Doug singing in the school's chorus and being the bass soloist in the school's operetta. Major Johnson, in his dress blues, then stepped forward. He told the crowd that Doug was "… a young man who paid the supreme sacrifice in the service of his country." The ceremony closed with everyone singing "My Country 'Tis of Thee."

Leona Dickey was deeply touched by the ceremony to honor her son and told them she was "Greatly honored—by the greatest little community in the world."[12]

Articles and photos of the Dickeys accepting Doug's Medal of Honor were published in papers around the country and even some newspapers overseas. The episode that Brelis and his crew produced was broadcast nationally.

The Dickeys were stunned by the response. "People called us from all over the United States," Leona said. "I knew the Medal of Honor was a wonderful thing, but I didn't know that people from all over the nation would send cards and call you and everything. I didn't know that until it happened to us."

Many of the men from 2nd Platoon didn't know Doug had earned the Medal of Honor until they saw it in the paper. Mac McClelland had no idea Doug Dickey had saved those men that day or that Doug had been nominated for the award. After being medevac'd back to the United States and spending months in the Great Lakes naval hospital, he was sent to Camp Lejeune. One day he saw a photo of Doug Dickey in the newspaper. He was stunned when he read about Doug diving on a grenade and saving his comrades that Easter Sunday, the same day he had been badly wounded.

The article reminded Mac McClelland of a discussion he had had with Doug one day in Vietnam. There had been a news article in *Stars and Stripes* about a Marine or soldier who had just been awarded a posthumous Medal of Honor for diving on a grenade to save his comrades.

> I said to Doug, "Man, it must take a lot of guts to think of jumping on a grenade to save your buddies," I said. "I guess if it came up ... I guess that's when you have to face it."
>
> And I remember he straight out looked at me—right in the eye, and said, "You know, Mac, I'd do it."
>
> And I said, "Are you serious? Wait a minute ... are you saying that ... but ... I mean ... really? You won't know that!"
>
> And he goes, "Yes, I do. I would."
>
> It just blew me away [when I read the article about Doug getting the Medal]. I thought, "God, Dickey! You said you would—but damn!"
>
> It was also heartbreaking. He was a good guy. I liked him. I don't think there was anybody that didn't like Dickey, really. He was just an all-around good guy.

Lionel Lawson was from Tamaqua, Pennsylvania, and was eventually medevac'd back to the naval hospital in Philadelphia. He had wanted to make the Marine Corps his career but was too badly wounded on Easter Sunday and was discharged in 1968. He, like Mac McClelland, had no idea Doug had earned the Medal of Honor. He found out while reading a copy of *Leatherneck*, the Marine Corps' monthly magazine. "I said, 'Oh my God, I served with this guy!'" Lawson didn't know what Doug had done until he read the article. "I was proud that I had served with a Medal of Honor recipient. When I read what he did to get it, I thought, 'Wow! It takes a lot of balls to do that.' Man, he saved four other guys that were in that hole with him!"

Eventually things calmed down for the Dickeys. Norman's wound was too severe for him to stay in the Marines and he was discharged in August 1968. He came home to Rossburg and moved into his old room for a while. His leg was still hard to bend and he walked with a pronounced limp for more than a year. His room was on the second floor of their home. His mother and father tried to convince him to move into one of the downstairs rooms so he wouldn't have to deal with the stairs. Norman refused to move downstairs and treated the painful and slow trips up and down the stairs as a personal challenge and point of pride. "It used to hurt me just to watch him struggle up and down those stairs," Leona Dickey said.

Just as his two older brothers had, Dennis Dickey went down to the Marine recruiter's office after he graduated from high school in 1969 and tried to enlist. "I might be the first guy the Marine Corps recruiter didn't want," he said with a laugh. The recruiter knew his two older brothers had both fought in Vietnam and that Doug had earned a posthumous Medal of Honor. He didn't want to face Harold and Leona Dickey if he enlisted another Dickey boy, while going to Vietnam was still a certainty. "He said, 'Why don't you go join the Air Force or the Navy or something?'" Dennis said with a laugh later. Dennis was adamant that he had to wear the same Marine Corps uniform his father and his two older brothers had worn so proudly. "I just said, 'No. That's what I wanted to do my whole life. I wasn't going to change my mind.'"[13]

They reached a compromise. The recruiter would enlist Dennis, but refused to put him in the infantry. "He said the only way I could join was on a four-year aviation contract," Dennis said, "so that's what I did."

When Dennis told his parents he was enlisting, he could tell it worried them. But they seemed to understand that it was something he had to do. Norman wasn't so circumspect. He had been to Vietnam and had seen the war. He had already lost one brother. "First, he told me if I did enlist in the Marine Corps, he was going to kick my ass," Dennis said. "But I told him I always wanted to be a Marine." Although Norman was worried, he knew how Dennis felt. "He didn't kick my ass," Dennis said with a laugh, "He didn't mess with me."

Just as his father and two brothers had; Dennis Dickey went to war. He was assigned as a plane captain in VMA-224, a Marine Corps fighter-bomber squadron flying off the USS *Coral Sea*. While he was safe from communist bullets, he was in one of the most dangerous jobs in the military. He spent months on the flight deck of the *Coral Sea*, dodging jets as they blasted off from the catapults or came slamming down onto the deck while landing at over a hundred miles an hour.

As a plane captain, Dennis was personally responsible for ensuring the aircraft were fully operational and combat ready. He had to check everything from the oxygen the pilots breathed to the bombs that were loaded on the racks beneath the wings. His squadron flew combat missions as part of Operation *Pocket Money*, supporting the mining of Hai Phong harbor after the North Vietnamese invaded South Vietnam in April 1972. Dennis was discharged as a sergeant in 1974 and returned to Darke County. He took up farming, married, and raised a family.

Steven Dickey had been plagued with health problems since he was a child. Joining the Marines was never an option for him. He went to work as a house painter and moved to Colorado for a while. However, he continued to miss his older brother in a very personal way. After working for a few years, he bought the plot next to Doug's and had his name carved into a stone marker. "I just wanted to make sure I ended up next to my brother," he said.

Vera's husband, George, was sent to Vietnam in 1970, working in intelligence. After returning from Vietnam, George and Vera spent several years assigned to bases in Europe. Harold and Leona went to visit them in 1976 and spent a month traveling around Europe. Visiting the great cities she had read about all her life was a wonderful treat for Leona Dickey. "We went to Switzerland, Germany, all over Italy, Luxemburg, just all over," Leona Dickey said. "We had a beautiful trip." They visited Rome and stayed in a hotel just up the street from St. Peter's Basilica. "It's the most beautiful church you've ever seen in your life."

Occasionally, Harold and Leona would hear from some of the Marines who had served with Doug in Vietnam. Larry Dickerson stayed in touch. Gary Hudson would call every year on the anniversary of the battle.

The other four boys from Darke County who had enlisted with Doug came home from Vietnam safely. During their first year home, they helped each other readjust after spending a year in combat. Roger Young remembered that year: "We drank every night at a bar and talked about all the stuff that happened over there to all of us—and what happened to Doug," he said. "We just had a nice little support group between the four of us guys." Within a couple of years, they all got jobs or started businesses and got married.

Roger Young became close to Norman Dickey in the year after they all got home. "The first couple of years were really hard on Norman," he said. Norman seemed restless and traveled around a lot. "He would come to the house and just want to talk and talk and talk," said Young. "It was his brother who got killed, and he got shot really badly…" Norman eventually went to work at the same GM plant where his father worked; then he worked for the railroad. After working there for several years, he got a job as a corrections officer. He eventually got married and settled down. "He seems to be very, very, very well adjusted and has finally accepted all of it," Young said. "He's a great friend of mine and I have total respect for the guy."

Norman Dickey, like his father, isn't much of a talker. He considers himself lucky despite all he went through. "There were seven guys on the C-130 that I flew in with the day we got there [to Dong Ha]." When he was wounded and evacuated two and a half months later, he was the last one of the seven left. "Everyone else was either dead or had been shot," he said. He became an accomplished woodworker over the years. One of his finest projects was a box for Doug's Medal of Honor.

Fifty-eight Marines eventually earned the Medal of Honor during the Vietnam War. Forty-four of those were posthumous awards. They went to young men who, like Douglas Dickey, died saving their buddies.

Going to Washington to accept Doug's Medal of Honor had been overwhelming for Leona Dickey. Shortly after the ceremony, as she had done before, she pulled out a piece of paper and began to write. When she finished the poem, she tucked it away with the others she had written over the years. It would be 29 years before she shared it with anyone:

The Medal

A police escort through our Nation's Capital
On April sixteenth sixty eight
We arrived at Marine Headquarters,
A dress blue General, at the gate.

Introductions!, then we're seated
Among the honored guests
This nation is paying homage
To one of its very best.

The Honor, and the Color Guard
Put on their best display,
And raised "Old Glory" proudly,
At the barracks, there, that day.

They talked for awhile in private
To me, and poor old dad,
They must have sensed our feelings,
It took All the courage we had.

A Salute! Then the band played a stirring march
The Marine Corps Hymn, the Anthem, too,
And two brown misty eyes looked up,
At dad's misty eyes of blue.

Then the dignitaries took their places,
And each one did his part,
They spoke their praise of my Darling,
And Oh! How it pierced my heart.

"Above, and beyond the call of duty,"
We heard the General say,
We present Douglas this "Medal of Honor,"
In the name of Congress today.

And when they gave us the coveted medal
For service "above, and beyond" the call,
A body could hardly contain this heart,
It was standing ten feet tall.

We reached out, and humbly accepted it,
With sorrow, and yet with pride,
It was not for poor old dad, and me,
But our dear little son, who died.

"No tears," I thought as I stood there
for all of the crowd to see,
He would want me to be composed, and strong,
And display the same courage, as He.

Then the ceremony was ended,
And soon the crowd was gone,
A Nation had called him a Hero,
We called him, Our loving son.

Leona Dickey
(4–16–68)

PART IV

HEALING

CHAPTER 21

Veterans

"He had rid himself of the sickness of battle. The sultry nightmare was in the past. He had been an animal blistered and sweating in the heat and pain of war. He turned now with a lover's thirst to images of tranquil skies, fresh meadows, cool brooks—an existence of soft and eternal peace."

STEPHEN CRANE, THE RED BADGE OF COURAGE[1]

In the two weeks following the battle, many of the wounded men were medevac'd back to the United States. They were sent to the hospitals closest to their hometowns, scattering them around the country. Some were discharged early because their wounds rendered them physically unqualified to continue their service. Some were returned to duty and eventually discharged after completing their enlistment in a quiet stateside assignment. A handful stayed in the Marine Corps and completed a career. Within a year, all of the men who had fought on Easter Sunday were home. Eventually, they all tried to get on with their lives. They got married; went to school; started businesses; raised families.

For those who were badly wounded, a second war had just begun. Jerry Idziak, Heywood Swearingen, Colin McClelland, Lionel Lawson, and the others joined the legions of badly wounded men in hospital wards all over America. In those hospitals, they started the steep painful climb up to a new life.

Their second war seemed to be against their own bodies. Healing meant pain. Lots of pain. It was months of pain that most can't imagine and that cannot be described with words. Rick Eilert, a Marine who had been blown apart by a booby trap in November 1967, realized during his first week at the naval hospital in Great Lakes, that healing and rehabilitation were going to be the greatest challenges he ever faced. He told his mother after his first few days at the hospital, "You know, I always wanted to find out what I was made of ... that's kind of why I went into the corps. But I've got a feeling that the battlefield was only step one in the guts course." Then he admitted, "I guess I'm scared."[2]

For those whose bodies had been burned and torn apart, the doctors and their staffs fought a race against bacteria every day. Deep wounds had to be debrided. Initially, most men had to go through the process three times a day. Corpsmen or medics had to tear away bandages and remove fist-sized clumps of pus-soaked gauze packing. Then they would scrub the inside of the wound to clear away the rotting tissue. It was the only way to prevent gangrene. They had to scrub the pus, scabs, and dead flesh away until fresh blood flowed, indicating they had finally hit healthy tissue. Only healthy tissue could grow and heal.

The scrubbing exposed nerve endings. The men tried not to scream during the daily dressing changes. It was a point of pride among them. Their pajamas became soaked with sweat and tears streaked down their faces. The pain was so intense men broke their fingernails and tore skin from the palms of their hands gripping the rails on the sides of their beds while their dressings were changed.

No matter how much the hospital staff cleaned, the air in those wards was always thick with the putrid smell of pus, rotting flesh, and antiseptic. For the badly wounded, it went on like that; day after day; month after month. "The horror of the war zone was only the start of the wounded man's agony," Eilert wrote later.[3]

The wounded men in the wards bonded as they had in the field. They helped each other. They became comrades in a different kind of battle. When the dressing cart started to make its rounds, they quietly encouraged each other. When a man awoke after a surgery, he often found the other men gathered around his bed to see how he was doing. The same sense of courage that made them walk point or rush enemy positions now pushed them to endure painful treatments and surgeries with grit.

They went through one surgery after another. Shattered bones were reassembled like pieces of broken pottery. The splintered pieces were lined up and fastened together with stainless-steel screws, rods, and plates. If the bones started to knit together properly, the doctors would start to close the outer wound. If infection set in, they were taken back to the operating room. The wound would be opened and the process would start all over again. Once the bones healed, the skin grafts began.

If the skin grafts took and infections were kept at bay, the wounded men would eventually begin physical therapy. Joints that hadn't bent in months were bent, and weakened bones were put to the test. The men went through new and excruciating chapters of pain. An injury that happened in a fraction of a second, often took years to heal; and its legacy lasted a lifetime.

The same coarse sense of humor that had buoyed them in combat became a staple in the wards. Among the wounded, no topic was off-limits—missing limbs and disfiguring wounds became fodder for off-color stories, punchlines, and practical jokes.

"Courage should be as important on the ward as it was on the battlefield," Eilert said of his time in the naval hospital.[4] A hierarchy of respect formed where the seriously wounded were treated. It was the men with the worst wounds and those who endured the non-stop pain with grit—and even humor, who were now the heroes and role models.

The other heroes were the doctors, nurses, corpsmen, medics, and orderlies who worked tirelessly to put the men back together. They were not only dedicated and professional; they were encouraging and cheerful. They were also tough and unyielding when they had to be. They lived with the men day in and day out for months, and were the only other witnesses to the depth of their pain and courage. Healers have special hearts. They are called to work in places most people never want to see. While most people see the horrifying wounds; a healer sees the rest. They see the bright soul beyond the damaged bone and tissue. They see the bright soul who can and will overcome the pain and trauma of his wounds. The men and women in the wards worked to make a future possible for each of their young patients.

As they had in Vietnam, they still endured the loss of comrades. Some bodies were just too broken. Infection could suddenly rampage through a man's weakened system, crashing one organ after another. The doctors would load his body with antibiotics and wheel him in for emergency surgery. Sometimes, despite every effort, his life still slipped away. Doctors would emerge from the operating room cussing and swearing in frustration. The next day there would be an empty bed in the ward.

Somewhere in America a Marine casualty team would appear at the front door of a family who had believed for weeks that their son was finally safe. The team would try to explain to the stunned family how their son had survived the Vietnamese rice paddies and jungles, but that he had died in a hospital a few miles from home. The cruelty of war is boundless.

William L. Moore, Doug Dickey's senior drill instructor, was one of the men who suddenly died in a naval hospital weeks after he had made it home. Moore completed his tour as a drill instructor in October 1967 and received orders to Vietnam. He and his wife, Rita, packed their seven children and their dog, Bobo, into the family station wagon and drove to South Carolina. Bill Moore was originally from Darlington and they had established a home in North Charleston.

An artilleryman, Moore had been promoted to gunnery sergeant and was assigned to Battery B, 11th Marines, headquartered in Phu Bai. On February 7, 1968, in the midst of the Tet Offensive, he was a member of a resupply column making its way from Battery B's position to the battalion headquarters. The column was ambushed by a much larger NVA force at 1400 that afternoon. The armored vehicles leading the column were knocked out and most of the Marines and soldiers were quickly killed or wounded in the ensuing battle. The column was eventually cut off and overrun.[5]

Bill Moore, shot in the arm and wounded by a grenade blast, played dead when the NVA soldiers started walking among the wounded Marines, shooting any survivors they found. An NVA soldier pushed his rifle into Moore's shoulder and pulled the trigger, blowing a hole through him. Moore managed to continue to play dead, even when the same soldier pushed the muzzle of the rifle against his head. At the last second, the soldier was called away by another soldier and walked off without firing the fatal shot. Moore lay among his dead comrades for more than five hours until an American rescue force fought its way to their position and evacuated him. He was the only survivor from 28 men in his group.[6]

Bill Moore was eventually evacuated back to the naval hospital in Charleston, where he recovered quickly. The local newspaper ran a photograph of him sitting up in bed on February 23 when Rear Admiral Ballanger presented him with three Purple Hearts.[7]

Rita, who was pregnant with their eighth child, was visiting her husband two weeks later on a Friday evening. "He was sitting up and laughing and talking..." she said. A few hours after she left, in the early morning hours of March 2, Bill Moore died in his sleep. The doctors later said it appeared that a blood clot had broken loose while he was sleeping. He was 37. He had been a Marine for 19 years.

Rita Moore made arrangements for her husband to be buried in Arlington National Cemetery. He was laid to rest there with full honors on March 11.[8] A month later, she packed her family into their little station wagon and drove to Cincinnati—to stay with her family while she figured out what to do next.

Before they left Charleston, the Moores made arrangements to leave Bobo, their dog, with the Marines at the barracks in Charleston. Bill Moore had bought the thoroughbred English bulldog puppy in San Diego to keep Rita and the kids company while he was in Vietnam. Originally, Bobo had been named Snowball because she was almost all white. However, Moore's youngest had trouble pronouncing Snowball and kept calling her "Bobo." The name stuck. They had never had a pet and Bobo quickly became part of the family.

On April 4, before they left for Cincinnati, the Moores attended a ceremony at the Marine Barracks where Bill Moore's son, 13-year-old Billy, officially handed Bobo over to Colonel Olsen, the barracks commander and the 75-pound puppy became the barracks' official mascot. The local paper joked that "Lance Corporal Bobo" was "the first female attached to the Marine Barracks at Charleston Naval Base in the unit's 160-year history."

Donating Bobo to the barracks wasn't an easy decision. "I just couldn't take care of the dog like I should," Rita said. She talked it over with Billy, who had been taking care of Bobo while his father was away, and they decided it would make his father proud to have Bobo become the mascot for the barracks.

"We all love her, just as my father did," Billy said at the ceremony. "But when mother said we should donate her to the Corps, I said yes." Billy thought it would make his father proud.[9]

The badly wounded who had to fight a long excruciating war to survive and heal became a small community within the community of combat veterans. They had fought two wars. Just as the combat veterans felt a little alienated from their friends and family after they returned; the men who endured the pain of the long-term care wards felt somewhat isolated from the men they had fought beside. While those men knew the panic and fear of the battlefield; they didn't know what it was like to have to lie helpless in a bed while another man changed your bedpan and wiped your ass for you. They had never felt the daily terror when the dressing cart was wheeled up to your bed. "In the hospital," Rick Eilert wrote later, "we made friendships based on a common denominator of pain and a different kind of courage, which up to that point none of us had ever needed before. It was frightening to go into combat. Sometime, the journey home required far more bravery."[10] There are no medals given for the courage it takes to heal and to try to live again. Maybe there should be.

Vietnam was unique in another way. The men returning from the war came home alone. Prior to September 1965, Marines were rotated into Vietnam as part of their unit. They trained together; arrived in Vietnam together; and left Vietnam together. However, the escalating troop requirements quickly made this system unsustainable.[11]

In September 1965, the Marine Corps went to the "individual replacement" system. Instead of moving as units, Marines rotated into and out of Vietnam individually. They were sent to Vietnam and reported to units already in the field. Their orders were to serve with that unit for 13 months. If they survived to the end of the tour, they were pulled out of their unit and flown home—leaving their comrades behind. They came home alone.

At the end of World War II, combat veterans spent months decompressing while they waited in reembarkation camps and while they sailed home with their units on board troopships. A Vietnam veteran often found himself suddenly in his old bedroom in his parents' house with Vietnamese mud still caked under his fingernails.

Charlie Runnels got his orders to go home on June 10, 1967, while the company was fighting up at Con Thien. "And at two o'clock in the afternoon of June 13th, I was sitting on my folks' front steps back in Bethel, Maine," he recalled. "I literally had been in combat less than four days earlier. There was no 'cool down period'— nothing," Runnels said. "And my mother told me later, that I had the craziest eyes she'd ever seen on anybody in her life—when I got home."

To the men who made it home from Vietnam, there was often a haunting sense of guilt. There was a sense of indebtedness to those who died there and who would never age. A young veteran stepping off an airliner in Southern California on the first leg of his trip home, couldn't help but recall the names and faces of his buddies who hadn't made it this far. During relaxed moments on patrols or while sitting in fighting holes or bunkers, they had shared plans about what they would do when they were finished with Vietnam. Some of the plans were ribald, grandiose, or outrageous. Most of the time, they were simple. Most of the plans revolved around the word "home."

America had changed while the men of 2nd Platoon had been in Vietnam. Unlike any group of returning American warriors in the nation's history, the men returning from Vietnam were not welcomed home. Those who objected to the war often attacked the returning soldiers, sailors, airmen, and Marines. The reception some of the men encountered when they got home was vile.

Today, it's hard to imagine the shameful way some of the young men returning from Vietnam were treated. Greg Long and Haywood Swearingen ran into some of the protesters. Long had finished his year in Vietnam and found himself getting off a plane at the Marine Corps Air Station in El Toro, California. To catch his plane home to Idaho, he had to go to the front gate of the base and catch a cab to the Los Angeles International Airport. He and six other men walked to the gate. When they got there, the Marine guard on duty at the gate offered them sheets of plastic to protect themselves after they left the base. He explained that the protesters gathered outside the base had been pelting servicemen with water balloons. He told them some of the balloons had been filled with urine. "There was a ton of protesters at El Toro all the time down there, I guess," Long said. "And they didn't treat us too good. They were spitting at us and calling us every name in the book—throwing balloons full of piss at us," said Long. "There was seven of us that caught one cab ... and we told him to haul ass to L.A.X. We just wanted out of there," he said. "We just wanted to go home."

Haywood Swearingen came home on a medevac flight to Andrews Air Force Base in Maryland. The plane was specially configured for the badly wounded. The inside of the plane was outfitted with racks to hold stretchers. The wounded men were carried on board and their stretchers were latched into the racks. The plane looked like it was full of bunk beds when it was loaded with wounded men. When the plane landed, teams of medical personnel lifted the stretchers out of the racks and carried them to a bus that was pulled up next to the plane. The bus was configured like the plane. The seats had been removed and replaced with racks. The wounded men were carried on board the bus and their stretchers were latched into the racks. Once loaded, the bus took the wounded men to one of the military hospitals.[12]

Haywood was in pretty bad shape and was one of the men loaded on the bus for the trip from the air base to the hospital. As at El Toro, there was a group of protesters gathered outside the gate at Andrews Air Force Base. When the medevac buses left the base, the protesters pelted them with balloons and rotten fruit, and screamed obscenities. "They were throwing tomatoes and everything at us—I'll tell you ... them flower children didn't give a damn about us," he said with a sarcastic laugh. He remembered thinking that the Vietnamese people had treated them better than they were being treated by other Americans. "I had a homecoming that

I didn't believe," he said. "Back then, we didn't have no decent welcome. They had a right-bad welcome for us."

The scars run very deep for the veterans who had to run one of those hateful gantlets when they got home from Vietnam. They love America and made tremendous sacrifices for her. They served because their country asked it of them. It was their duty as citizens and as men. When Vietnam veterans talk about that dark time and the poor way they were treated, they don't sound angry. They sound heartbroken.

Most of the new veterans, like the generations of veterans before them, learned not to talk about their wartime experiences. They learned not to talk about Vietnam or the banana grove, or Easter Sunday 1967. Those who went to college learned that being identified as a Vietnam veteran would subject them to abuse and ridicule. Even well-meaning and loving family members signaled that talking about Vietnam was unwelcomed. When the nightmares came, a man would go to the bathroom, splash cold water on his face to remind himself that it was just a bad dream and that he wasn't back in the banana grove, or in a trench at Con Thien, or sweating on a dark, humid jungle trail. He would reassure his wife, saying, "It's all right." Then he would climb back into bed and try to get some more sleep before he had to get up and go to work.

Most ended up around people who hadn't ever been in combat and couldn't relate. Those who stayed in the military or went into law enforcement were luckier. They found they were surrounded by men who carried similar memories. They had someone to talk to. For those who joined veterans' organizations like the Veterans of Foreign Wars or the American Legion, the experiences varied. While some found a haven of men like themselves, others found that the leaders of some of the chapters were hostile to Vietnam veterans. Some of the older veterans of World War II and Korea viewed the returning veterans with suspicion or even hostility. Like the rest of the country, they had been fed an endless succession of stories about rampant drug abuse, dereliction of duty, atrocities, and even soldiers and Marines murdering their leaders.

After the fall of the South Vietnamese government in April 1975, America's Vietnam veterans were unfairly tied to another word that had never been attached to a group of American veterans before: "defeat."

In the years after the war, most of the men who fought in Vietnam built a wall in their minds around their memories of Vietnam and tried to live their lives as if it had never happened. But every once in a while, a memory from Vietnam would escape its prison and come charging into the present day, and the man would wrestle with it all alone. That's when he felt more alone than ever.

After Lionel Lawson got out of the hospital and was discharged from the Marines, he went to school and had a successful career in banking. He and his wife raised two children. He wore suits to work, and the bank was usually quiet and peaceful.

Every once in a while, on a sunny day, while sitting at his desk, he would look down at his hands and see the scars. He would think about that day; and lying in the crater frantically twisting rounds out of the machine-gun belts so they could use them in their rifles. It was like a memory from a dream—an unreal world from a different universe.

Jerry Idziak spent more than a year and a half in the naval hospital in Great Lakes. Most of that time he was in traction. "I had tubes running out of me everywhere." The highlight of his hospital stay was getting busted for assault and battery while he couldn't even get out of bed.

There was a navy corpsman working on his ward who hadn't been to Vietnam. For some reason, the man seemed to take sadistic pleasure in inflicting pain on the badly injured Marines he was supposed to be helping. "Most of them [the corpsmen] were great, but this guy was an asshole," Idziak said. This particular corpsman often neglected the wounded men, leaving them in their own waste. He seemed to take perverse pleasure in taunting the helpless combat veterans.

Jerry had just come out of surgery one night and needed help with a catheter. He was in a lot of pain. Instead of helping him, the corpsman started mocking and ridiculing him. Jerry was in a body cast and appeared helpless. The corpsman underestimated the situation and got too close while he was taunting Idziak. "I got a hold of his thumb—and I broke it!" Idziak said. "I had just been promoted to sergeant and got busted back to corporal," he said with a laugh. The corpsman and his broken thumb were transferred.

Gary Hudson, one of the men saved by Doug Dickey, finished his tour in Vietnam and went home to Louisville, Colorado. He married Susan, his high-school sweetheart. Wounded during his tour, he went home with a Purple Heart. He spent a couple of years as a police officer while attending the University of Northern Colorado in Greeley, graduating in 1971 with a degree in political science.

Gary decided he missed the Marines and joined up again, this time to be an officer with a contract to go to flight school and become a pilot. "He always wanted to fly," his mother said. However, while going through the Officer Candidates School at Quantico, he injured his knee and was told he was no longer qualified for flight school. He was discharged.

However, when he got back home to Colorado, he found out he still met the Air Force's physical qualifications. He joined the Air Force and went through training in Texas, and was commissioned as an officer in 1973. He then became a bomber pilot.

Gary was very proud to be an air force pilot, but his heart was still with the Marines. Isabelle Hudson remembered an exchange between Gary and his father shortly after Gary finished his air force training. Gary's father had been in the Army Air Corps during World War II. "Chuck asked Gary what he thought about the Air

Force and the Marines, and he [Gary] said, 'Well, I don't want to hurt your feelings, dad, but the Air Force is like Boy Scouts compared to the Marines.'" Isabelle laughed softly remembering the scene. "It kind of deflated his father a little bit."

After he got home from Vietnam, Gary told his parents about Doug Dickey. Gary was one of the men invited to the award ceremony in Washington, D.C. "He always had nice things to say about Dickey," Isabelle Hudson said. Other than that, Gary didn't say much about Vietnam. "When he came home, he was very quiet for quite some time." His mother only heard him talk about Vietnam when he got together with his Marine buddies. She wanted to understand the part of her son's life that had shaped him so much—but that he avoided talking about it. "They would start talking—it was none of my business—but I would try to listen in on it," she said. Surviving war was an experience Gary and his father shared and it brought them closer. Chuck Hudson was able to help his son come to terms with the war. "They talked a lot," Isabelle Hudson said.

Gary Hudson phoned Harold and Leona Dickey on the anniversary of the Easter Sunday battle every year. He was one of the few people who had served with Doug who stayed in touch during the years right after the war. Gary and the Dickeys became close. It was good for all of them. "That was very difficult for a 19-year-old boy to see that happen to your friend. Doug Dickey was one of his very good friends in Vietnam," Isabelle Hudson said.

Tragically, Gary Hudson was killed on April 1, 1977, when the B-52 bomber he was copiloting crashed while making its final approach to K. I. Sawyer Air Force Base in Michigan. He and Susan had a three-year-old boy, Travis Scott, at the time. Shortly after Gary was killed, Susan found out she was expecting their second son. Jeremy was born later that year.

Leona Dickey was one of the people who called the Hudsons right after Gary was killed. She had seen an article about the crash in the newspaper. Leona Dickey was heartbroken. She had just talked to Gary; he had just phoned the Dickeys earlier that week on the anniversary of Doug's death. Leona Dickey was one of the few people who could understand what Gary's parents were going through. "They were very supportive, as they would be—going through something like that. They were really nice people," Isabelle Hudson said.

Blackjack Westerman came home from Vietnam and served one last tour at the Puget Sound Naval Yard in Washington. He retired in 1973 and settled in nearby Sequim. He never talked much about Vietnam after he came home. "The stories I got were never really from him," his son, Jack Westerman III, said. "They were either stuff that I happened to read or what other Marines would tell us as we were growing up."

Jack Westerman and his wife, Nan, had been together since they were teenagers. They had chopped cotton to survive during the Depression. They escaped from the crushing rural poverty of dusty Keota, Oklahoma, together. The Marine Corps had been his salvation in many ways according to his son. Jack and Nan raised a son and three daughters together. Nan passed away in 1975. Blackjack Westerman passed away from a massive heart attack in 1981.

His son said it was clear that Vietnam weighed on his father even though he didn't talk about it much. "I think Vietnam was difficult, obviously, for the entire country," he said. "But for the Marines who served during World War II and Korea, and came back and were recognized [for that service]. And then, for a long time, Vietnam vets weren't." Thinking about his father, Jack said, "And in a war where I think the senior officers knew they couldn't win—or weren't given the ability to win, and yet they were writing letters [to the parents of killed Marines] and sending those boys home in the body bags—I think that always really, really burned," he said. "I think it really crushed him in a way."[13]

The Vietnam War left thousands of children to grow up without their fathers. Among them were John Szymanski's son and daughter, Jim and Stephanie; Dick Housh's two boys, Mike and Tim, and his daughter, Terry; Bob Bryson's daughter, Lisa; and Doug Lee's daughter, Cindy. In his book, *We Were Soldiers Once ... And Young*, Lieutenant General Harold G. Moore summed up the unique sense of loss those children feel: "They are the gold star children, war's innocent victims, and their pain shimmers across the years pure and undimmed. They pass through life with an empty room in their hearts where a father was supposed to live and laugh and love. All their lives they listen for the footstep that will never fall, and long to know what might have been."[14]

Larry Normand survived Vietnam and came home to Baton Rouge in September 1967 with two Purple Hearts. He married Cheryl and worked in construction. Eventually, he had a thriving business of his own. He and Cheryl had two daughters, Cherilon, and Lauren.

In 1975, the country that had been the source of so much suffering for Larry Normand ended up giving him his son.

By April 1975, the South Vietnamese government was collapsing. Communist tanks had rolled up to the outskirts of Saigon and the North Vietnamese were shelling the city. Tens of thousands of people were trying to get out of Vietnam before the communists took over. The city was in chaos. It was heartbreaking for those who had served there to see all their sacrifice and hard work end up going for naught.

Cheryl Normand was watching the news on television. What struck her was the footage of terrified children running in the streets—seemingly abandoned. It broke her heart. She said a prayer to herself that day: "Lord, if you will send me one of those children, I promise you I will raise that child as my very own and to know you all the days of their lives."[15]

Larry Normand on the battlefield with a captured AK-47 rifle after the Easter Sunday battle. Eight years later, Larry and Cheryl Normand adopted a child from Vietnam. (Larry Normand)

About a month later, the minister at their church told the congregation about a group of missionaries who had managed to fly 23 Vietnamese orphans out of Saigon at the last minute. The missionaries were now trying to find homes for the children. Larry and Cheryl drove to Oklahoma, where the children were living, and adopted six-year-old Neng.

Neng's family had been Montagnards. The Montagnards are tribesmen who live in the mountains along the western Vietnamese border. They are fiercely independent people who have little regard for the ethnically distinct Vietnamese who live along the coast and the lowlands. Although the Montagnards had little use for the Saigon government, they hated the communists more and became very loyal to the America military—particularly the Special Forces units operating in remote mountain outposts. The tribesmen were ferocious warriors and were feared by the North Vietnamese and Viet Cong. It was certain the victorious communists would take revenge on them. Fearing the worst after the Saigon government fell, the Montagnards brought their orphans to the missionaries and pleaded for them to get the children out of Vietnam.

Ulrich Huyssen was a 31-year-old German missionary who had escaped from behind the Iron Curtain with his parents as a child. He had followed his father into the ministry and became a missionary, spending time in Biafra, India, and Nigeria.

At his home in Oklahoma, he received an urgent call for help from a fellow minister in Vietnam. Quickly arranging travel, he and his wife, Gisela, flew to Saigon and arrived on April 14. After arriving, they made arrangements to get four orphan children out of Vietnam.

As Huyssen was making those arrangements, he was approached by a Vietnamese pastor who told him he had 19 Montagnard children they had to get out of the country. The pastor and his wife had whisked the children out of an orphanage in Kontum, a province in the mountains about 350 miles north of Saigon, just before the NVA swept through the area on their march south. The pastor had no paperwork on the children, who ranged in age from four to ten. He didn't even have a single birth certificate. Getting the children out of Vietnam seemed an impossible challenge. Regardless, the idea of leaving the children behind was unthinkable. "He told me that these children would almost certainly be slaughtered if the Viet Cong came into power," Ulrich Huyssen said later.[16]

The ministers quickly devised a scheme to get the kids on one of the American planes leaving from Ton Son Nhut Air Base in Saigon. It was a long shot at best. They divided the children into three groups, with a missionary couple assigned to escort each group. They were going to try to get everyone on a plane by posing as families. The missionaries would tell the officials at the air base that the orphans traveling with them were actually their sons and daughters. To anyone looking at the group, this was clearly preposterous. But it was the only plan they could think of. They had to try something.

In the first of several miracles, they all made it through the base checkpoint and got to the airfield. It's unlikely the guards were fooled. For some reason, they disregarded the rules and let them all through.

Eventually, the entire group managed to get on a plane bound for the Philippines. The American and Philippine officials at the Cubi Point Naval Air Base were dumbfounded to discover they had a group of Vietnamese children on their hands who had absolutely no documentation. The situation was unprecedented.

Luck stayed with the missionaries and their orphans. Rather than try to return the group to Vietnam or send them to a refugee camp, the officials at Cubi Point put them on a plane bound for the United States. Huyssen and his team of missionaries had pulled off a minor miracle. They had managed to get a group of Vietnamese orphans from Saigon to Oklahoma without a single scrap of paper. Dozens of government officials along the way had ignored rules and regulations and allowed the group through. Once in Oklahoma, Huyssen and his team soon found homes for the children.

Although he couldn't speak any English when Larry and Cheryl brought him home in May, Neng proved to be very bright and outgoing. Surprisingly, over the summer months he had learned enough English to start school that fall. "He was a typical little boy," Larry said. "Shucks, he learned English by watching cartoons."

Larry Normand has always been very proud of his son. Neng played sports in high school and was popular. He graduated from Louisiana Tech and married Debbie Nguyen. Debbie and her parents had fled Vietnam in 1981 in the "boat people" exodus. Neng and Debbie had a set of triplets—adding to Larry Normand's growing number of grandchildren. Neng went to work in his father's business after he graduated from college. He supervises most of the high-tech computerized production that has become a large part of their custom woodworking business. Father and son work side by side every day. "I couldn't run the place without him," Larry says.

Larry Dickerson had finished his year in Vietnam and returned to Delaware with a Purple Heart and a Bronze Star Medal. He married and had two sons. He went to work as a schoolteacher at the same school he had attended as a boy in his hometown of Smyrna, Delaware, and eventually became the principal of the school. He loved his job and was known for spending little time in his office. He preferred to walk the halls and banter with the kids. At lunchtime, he would go into the lunchroom and joke with the kids and "collect high-fives."

Those who worked with Dickerson knew he had been a Marine and that he was proud of it, but they didn't know much about his service. He carried himself with the posture and bearing of someone who had been in the military, and military jargon occasionally crept into his conversations. Most of his colleagues didn't pay much attention to the two framed photos hanging on the wall of his office. One was the group photo of 2nd Platoon taken on Okinawa on New Year's Day, 1967. If someone asked about it, Dickerson would just say it was a picture of "my men." The other photo was of a smiling young Marine—Douglas Dickey. Dickerson said later that he kept the photos in his office "to keep things in perspective."

Tim O'Toole came home to Pensacola in July 1967. He reunited with Theresa and met his eight-month-old daughter, Colleen, for the first time. His 13 months in Vietnam had been unusually charmed. "I went through that whole thing and never had a scratch—never even had a nick," he said. It was an almost miraculous run of luck, considering his helicopters were often shot to pieces and several times other men in his aircraft were hit. By the time he rotated home, he had flown 561 missions. "I can't remember all 561 missions, but I remember about 100 of them vividly," he said softly. He earned three Distinguished Flying Crosses and dozens of Air Medals.

The Marine Corps desperately wanted to retain men like Tim O'Toole in 1967. They needed skilled helicopter pilots in Vietnam more than ever. They offered him a number of incentives to stay on in the Marines. Among other things, they offered him a regular commission and his choice of aircraft to fly. The venerable UH-34D was being phased out.

But life had changed for Tim O'Toole. "I had my wife and my daughter now—everything to live for." He turned down all the Marine Corps' offers and left active duty in 1969. He stayed in the reserves for a while, flying CH-46s. He also turned down several offers from the airlines. The vagabond lifestyle of an airline pilot didn't appeal to him either. He decided to go back to college. He got a degree in Building Construction from Virginia Tech and went on to a successful career in the building industry.[17] He and Theresa had two more children, Tara, and Kevin.

In his reflection on the Vietnam War, written more than 10 years after the war ended, former President Richard Nixon paid tribute to the generation of warriors who went to Vietnam:

> Our best young men did not go to Canada. They went to Vietnam. When I visited our servicemen in South Vietnam in July 1969, I found the most idealistic young Americans of an idealistic generation. But they knew better than their contemporaries at home what it took to give life to ideals in a world that was far from ideal. Any war is difficult to fight in. But the war in Vietnam was the most difficult one in which American soldiers had ever fought. Front lines were seldom clearly drawn. Enemy soldiers were often hard to identify. Our men were constantly bombarded by media reports telling them the war was unwinnable, that our cause was unjust, and that a majority of the American people opposed it. But to their credit, our men did their duty. They honored their country. They served well the cause of freedom and justice.[18]

Vietnam veterans were always proud of their service. However, after they returned, they quickly realized they could only rely on their fellow veterans from South East Asia for support. In 1979, Jan Scruggs, a soldier who had fought in Vietnam and had been wounded during his two tours, decided that his comrades who died in Vietnam deserved to be recognized with a suitable memorial. Initially, his effort to raise money for the memorial was met with little success—and even ridicule in the national media. After months of fundraising, Scruggs had raised a total of $144.50. Nobody wanted to think about Vietnam, much less build a memorial to the war.

Eventually his efforts began to succeed—but it was almost all due to the donations of fellow Vietnam veterans and the families who had been touched by the war. Many of the $5 and $10 donations Scruggs received were accompanied with heartbreaking notes from people who had lost friends, comrades, fathers, sons, or husbands in the war. They wanted to make sure they weren't forgotten.

Through dogged determination, Scruggs and his band of veterans began to garner support for the project. Even the legislation to get the project going in Washington was ushered through the government by a network of Vietnam veterans.

Their growing success was largely due to an emotional sea-change taking place in America. The American people seemed to be awakening to the sacrifices of the men who had fought in Vietnam—regardless of the politics surrounding the war. The fund started to grow. However, it was still the veterans' organizations who wrote the biggest checks.

The Vietnam Veterans Memorial Fund (VVMF), the nonprofit organization founded by Scruggs and others overseeing the project, eventually held a competition to select a suitable design for the memorial. There were 1,421 entries submitted.[19] The winner of the competition was a 21-year-old undergraduate architecture student at Yale named Maya Ying Lin. Lin was born and raised in Ohio. Her parents, however, had escaped from communist China 10 years before she was born. By her own account she was "a typical Midwesterner." She had a normal American upbringing and had even worked at McDonalds as a teenager. She knew little about the Vietnam War and hadn't been personally touched by the war in any way.[20]

Maya Lin's design was to have all the names of the war's dead etched into a series of polished black granite tablets that would form two walls. The walls would be set down into the earth on a stretch of land adjacent to the National Mall. She saw the two walls meeting as analogous to a set of silent, welcoming hands.

As with every proposed memorial, Lin's design was controversial when it was first introduced to the public. However, there was a simple poetry to it that resonated with most of the organizers. Many who saw her design were initially perplexed by it; but, like a poetic phrase, they found that it planted itself in their minds and stayed with them—and began to resonate with them in a deeper way. Her design was haunting and reverent without being morose or depressing. The principal design feature was the names of the 57,939[21] dead, arranged chronologically. This immortalized each of the men and women who had died in the war—personalizing the sacrifices and memorializing each loss, while at the same time, graphically illustrating the cumulative cost and sacrifice the American people had paid during the Vietnam War.

While the Carter administration had been cool to the idea of memorializing the Vietnam War, President Reagan made recognizing Vietnam veterans a priority when he took office in January 1980. In an elaborate ceremony on February 24, 1981, Reagan presented the Medal of Honor to Roy Benavidez, a Green Beret whose Medal recommendation had languished in bureaucratic limbo for more than a decade. Reagan declared April 26, 1981 a Day of Recognition for Veterans of the Vietnam Era.

The announcement of the memorial design, combined with the clear blossoming of public support for Vietnam veterans, propelled the project forward in the next year. Funding began to flow in to the VVMF. By the end of 1981, the VVMF had collected more than eight million dollars—enough to build the memorial. The American Legion had written the largest check—one million dollars. However, most of the funding came from small, personal donations. Over 650,000 people had contributed $10 or less.[22]

The dedication of the Vietnam War Memorial was scheduled for the Saturday after Veterans Day, 1982. As news of the dedication spread, veterans and family members started converging on Washington, D.C. from all over the United States. By the second week of November, hundreds of thousands of Vietnam veterans and family members had descended on the capital to take part in the "National Salute to Vietnam Veterans."

The dedication was preceded by the Candlelight Memorial Ceremony at the National Cathedral. Around the clock, over three days, starting on Wednesday, November 10, a succession of volunteers took turns reading the names of the fallen. Often comrades and family members tearfully read the names of those they knew personally. The last name was finally read at midnight on Friday, November 12.

On Saturday morning, November 13, a long-overdue welcome-home parade was held down Constitution Avenue to honor the Vietnam veterans. The parade was planned so it would lead into the Memorial dedication that afternoon.

Led by formal marching units and color guards from the military services and veterans' organizations, the parade began with a sea of flags and patriotic music. Tens of thousands of men, women, and children lined the route, cheering and waving flags as the veterans made their way down the Mall to the memorial. More than 15,000 veterans marched down Constitution Avenue that day. Some marched smartly; some limped; some rolled along in their wheelchairs. Among the marchers was William Westmoreland. It was "quite an emotional experience," he said, "something I never thought would take place."[23]

The Vietnam War Memorial, which has become known widely as "The Wall," was dedicated on Saturday afternoon, November 13, 1982. More than 150,000 people crowded around the memorial. A number of speakers gave brief, impassioned speeches. At 2:55, the crowd sang "God Bless America." With the last note fading, Jan Scruggs announced simply: "Ladies and Gentlemen, the Vietnam Veterans Memorial is now dedicated."[24]

Seconds later, the crowd pushed down the small retaining fences and moved toward the black granite slabs. Then something happened which the designers and organizers hadn't anticipated. People wanted to touch the names. Reflexively, people would reach out and touch the names of loved ones and comrades. Another thing started to happen. A person would go to a name on the Wall and find another person there touching the same name. The Wall started bringing people together. As the organizers had hoped, "The Wall" became a place of healing.

The greatest fear for those who lost loved ones in the war was that they would be forgotten. The Vietnam War Memorial became a place where the living began to fulfill their promises to never forget the killed. The Wall became a place where families and comrades could assure themselves that there is a lasting commitment to the memories of the lost.

Carl Martin's first letter home after Operation *Beacon Hill* gives insight into the spirit that has made the Vietnam War Memorial the most visited monument in Washington, D.C.

Before deploying to Vietnam, Martin had made an arrangement with Mr. W. E. Elkins, an elderly neighbor whose farm was near his parents' place in

Florida. Carl had somewhat adopted Mr. Elkins as a grandfather while he was growing up. Carl wanted to write about the war he was about to experience, but guessed that some of it might be pretty grim and he didn't want to alarm his parents—especially his mother. He asked Mr. Elkins if he could write to him instead—and tell him the unvarnished truth about what he was seeing and experiencing in Vietnam. Carl told Mr. Elkins that if he made it home, he would go by his place later and collect the letters. If he was killed, he asked Mr. Elkins to deliver the letters to his parents. He knew they would want them. Mr. Elkins agreed. For months, Carl wrote to the elderly man describing the horrors and heartbreak he was living through.

On April 3, 1967, Carl Martin finally got some time to write a letter. He and the rest of the battalion had just arrived back at Dong Ha after completing Operation *Beacon Hill*. Carl wrote a 10-page letter to Mr. Elkins. The 21-year-old sergeant recounted in detail losing three of his men on Good Friday and described what it was like to be in a firefight: "… you could smell the sweat and the blood and most of all the fear of the men around you," he said. "Yet everyone was so determined to live."

Carl Martin described being heartbroken when he found Doug Lee's body after the Easter Sunday battle. "He was twenty years old, had just gotten married before he came to Vietnam and what is saddest of all … he left a child behind that he had never known."

Martin had seen four of his friends die in three days. "One thing I've learned about this war," he wrote, "it claims the heroes among its dead, because they are the ones who stand up and do their job when the shooting starts…"

Martin told Mr. Elkins, "I've decided to write a personal letter to each family of the men I lost. I think it will be the hardest thing I've ever had to do." He tried to process the losses. "After everything's over, you can think of a thousand ways you could have saved each man if you had only done this or that. Sometimes it's so hard to be a leader, because you know everything depends on you."

On the last page of his letter to Mr. Elkins, Carl Martin scratched out words that echo within the heart of every man who has been to war. "Two more months and I'll be out of the war, but the war will never be out of me. I'll remember it and the men I shared it with for the rest of my life! Keep writing and saying your prayers, as I need both of them."

CHAPTER 22

Rally Point

"The initial rallying point and rallying points en route are selected to enable the patrol to reassemble if it is unavoidably dispersed ... The success of the patrol is jeopardized if it is dispersed."

"Patrolling," FMFM 6-5: Marine Rifle Squad[1]

A chance encounter in late 1996 set the wheels in motion to bring the men from 2nd Platoon together again after 30 years.

Steve Pruitt left Vietnam in August 1967. He earned a Purple Heart after getting hit with some shrapnel before he went home. "It wasn't nothing major," he said with a chuckle, "a piece in my arm, and a piece in my butt."

After returning from Vietnam, Steve was assigned to the Marine Barracks on the U.S. Navy's base at Guantanamo Bay, Cuba. The American naval base was established in 1903 as one of the U.S. Navy's coaling ports. The United States refused to surrender the base to Fidel Castro after he and his communist rebels seized power in 1959. After the communist takeover, the base became a besieged Cold War outpost. Relations between the United States and Castro were extremely hostile, and almost triggered a nuclear war with the Soviet Union in October 1962.

The American base was surrounded by elaborate fences and minefields and maintained a high level of alert. The Marine Barracks provided the security for the base, manning the guard towers along the fence line and patrolling the 24-mile perimeter,[2] which was often called "the Cactus Curtain," likening it to the Iron Curtain that divided Cold War Europe.

Despite the Cold War tensions, the base felt much like a small town to the Americans and Cubans who lived there. The isolation bred camaraderie among the thousands of sailors, Marines, and civilians who called the 45-square-mile base home. The navy tried to make life at the base as pleasant as possible and maintained an array of recreational facilities, including some of the most beautiful swimming beaches in the Caribbean.

Steve met Maggie Siaca shortly after he arrived at Guantanamo. Maggie was living on the naval base because her father was one of the civilian engineers working there. Steve was immediately smitten by the feisty Cuban girl. Between guard shifts, Steve and Maggie picnicked and swam at the base's beaches, went to the movies, and enjoyed the simple life on the base.

After a year at Guantanamo, Steve's enlistment was done, and he was flown to Camp Lejeune to be discharged. His top priority was to get back to Guantanamo as fast as possible so he could be with Maggie. While working through the discharge process at Camp Lejeune, he wrangled a civilian job back at Guantanamo, working at the base's desalinization plant.

He and Maggie were married shortly after Steve got back to Cuba. A little while later, they decided it was time to start a family. Steve convinced Maggie to come back to Delaware with him. They settled in Newark and had two boys. Steve worked as a mechanic for a couple of construction companies and spent some time as a sales representative for an equipment company.

Steve Pruitt had known since 1967 that Larry Dickerson was from Smyrna, Delaware, not far from his hometown, Wilmington. As he had been taught at Quantico, Dickerson had studied the service record of every man in his platoon. While going through the records, he noticed that Steve was from Wilmington. The first time Dickerson inspected the platoon, he surprised Steve by asking him, "Did you know that Middletown beat Salesanum?" Steve was dumbstruck when he heard his new platoon leader mention the cross-town football rivalry between the two small schools back in Delaware. Seeing the baffled look on Steve's face, Dickerson smiled and told Pruitt he had grown up in Smyrna.

Over the next seven months, Dickerson and Pruitt shared newspapers from Delaware and kept each other updated when either of them got interesting news from home. Dickerson was still in Vietnam when Steve finished his tour in August 1967 and rotated back to the States.

Steve thought about Larry in the decades after he returned to Delaware. However, he was always reluctant to phone the number he saw listed in Smyrna. "I was afraid he might have got killed and I didn't want to be talking to his dad or his mother…"

One day in 1996, Steve was down in Smyrna on business and ended up chatting with one of the mechanics on the job site. Making conversation, Steve asked him if he had ever heard of anyone in Smyrna named Larry Dickerson. The man said, "He's teaching here. He's my son's football coach," then he added, "He's the principal of the school too." He told Steve he'd probably see Dickerson that evening at his son's football practice.

Steve told him he had served with a guy named Dickerson in Vietnam, although he doubted it could be the same guy. Steve handed him one his business cards and said, "Take this card and give it to him. If that's him, tell him to give me a call."

As the school's principal, Larry Dickerson often found himself standing on the sidelines of one of the athletic fields at the end of the day, rooting for one of the teams or encouraging the kids during practice. He often spent the time chatting with parents. It was on one of these afternoons that things began to change for him and the veterans of 2nd Platoon.

Dickerson was standing alongside a field when the mechanic Steve had met earlier walked up with Steve's business card. Dickerson described the meeting later: "I had a parent come up to me, and he asked me if I was in the Marine Corps, and I said, 'Yes, I was' ... and he also asked if I was in Vietnam, and I said, 'Yes.'" Dickerson, like most Vietnam veterans, had become leery of questions about his Vietnam service. He braced himself for some type of unpleasant question or comment.

Instead, the man just handed Steve's business card to him and said, "This fellah wanted me to give you this card to see if you would recognize him."

Larry Dickerson looked down at the card. "And when I saw Steve's name, I had to leave," he recalled. A sudden wave of emotion swept through him. "I almost broke down there," Dickerson said. He quickly walked back to his office, brushing past students and parents. "It was a very emotional experience for me."

When Larry Dickerson got back to his office, he looked up at the platoon photo hanging on the wall. "I looked up there and I reflected back on a lot of things and tried to get myself together again," he said. "Then I went back out and I told the father, I said, 'I'll be calling him tonight—and I appreciate very much that you brought me this card.'"[3]

Larry Dickerson phoned Steve Pruitt that evening. Steve had been living a few miles away in Newark the whole time. "It was emotional for both of us," Dickerson said. "It was like you were calling from the jungle the first time [we talked]." They spent more than two hours on the phone. They threw names back and forth and wondered about men they hadn't seen since Vietnam. At times, they laughed, remembering some comical mishap or goofy personality. And there were some long, pained pauses at times when they talked about men who had been killed or wounded.

After realizing how good it felt to reconnect with someone who had shared those experiences, Larry and Steve decided to find other members of the platoon. Their two families quickly became part of the project as they tried to track down men they hadn't seen in almost 30 years. Steve's wife, Maggie, became an accomplished detective, finding men with only the slimmest of leads.

Dickerson put ads in all of the military and veterans' magazines asking for members of his platoon to contact him. Although he didn't get any calls from his platoon members, he ended up getting calls from other Marines who had fought in the same area around the same time. Even though the men hadn't been in Dickerson's unit, they had seen his notice and called because they just needed to talk to someone who had been there and shared their experience.

They made hundreds of phone calls trying to find men, often based on vague recollections of where men were from or where they said they were going after they were discharged. The cruise book Blackjack Westerman had printed when they were in Okinawa in 1967 helped. There was a directory in the back that listed the hometowns of the Marines in the battalion.

Bill Dorsey remembered getting Dickerson's call. Dickerson called him on New Year's Day, 1997. "It just really freaked me out," said Dorsey. He also had a copy of the platoon photo hanging on his wall, taken thirty years—to the day—that Dickerson phoned him. Bill told him he had written some addresses and other information on the back of the photo. "He said, 'Great! Let's use that to try to locate some more of these guys.'"

Kent Hansen was one of the last to be located. Kent had gone back to college after Vietnam and became a successful businessman. He had moved several times for his career. He was in Baton Rouge when Dickerson finally tracked him down. Kent remembered getting the call. "One Sunday night, the phone rings and the guy on the other end said, 'My name is Larry Dickerson. Does that name mean anything to you?'" Kent had met several Dickersons in the last 30 years. "I said, 'Yeah, the name's familiar … now, what the hell do you want?'"

"Vietnam" was all Larry Dickerson said.

It stopped Kent Hansen cold. "I just said, 'Oh my God!' It was like a closet door that's been closed for 30 years and all of a sudden is flung open and everything comes out." He and Dickerson talked for hours that night.

Dickerson had heard that Greg Nichols was living in California. He called more than 50 Gregory or "G. Nichols" listed in the phone book. He found Doc Nichols with the very last number on his list. Dickerson got his answering machine and started to leave a message, as he had on several other answering machines, explaining that he was looking for a Greg Nichols who had been his corpsman in Vietnam. Before he could finish leaving the message, Doc Nichols picked up the phone, screaming, "It's me! It's me!"

The plans for a platoon reunion started to take shape. Larry Dickerson had kept in touch with Harold and Leona Dickey since meeting them at Doug's award ceremony in 1968. After discussing it with the Dickeys, he suggested that the reunion be held in Doug's hometown. The platoon could meet Doug's family and the Dickeys could meet the men who were with Doug in Vietnam. Everyone liked the idea. They decided to hold the reunion over the Memorial Day weekend. By then, Dickerson had tracked down Greg Long, Bill Dorsey, and Charlie Runnels. Harold and Leona Dickey would get to meet the men Doug saved that day. Garry Hudson had died in 1977. No one was able to find Walter Smith.

In the course of their research, Dickerson had also located Jim Ver Helst's parents in Iowa. Knowing how badly they wanted to meet the men who had served with Jim, Dickerson also invited them to the reunion.

The men of 2nd Platoon began converging on Greenville at the end of May 1997. It was just over 30 years since the Easter Sunday battle in the banana grove. The platoon quickly took over the lounge at the Greenville Inn. One of the most emotional moments was when Jerry Idziak walked into the room. For the last 30 years, most of them had assumed Jerry was dead. No one had imagined he could have survived after being so badly wounded.

It was the first day of the reunion that brought Bill Dorsey to Mrs. Dickey's kitchen door—still unable to find any words for the woman whose son died saving his life.

Many of the other platoon members had already met Harold and Leona Dickey the day before. Dorsey had kept putting it off, making excuses. Finally, a group decided they were going to head out to the Dickeys' farm and told Dorsey he had to go with them. He and his wife, Becky, headed out ahead of the group. It was then that Bill Dorsey found himself standing outside the kitchen door watching her make lunch.

Bill Dorsey never did find the words to say to Leona Dickey. He didn't have to. "I didn't even knock," he said. "She turned around and seen me," he said, "and she knew me."

When she turned and saw Bill standing outside her kitchen door, Leona Dickey smiled and said, "I know you." Then she pushed through the screen door and hugged him.

"She threw that apron down on the floor and came out that door and went up around my neck," Bill Dorsey said, "and it was like 40 years lifted off of me." Leona hugged him tightly. "When she did that, it took a load off of me," Dorsey said.

The other men and their wives were out at the front of the house by then. They all went into the living room and Leona gave them a tour of her little home. The walls in the living room were covered with photos of her family and she explained who they all were.

Leona Dickey came over to Bill again after things calmed down a bit. Bill Dorsey vividly remembered that afternoon years later:

> And she pointed to a chair over on the side of the living room there, just a little country living room, and she said, "That's where Doug used to set when we watched TV as a family."
>
> Then she said, "Would you take a picture of me and you in that chair?"
>
> And I said, "Sure, I'd be glad to." So, she went and set down on the chair and I got down on my knee beside her to get the picture made ... and I broke down like a three-year-old. And I squalled, and I cried, and that done me more good than 150 psychiatrists could have done.
>
> I bawled it all out right there in her lap.
>
> And we got our picture.
>
> And from then on ... I felt, like I said, 40 years lifted off my shoulders, you know.

The next morning, the platoon accompanied the Dickeys to a service at the Rossburg Methodist Church. There had been a fair amount of celebrating the night before and several of the men looked worse for wear as they took their seats—filling up the side section of the church. The minister explained to the congregation who the men were and that they were there to honor Doug. Everyone in Rossburg knew about Doug. A picture of him hung in the entrance of the church. It meant a lot to Leona and Harold Dickey to have the platoon in their church. It made her very proud.

That evening, they had a dinner at the Ansonia American Legion. The Legion had had Doug's name added to it in 1982. The reunion was a big event in the community and the hall was jammed with all sorts of community leaders, and family members from the large Dickey and Schlecty families. Bob Birt, Tim Barga, and Roger Young were there and blended in with the 2nd Platoon Marines. David Thornhill had died in 1993. His funeral, like Doug's, had been conducted at the Rossburg Methodist Church.

After dinner, Larry Dickerson went to the lectern for the ceremonial part of the evening. Serving as the master of ceremonies, he began by thanking the Dickeys for welcoming them to their town. He also went around the room introducing some of those who had helped organize the reunion. He then introduced each man from the platoon and had each man stand so the guests could see who they were. When Dickerson introduced Jerry Idziak, the whole room stood and gave him a standing ovation.

Becoming more formal, Dickerson then read the names of all the men from 2nd Platoon who had been killed in action. The first name he read was Doug's. When he had finished reading the names, he signaled and the sorrowful notes of "Taps" filled the hall.

After the last notes faded, Larry Dickerson pulled a sheet of paper from his jacket pocket and spread it on the lectern. He had been working on the speech for months; many of the words had been in his heart for 30 years. The room became quiet. Larry looked up from his notes and began to speak:

> We are also here today to honor you, the men of Second Platoon and others we have today that served with us in Vietnam. Many of you have suffered wounds physically and psychologically and we want you to know that we care about you and appreciate deeply your sacrifices.
>
> Our gathering here today is meant to be one of healing and comradeship. We're especially honored to have the reunion here at American Legion Post 353, named after Douglas Dickey, a Medal of Honor recipient from our platoon who saved a number of us from certain injury and possible death by throwing himself on a grenade on Easter Sunday, 1967. Doug exemplified the traits that James Ver Helst, Victor Van Vactor, Larry Larson, John Szymanski, Marvin Cole, Robert Bryson, Floyd Larrabee, James Rader,[4] Joseph Klein,[5] and the members of Second Platoon demonstrated during those difficult times, that of courage, sacrifice for others, heroism, valor and brotherhood.
>
> This was a great platoon of outstanding young men ...

At that point emotion started to overwhelm Dickerson and his voice began to crack. "... who I have always thought about and have always felt thankful and honored ..."

He choked out the rest of his remarks through sobs. "… and privileged to be their platoon leader. I could not have served with a finer group of young men—for which I will always be thankful. All of you will be in my heart—until the day I die. Thank you."

As he walked back to his seat, wiping tears from his eyes, the crowd rose and gave him a standing ovation, many of them were also wiping their eyes.

Later that evening, Dickerson asked Leona Dickey to speak. She walked to the lectern and took the microphone, and said, "Can you hear me?" The group said they could. "I'm not used to doing this," she said. The room became quiet. She looked down at the piece of paper in her hands and then looked up at the room full of people. "I wrote this after we'd been to Washington and—I don't know why—I write a lot of things. I'll try and stumble through it for you." She looked down at the paper. "I call this poem 'The Medal.' None of my kids have ever heard it because I write and then I hide the stuff, because I think it's so poor…"

Leona Dickey then read the poem she had written after attending the Medal of Honor ceremony. When she finished reading the poem, Leona Dickey looked up at the crowd and said quietly, "That's it." Everyone in the room stood and applauded. She looked around the room, smiled, paused, and then walked back to her seat.

Harold Dickey said little throughout the evening but stayed close to his wife, often reaching over to hold her hand. When he was asked to say something to the group, Harold Dickey thanked everybody for coming. Then, gently pulling Leona to his side, he proudly said they had celebrated their 50th wedding anniversary last year. Everyone applauded. For the rest of the evening, Harold Dickey beamed proudly, his eyes glistening as he looked over the group of men who had come from all over the country to honor his oldest boy.

Given an opportunity to speak, one of the men from the Marine Corps League stood. He took the microphone and explained that he had fought on Guadalcanal. He congratulated the platoon for finally having a reunion, although he thought it was a shame it had taken them 30 years. He said his unit from Guadalcanal had just held their 50th reunion. Then he told them he was sure this wouldn't be their last reunion. "Because, once you've found each other, believe me, you won't let loose, because you are a family."

Doc Long said the closing prayer at the end of the evening. He began by thanking the Lord for bringing them together. He ended the prayer: "And we ask Thee to say hello to our departed comrades. We haven't forgotten them in 30 years. We'll never forget them."

The platoon got together for a short meeting before they left Ohio to go back to their homes. They decided they should have a reunion every year. They also decided they would move their reunion around the country so they could meet the families of the other men they had lost in Vietnam.

Lionel Lawson said of that first reunion: "It was *very* emotional to see all the guys after 30 years ... and what we went through. It was a good time, it was a fun time—a lot of joking, a lot of laughing ... a *lot* of crying."

"We were all afraid to go there," Doc Long said of the first reunion and meeting the Dickey family. "We were all a little bit shook up," he said, "but it was kind of like if you left home—and never talked to your mom and dad for like ten years—and then went home, without causing them any trouble while you were gone—and you went home—and how happy they would be to see you. That's kind of how it was. They were really really happy to see us and really glad that we came to pay our respects, and to see them."

"That was probably the best feeling of my life," Greg Long said, "'cause up till then—it's been 30 years—and up till then, I'd often wondered what happened to them [the platoon] and what happened to Doug's family."

"It's something you learn to live with," Bill Dorsey said of having a man die to save his life. "It's something that you often question. There's a great amount of grief that goes along with it, because, in a lot of ways, maybe you blame yourself. It was a situation we were all put into," he said. Then, thinking of Doug Dickey, he said, "And he was just brave enough to do what he felt, and wanted, to do—to keep all of us from dying. He was there at the time and took it upon himself, and yeah, it's a load to carry." Then Dorsey added, "But after I met his mom and his family, there was a lot of that [grief] went away—a lot of it—that I had lived with for a long time."

After the 1997 reunion, Leona Dickey kept in regular contact with the members of the platoon. She called them "my boys." As far as she was concerned, they were family. They phoned her often. They called her "Mama Dickey" or "Ma' Dickey." She loved that.

CHAPTER 23

A Brotherhood

"From this day to the ending of the world, but we in it shall be remembered—We few, we happy few, we band of brothers; For he to-day that sheds his blood with me Shall be my brother..."

SHAKESPEARE, *HENRY V*

The following year, the platoon's reunion was held in Mason City, Iowa—the hometown of Jim Ver Helst. Jim's mother and father were elated to have the men come to their town. Ray and Isabelle Ver Helst had wanted to know about their son's time in Vietnam for decades. Ray Ver Helst had even put an ad in the "Mail Call" section of *Leatherneck* magazine eleven months after Jim was killed asking for anyone who knew their son to contact them. Having the platoon come to their hometown was an answer to their prayers.

Jim Ver Helst

Isabelle and Dale Layman had two children. Jim was their second boy. He was born on April 1, 1947, in Kewanee, Illinois. His older brother, Jack, had been born two years earlier. Dale Layman unexpectedly died of a massive heart attack, just short of his 28th birthday. Isabelle found herself a young widow with two little boys. Jim was not quite two when his father died.

Isabelle and Ray Ver Helst were introduced by some family friends. Ray was a mechanic from Mason City. He was immediately smitten by Isabelle and loved her two little boys. It didn't take long for Ray to ask Isabelle to marry him. They moved to Nora Springs and Ray adopted Jack and Jim. David was born in 1951 and the family moved to Mason City a year later.

Mason City might be the ideal American town. Meredith Willson grew up in Mason City and immortalized his hometown in his hit musical, *The Music Man*. Like the mythical River City, Mason City is a distinctly musical community. It's a cheerful patriotic town which marks its holidays with concerts, festivals, and parades. When the film version of the musical starring Robert Preston and Shirley Jones was released in 1962, it was premiered in downtown Mason City at the Palace Theater. Despite a glamorous life spent on Broadway and in Hollywood, Meredith Willson never forgot his hometown. He returned often and when he passed away, he was brought home from California and laid to rest alongside his family in the cemetery in Mason City.[1]

The Ver Helst boys all participated in sports and, like just about everybody in Mason City, they all played some type of musical instrument in school. Jim played a drum in the school band.

Ray Ver Helst had been diagnosed with diabetes when he was a child. It was the reason he was turned away when he tried to enlist during World War II. However, Ray never let it slow him down. He was an outdoorsman and athlete. His family had a farm in nearby Nora Springs and he took the boys out there regularly and taught them to hunt and fish. When they weren't at school or doing chores, his sons were often swimming or using the gym at the YMCA downtown. Ray was a skilled mechanic and earned a good living fixing everything from automobiles to washing machines. He earned some extra money teaching classes on repairing equipment or tuning carburetors.

Jim Ver Helst distinguished himself as an athlete and became one of Mason City High School's best wrestlers. He worked hard to be a strong wrestler and gathered an assortment of barbells and weights and put together a gym in their basement. The local newspaper often mentioned his wrestling victories while he was in high school.

Jack learned how tough his younger brother was one day after his father brought home some boxing gloves. The two boys decided to go out in the front yard and do a little boxing. They hadn't been sparring for more than a few seconds when Jim landed a solid punch. "He hit me in the nose," Jack said. "I said to myself, 'Well, that was just luck.'" Jack regained his composure and moved in on Jim again. "And the next time—he hit me again!" Jack laughed telling the story. It dawned on him that Jim was a lot faster and could hit a lot harder than he could. "I realized I was going to get the worst of it," he said with a chuckle. "I never put the gloves on with him again."

Although Jim was a good athlete, most people remember that he was always building something, especially mechanical things. As a little boy, he built a go-cart. Then he built a motor scooter. He not only built the motorbike, but also researched the motor vehicle regulations and made sure it was street-legal. He even got it registered. He could be seen zipping around Mason City on his little motorbike. He taught himself to weld, and then built his own arc welder.

Jim was four years older than Dave. Dave looked up to his older brother. "He was a tough guy," Dave Ver Helst said, "but he was a gentleman. He was my example for how I should behave and act around girls." Dave remembered Jim talking to him one day when he was in junior high. Jim said he had seen Dave walking downtown with one of the girls from school that afternoon and had noticed that Dave had been walking on the inside of the sidewalk, while the girl had been walking along the curb. Jim reminded his little brother that a gentleman should always walk on the curb-side of the sidewalk when walking with a lady. He told Dave it was a sign of respect. "He reminded me to be considerate and respectful of other people and especially the opposite sex," Dave Ver Helst said. "He was my role model."[2]

By the time Jim graduated from high school, he was not only a top athlete, but also a skilled mechanic and welder. While the new graduates scrambled to find a job after high school, Jim Ver Helst's talents, particularly as a welder, gave him a number of opportunities. He was hired by the Kewanee Boiler Corporation, located in his mother's hometown. He lived with his grandparents while working there. They were delighted to have him.

The managers at the factory were impressed by Jim's skill and put him to work as one of their micro welders. He was making so much money as a welder, he was able to buy his dream car. It was a 1966 Mustang. "He loved that car!" Jack Ver Helst said with a laugh. "It was brand new when he got it," he said. "A burgundy Mustang with black leather interior; four-on-the-floor—with a tach' and the whole bit." Jim and his father shared a love of mechanical things. "He really enjoyed that car too," Jack said with a laugh remembering his father's obvious joy when Jim brought the Mustang home.[3]

Jim Ver Helst knew it was just a matter of time before he got his draft notice. The managers at the boiler plant told him they could get him a deferment. It was considered an essential wartime industry because many of the boilers they made were used by the military. They told him he could probably qualify for a II-A deferment. "But he didn't want anything of that," his brother Dave said. "He wanted to be a Marine."

After working in Kewanee for about a year, Jim went down to the recruiting office and enlisted in the Marines. Ray and Isabelle were very proud that Jim had decided to enlist. "He was just a patriotic individual," Jack Ver Helst said. "And he wanted to serve his country." Then he laughed remembering his brother. "And he was a hard-nosed kid."

While Jim was in Vietnam, Isabelle mailed him packages. He wrote once and told her Slim Jims were particularly popular. Most importantly, the meat sticks, vacuum-packed in plastic wrappers, didn't spoil in the Vietnamese heat. After that, he received hundreds of Slim Jims in the mail. He shared them with the other guys in the platoon. They were always happy when Jim got a package from his mother.

Ray was working at Mason City Appliance in March 1967. Jack had moved to Boone, Iowa, and was attending college and working at the YMCA there. Dave was a sophomore at Mason City High School. Ray kept the store's repair van at his house and drove it to work every morning. He would drop Dave off at school on his way to the store. "We were just about to walk out the door when we saw the Marines coming up," Dave said. "And, of course, it didn't really need any explanation when we saw that," he said. "That's something I will always remember."

Jim was escorted home by Lee Cornick, a friend from high school. Lee had enlisted in the Marines and had also been sent to Vietnam. Jim was buried with full military honors.

A few weeks after Jim was buried, a letter from Bob Kelley arrived. He was frank and honest with Ray and Isabelle, explaining that 2nd Platoon was leading the company in an operation near the DMZ. "James was one of the four front Marines in his platoon and was killed instantly by machine gun fire when the attack commenced." Bob Kelley closed his letter to Ray and Isabelle Ver Helst: "Lance Corporal Ver Helst was one of the bravest, most courageous Marines I have ever known. Your deep loss is felt by every officer and Marine in the company. Please accept our most sincere sympathy in your bereavement."[4]

In the months following Jim's death, Ray and Isabelle yearned to know more about their son's last months and days. They contacted the Marine Corps, but the officials there didn't know any more than the few sentences in the telegram notifying them that Jim had been killed. They tried to contact Bob Kelley, but he had been medically evacuated from Vietnam. All Jim's other friends had left the battalion and were scattered all over the country.

Unable to reach anyone, Ray put an ad in the "Mail Call" section of *Leatherneck* magazine. His ad appeared in the February 1968 issue, and read: "Mr. and Mrs. Ray Ver Helst, 516 N. Madison, Mason City, Iowa 50401, to hear from anyone who served with their son LCPL James L. Ver Helst, "C" Co., 1st Bn., 4th Marines, who lost his life near Gio Linh, Easter Sunday, 1967."[5]

By then, Kent Hansen was home. He had been discharged and was getting ready to go back to school. He had subscribed to *Leatherneck* in boot camp and the magazines still came to his parents' house in Utah. "I would thumb through them when I stopped by," he said. "I saw that issue and noticed the note about Jim and remarked to my parents, 'Hey, I knew this guy.'" A few weeks later, his parents told him the Ver Helsts were coming by. They had written Ray and Isabelle and told them Kent had served with Jim. Ray and Isabelle had driven all the way from Iowa to talk to Kent. "I didn't have any idea what I would say to them," Kent said. He had only been home for a few months himself. He couldn't imagine trying to tell them about Jim being shot to pieces by a machine gun. "I don't really remember what I said—It wasn't much."[6]

Ray and Isabelle had been looking forward to having the platoon come to Mason City since they had met most of them in Ohio the year before. It meant the rest of their family could meet the men Jim had served with in Vietnam. The reunion was scheduled over the Memorial Day weekend and members of the platoon began arriving in Mason City on Thursday and Friday.

The platoon had located Bob Kelley in California after the reunion in Rossburg and invited him to Mason City. Kelley had stayed in the Marines and had returned to Vietnam in 1972 as an advisor. He was one of the Americans who fought alongside the Vietnamese Marines during the 1972 Easter Invasion. Kelley retired as a lieutenant colonel after more than twenty years as a Marine officer. He came to the reunion with some trepidation. "I was afraid they would hate me," he said. "I had been the guy in charge and you never know how people process that." His fears were unfounded. "It turned out great for me," he said. Kelley was able to answer questions some of the men had had for years regarding decisions and events in 1967. It was reassuring for many of the men to learn there had been thought and planning behind events that seemed random, or even absurd, to 19- or 20-year-old riflemen in 1967.

Kelley had commanded Company C for about five months. Those five months, however, had changed his life. Nothing before or since compared with the responsibility he shouldered while he was commanding his company in Vietnam. He had won battles, but he had also written dozens of letters to the parents and the widows of those killed. He had thought of the men he had commanded in Vietnam every day since. To Kelley, they would always be "my men." At the reunion, he told them that commanding Company C was the "greatest event in my life." Then, flushed with emotion, he told them, "I remember each one of you simply as a hero that I was privileged to serve with."[7]

On Sunday, the platoon and the Ver Helst family gathered at Jim's grave to hold their memorial service. "We are here today for James Ver Helst, whom we loved," Dickerson said. "We want him to know that he and others who were killed in action are always in our hearts."[8]

The reunions also helped resolve unanswered questions. "We went through hell getting those guys [the dead] out of there, and now we know where their final resting place is," said Ray Baer. "It just makes us feel so much better."[9]

The weekend was especially healing for Ray and Isabelle. As with most parents, they knew very little about the circumstances of their son's death. "I was never in the service," Ray Ver Helst said. "It's hard for me to realize what they went through."[10]

They heard the men tell their stories and the Ver Helst family got answers to questions they had asked themselves for more than 30 years. They met men who had been mentioned in Jim's letters. Isabelle said after the reunion, "Last night at dinner, hearing them talk about Jim, it was almost like he was with us again. I know today he would just be grinning down at these guys."[11]

CHAPTER 24

The Last Casualty

None of the men in 2nd Platoon were ready for the tragedy that struck in the year after the Mason City reunion. On September 4, 1998, Larry Dickerson rode his bicycle out to a forested area and shot himself.[1] No one knows for sure why he decided to take his own life four months after the Mason City reunion.

Most of the men in 2nd Platoon count Dickerson as the platoon's last casualty from Vietnam.

Combat leadership carries a terrible paradox. Young officers, like Dickerson, were expected to love and care for the Marines they led. One of the first lessons new officers were taught when they began their training at Quantico was John Lejeune's *Marine Corps Order No. 29*, titled: "Relations between officers and men." An excerpt was printed in the first pages of the *Marine Officer's Guide*.[2] Lejeune stressed that there should be a "spirit of comradeship and brotherhood in arms" among all Marines. When he wrote it, Lejeune sought to make sure there wasn't a class divide among Marines as there was between officers and enlisted men in European armies. Lejeune defined the leadership responsibility of Marine officers:

> The relationship between officers and enlisted men should in no sense be that of superior and inferior nor that of master and servant, but rather that of teacher and scholar. In fact, it should partake of the nature of the relation between father and son, to the extent that officers, especially commanding officers, are responsible for the physical, mental, and moral welfare, as well as the discipline and military training, of the young men under their command who are serving the Nation in the Marine Corps.[3]

The cruel irony, however, is that young officers also have to lead those young men into battle. Platoon leaders, like Dickerson, saw the immediate results of their decisions. Despite their best efforts, their Marines were killed and maimed right in front of them. They gave orders and then had to hear the screams after enemy bullets and explosives had torn their men apart.

Dickerson's concern for the lives of his men had driven him to become a skilled tactician and battlefield leader. He shared the dangers and hardships of his men. He was wounded himself and was decorated for his bravery on the battlefield. The men in the platoon felt they had been fortunate to have Dickerson as their platoon leader—and they told him that often. Despite those assurances, it seemed that Larry Dickerson counted every man lost in Vietnam as a personal failure. He seemed to harbor a deep unresolvable guilt about those losses. It didn't seem to matter how many times his men assured him he had done the best job any human could have done in his position. Larry Dickerson just couldn't seem to forgive himself.

Bringing the platoon and the families together with the reunions had been a tremendous blessing to everyone and had helped heal many broken hearts. Despite all he had done for his men and their families, it seemed Larry Dickerson still couldn't forgive himself.

Steve Pruitt had gotten to know Larry Dickerson well since their first phone call in 1996. They often met and their families had become close. But Steve had noticed Larry never really seemed to be at ease when he met the families of those killed or talked with the men who had been badly wounded. "He had this smile on his face, but you could tell it was eating his heart out," Steve said.

Doc Long remembered a discussion he had with Larry Dickerson one night. "'Doc,' he says, 'You know, I loved you guys—you were my family,' he said. 'But I was the one who had to send you out to...get yourselves killed,' he says. 'I always had to make those decisions.'" Then Greg Long added, "You know, the day Doug died—he landed on Larry..." Then Long said of Dickerson, "He had too big of a heart..."

Larry Dickerson's wife was asked later if she thought the reunions had triggered his suicide. She said they had actually helped. Her husband had struggled with Vietnam for years. The reunions actually seemed to help—but just not enough.

CHAPTER 25

A Living Memorial

They shall grow not old, as we that are left grow old:
Age shall not weary them, nor the years condemn.
At the going down of the sun and in the morning
We will remember them.

ROBERT LAURENCE BINYON: *FOR THE FALLEN* (1914)

Larry Dickerson's suicide was devastating for the men in the platoon. Many were furious at him for doing it. It was senseless. Several of them asked themselves what they should have done to help him. In the course of discussing Larry's death, they questioned continuing the reunions. They decided the reunions had to go on.

Larry Larson

The year after Mason City, the platoon held their reunion in Carmel, California, Larry Larson's hometown. Larry Dickerson had contacted Robert Larson, Larry's father, after the first reunion. Robert Larson was struggling with health problems at that point and relayed the information to his son, Bob. Bob was Larry's older brother. Bob and his wife, Mona, flew out to the reunion in Mason City. Bob was somewhat leery of attending at first. "We wanted to see what this was all about," he said later.

Bob was surprised by the emotional impact of meeting his brother's buddies. "It was pretty incredible," he said. "It was great!" While in Iowa, Bob and Mona offered to host the next reunion in Carmel. Bob wanted his father and the rest of their family to meet the platoon.

Robert and Jessie Larson moved to Carmel from San Jose in 1959. Robert worked for Kelly-Moore Paints and was offered a transfer to the Monterey area. He jumped at the chance to move his family from the sprawling city and settle on the sleepy, picturesque Monterey Peninsula. Robert and Jessie had two boys, Bob and Larry. Bob was the eldest. Larry was 19 months younger than Bob. The Larsons moved into a comfortable little house a few blocks from the Carmel Mission. Bob enrolled at Carmel High School; Larry was enrolled at Junipero Serra School, the parochial school at the Carmel Mission.

Jessie Larson was raised in a large lively Mexican clan in San Jose. Family was everything to her. Jessie Larson's home was always filled with music and the smell of cooking. "It was always a very musical home," Mona Larson said about her husband's family. Their home was also always full of kids. Jessie liked young people and welcomed all the neighborhood children, and she loved getting a chance to feed them.

While Bob became a star athlete at Carmel High, Larry embraced his religious classes at Junipero Serra. Larry served as an altar boy at Mass and volunteered to lead youth ministry groups. The Carmel Mission became his home-away-from-home and he was well known and liked by the nuns and priests. He eventually told his parents he wanted to be a priest.

Bob went on to San Francisco State after he graduated. Instead of following Bob to Carmel High when he finished Junipero Serra, Larry went to Holy Redeemer, a Catholic seminary high school in Oakland. Larry's plan was to graduate from Holy Redeemer then enroll at St. Mary's College in nearby Moraga to begin his studies for the priesthood.

However, in his last year at Holy Redeemer, Larry began seeing more and more obituaries in the newspapers for local boys killed in Vietnam. As a seminary student at St. Mary's, Larry would be exempt from the draft. Every week, however, Larry saw more and more articles about young men killed in the rapidly expanding war. What bothered him deeply was reading that many of the young men were married and left behind widows and children. It weighed heavily on his conscience.

Larry Larson came to a decision. He decided he would enlist and go to Vietnam before becoming a priest. He felt it was his duty to spare at least one young father or husband from having to go to war. Furthermore, Larry decided he would enlist in the Marines. His uncle Carl had been a Marine during World War II and the family admired him. Larry didn't tell his family about his decision. The issue was deeply personal for him.

Unlike his older brother, Larry had never been too athletic. He knew he had to get in shape before he went in the Marines and embarked on a program to lose weight and build up his muscles. His newfound enthusiasm for exercise was curious to his family, but they just accepted it as a healthy change.

Robert and Jessie had no idea what Larry was planning until he came home one day and announced that he had just enlisted in the Marines. They were stunned.

He explained that he had gotten a leave of absence from St Mary's and planned to continue his path to the priesthood after he returned from Vietnam.[1]

Bob had always been protective of his little brother. Larry was a gentle soul and Bob never imagined his younger brother would end up in Vietnam, much less as a Marine. Bob always assumed he would be the one who went to Vietnam. He figured he would enlist or be drafted after he graduated from San Francisco State. Bob had always taken comfort from knowing that his little brother would be exempt from the draft as a student at the seminary.

After learning Larry had enlisted, Bob disenrolled from San Francisco State and enlisted in the Army. He hoped that somehow he could take Larry's place in Vietnam. Regardless, Bob knew one thing for sure: he wasn't going to stay in college while his little brother went off to fight in Vietnam. By the time Larry was going through boot camp in San Diego, Bob had also enlisted and was on his way to the army's boot camp.

Larry graduated from the recruit depot in San Diego in April 1966. After finishing boot camp, he was sent up to Camp Pendleton for infantry training. Larry's plans changed again while he was training at Camp Pendleton. While on liberty in San Diego, Larry met a petite strawberry blonde named Sharon—and fell in love. Larry brought Sharon with him when he went home to Carmel just before leaving for Vietnam. He wanted her to meet his family. "You could see it was pretty serious for him," Bob said.

Deployed to Vietnam in October 1966, Larry joined Jack Westerman's battalion. He wrote home regularly. He and Sharon kept up a steady exchange of letters and their relationship deepened despite the distance. Jessie Larson worried about her son and sent him boxes of food and goodies almost every week.

Larry's letters became more serious while he was in Vietnam. War was more brutal than he had imagined. He especially felt sorry for the Vietnamese villagers. As his months in Vietnam passed, it seemed more and more that Larry yearned to build a simple, peaceful life when he came home. "I think he wanted to have a family of his own," Bob said.

On March 18, 1967, 2nd Platoon was on board the USS *Ogden* making final preparations for the landing that would mark the beginning of Operation *Beacon Hill*. The amtracs were fueled and loaded and the company gunny was distributing ammunition and grenades. The corpsmen were stuffing their kits with extra battle dressings and signing for their allotment of morphine syrettes.

Sharon had recorded a tape and sent it to Larry a couple weeks earlier. He listened to it over and over. He loved hearing her voice. Larry decided to borrow a tape recorder and make a tape to send home to his family. Sitting in the troop compartment on board the *Ogden*, Larry recorded a 20-minute message to his family. He dropped the tape and a bundle of letters in the mailbox on the *Ogden* a few hours before 2nd Platoon squeezed into the amtracs and headed for the beach just north of the Cua Viet River.

Larry had earned the respect and admiration of his fellow Marines in Vietnam. He was courageous in firefights, yet was kind and considerate, especially to the villagers they encountered. The men in the platoon nicknamed him "Packrat" because he squirreled away all sorts of things in his pockets and backpack. He seemed to pack the stuff away knowing that someone would eventually need it. Then, when someone needed something, whether it was a bayonet or a set of bootlaces, Larry would pull it out of his pack and hand it to the man with a big smile.

Larry Larson was the first member of the platoon killed on Easter Sunday. He had just taken over as the platoon's point man when they hit the NVA position. Larry Larson was killed instantly in the first seconds of the ambush.

On Tuesday, March 28, Jessie Larson saw a dark-colored government sedan pull up in front of the house. A Marine officer knocked on their door a few moments later. The officer was in his dress uniform. She could see Bishop Harry Clinch and Monsignor Marron standing on the walkway behind the officer. Jessie Larson knew her worst nightmare had come true. "When my mother saw the Bishop standing there, she knew my brother was dead," Bob Larson said.

Bob had managed to get leave over the Easter weekend on his way to the Officer Candidate School at Fort Benning, Georgia. He wanted to spend Easter with his mother and father. With Larry in Vietnam, he wanted to be home for the holiday. He especially wanted to be there for his mother. He and a friend had decided to walk into Carmel to do some shopping that day. "All of a sudden, I had this overwhelming feeling that I had to go back to the house," he said. Bob got back just after the Marines had left. Bishop Clinch was sitting with his parents.

When Larry's body came home to Carmel, the mortuary told Bob the military had designated it a "closed casket." They weren't supposed to open it under any circumstances. Bob had heard troubling stories about carelessness in the military morgues in Vietnam. He had heard about bodies being mixed up and sent to the wrong families. He went to the Carmel mortuary and demanded they open the casket. Bob was insistent. "I just had to make sure it was him," he said. "I just wanted to make sure it was him." They reluctantly agreed to open the casket. "It was him," he said softly. Larry was buried with full military honors at the Golden Gate National Cemetery in San Bruno. Sharon was there. A couple of weeks later, the package with the tape recording he made on the *Ogden* arrived in the mail.

One day, months after Larry had been buried, Bob came home to Carmel on leave. The house was still quiet and dark. He was really worried about his mother. She had always been such a lively little woman. Since Larry had been killed, she seemed to have lost interest in life. She couldn't even bring herself to say Larry's name. She would leave the room if people started talking about him. It broke his heart. "This isn't what Larry would have wanted," Bob said to his parents. He went to the front window and yanked the drapes open, flooding the living room with sunshine. He went over to the console stereo that had always filled the house with music and turned it on. "Our lives have to go on," he said.

On September 22, 1968, the Catholic Diocese in Carmel named the Little League baseball field next to the Carmel Mission and the Junipero Serra School after Larry. Greg Nichols had been discharged from the naval hospital in Oakland by then, although he was still recovering from his wounds. He heard about the dedication and came down for the ceremony. During the dedication, Bishop Clinch and Monsignor Marron spoke about Larry—and how he had so much faith for such a young man.

Bob finished the officer course at Fort Benning and was commissioned as an infantry officer. He was told he was exempted from service in Vietnam because his family had already lost a son in combat. Bob, however, refused to consider the exemption and volunteered to go to Vietnam. "I was pretty angry," he said, reflecting on those times almost 50 years later. "I think I had some idea that I was going to get some kind of 'revenge' for Larry."

Before he left for Vietnam, Bob rekindled his romance with Mona. She had been his sweetheart when he was attending middle school in San Jose. Mona had always been close to the family and Bob had phoned her when Larry was killed. They started dating seriously.

Bob saw action in Vietnam although his one-year tour was cut short when the army had to reinforce the Demilitarized Zone in Korea after the North Koreans seized the USS *Pueblo*. He finished his overseas assignment leading patrols along the DMZ in Korea.

After two years as a soldier, Bob came home and went back to finish college, this time at San Jose State. He and Mona married and Bob went to work for Bank of America. They raised two boys, Adam and Keith.

In the following decades, Jessie Larson sprang back to life, although she was never quite the same woman she had been before Larry was killed. She loved having children in her home and started babysitting for several families in the area. The kids loved her and their parents trusted her. There were always people coming and going. Once when Bob stopped by the house, he found Clint Eastwood sitting between his mother and father on the couch, watching television with them. His mother explained that "Clint" had come by to pick up his kids and she had asked him to stay for dinner. Jessie Larson had that kind of home. You didn't want to leave.

Jessie was thrilled when Bob and Mona brought their two boys down for visits. Her grandchildren seemed to help her come to terms with Larry's loss. On one visit, she took little Adam aside. She went to the closet where a lot of Larry's things were stored and pulled out the little phonograph Larry had used as a boy. Then she pulled out the carrying case where Larry had kept his collection of 45 rpm records.

Somehow, she seemed to know that Adam would like Larry's record player and records. She was right.

Adam played Larry's records over and over and never seemed to tire of listening to the collection of rock and roll songs and ballads from the early sixties. Adam and Keith would play the records and jump around, dancing to the music. It made Jessie happy to see her grandsons enjoying Larry's records. At a memorial for Larry years later, Adam told the group that, although he had never met his uncle, he felt he had gotten to know Larry through the music they both loved. Larry had helped bring the love of music to another generation of Larsons.

In May 1999, the platoon converged on Carmel for their third reunion. Jessie Larson had passed away in 1993. Larry's father, Robert, was thrilled with the show of respect and love for his son. Many other members of the Larson family came to Carmel to meet the men from Larry's platoon. The Larsons gave the men in the platoon and their wives a tour of Point Lobos and took them for a drive around Pebble Beach. They went to Mass at the Carmel Mission in honor of Larry and visited Larson Field to see the baseball field that had been named after Larry.

On Sunday night, the Larsons hosted a spaghetti dinner at their home in Carmel. Bob had mentioned earlier that he had a tape Larry had recorded just before they went ashore on *Beacon Hill*. He asked them if they wanted to listen to it. Everyone said they wanted to hear it.

Later, after dinner, they gathered around the portable tape player. When Bob turned on the tape recorder, Larry's voice filled the room. His first words were: "March eighteenth, the day before Operation *Beacon Hill* ..."

It was like a portal through time for the men standing there—it took them back to Vietnam. While Larry talked, they could hear the shipboard sounds in the background. They could hear their own voices from 32 years ago coming out of the recorder. Doc Long could hear himself joking around and teasing someone. Lionel Lawson could hear himself asking the guys in his squad if they had taken care of one chore or another.

Larry's voice sounded upbeat, but also a bit weary. There are jaunty, cheerful voices in the background. Larry began the tape to his family by explaining the racket in the background. "The voices you hear in the background are those of my comrades," he said. There were loud outbursts in the background—the sound of young men horsing around in the cramped troop compartment. "That's how we are. It's war ... it's war. We're fighters—our job is to fight. It's no thrills—mostly chills. But, we do what we do—what has to be done."[2]

Larry explained he was making the tape on board the USS *Ogden* as they were getting ready to make a landing. He mentioned he had been considered for meritorious promotion, but dismissed it as unimportant. "I don't give the sole of my boots for rank—as long as I'm doing my job, that's all that matters. I risk my neck for that, and, I think, in the end, for the others. But as long as I know I'm doing my best for the Marine Corps and for our country, for the love of God; that's all I want."

Larry then dictated a series of messages to family members and close family friends. "I miss everyone so much. Please tell them," he said.

He told his family he had gotten a tape and photo from Sharon and that he had to kick everybody out of the room when he listened to her voice because he missed her so much. "I just about started bawling," he said.

He joked about the battalion's recent liberty in the Philippines. "The town will never be the same—especially after One-Four has left it." He laughed and mentioned brawling with sailors in town and that the bars would be replacing mirrors and fixing broken furniture for a while after they left.

For the last half of the tape he spoke to his mother and father. "Pop, if I do become a father, I hope to be like you, with all your goodwill. My father, I love you very much," he said. "Pop, please don't let the pressures and worries of the job get you down. Remember, we all love you. Nothing but you is all we want."

To his mother, he said: "I long to hear from you. For, by your words, I gain my courage. Mother, please don't sob. For there will always be worries and concerns as long as we live. But we must accept what we have in front of us and do the best. I love you very much and I hope for the day when we will all be together again." He went on, "Please do not be sad, for with your song and your smile we have love and let us be in appreciation for what we have. And thank God for our blessings."

Twenty-year-old Larry Larson could see the tape was about to run out. He finished by telling his family: "All I can say is I love you, I love you! I would have said this all through the whole tape and all the tapes there ever is in this whole world. Just remember, I do love you and all I do is for you. Pray for the Lord thy God."

The tape cuts off at that point.

Greg Nichols described the scene when the tape ended: "There wasn't a dry eye in the place."

Bob and Mona were made honorary members of 2nd Platoon. They have attended just about every reunion since.

Victor Van Vactor

In 2000, 2nd Platoon held their reunion in Louisville, Kentucky, and met with Victor Van Vactor's brothers. Victor was the youngest of four boys. His older brothers, Paul, Bobby, and Richard, welcomed the platoon. Victor's parents, Walter and Mabel, had long since passed. The Van Vactors and the platoon members socialized while they cruised up and down the Ohio River on board the *Belle of Louisville*, a restored paddle wheeler. On Sunday, the Marines and the family held a memorial service at Victor's grave.

The Van Vactors are a close and hardworking family. Their father, Walter, only made it through the third grade and supported his family by working in a government warehouse. Yet, he was determined that his boys would be educated. He and Mabel scrimped and saved and managed to send all of their boys through parochial schools. With the exception of Victor, all the Van Vactor boys eventually went on to college.

Victor's oldest brother, Paul, had been a Marine. Victor tried to join the Marines right after he graduated from Trinity High School in Louisville in 1965. The Marine recruiters turned him away because he had a history of asthma. Victor then tried to enlist in the army, and was also turned away because of his asthma.

Unable to get in the service, he took a job as a go-fer at a car dealership. The dealership fired him after he got in an accident ferrying a van from one car lot to another. Richard remembered that the van had flipped over in high winds while Victor was driving it.

After losing his job at the dealership, Victor decided to try his luck with the Marine recruiter again. By then, the Marine Corps had somewhat relaxed its standards due to the rapid escalation of the war in Vietnam. This time, the Marines took him. "He was really proud of being a Marine," Richard Van Vactor said of his little brother.[3]

"I believe Victor graduated from high school with the idea that he was going to join the Marines," Richard said. "I'm sure he liked being a Marine. From his letters, he was enthusiastic. I don't remember him complaining about anything. My recollection was that he went there [Vietnam] with relish. He really was happy," Richard said. "That's my remembrance of him. He was just a really great kid."

"I remember it like it was yesterday," Richard said of the day he was told Victor had been killed. "I was at work over at the bank. I was a clerk—going to school and working at the same time. And I got a phone call," he said. "And you can imagine sitting in a room with four or five other people and someone calls and tells you your brother's been killed. What do you do?" Richard Van Vactor said. "Actually, I remember thinking to myself: 'I'll be glad when five years pass because, surely, this will be a lot better.'" He then added, "Well, of course, it does diminish with time … but you still … I say Victor's name to myself every day."

It was much worse for their mother. Victor was the youngest and the family doted on him. His mother adored him. "I'm telling you, there's nothing like a mother," Richard said. "Mothers are the most special people," he said. "Try to imagine the horror of a mother seeing a Marine in uniform and a chaplain come to your door," he said. "And of course, she knew when she saw who was at the door. You know right away. You don't even need someone to tell you," he said. "The telling is just the details. You already know the story." Victor had always been outgoing and friendly. He made friends wherever he went. Richard remembered that the funeral home was full of people the entire time Victor was there.

Mabel Van Vactor died in 1977. She was buried beside Victor. Victor's medals and the flag from his casket were buried with her. That was one of her last requests.

The three Van Vactor brothers still get together for lunch at least once a month. They joke around and argue about current events. Victor frequently comes up at some point during the lunch. "It would have been fascinating to see how he would have grown up and matured and what his views would have been," Richard said. "We wish there could be four of us here at lunch—not three."[4]

John Szymanski

The platoon held its fifth reunion in Carson City, Nevada, in the summer of 2001. They came to Carson City to honor John Szymanski. Loretta Szymanski was thrilled when the platoon finally found her. She always had a feeling she would hear from them. "I used to tell my mom, 'One of these days, I'm going to hear from those guys, because he [John] was so well loved.'"

John Szymanski grew up in Trenton, New Jersey, and enlisted before he turned 18—his father had to sign for him to join the Marines. After he graduated from boot camp, the Marine Corps sent him to the guard force at the Naval Ammunition Depot in Hawthorne, Nevada.

The ammunition depot was established after a disaster at the Lake Denmark Naval Ammunition Depot in New Jersey. On July 10, 1926, a bolt of lightning struck one of the buildings and set off a cascading series of explosions and fires that lasted four days and killed 19 people.[5] As a result of the Lake Denmark disaster, it was decided to move the depot to remote Nevada, away from any population centers. The dry desert climate was also ideal for storing the explosive materials. Eventually, the depot had thousands of bunkers sprawling over more than 200 square miles. The tiny town of Hawthorne is located right up alongside the depot—also putting it in the middle of nowhere. It is 120 miles from Carson City. Most of those in Hawthorne worked at the depot.

Loretta's father was a career Marine who had served in both World War I and World War II and had fought on Iwo Jima. He had been assigned to the ammunition depot as a Marine and then went to work there as a civilian after he retired. Loretta went to high school in Hawthorne and got a job working for the Mineral County Treasurer's office after she graduated. One night, while in town with her girlfriends, she met John Szymanski. He asked her if she wanted to go to the movies the next night. She said yes. When they were leaving the theater after that movie, John asked her if she would like to go to the next movie with him. "He told me he knew he was going to marry me," Loretta said. A year later they were married.

John reenlisted in the Marines and he and Loretta were sent to Niagara Falls, New York, where John was assigned as a recruiter. He worked long hours and was often recognized as the outstanding recruiter for the area.[6]

John and Loretta started their family in 1964 when Jimmy arrived. Stephanie came along a year later. John loved being a father, but like a lot of young dads, he often found himself exhausted by toddlers. Loretta remembered returning to the house after leaving John with little Jimmy for a few hours. "And when I came home, here he was—asleep on the couch—and Jimmy's laying on his chest. They were both just sound asleep." She slipped by them, got the camera, and snapped a picture before they woke up.

Toward the end of his assignment, the commanding officer of the recruiting station asked John if he would consider staying on for another year or two. At that time, anyone who was a successful recruiter was a prized asset. John turned down the offer. The war in Vietnam was rapidly escalating and John knew that just about every young man he recruited into the Marines was on his way to Vietnam. He had attended funerals for some of the young men from the area who had been killed in Vietnam. He had learned to play the trumpet in high school and often volunteered to play "Taps" at the funeral ceremonies.

John requested a set of orders to Vietnam. "You know, he was 'all infantry,'" Loretta recalled. "He said, 'I've got to go to Vietnam—I didn't join the Marine Corps to sit behind a desk.'"

When John got his orders to Vietnam, they decided it was best for Loretta to take the kids back to Nevada so she could be close to her parents while he was in Vietnam for the year. They drove out to Nevada and got a house in the Babbitt housing area near Hawthorne. She and her mother then drove John out to Camp Pendleton, to catch his flight to Vietnam. "We got there at nighttime and that's the last time I ever saw him." John kissed Loretta goodbye and then walked around one of the old wooden barracks buildings to the embarkation point. "The barracks were kind of lifted off the ground and I could see his legs walking around to the back—that was the last I saw of him."

Loretta sent care packages of salami, cheese, Vienna sausages, and other food to John regularly. After he had taken out her letter, he would pass the box around and let his men have what they wanted. Some of them didn't get letters, much less boxes of food.

Before he left, Loretta made John promise he would tell her everything that was going on in Vietnam. She had been raised in a Marine family and knew her husband was about to go through something horrendous. She wanted to go through it with him—as much as she could. He promised he would—and he did. He told her about some of the horrors he saw. In one letter, he described leading a patrol that recovered the body of a Marine. The man's body had been obscenely mutilated and hung up in a tree by the Viet Cong. One day a small package arrived. "He sent me a pungi stake that he almost fell on," she said.

Loretta and the kids were up at Fernley, northeast of Lake Tahoe, with her parents when she found out John had been killed. The phone rang and her mother handed it to her father. "My father never got phone calls," she said. "I could hear him say, 'Yes, yes … OK.'"

Her father hung up the phone and said to her, "Ski's [John's] been wounded …" Then he told her a couple Marines were on their way to talk to her.

While waiting for the Marines to arrive at the house, Loretta called her brother, Jack. She told him, "I think Ski's been killed." Jack assured her that it wasn't true and told her not to worry. But Loretta Szymanski could feel in her heart that her husband was gone. "I knew," she said. The Marines arrived a little while later. "They came in and said, 'We're sorry …'" Remembering that day still brings Loretta Szymanski to tears. "I can tell you what a wonderful man he was. He was so happy-go-lucky. He would always say to me, 'Baby—don't worry, baby, don't worry.' He loved life—he was always an optimist."[7]

A letter arrived from Bob Kelley about two weeks later. Kelley began the letter: "My dear Mrs. Szymanski, It is with my most heartfelt sympathy that I write to you concerning the recent death of your husband, Staff Sergeant John S. Szymanski …" Bob Kelley then described the action on the afternoon John was killed. He wrote: "Staff Sergeant Szymanski's courageous act saved the lives of at least three of his fellow Marines." He told her they were going to have the Catholic chaplain conduct a requiem Mass for John in the next few days. "All of the officers and the men of the Company will attend in addition to John's many other friends throughout the Battalion."

Bob Kelley closed his letter: "Your husband was one of the bravest, most courageous Marines I have ever known. His men idolized him and patterned their actions after his exemplary leadership. Your deep loss is felt by every officer and Marine in the Company. Please accept our most sincere sympathy in your bereavement."

Although John Szymanski never made it to Quantico, the Marine Corps posthumously promoted him to second lieutenant. He was also posthumously awarded the Silver Star for his actions on March 23, 1967.

Loretta had John buried in the little cemetery in Carson City and bought a house there at about the same time. She chose Carson City because she and John had often driven up there when they were newlyweds. John had said he would like to retire in Carson City or Reno. John loved Nevada. Although he was raised in an eastern city, he felt more at home in the West. A man with his imagination and ambition needed space. The wide-open horizons and untamed nature appealed to him. Loretta raised their two children there.

Loretta received a package in the mail after John was buried. It was a pile of letters she had written to him that were being returned. "I had about ten letters returned to me that I had written him that he never got," she said. "And that just broke my heart."

It was tough to live her life without John in the months and years that followed. "When you love somebody like that, you just—I don't know. You just keep going, day after day after day. And try to make it." Raising Jimmy and Stephanie kept her going.

The platoon had found Loretta Szymanski just before their reunion in Carmel and had invited her to meet them there. She was looking forward to meeting Larry Dickerson. "I was so excited because they were telling me that Dickerson was going to be at the reunion and I was going to get to talk to him about Ski. Because they told me he was with him quite a lot." One of the men from the platoon phoned her later and told her about Dickerson's death. "I was heartbroken," she said.

During the reunion in Carson City, the men in the platoon were able to tell Jimmy and Stephanie Szymanski about their dad. They told Loretta about John and how much they admired him and relied on him. "They said they would always go to town, but Ski would stay back and write letters home to me."

In 2008, Loretta Szymanski had John disinterred from the little cemetery in Carson City and reinterred at the Fort Rosecrans National Cemetery overlooking San Diego Bay.

It had been important to have John nearby while she was raising their family in Carson City. However, Loretta Szymanski began to feel that it was time to move John to the National Cemetery after Jim and Stephanie moved out. She had been considering the move for some time.

On one trip to Fort Rosecrans while she was making the arrangements, she ended up talking briefly to a priest who was at the cemetery conducting a service. The short discussion resonated with her. She told the priest about John and how he had been killed saving some of his men in 1967. "He said that a man like John should be resting in 'hallowed ground,'" she said. The priest told her John belonged in a place where he was surrounded by other warriors—men who had died serving the country as he had. She had John moved shortly thereafter. He is now in hallowed ground and his grave will always be tended.

John Szymanski would be proud of his two children. "My kids are just like him," Loretta said. "And that's so funny to see that. It's wonderful. So, he's still living in them." Loretta Szymanski loves to talk about John although it often brings her to tears. "He's always around," she said. "Everybody's guardian angel."

*

The following year, 2nd Platoon went to Washington, D.C., to honor Dick Housh and met with his daughter and one of his two sons. The platoon also used the trip to make a pilgrimage to the Vietnam War Memorial, "The Wall." Many of them hadn't been to the Memorial yet. Visiting The Wall is an emotional experience for anyone. For those who fought in Vietnam, the experience is often overwhelming. Most of the men from the platoon were moved to tears as they touched the familiar names etched into the black granite at the center of Panel 17 East. Leona and Harold Dickey came out for that reunion and stood with the platoon at The Wall.

On years when they couldn't coordinate the reunion with one of the Gold Star families, a platoon member would volunteer to host it. They went to Bill Dorsey's home in 2003. Bill's wife had passed away two years earlier and the platoon wanted to go to the Dorseys' hometown to show their respect for her. "I think that was one of the greatest honors that could have ever been bestowed on me," Bill Dorsey said. "They all wanted to honor my wife because she'd been a part of it [the reunions] from the time it started up, until that point," he said. "And they made the trip from all over the United States to come here to honor her and that was just—again, unbelievable."

"Hedge" Deibert and his family hosted the platoon at their home in Oceanside, California, in 2004. Deibert had led the platoon before Larry Dickerson arrived in Okinawa. "I love my men so much in heart and soul," he said of the Marines he led in Vietnam.

Charlie Runnels hosted the reunion at his home in Maine, in 2005.

They returned to Greenville, Ohio, in 2006 to honor the Dickeys. Harold Dickey had passed away after a fight with cancer in 2004. It had been very tough on Leona. The platoon wanted to show their support for her and her family.

In 2007, Steve Pruitt hosted the reunion in Delaware. Barbara Dickerson and her sons joined the platoon in honoring Larry that year. She and her sons gave them tours of the school Larry had loved so much and the platoon held a memorial service at Larry's grave.

Bob Kelley and his wife, Pat, hosted the reunion in Millbrae, California, in the summer of 2008. Larry Larson is buried in the Golden Gate National Cemetery nearby. As part of the reunion, Bob Larson and the platoon held a memorial service at Larry's grave.

In 2009, the platoon returned to Mason City, Iowa. Ray Ver Helst had passed away that October and they gathered to support Isabelle Ver Helst. Mrs. Ver Helst was doing well, and was happy to see the gang again. Her 16-year-old grandson, Matt, wanted to do something special for his uncle's comrades. He had an afterschool job working at the local Wendy's restaurant and arranged to throw a free lunch for the platoon at the Wendy's. It was quite a spectacle and a lot of fun for everyone when the members of 2nd Platoon and the Ver Helst family took over the Wendy's in Mason City that Sunday afternoon.

*

Larry Normand hosted the reunion in June 2010 in Baton Rouge, Louisiana. He treated the platoon to an authentic Cajun barbeque at his house on Saturday. On Sunday, the platoon had a private dinner at the hotel. Larry had arranged for Neng's father-in-law to be the guest speaker at the dinner. Hung Van Nguyen described how he and his family had escaped from Vietnam in 1981 and how he had made a new home in America for him and his family.

Hung was a Roman Catholic and had been a member of the South Vietnamese Air Force. He wasn't able to get out of Vietnam before the fall of Saigon in April 1975. He, along with most of those in South Vietnam, had hoped the communist regime wouldn't persecute the South Vietnamese after the Republic of Vietnam was defeated. Those hopes were quickly dashed. Within two weeks of the communist victory, it became clear the North Vietnamese came as conquerors—not as "liberators" as their propaganda had claimed for years.[8] To mark their conquest, one of their first acts was to rename Saigon, "Ho Chi Minh City."

The communist leaders from the north had no intention of sharing power with any of the southerners—not even those who had been loyal communists and had fought for the communist cause. In one of the most profound ironies of the era, Viet Cong leaders were often rounded up and imprisoned alongside their former enemies from the South Vietnamese Army. Both groups of men posed a threat to the power and authority of the new regime as far as Hanoi was concerned.

Hung's story was illustrative of the larger tragedy that unfolded in Southeast Asia after the fall of the Saigon government in April 1975. Within two weeks after the fall of Saigon, the North Vietnamese leaders announced a "reconciliation" program. Those who had been associated with the former South Vietnamese government were told they would have to attend reeducation courses. They were told the reeducation courses would last between three and 30 days.

It was a well-worn blueprint used by communist regimes to consolidate power. Stalin and Mao had used it against millions in the Soviet Union and China. Ho Chi Minh had used the same type of campaign to consolidate his regime's control over the North Vietnamese people when he took power in 1954.

The North Vietnamese quickly rounded up and imprisoned any citizens who could be distinguished as educated, successful, or who had occupied any position of responsibility. More than 300,000 people were swept up in the following weeks. Soldiers, teachers, clerks, businessmen, students and anyone who held any position associated with the Saigon government disappeared into the prison system. The length of the course was supposed to depend on the degree to which someone had been associated with the Saigon government. Thirty days passed, then a year, and few of those who had entered the reeducation camps returned. Some were held for 17 years.[9]

In 1978, the communist government decided to institute "complete socialism" in the conquered southern half of the country. They did this by ending all private trading and business. Soldiers went into shops and confiscated everything from the shelves. At the same time, the government changed the currency. This wiped out the savings for those in the south whose savings were still held in the currency of the Saigon government. Hanoi also instituted a licensing system that denied jobs to anyone who had been associated with the former South Vietnamese government. The communist regime forced tens of thousands of southern Vietnamese to move into "New Economic Zones." These were sprawling government-created ghettos.[10]

Destitute and deprived of any way to earn a living, millions began to flee Vietnam. They fled the country in every direction. Initially, they flooded into the neighboring countries. However, war and genocide erupted in neighboring Laos and Cambodia, eventually shutting down those avenues of escape.

Unable to escape to the west, more and more Vietnamese tried to escape to sea. Approximately a million people decided to take their chances against the South China Sea rather than find out what horror the communist government would inflict on them next. The helpless refugees went to sea in just about anything that would float, trying to make it to Hong Kong, the Philippines, or one of the other nearby countries. Many of the boats were unseaworthy and sank in the open ocean.

In addition to surviving the forces of nature on the open seas, the refugees had to contend with the savage pirate bands who infested the waters. The refugees on the overloaded boats usually left the country with all their savings and valuables. Pirates descended on the helpless boats, robbing, raping, and murdering the refugees.

As the exodus continued, human bodies floating in the South China Sea became a common sight.

The free world had largely ignored Vietnam after the communist victory. It wasn't until the mass exodus of "boat people" refugees became an international humanitarian crisis that the desperate situation inside communist Vietnam made the news. The United Nations eventually recognized the exodus as a humanitarian disaster. Ships from member nations began patrolling the international waters around Vietnam to rescue as many of the refugees as possible.[11] Hundreds of thousands of the former South Vietnamese citizens were eventually brought to the United States. Despite the international efforts to help, it is estimated that up to 300,000 Vietnamese refugees were lost at sea in those years.

At about the same time the communists took over in Vietnam, Pol Pot and his communist Khmer Rouge seized power in neighboring Cambodia. For the next four years, the Khmer Rouge carried out a methodical genocide that killed up to three million of their own people—about a fifth of the country's population. The genocide in Cambodia eventually triggered a war between China and Vietnam. Thirty-five thousand Vietnamese and Chinese soldiers were killed in the two-month war.

It became undeniable in the years following the communist victory that the defeated South Vietnamese government had yielded a much better life for the Vietnamese people than the communist regime from Hanoi. The contrast between the two regimes was stark. The government of the Republic of Vietnam had been much more humane despite its flaws and corruption.

Joan Baez had been a rabid anti-war activist and had even traveled to Hanoi during the war to show her support for the communist regime. After the fall of Saigon, Baez began to hear increasingly credible accounts of the communist regime's reign of terror. The situation in Vietnam became so horrific that even Joan Baez eventually felt compelled to act.

In April 1979, she paid to publish a one-page plea to Hanoi in several major U.S. newspapers. In her "Open Letter to the Socialist Republic of Vietnam," Baez recounted in detail the atrocities committed by the communists since their victory in 1975. She called the situation in Vietnam under communist rule a "nightmare" and said that, "For many [in Vietnam], life is hell and death is prayed for." Baez called upon the communist government to release thousands of prisoners and allow international agencies to inspect and investigate claims. Her letter was also signed by 85 other prominent American leftists. The official response from the communist government was to call Baez "a liar."[12]

The true character of the communist government was finally clear even to people like Joan Baez. It wasn't possible to excuse the communist excesses anymore by claiming it was American propaganda. Unfortunately for millions of Vietnamese and Cambodians, this epiphany by Americans like Baez came decades too late.

Reflecting on the millions who were slaughtered in Southeast Asia after Saigon fell, Richard Nixon reflected on the tragic irony of the age: "Certainly today the record is clear for all to see: A Communist peace kills more than an anti-communist war."[13]

At the reunion in Baton Rouge, Hung Van Nguyen told his story to the platoon and their guests at the dinner. As life had gotten worse, he had decided he had to get his family out of Vietnam. Furthermore, he decided their best chance was to escape to sea as many of his neighbors had done since the communist takeover.

It was essential to keep his plan secret. The communist government had become embarrassed by the refugee exodus from South Vietnam and had instituted draconian punishments for anyone caught trying to escape.

The first thing Hung did was begin building a boat in his backyard. He told his friends and neighbors he was building a boat because he wanted to start fishing in the nearby river to help support his family. It took months to complete the hull.

The most dangerous part of the plan came when he started to build the small motor. Mechanical parts were rationed and closely monitored. Hung said he was building a generator for his house when he bought the motor parts. In the course of building the boat, he had to reveal his plan to a few trusted confidants. Their only condition for helping him was that he had to find space for them on his boat so they could escape also. When the boat was completed, Hung made a few fishing trips up and down the river to give credence to his cover story.

On a dark night in 1981, Hung Van Nguyen and his family took the boat down to the river near their home and slipped it into the water. By the time they had loaded everybody, there were more than a dozen people on board. The boat drifted toward the ocean. At one point, they held their breath and prayed as a government patrol boat crossed ahead of them in the darkness. Once they made it to the open ocean, Hung started the motor and navigated as best as he could for the shipping lanes. He hoped to intercept one of the ships cruising off the coast. After several days at sea, they made it to a set of oil rigs, and were taken on board one of the rigs. From there, they were taken to a refugee camp. Eventually, he and his family made it to the United States. Hung and his family started a business in Baton Rouge and quickly established themselves in the community.

When Hung and his family were taken on board the oil rig, the crew on the rig had to sink Hung's boat to keep it from becoming a hazard to the ships in the area. He was sad to see something he had put so much labor into, and which had brought him and his family to safety, disappear into the blue water beside the rig. Later, Hung built a scale model of his little boat, carving the individual pieces of wood for the model just as he had for the actual boat. He did this so later generations would understand how their family managed to get to America. Hung brought the model of his boat to the dinner that night and showed it to the group.

Speaking to the group that night, Hung said of the decision to attempt such a dangerous escape: "We were going to die anyway if we stayed. I would rather die trying to be free."

Marvin Cole

The platoon was able to find members of Marvin Cole's family and held the reunion in Fort Smith, Arkansas, in 2011. Marvin had been the youngest of 14 children. The platoon was met in Fort Smith by Marvin's three surviving sisters and two brothers, along with dozens of nieces, nephews, cousins and other members of the family. Three generations of Marvin's family filled the VFW hall on Saturday night. The gathering was very moving for the Coles. Like all the other Gold Star families from the platoon, the Coles knew almost nothing about Marvin's last months or days. The Coles were a very close family. Marvin had been the baby. His older brothers and sisters adored him. Losing Marvin tore a hole in the family.

On Sunday morning, the Cole family and the members of the platoon held their memorial service at Marvin's grave in the Fort Smith National Cemetery. A 21-gun salute was fired over his grave by the honor guard from the local Marine Corps League. The platoon then went to the King Solomon Missionary Baptist Church in Fort Smith where Reverend Stanley Whitmore presided over the service. Whitmore is one of Marvin Cole's great-nephews.[14] Reverend Whitmore introduced the platoon to his congregation. His sermon was about service to our fellow man.

After the service, they had a picnic lunch at the River Front Pavilion. There were enlarged photos of Marvin hanging on the wall of the pavilion. They were enlargements of him from the platoon's group photo taken New Year's Day 1967. The photos showed Marvin the way both the family and the platoon remembered him—a kid with a big broad smile. When people talked about Marvin that weekend, the word heard most often to describe him was, "happy."

Floyd Larrabee

The reunion was held in Olathe, Kansas in 2012, where they met with Floyd Larrabee's family. Floyd had grown up in rural Kansas. He was the oldest of five children, with a younger brother, Raymond, a sister, Patsy, and two younger stepbrothers. By the time he was 10, Floyd was going out into the woods to hunt on his own. The family moved to Stanley, Kansas, before high school. "It was just a little town with a bank and a grocery store and not much else," Patsy Puckett said. Floyd played football and ran track in high school. He got good grades, but had to work hard for them.

After graduating from high school, Floyd married Evelyn Dixon, his high-school sweetheart. He and Evelyn moved into a small cottage in Olathe, and Floyd got a job working in the plywood factory nearby. Floyd got his draft notice shortly after they settled down. Like Bill Dorsey, Floyd was told he was being drafted into the Marine Corps when he reported to the local draft board. "He wasn't too fond of the idea, but he went in," his sister said.[15]

They had a going-away party at Floyd and Evelyn's house before he left; the house was decorated with red, white, and blue bunting. He came home on leave after finishing boot camp. Floyd's mother and Evelyn drove him to Camp Pendleton at the end of his leave. He left for Vietnam from Camp Pendleton. "That was the last we saw of him," Patsy said.

Floyd wrote home regularly while he was in Vietnam. "He said he felt sorry for the people there," Patsy said. Floyd identified with the Vietnamese he saw trying to survive in the middle of a war. He wrote home once about seeing a group of villagers cutting up a bloated rotting water buffalo carcass—trying to find some edible meat. He and his family had grown up poor and he was sympathetic. "He felt sorry for the little kids there," Patsy said. "For a kid his age, that would be hard stuff to see." He mailed a photo home of him surrounded by Vietnamese children while he shared candy bars with them. "He didn't consider them his enemy," Patsy Puckett said.

Patsy was a senior in high school in 1967. She was in gym class when the Marines came to her school to get directions to the family house so they could to notify her mother that Floyd had been killed. "I think they went to Evelyn first and then came looking for us," she said. "I had to change out of my gym clothes, and I could hardly do it because my hands were shaking so bad."

Floyd was buried in Memorial Gardens Cemetery in Overland Park. He had a military funeral with the honor guard. "I wasn't ready for the gunfire," Patsy said. Floyd's death meant Raymond was exempt from the draft. Raymond got a job working in the cemetery where his older brother was buried. "I think he was working through something then. It affects people different ways," Patsy said. Evelyn eventually remarried and had a family of her own and moved out of state. "We didn't see too much of her afterwards. I imagine it was just too painful," Patsy said.

Dave Rumsey organized the reunion in 2012 after he and his wife found Floyd's brother and sister. Dick Housh's son, Mike, and daughter, Terry, also came to the reunion from their homes in Missouri.

The reunion was particularly important for Floyd's brother, Raymond, and his sister, Patsy. They had heard different stories over the years about how Floyd had died. Their mother had asked the military about his death and had gotten different stories. One version had him killed while riding in a jeep that hit a mine. The reunion was the first time they learned about the battle on Easter Sunday. Mac McClelland told Raymond and Patsy how Floyd had gone forward again and again to help his wounded friends during the battle even though he had been wounded, and how he was eventually killed doing that. It was comforting for Patsy to see that her brother had real friends while he was in Vietnam. "I was impressed by their friendships and how they had each other's backs," Patsy said.

On Sunday, the group went to a Kansas City Royals game. Rumsey had arranged to have the Royals honor the families. At the end of the second inning, the announcer explained to the fans that the Royals were honoring a couple of men who had been killed in Vietnam. Then, they projected photos of Dick Housh and Floyd Larrabee on the stadium's giant screen. The photos were snapshots taken in Vietnam. The stadium camera then zoomed in on the family and platoon members grouped in the stands while the announcer explained the reunion. The baseball fans applauded and cheered for the 2nd Platoon Marines and the Larrabee and Housh families. "I'm still very much moved by it," said Patsy Puckett. "It was vindication for the guys who fought. Because our guys weren't honored, they were vilified when they came home," she said. "I'm glad that has changed. I have a grandson who has put eight years in the Marines and I'm very proud of him."

Patsy Puckett said of her brother: "He was just a good honest person," she said. "I know he missed his wife a lot while he was over there. I know he really enjoyed being married to Evelyn and loved her a lot," she said. "I'm glad he got at least that opportunity—to experience that part of life."

Bob Bryson and Ed Gutloff

In June 2013, the reunion was held in Commack, Long Island. Both Bob Bryson and Ed Gutloff are buried at the nearby Long Island National Cemetery in Farmingdale, New York. Bob Bryson's daughter, Lisa, came to the reunion with members of her family and met the men who had served with her dad in Vietnam.

Bob Bryson was born on December 29, 1944 in Rochester, New York. His parents died when he was young and he was raised by his mother's parents in Rochester. He enlisted in the Marines in September 1962, after graduating from Aquinas Institute that year. His first duty station was at the naval station in Newport, Rhode Island.

While he was stationed in Newport, Bob met Jo-Ann Walsh, the daughter of a career sailor. She was studying nursing at the Newport School of Nursing. The rest of her family had recently moved to Madrid, Spain, when her father had been assigned to the advisory command working with the Spanish navy.

David Flaherty was also assigned to the Marine Barracks with Bob Bryson. They became friends because Flaherty was also from New York and would ride home with Bob on long weekends or vacations. Often, Jo-Ann would go home with Bob. "They were a really nice couple. I really liked being around them," Flaherty said. "It seemed like we laughed all the time during the drive back and forth."[16]

Bob and Jo-Ann were married in March 1966. Jo-Ann found out she was expecting their daughter shortly before Bob got his orders to Vietnam. Bob arrived in Vietnam in May 1966. With their baby on the way, they had decided Jo-Ann should go to Spain and live with her folks until Bob got back from Vietnam.

Rick Walsh was Jo-Ann's little brother. He remembered the day the Marines from the American embassy brought the news that Bob had been killed. He was coming home from school. Their family lived in an apartment building with an open courtyard in the middle. As he started up the stairs, he heard his sister wailing. It filled the courtyard. "I remember that. Something like that, you'll never forget," he said. Rick Walsh still fondly remembers Bob Bryson. "He was really nice to me, like an older brother."

Lionel Lawson was finally able to fulfill the promise he made to Bob Bryson while they were lying in the banana grove in 1967. Through tears, he managed to tell her that her father's last thoughts were of her and that his last words were that he loved her. Bob Larson had found a photo of his brother and Bob Bryson among Larry's collection of photographs. He had the photo framed and presented it to Lisa on behalf of the platoon. On the back of the photo, Larry Larson had written that the other Marine in the photo was, "Bob Bryson, a new father."

The weekend was an overwhelming experience for Lisa. She told the platoon later: "What a gift to spend time with all of you. I am so honored and grateful to have met you all. I know it is what my father wanted and probably by his very own design. He has always lived on in me and I know he was smiling over us when we were all together. I will treasure your kindness always. God bless you and thank you."[17]

The platoon was unable to locate members of Ed Gutloff's family despite a year-long search. They held a ceremony at his grave to honor and remember him.

*

The platoon returned to Oceanside for the 2014 reunion. On Saturday, they made a trip to the Fort Rosecrans Cemetery with the Szymanskis and held their memorial at John's new and final resting place. Loretta Szymanski's father, a career Marine, is also buried at Fort Rosecrans. It is comforting for her to know her father and John are now resting close to each other.

On Sunday, Mary Jane Deibert had the platoon over to her home and hosted a brunch in her backyard. Hedge Deibert had passed in 2010. "I say prayers for all of you every day," she said to them that morning. That evening, 2nd Platoon had a banquet in the SNCO Club at Camp Pendleton, overlooking the Pacific Ocean. As at their other dinners, there was a table with a single solitary setting. A camouflage-covered helmet sat on the table next to the place setting: An M1955 flak jacket was draped on the back of the chair. The table is set for the missing men from their platoon.

In June 2015, the platoon converged on Racine, Wisconsin to pay their respects to Ray Baer. Baer had returned from Vietnam with three Purple Hearts and a Bronze Star Medal. He stayed on in the Marines for a while and did a tour as a drill instructor. He married—a couple of times, and had three daughters. He worked as a welder for 30 years and then moved to Hawaii for a while.

Ray Baer never ceased to live his life with gusto. He was happiest when he was out in the weather, hunting. Ray was one of the first men Larry Dickerson contacted for the platoon's first reunion and he stayed close to the platoon in the following years.

He died peacefully at home in May 2011 surrounded by his family. In his obituary, Baer first listed his family as his survivors. Ray then had it written: "He is also survived by his Brothers in Arms." His obituary then listed each member of 2nd Platoon by name. He was buried with full military honors in the Southern Wisconsin Memorial Cemetery in Union Grove.

On Sunday, June 28, 2015, 2nd Platoon and Ray Baer's family assembled at his grave. The platoon held their yearly memorial service—reading the names of each of their comrades who fell in Vietnam, followed by the names of those who had passed since returning from Vietnam. After each name was read, they rang a single chime on the ship's bell that is brought to every reunion.

After they had finished the formal ceremony, Doc Long and Lionel Lawson announced that Ray had told his family that one of his last wishes was for everybody in the platoon to have a beer with him. Long and Lawson then pulled out a cooler filled with Ray's favorite beer. Doc Long popped open a beer and rested it on Ray's grave. "There you go, Ray," he said. Everyone else grabbed a beer out of the cooler. When everyone had a beer in hand, Doc led the toast: "To Ray…" he said, and raised his can toward Ray's marker. Everybody laughed, raised their can of beer toward Ray, and shouted, "To Ray!" If you knew Ray Baer, you would know there was no more fitting salute for him.

The reunion in 2016 was scheduled to take place in the Tampa area. The platoon wanted to visit Gordy Cardinal's family. Gordy had survived Vietnam and had attended reunions. He had passed away in 2006.

On Sunday, members of Gordy's family and the platoon gathered at Gordy's grave in the Bushnell National Cemetery and held their memorial service. Following the gathering at his grave, they went to the VFW Post in Bushnell and had dinner together.

Another trend began to take shape at the Tampa reunion: grandchildren started coming to the reunions. Larry Normand's granddaughter, Abby, was moved to hear about her grandfather's experiences in the war. Seeing a photo of him on the battlefield in Vietnam when he was 20 years old, she nudged him in the side and said, "Pop-Pop—you were hot!" While enjoying the weekend reunions in interesting places, the growing cadre of grandkids also learn a lot about their grandparents—and about a war that they've heard very little about.

For years, members of the platoon had tried to find members of Doug Lee's family. The search had been difficult because Doug had actually been a member of 1st Platoon and his platoon leader, Dennis Dooley, had died of cancer in 1974. However, in August 2015, by happenstance, Donna Runnels was put in touch with Doug's widow, Sandy. Donna invited Sandy and any other members of Doug's family to the platoon's upcoming reunion in Tampa. Sandy came to Tampa and met with the members of 2nd Platoon and their families.

Doug Lee

Doug Lee was the oldest child in the family, with three younger sisters. Their parents divorced, leaving Doug as the man of the house when he was young. The family struggled financially while he was growing up in Winston-Salem, North Carolina. According to his sisters, Doug shouldered a lot of responsibility early in life. "He was very protective of mom and me because mom was a single mother; and that wasn't very common at that time," Vicky Young said of her brother.[18]

Doug and Vicky were only two years apart and were best friends growing up. They watched television shows like *American Bandstand* together and learned the latest dance moves, particularly the twist. They would practice their dance moves all week and then enter the dance contest held in the theater downtown on Saturday afternoons. "We had a good time," Vicky said, "and we could win a lot because we had a lot of time together to practice," she said. "So, I think it gave us a little bit of an edge." The contest was sponsored by a local radio station and the first prize was a pair of tickets to next week's contest. "Doug was a really good dancer," she said. "It was just a thing to win the twist contest—and then you could go free to next week's contest," Vicky said with a laugh.

Debbi was 12 years younger than Doug. She remembers him teaching her the fundamentals of boxing when he came home on leave one time. "I was seven," she said. He taught her how to duck a punch and then return a punch. "He'd keep tagging me until I got mad and I'd hit him. And I did—right in the nose," she said with a laugh. His lesson was meant to be serious. "He said, 'Don't let anybody ever hurt you,'" Debbi Nance said. "I took it to heart."[19]

Doug's sisters remember his playful, fun-loving side most though. "He was an absolute nut!" Debbi said. On one trip home after joining the Marines, he and the family went out to a restaurant for dinner. While they were eating, he implied that he was privy to secret information now that he was a Marine. Later, during the meal, he said, "Excuse me," and reached down, pulled his shoe off, and started seriously talking into it, like Maxwell Smart, the bumbling secret agent from the TV show *Get Smart*. There was a moment or two at the table before everyone realized he was putting them on. "He was just always that way. He was just a cut-up," Debbi Nance said.

No one was surprised when Doug enlisted in the Marines. He had always been interested in the military and both sides of the family had proud military legacies. Doug's father fought in Europe during World War II and survived 150 days in a German POW camp after being captured when Nazi panzer units overran his regiment in the opening days of the Battle of the Bulge in December 1944.[20]

Sandy met Doug when a friend invited her to go to the pool on the base one afternoon. "He was the cutest redhead you've ever seen," she said with a quiet laugh. Doug was on the guard force at the Goose Creek Naval Weapons Station outside Charleston. Sandy's father was a career navy man stationed in Charleston.

One of Sandy's fondest memories was the day Doug instigated a water fight with all the kids in her neighborhood. He chased the kids all around the block, while they battled each other with squirt guns. He went so far as to remove the screens from the windows in her mother's house so he and the kids could chase each other in and out of the house. "He played cops and robbers—with the kids climbing out of the windows—shooting them with a water gun," she said with a laugh. "He took all the screens off to play with the kids."

Doug proposed to her on Folly Beach on James Island near Charleston.

"We were young. God, we were young," Sandy Evans said. "He was just a good guy. He was happy. Even when I was pregnant, he'd come in … the dishes were dirty and he looked at me and he said, 'You don't feel good, do you?' And of course, I'm throwing up … and he goes in and he washes the dishes and he never said a word. He just said, 'What can I do to make you feel better?'"[21]

Cindy was born in August 1966, a week or so after Doug left for Vietnam. "She wasn't supposed to live through the night," Sandy said. Cindy was born with Tetralogy of Fallot—a heart defect. A Marine officer at the hospital told Sandy she shouldn't tell Doug about Cindy's health problems because he needed to stay focused to survive in combat. Sandy followed his advice and didn't tell Doug about Cindy's heart problems. She still wonders if it was the right decision. The baby girl went through one open-heart surgery after another. But, Cindy was tough and she survived, despite the doctors' predictions. Her last surgery was when she was eight. She got stronger and stronger. Eventually, Cindy joined the Marines—just like her dad.

In his letters from Vietnam, Doug wrote about their future together. "It was all about planning our future," Sandy said. "He was a joker, but he was serious too." After his parents divorced, Doug's mother often struggled to support him and his sisters. He was determined their children wouldn't ever live like that. They set up a household budget and kept a ledger to track all their expenses. They were budgeting because they had their hearts set on buying a house. "It was going to cost $6,000 for the house. It was a three bedroom, two bath …" Sandy said. When Cindy came along, they started a fund for her. "We would save for Cindy's future, so that she would go to college and not have to work to go to college," Sandy said. "His letters were full of dreams and hopes." Doug wanted to get out of the Marines and go to college. Then he planned to go back in the Marines as an officer. "He'd go back into the Corps—and we would travel the world!" Sandy said.

Sandy moved in with her mother when Doug deployed to Vietnam. She enrolled to take some classes at the local college. Her father was also deployed to Vietnam at the time.

On Easter Sunday 1967, a dozen red roses were delivered to the house. "I got a dozen long-stemmed red roses from him," Sandy said. Doug had arranged to have them delivered weeks earlier while he was in the Philippines.

Sandy was returning from her classes later that week when she saw a Marine Corps sedan parked around the corner from her mother's house. A neighbor was babysitting Cindy. "I noticed because I was the only Marine in the neighborhood. Everybody else was navy or air force," she said. "And they waited …" Sandy recalled. "I just knew something was wrong … but I just went on in and started studying."

It turned out the Marines were waiting for Sandy's mother to get home. "She came home from work; and once they saw my mother drive in, they waited a few minutes and then approached the door." They told her about Doug's death while the roses he sent were still sitting on the table. The recent wars in Iraq and Afghanistan have dredged up a lot of pain for Sandy. "My heart breaks every time I see that another serviceman has died."

"It's been 49 years; and it's like yesterday some days," Sandy Evans said in 2015. "Other days; it feels like a hundred years ago." After meeting the platoon in Tampa, she has stayed in touch with them.

*

The size of the group at the reunions has fluctuated over the years as some men are not able to attend due to other commitments: graduations, weddings, or health problems. Sadly, the platoon has begun to lose men to disease. Hedge Deibert passed in 2010 after fighting heart disease for years. Bill Dorsey died in 2012 after a battle with cancer. Bob Kelley passed away in 2014, Ralph Grant in 2018.

Over the years, members have been found and have joined the group. Dave Koziczkowski and his wife, Marcie, surprised the platoon by showing up in Mason City in 2009. He had heard about the platoon's reunion through another veteran of 1st Battalion, 4th Marines. Dave had been one of the 3.5-inch rocketmen assigned to the platoon like Larry Normand and Gary Hudson. Dave had joined Company C in December 1966 and spent most of his time with 2nd Platoon. He had fought with them on Easter Sunday and then through the brutal months that followed up at Con Thien and along the DMZ in Operations *Prairie IV, Hickory, Cumberland,* and *Choctaw.* He managed to survive those operations largely unscathed.

Dave was walking along the side of the road with the platoon during a patrol on July 16, 1967, when a tank came rumbling up behind them. "I always hated tanks," he said later with a chuckle. Just as the tank came alongside him, it hit a huge mine buried in the road. The explosion disabled the tank and blasted Dave over a tree and into a nearby field. The other men in the platoon were blown off their feet by the explosion. They couldn't imagine how anyone could live through such a massive blast. They figured Dave had to be dead. Doc Long found him in a field with all his clothes blown off; his body a bloody mess of shredded and burned flesh. Long patched up the worst wounds while Dickerson called in an urgent medevac. Dave had so many broken bones that Long used all the splints he had in his kit and had to resort to using pieces of branches. They loaded Dave on a helicopter and flew him out. Everyone figured "Ski" would probably die before the helo made it back to the aid station.

Miraculously, Dave Koziczkowski survived. He spent a year and a half in the Great Lakes naval hospital. After he was discharged, he bought a rundown farm in

Wisconsin. The farm represented a huge challenge. He poured his heart into the farm. Piece by piece, he cleared the rocks out of the fields and rebuilt the farmhouse. Decades of hard work converted the farm into a picturesque sanctuary. A tree-lined drive leads to the immaculate house with broad porches. The fields around the house are lined with rock walls. "It's just heaven," Marcie said when asked about their home. According to Dave, the long hours and hard work kept him out of trouble and helped him avoid the heavy drinking and other self-destructive behaviors that have destroyed so many other badly wounded veterans.

Dave Koziczkowski is a man with a sunny and optimistic disposition. He considers every day he's lived since Vietnam a gift. He and Marcie made the trip to Iowa so he could personally thank Doc Long for saving his life that day in 1967. Dave and Marcie have made it to most of the reunions since.[22]

The wives in the platoon have also found companionship through the reunions. As wives, they have also felt isolated at times. They have spent their lives loving men who've had experiences that many husbands haven't had. Some of the women lived through the war with their husbands. They spent months panicking every time someone knocked on their front door. Those who met their husband after he came home from Vietnam have tried to understand that shadowy part of his life—that part he never wanted to talk about but that seemed to affect him so much. It is at the reunions that they get to hear about that part of his life. They learn about their men from the other men in the platoon. They hear heartbreaking stories that help them understand those pained silences they have endured for decades. They find out the stories behind those medals and ribbons stashed away in the footlocker down in the basement. They understand the names that are shouted in the dark when the nightmares have come.

There is always a lot of laughter at the reunions. Greg Long is still the life of the party and the platoon's chief prankster. At one reunion, he stood in front of the group and said in a solemn voice that he wanted to read a poem he had written about their time in Vietnam. The men and their wives sat quietly, wanting to be respectful of any heartfelt expression. Long then launched into a poem that was not about heroics, but rather was about the time they forded a filthy, sewage-filled stream. He poetically explained that when they emerged from the filthy water, they discovered that every one of them had picked up leeches. This had happened many times. They began stripping off their uniforms, exposing the thick black slugs. The usual procedure was for Doc Long to light a cigar and then go from man to man and remove the leeches by singeing them with the burning tip of the cigar.

He then explained to the room full of men and women that when Steve Pruitt pulled down his trousers, he found to his horror that a leech had attached itself to "his very delicate part." Steve and his wife, Maggie, were sitting in the back of the room. Then Doc Long described that Steve, for some reason, was more afraid of the burning cigar than he was of the leech attached to him. He described how he kept chasing Steve with the burning cigar while Steve kept trying to run away from him with his trousers halfway down his legs.

Doc Long finished the "poem" by explaining that the platoon decided to name Pruitt's leech "Greta." Greta became a running joke in the platoon. For weeks they would ask Steve if "she" had written, "… after all they were practically engaged," Long said. Maggie Pruitt hadn't ever heard the story and she looked at her husband and laughed so hard she had tears in her eyes. The rest of the platoon howled for minutes, remembering the day and adding details. Steve Pruitt just blushed, chuckled, and said, "Doc … you son of a bi …"

Greg Long and Greg Nichols always get a lot of ribbing at the reunions because, as corpsmen, they were actually members of the U.S. Navy; "squids" in Marine parlance. However, both men are considered, "more Marine than navy." Long went on to earn two Bronze Star Medals for valor while he was with the platoon. He was eventually wounded twice himself. "He saved my life," is a common tribute paid to both the corpsmen by the men who survived the war. "I never saw Long or Nic' hesitate when someone yelled, 'Corpsman up!'" Lionel Lawson said. "They were there! Never hesitated. I consider them two of the bravest guys I ever served with. They would just jump up in a line of fire to go get a Marine that's hit," he said. "It takes a lot of balls."

Although Dennis Heider survived the counter-ambush assault with Lionel Lawson, he was badly wounded later in the battle. While trying to rush from one position to another, an NVA bullet took him out. "It hit me in the chest—went right through me and really put me down," he said. The next thing he remembered was Doc Long over him, cutting his pack off with his KA-BAR knife. "I couldn't move, I was really messed up," Dennis said. "Then all these grenades started coming in—all around us." What happened next is vivid in his mind: "Doc laid on top of me to protect me from the grenades … he covered me with his body," Heider said. "I'll never forget him doing that."

According to surveys done since the end of the war, Vietnam combat veterans are still intensely patriotic and have faith in the United States, despite the horrors they witnessed in combat. Their faith in their country is still strong: 66 percent of Vietnam veterans say they would serve again today if called upon.[23]

Photographer David Douglas Duncan was a Marine veteran of the Pacific war and documented some of the Marines' toughest fighting in both World War II and Korea, including the battle of the Chosin Reservoir. He praised the generation of Marines who fought in Vietnam. In 1967, Duncan said of the Marines he met up at Con Thien: "But they are all professionals, practicing a trade for which they volunteered. In the 10 days at Con Thien—though this seems hard to believe—I never heard any griping at being there. The men view Con Thien in the same light as Tarawa and Iwo Jima and are proud and happy to have held this hillock in a remote land."[24]

Jerry Idziak suffered incredible physical and mental pain since being wounded on Easter Sunday. He went through more than 35 major surgeries to put him back together. Jerry married; and he and his wife had two children. "I was told I would never be able to have kids—and my wife got pregnant on me two times and we had two wonderful kids," he said. Fifteen years after being wounded, he became critically ill again from an infection stemming from his combat wounds. He spent another 18 months in the hospital that time.

Jerry doesn't regret being a Marine or fighting in Vietnam despite his suffering. "I tell you what, if my country wanted me to do the same thing, for my country, I would do it. That's just the way I feel. And I think most of the guys I served with feel that way," he said.

Millions of South Vietnamese, Americans, and allied forces, fought to keep the people of South Vietnam free between 1954 and 1975. The failure to win that war was a tragedy for the Vietnamese people. Whether America's commitment in Southeast Asia was in America's best interest can certainly be debated. Sadly, the list of strategic blunders committed by a succession of American administrations while fighting the war is both indisputable and tragic.

However, the calculated and deliberate brutality by the communists after 1975 proved America's cause in Vietnam had always been honorable. The Americans who fought and died in Vietnam wanted to give the Vietnamese people a chance to experience the gift Americans value most—freedom.

President Ronald Reagan summed up the American experience in Vietnam during his Veterans Day address in 1988. He said: "Who can doubt that the cause for which our men fought was just? It was, after all, however imperfectly pursued, the cause of freedom; and they showed uncommon courage in its service."[25]

The reunions have helped them make peace with their experiences in Vietnam. Most of the men have struggled at times with Post-Traumatic Stress. In World War I, physicians working with combat veterans developed the "talking cure." They found that the most effective treatment for "war neurosis" was to have men talk about the trauma they had lived through. The platoon reunions have accomplished this and much much more.[26]

The men and their families have grown closer every year since their first reunion. They talk and often meet in the months between the reunions. No man has to carry the burden of Vietnam alone any longer. When the dark phantoms of Vietnam begin to pull a man down, he knows help is only a phone call away.

Doc Long summed up a sentiment that resonates with most of the men in the platoon: "I'll tell you," Doc Long said, "before we got together, I mean, I was a wreck." He had sunk to some very dark points in his life—mentally reliving his time in Vietnam. He lived alone with the visions of his friends who were killed and wounded—many died in his arms while he tried desperately to save them. One of the worst visions that visited him over and over was Doug Dickey and the horrendous blast that killed him. "That was horrible … to have Doug get blown up and almost land on me…" he said. At points, he would cuss Doug for saving his life.

Today, he laughs remembering those days. "I used to be so mad … I used to yell at him. I'd say, 'Goddamn you, Doug! I don't know why the hell you saved my life—my life is a shit hole!'"

The reunions, however, have helped change that. Talking to the other men in the platoon has worked wonders. "Because you can get a lot of stuff out there that you can't get out talking to anybody else," Long said. "It did me a world of good. It did me an absolute world of good." He remembers Doug Dickey differently today. He now remembers Doug Dickey as one of his angels. "Now, I've been able to see the few things that I've done that are maybe the reason I'm still here." He thinks of Doug every day. "And he's still kicking me in the butt, going, 'Keep going … keep going!'"[27]

Larry Alley was one of Jim Ver Helst's best friends. "We thought we couldn't be killed," he said. "We done some crazy things," he said. "We carried a flag with us on every operation. We wanted to be like Iwo Jima," he said with a quiet laugh. Larry was just a few feet away when Jim was killed. "I can't really say enough about him. He was just one great guy," Larry said. "We were always together."

Larry was one of the few men who not only survived Easter Sunday but managed to make it all the way to the end of his 13-month tour of duty in Vietnam. He has struggled with the same "survivor's guilt" that a lot of combat veterans struggle with. Over the years, he found it was helpful to do something to remember the friends he lost. He ended up building a small memorial in the land behind his house. "That helps me," he said.

Larry had prayed and thought about all those men for years. Then one night he had a dream that gave him a sense of peace that has lasted since. In his dream, the platoon was back on the *Ogden* getting ready to make the landing for *Beacon Hill,* and all of the men they lost were there. "Jim and Larrabee and all of them were there, but they were in their dress uniforms" he said. They were smiling and happy. "And they told me, they said, 'Alley, it's OK, it's OK.'" The dream was deeply powerful. "For two or three days or more, I wouldn't say a thing. I was just happy. It's the greatest feeling I've ever had," he said. Unlike most dreams that fade quickly, Larry Alley still remembers the dream vividly years later. "Boy, I wish everybody could have a dream like that, because, I mean, it was beautiful."[28]

"I came home feeling like I'd done my part," Tim O'Toole said. For decades he didn't talk much about Vietnam. He was busy raising his family and overseeing large construction projects. However, at about the same time 2nd Platoon began having reunions, Tim O'Toole began playing golf with eight other Marine combat veterans a couple of times a month. In addition to playing golf—they talk. "It's probably some of the best therapy you could ever have," he said. "What's really nice about the group is that there is nothing that is off-limits—absolutely nothing." Over the years, a lot of ghosts from Vietnam have been laid to rest out on that golf course, or over a few beers back at the clubhouse.

Tim O'Toole is proud of his service in Vietnam. "I wanted to do my family proud," he said. "I decided that I was going to do everything I had to do so that I could come home and not feel bad about it. And I never have felt bad about it." However, the names of his comrades from HMM-363 who didn't make it home are never far from his mind. When he talks about Vietnam he will eventually start to talk about those men. He will say each man's name and mention something unique about him; a particular trait or gift. He will tell you they were some of the finest men he's ever known.

The Marines from 2nd Platoon have always admired the crew of YZ-69. O'Toole and his crew got shot out of the sky trying to get their wounded buddies out—and they've never forgotten that. They know many pilots wouldn't have even attempted the medevac through the tiny opening in the trees—in fading light—through a hail of antiaircraft fire. "I was in the crater with the other guys," Mike Helton said. "I remember the helicopter. I couldn't believe that. What a bunch of guys with big brass balls those guys are. They brought that damn helicopter down. I remember him coming in and as he was sitting down, you could see the tracer rounds going through the helicopter. He came down and set on the edge of that hole with one wheel on the ground."[29]

"I'm proud of the job I did over there and I'm a lucky man," O'Toole said. Nevertheless, he still chafes a little at the memory of Easter Sunday. Pilots see things a little differently. "Out of 561 missions, that is the only one I didn't finish. Still bothers me today," he said.[30] Retired now, Tim O'Toole is often surrounded by grandchildren and great-grandchildren. "I loved construction and I loved flying for the Marine Corps. I have been happy for my entire life and I know some it has been hard work but, I have to say—I have been very lucky."[31]

Before he died in 2012, Bill Dorsey said of Vietnam and the reunions: "It's like a long, drawn-out movie, if you would. Of all the hardships—pain and suffering and everything that everybody went through, and we're kind of winding down to a happy ending now, and that, in itself, is not only totally amazing, but a blessing from God."

Lionel Lawson has made it to every reunion. "It's hard to believe how old the rest of us of got," he said. "I mean, we were all 18, 19 years old back then ... just a bunch of kids, but I couldn't be prouder of any bunch of guys I ever served with, I'll tell you that. Brothers forever, that's what we are."

CHAPTER 26

The Legacy

It hurt me a great deal to lose him. But I can't feel bitter. There are so many people who die for no reason at all; and this was a definite reason—giving his life in this way.

LEONA DICKEY

Doug Dickey left behind a rich and lasting legacy of his twenty years. To his nation, he became an inspirational hero. To his friends and comrades, his selfless sacrifice on the battlefield changed the course of their lives. To his family, Doug will always be their loving brother and cherished son. While Doug Dickey's life was cut much too short, it was a life well-lived.

Douglas Dickey is known most widely as a Marine hero who earned the Medal of Honor in Vietnam. An American president explained the importance of recognizing and remembering the valor and sacrifices of men like Douglas Dickey during a ceremony where he presented the Medal of Honor to a soldier: "War is a terrible thing, wasting the young before they have a chance to reach their full potential," he said. "But there are moments, terrible in their danger and devastation, that can bring out unimaginable courage and leadership that cannot be fully described; but once seen and felt, can never be forgotten." He concluded his remarks with a timeless reminder: "As a people we need heroes, real heroes, who when tested excel and in doing so inspire others to reach for greatness within themselves. We need heroes not just for the victories that they make possible on the battlefield but in the later days to remind us of what America at its best can be now and in the future—the greatest nation on earth."[1]

The people of Darke county have embraced and honored their native son. Two months after he was killed, the Ansonia High School Class of 1967 memorialized Doug in their yearbook. Since Harold and Leona Dickey accepted Doug's Medal of Honor in 1968, many official honors have been paid to Doug by their neighbors. Rossburg declared Sunday, May 19, 1968, as "Doug Dickey Day." They had a parade through town in his honor. There is a bronze plaque at the base of the flagpole at the end of the Ansonia High School football field commemorating him. Doug's name was added to the Eck Arey American Legion Post in Ansonia in 1982. In May 2013, a section of State Route 47 near Ansonia in Darke County was renamed the "Pfc. Douglas E. Dickey Memorial Highway." The Garst Museum in Greenville unveiled an impressive exhibit honoring Doug in 2014. These monuments will serve to teach following generations about Douglas Dickey—and the other Americans who fought in Vietnam.

Doug will always rest in the rich soil of Darke County, where he is, fittingly, only a few paces from Annie Oakley.

The Marine Corps continues to honor and remember Doug. Among its tributes, it named a barracks after him in 1973. "Doug Dickey represented the finest of the finest," Major General James Livingston said while dedicating Doug's exhibit at the Garst Museum in 2014. Livingston earned the Medal of Honor as a company commander in Quang Tri in 1968. "His selfless act is, and always will be, a part of the legacy of this great Marine Corps," Livingston said.

Today, Doug's unit, 1st Battalion, 4th Marines, is headquartered in the Camp Horno area of Camp Pendleton. They still proudly call themselves "China Marines." More than two generations of Marines have served in the battalion since Blackjack Westerman commanded it and Doug Dickey earned the Medal of Honor. Doug's photo and citation hang on the wall of the battalion's headquarters beside those of the other heroes from the battalion—inspiring the current generation of Marines who proudly carry the battalion's colors.

Doug Dickey's Medal of Honor is, above all, a testament to his boundless love for his friends. His sacrifice on Easter Sunday changed their lives. Reflecting on that day, Larry Alley said: "You can't ever really get over that for the rest of your life."[2] Doug's comrades will never forget him.

The platoon's first reunion in 1997 was held to honor Doug and his family. Every summer since then, the men from 2nd Platoon have gathered from around the country to honor their comrades. They always hold a memorial ceremony on the Sunday of their reunion. They solemnly gather and read the names of all of their comrades who made the ultimate sacrifice in Vietnam. Then they read the names of their comrades, who, like Bill Dorsey, have passed since coming home from Vietnam. After each name is read, they pause and then ring a single chime on a small ship's bell. The first name read at the ceremony every year is Doug's.

Doug's sacrifice in 1967 created a living legacy that will stretch on and expand for generations. They are the children and the families that were made possible when he saved the lives of his comrades in 1967. Bill Dorsey came home and raised three sons and a daughter. Larry Dickerson had two boys. Greg Long had a son and a daughter. Gary Hudson had two sons. Almost every year there are more children born who can trace their lives to the actions of a young man named Douglas Dickey who sacrificed his life to save his friends in 1967.

During their first reunion, the men from the platoon took a bottle of Jack Daniels and made it their "Last Man Bottle." They pasted a label on it which reads:

"This bottle is to be consumed by the last surviving member of 2nd Platoon, "C" Company, 1/4, who served in Vietnam in 1967. Placed at the Eck Ary—Douglas Dickey Post 353 on Sunday, May 25th, 1997." The bottle is safely stored away. It is a reminder that as long as one man from the platoon is alive, Easter Sunday 1967, and the men who fought there, will not be forgotten.

For those who grew up with Doug—his family and friends, the legacy can be more complicated at times. They are all proud of him but there is no award that could ever fill the void they feel or mend their broken hearts.

"Everybody liked Doug," Tim Barga said, remembering his boyhood friend. Barga came home to Darke County after his time in the Marines and has lived a relatively quiet and peaceful life since. "It just shows me that nobody knows what men will do under the pressure of a battle," he said. "Some people just rise to an occasion that's extraordinary—and I think he did." The memory of Doug being humiliated in boot camp still haunted him almost 40 years later. "I always think of the ridicule he took and if those guys only knew how brave he was." Barga said of his time in in Vietnam: "I was very proud of the men I served with, and I still am. When they were told to do something they did it, and under some pretty rough conditions."

When asked to speculate on what Doug would have done if he had survived Vietnam, those who knew him suppose he probably would have come home to Darke County and had a little farm like his father. Most believe he would have married a local girl and raised a family. He would have been active in the church like his mother. Doug would have blended back into the community. He would have been a wonderful husband and father. Doug fell in love with the Pacific Ocean while he was in California. It's easy to imagine him taking his kids to see it one day so they could swim in it and love it as much as he did.

"Sometimes, it's hard," Dennis Dickey said of participating in ceremonies to honor Doug. He's proud of his brother, but the events can also make him feel that ache in his heart—that empty spot in his life where his big brother should be. He wishes Doug was here—growing old with him, and Norman, and Vera.

"He was just the kind of son any mother would cherish," Leona Dickey told Dean Brelis in 1968. War is cruelest to mothers. It's a mysterious dark beast that ravages and destroys precious lives. Mothers don't remember uniforms and ranks; they remember tiny arms, soft hands—and happy smiles. They remember the little boy who smiled and cooed with bright eyes as he tottered toward them on unsteady legs. War robs a mother of that precious life.

Leona Dickey passed away in April 2013. She was 90 years old. Her memorial service was packed. She had been a pillar of the community for most of her life. Her quiet strength and the way she had endured tragedy with grace and courage had been an inspiration to those around her over the years. In 2010, her youngest son, Steven, unexpectedly died of a heart attack. His death was a severe blow to Leona. She had come to believe that she wouldn't ever have to bury another one of her children. The source of her strength was revealed in one of her poems her grandson, Bill, read at her memorial service:

Second Chance

Will you give it another try, Dear Lord,
To make something out of me
I'll try to follow your footsteps,
Up there to the lonely Tree.

I'll hang on the cross beside Thee;
And suffer the pangs of death,
As you did that day, so long ago,
Paying our sinful debts.

Then I'll take up the cross, and follow
The way you would have me go,
For the life of a wretched soul like me,
Is laden with grief, and woe.

There's no one to turn to, here below;
Who can calm the storms within,
So I'll share with you all of my burdens,
If you'll only take me in.

I'll trust Thee with all of my troubles
I've tried to deal with, all alone,
And I'll lay my head, on your weary breast,
Until you call me home.

Leona Dickey was proud her son had earned America's highest award for valor. She was proud that Doug's name will always be listed among America's greatest heroes. But if you asked her about Doug, she wouldn't say he was a Marine hero. To her, Doug was her oldest son—her first baby. She would mention softly that he came into her life on Christmas Eve and left it on an Easter Sunday. She found some comfort in that. "He was just a special little kid you know—from the time he was born, he was just a special little kid," she said. "And everybody respected him and liked him ... everybody ... church, school, everybody."

Then Leona Dickey added softly, "The guy who threw the grenade—he would have loved him, if he could have just met him."[3]

Douglas E. Dickey's Medal of Honor Citation

The President of the United States in the name of The Congress takes pride in presenting the MEDAL OF HONOR posthumously to

PRIVATE FIRST CLASS DOUGLAS EUGENE DICKEY
UNITED STATES MARINE CORPS

For service set forth in the following

Citation

For conspicuous gallantry and intrepidity at the risk of his life above and beyond the call of duty while serving with the Second Platoon, Company C, First Battalion, Fourth Marines, Third Marine Division in the Republic of Vietnam on 26 March 1967. While participating in Operation Beacon Hill 1, the Second Platoon was engaged in a fierce battle with the Viet Cong at close range in dense jungle foliage. Private First Class Dickey had come forward to replace a radio operator who had been wounded in this intense action and was being treated by a medical corpsman. Suddenly an enemy grenade landed in the midst of a group of Marines, which included the wounded radio operator who was immobilized. Fully realizing the inevitable result of his actions, Private First Class Dickey, in a final valiant act, quickly and unhesitatingly threw himself upon the deadly grenade, absorbing with his body the full and complete force of the explosion. Private First Class Dickey's personal heroism, extraordinary valor and selfless courage saved a number of his comrades from certain injury and possible death at the cost of his life. His actions reflected great credit upon himself, the Marine Corps and the United States Naval Service. He gallantly gave his life for his country.

Sources

This book began as part of a broader effort to research all the Marines who earned the Medal of Honor in Vietnam. During two weeks of leave in 2002, I went to the Archives and copied the files they had on the 57 Marines who had been awarded the Medal of Honor in Vietnam. Bob Aquilina was in charge at that time and was exceptionally patient and hospitable in accommodating my undoubtedly intrusive invasion of their cramped work area with my new laptop computer and scanner. My first thanks go to Bob and his crew at the Marine Corps Archives. Allowing me to copy the files gave me the essential foundation for my research.

While driving from Washington, D.C. to my next assignment at Camp Pendleton, California, a few months later, I took a detour off the interstate while driving through western Ohio. I remembered from the official file I had copied at the archives at the Navy Yard that Douglas Dickey was from Rossburg, Ohio. On a whim, I decided to take a break from driving and find the little town listed as the hometown of the young Marine. I found Rossburg, Ansonia, and Greenville. After a while, I found the Brock Cemetery where Doug is buried. I took a couple of photos of the area and then got back on the interstate and continued to Camp Pendleton.

Driving around the farmland that afternoon had made Doug Dickey very real to me and made me more curious about the story behind the smiling face in his unusual official photo. After I retired, I decided to dedicate my time to researching the Marine Medal of Honor recipients from Vietnam. A quick search on the internet yielded the phone number for the Dickeys. I phoned the number and got Leona Dickey, Doug's mother, on the phone. Unfortunately, Doug's father, Harold, had passed about a year earlier. Leona Dickey enjoyed talking about her son and was very supportive and understanding. She chided me for not dropping by when I was driving through the area in 2002. I told her I thought that would have been rude. She dismissed that concern as silliness. I had no idea in 2002 how friendly the people in Darke County, Ohio, are—particularly, Leona Dickey and her family.

By that time, the men from Doug's platoon had been holding their annual reunions for nine years and she had contact points for most of them and gave me their phone numbers. I called several of them in the next month or so.

In early 2006, Leona Dickey phoned me and told me the platoon had decided to hold their reunion in Greenville again that year and she invited me to come out and meet everybody in person. I came to the reunion reluctantly, fearing that I was intruding on a personal and intimate affair. The men of 2nd Platoon and their families welcomed me and were, like the Dickey family, supportive, patient and helpful.

I first met Leona Dickey at that reunion in Greenville in 2006. She was sitting in the corner of the room at the hotel the platoon was using as a hospitality suite. She was quietly talking to one of the wives. The gathering was starting to pick up steam as more and more men and their wives arrived. Every once in a while, a profanity would burst from the crowd. The offender would quickly apologize when he realized "Ma' Dickey" was in the room. They all knew she didn't approve of that kind of language. Leona Dickey would just smile and sometimes roll her eyes. There was no place she would rather be than among the graying warriors she called "my boys."

I got to be friends with Leona Dickey. We talked often over the years. In the later years, we rarely talked about Vietnam. We usually talked about everyday stuff. She liked to talk about cooking and her grandkids a lot. She was also a big sports fan and followed several teams closely. She was someone who always left me feeling calmer and happier. Leona Dickey's friendship was a tremendous gift in my life. Everyone who knew her, misses her greatly.

Lastly, I was eight years old when the men from 2nd Platoon were battling for their lives in Vietnam. My mother graduated from high school in 1941, as did Leona Dickey. Their generation was devastated by World War II. My father and uncles all fought overseas during the war. I'm sure my mother silently thanked God she had started her family later in life, which made her two sons too young to be called to fight in Vietnam. She did, however, agonize as many of her friends' sons went off to fight in Vietnam.

At bedtime in our home, my mother sat on the edge of the bed while we said our prayers. We said the familiar, "Now I lay me down to sleep…" prayer. At the end of the prayer, we listed those we specifically wanted God to take care of, "God bless mommy and daddy and Tippy (our dog)…" and so on. Beginning in 1965, my mother always had us end the prayer with, "…and God bless all the men in Vietnam." I believe, as I think my mother believed at the time, that a child's prayer is particularly powerful. I like to think that one of our prayers made it across the Pacific and into a rice paddy or jungle foxhole somewhere in Vietnam and helped to bring one of those sons home to his mother.

The most important part of this research has been the interviews with the men and women who lived through this time. I have been humbled by their willingness to share these often-painful memories. Many times, talking about the events caused tears to flow again. While time has dulled some of the pain of the losses, the voids left when these young men were lost have never been filled. I pray that I have been a faithful steward of your memories.

Interviews by author (in alphabetical order):

Doug Dickey's Family and Friends from Ohio

Tim Barga, Diane Birt, Robert Birt, Dennis Dickey, Leona Dickey, Norman Dickey, Paul Dickey, Steven Dickey, Vera (Dickey) Moore, Roger Young.

Marines and Comrades from 1st Battalion, 4th Marines

Larry Alley, William Dorsey, Sandy Evans (widow of Douglas Lee), David Flaherty (Bob Bryson's friend from MCB Newport, R.I.), 1stSgt Ralph Grant, USMC (Ret.), David C. Gregg, Dennis Heider, Kent Hansen, Mike Helton (1st Platoon), Isabelle Hudson (mother of Gary Hudson), Jerry Idziak, Col John F. Juul, USMC (Ret.) (Company D commander), LtCol Robert Kelley, USMC (Ret.) (Company C commander), Phillip Key (1st Platoon), Marcie and Dave Koziczkowski, Bob Larson (brother of Larry Larson), Lionel Lawson, Greg Long, Carl Martin, Colin McClelland, Debbi Nance (sister of Douglas Lee), Greg Nichols, Larry Normand, Tim O'Toole (HMM-363), Steve Pruitt, Patsy Puckett (sister of Floyd Larrabee), Dave Rumsey, Charlie Runnels, Robert F. Sheridan (Operations Officers, 2nd Battalion, 3rd Marines), Haywood J. Swearingen, Loretta Szymanski (widow of John Szymanski), Richard Van Vactor (brother of Victor Van Vactor), David Ver Helst (brother of Jim Ver Helst), Jack Ver Helst (brother of Jim Ver Helst), Jack Westerman III (son of "Blackjack" Westerman), Rick Walsh (brother-in-law of Bob Bryson), Larry Wilson, and Vicky L. Young (sister of Douglas Lee).

Another invaluable resource for interviews was the Gray Research Center's Audiovisual Archives in Quantico, Virginia. Thanks to Susan Dillon, Tony Magnotta, Tom Baughn, Fred Allison and others for combing through the thousands of tape-recorded interviews they have archived from the Vietnam War. These are some of the most valuable interviews they found for me: BGen Frederick J. Karch, 15 Jan 1972, (Transcript); LtCol Jack Westerman (File #269A); interview of CDR Ronald Bouterie (MC), within the collected interviews conducted by Maj William Thurber, USMC, for Operation *Beacon Hill*, (File #932A); 2ndLt Salvador Martinez (File #3948A); Sgt Jimmie L. Blick (File #2181–1B); Cpl James M Couch II (File #1878A).

Primary Source Documents

1st Battalion, 4th Marines, 1967 Battalion Cruisebook.
Ansonia High School yearbooks, *The Oracle*, for graduating classes: 1961, 1963, 1964, 1965, 1967, 1969.
PFC Douglas E. Dickey biographical file (Marine Corps Archives).
PFC Douglas E. Dickey biographical file (Congressional Medal of Honor Society).
Command Chronologies and Combat After-Action Reports for U.S. Marine Corps commands in Vietnam.
 (Gray Research Center, Quantico, VA., and National Archives and Records Administration (NARA)).

U.S. Navy Ship Deck Logs (NARA).

U.S. Marine Corps Official Photographs and 16mm motion picture footage (NARA, College Park, Maryland).

Motion Picture and Video Resources

A Fellowship of Valor: The Battle History of the United States Marines. A&E Home Video and the History Channel, VHS, 1998.

First reunion of 2nd Platoon, held in Rossburg and Ansonia, Ohio, 25 May 1997. (Video tape footage of various events at the ceremony courtesy of Dennis Dickey).

Marines 1965. (Official U.S. Marine Corps film documenting Marine Corps operations in 1965. Courtesy of Gray Research Center, Quantico, VA.).

Marines 1966. (Official U.S. Marine Corps film (MH-10422) documenting Marine Corps operations in 1966. Courtesy of Gray Research Center, Quantico, VA.).

Marines 1967. (Official U.S. Marine Corps film (MH10527) documenting Marine Corps operations in 1967. Courtesy of Gray Research Center, Quantico, VA.).

PFC Dickey award ceremony (Unedited 16mm footage), 16 April 1968, U.S. Marine Barracks, Washington, D.C. (NARA Index # 6457 and # 6765).

The D.I.: A Builder of a Few Good Men. (Official U.S. Marine Corps documentary (MH-11082) about Drill Instructors. Courtesy of Gray Research Center, Quantico, VA.).

This is Parris Island. (Official U.S. Marine Corps documentary (CMC-TFR 1-63 (Revision Two) about recruit training at Parris Island, SC. Courtesy of Gray Research Center, Quantico, VA.).

Vietnam: The War This Week. NBC, narrated by Dean Brelis. (Copy of broadcast courtesy of Dennis Dickey).

I owe a public thanks to Carolyn Fisher, the genealogy assistant at the Greenville Public Library, in Greenville, Ohio. In addition to pointing me to a number of valuable resources during my visits to Greenville, she also unfailingly found answers to the often-odd questions I came up with after I had returned home. It was a distinct pleasure to find someone along the way who was genuinely enthusiastic about my work while I plodded along. Thank you, Carolyn, for your support and encouragement.

Selected Bibliography

The greatest and indispensable published resource for the history for the Marine Corps' operations in Vietnam is the set of volumes published by the History and Museums Division at Headquarters Marine Corps. In chronological order, according to the history of the war, the volumes are as follows:

Witlow, Captain Robert H., USMCR. *U.S. Marines in Vietnam, 1954–1964, The Advisory and Combat Assistance Era.* Washington, D.C.: History and Museums Division, Headquarters, U.S. Marine Corps, 1977.

Shulimson, Jack, and Major Charles M. Johnson, USMC. *U.S. Marines in Vietnam, 1965, The Landing and the Buildup.* Washington, D.C.: History and Museums Division, Headquarters, U.S. Marine Corps, 1978.

Shulimson, Jack. *U.S. Marines in Vietnam, 1966, An Expanding War.* Washington, D.C.: History and Museums Division, Headquarters, U.S. Marine Corps, 1982.

Telfer, Major Gary L., USMC, Lieutenant Colonel Lane Rogers, USMC, and V. Keith Fleming, Jr. *U.S. Marines in Vietnam, 1967, Fighting the North Vietnamese.* Washington, D.C.: History and Museums Division, Headquarters, U.S. Marine Corps, 1984.

Shulimson, Jack, Lieutenant Colonel Leonard A. Blaisol, USMC, Charles R. Smith, and Captain David A. Dawson, USMC. *U.S. Marines in Vietnam, 1968, The Defining Year.* Washington, D.C.: History and Museums Division, Headquarters, U.S. Marine Corps, 1997.

Smith, Charles R. *U.S. Marines in Vietnam, 1969, High Mobility and Standdown.* Washington, D.C.: History and Museums Division, Headquarters, U.S. Marine Corps, 1988.

Cosmas, Graham A., and Lieutenant Colonel Terrance P. Murray, USMC. *U.S. Marines in Vietnam, 1970–1971, Vietnamization and Redeployment.* Washington, D.C.: History and Museums Division, Headquarters, U.S. Marine Corps, 1986.

Melson, Major Charles D., USMC, and Lieutenant Colonel Curtis G. Arnold, USMC. *U.S. Marines in Vietnam, 1971–1973, The War that would not End.* Washington, D.C.: History and Museums Division, Headquarters, U.S. Marine Corps, 1991.

Dunham, Major George R., USMC, and Colonel David A. Quinlan, USMC. *U.S. Marines in Vietnam, 1973–1975, The Bitter End.* Washington, D.C.: History and Museums Division, Headquarters, U.S. Marine Corps, 1990.

Shulimson, Jack, ed. *The Marines in Vietnam, 1954–1973, An Anthology and Annotated Bibliography.* Washington, D.C.: History and Museums Division, Headquarters, U.S. Marine Corps, 1974.

Shulimson, Jack, ed. *The Marines in Vietnam, 1954–1973, An Anthology and Annotated Bibliography, Second Edition.* Washington, D.C.: History and Museums Division, Headquarters, U.S. Marine Corps, 1985.

Published Works

A Marine's Guide To The Republic Of Vietnam. MCBul 3480. Prepared by G-2 HQ FMFPAC, 11 May 1966.

Advanced Base Operations in Micronesia (FMFMRP 12-46), 21 August 1992.

Allen, Lieutenant Colonel Alfred M., MC, U.S. Army. *Internal Medicine in Vietnam, Volume I: Skin Diseases in Vietnam, 1965–72.* Washington, D.C.: Office of the Surgeon General and Center of Military History, United States Army, 1977.

Amphibian Vehicles, (FMFM 9-2). Washington, D.C.: Headquarters, United States Marine Corps, 17 September 1964.

Anderson, David L. *The Columbia Guide to the Vietnam War.* New York: Columbia University Press, 2002.

Baez, Joan. *And a Voice to Sing With.* New York: Summit Books, 1987

Bui Tin. *Following Ho Chi Minh: Memoirs of a North Vietnamese Colonel.* Honolulu, HI: University of Hawaii Press, 1995.

Bui Tin. *From Enemy to Friend.* Annapolis, MD: US Naval Institute Press, 2002.

Carter, Jimmy. *Public Papers of the Presidents of the United States: Jimmy Carter, Volume 2.* Washington, D.C.: Office of the Federal Registrar, National Archives and Recources Service, General Services Administration, 1980.

Cavendish, Marshall. *The Vietnam War: Volume 12: After the War.* New York: Marshall Cavendish Corporation, 1989.

Chanoff, David, and Doan Van Toai. *Portrait of the Enemy.* New York: Random House, 1986.

Coan, James P. *Con Thien: The Hill of Angels.* Tuscaloosa, AL: University of Alabama Press, 2004.

Collier, Bill. *The Adventures of a Helicopter Pilot: Flying the H-34 Helicopter in Vietnam for the United States Marine Corps.* Sandpoint Idaho: Wandering Star Press, 2014.

Condit, Kenneth W., and Edwin T. Turnbladh. *Hold High the Torch: A History of the 4th Marines.* Washington, D.C.: Historical Branch, G-3 Division, Headquarters, U.S. Marine Corps, 1960.

Conroy, Ken, Ken Bowra, and Simon McCouaig. *The NVA and Viet Cong.* London: Osprey Publishing, 1991.

Cowing, Kemper F. (compiled by), and Courtney Ryley Cooper (edited by). *"Dear Folks At Home -- -- --": The glorious story of the United States Marines in France as told by their Letters from the Battlefield.* New York: Houghton Mifflin Company, 1919.

Crane, Stephen. *The Red Badge of Courage.* New York: Barnes & Noble Books, 1992.

Doan Van Toai, and David Chanoff. *The Vietnamese Gulag.* New York: Simon and Schuster, 1986.

Doyle, Edward, and Terrance Maitland. *The Vietnam Experience: The Aftermath: 1975–85.* Boston: Boston Publishing Company, 1985.

Doyle, Edward, Samuel Lipsmen, Terrance Maitland, and the editors of Boston Publishing Company. *The Vietnam Experience: The North.* Boston: Boston Publishing Company, 1986.

Duiker, William J. *Ho Chi Minh.* New York: Hyperion, 2000.

Duiker, William J. The *Communist Road to Power in Vietnam.* Boulder, Colorado: Westview Press, Inc., 1981.

Duncan, David Douglas. *War Without Heroes.* New York: Harper and Row Publishers, 1970.

Dunnigan, James F., and Albert A. Nofi. *Dirty Little Secrets of the Vietnam War.* New York: St. Martin's Press, 1999.

Eilert, Rick. *For Self and Country.* New York: William Morrow and Company, Inc., 1983.

Fails, Lieutenant Colonel William R., USMC. *Marines and Helicopters: 1962–1973.* Washington, D.C.: History and Museums Division, Headquarters, U.S. Marine Corps, 1978.

Fall, Bernard B. *Reflections on a War.* Garden City, NY: Doubleday & Company, Inc., 1967.

Fall, Bernard B. *Street Without Joy.* Mechanicsburg, PA: Stackpole Books, 1961.

Fenlon, Holly S. *American Gold Star Mothers Inc: 1928–2010.* Doylestown, PA: Platform Press, 2010.

Ferling, John. *The Ascent of George Washington: The Political Genius of an American Icon.* New York: Bloomsbury Press, 2009.

Fitzpatrick, John C., ed. *The Writings of George Washington, Volume 24: February 18, 1782–August 10, 1782.* Washington, D.C.: United States Government Printing Office, 1938.

Fleming, Keith. *The U.S. Marine Corps in Crisis: Ribbon Creek and Recruit Training.* Columbia, SC: University of South Carolina Press, 1990.

Gaffen, Fred. *Unknown Warriors: Canadians in Vietnam.* Toronto, Canada: Dundurn Press Ltd., 1990.

Geer, Andrew. *The New Breed: The Story of the U.S. Marines in Korea.* New York: Harper & Brothers, 1952.

Gravel, Mike, ed. *The Pentagon Papers: The Defense Department History of United States Decisionmaking on Vietnam.* 5 vols. Boston: Beacon Press, 1971–1972.

Guidebook for Marines (Eleventh Revised Edition). Washington, D.C.: Leatherneck Association, Inc., May 1, 1966.

Heinl, Robert Debs, Jr. *Handbook for Marine NCOs.* Annapolis, MD: Naval Institute Press, 1979.

Heinl, Robert Debs, Jr. *Soldiers of the Sea: the U.S. Marine Corps, 1775–1962.* Annapolis, MD: U.S. Naval Institute Press, 1962.

Hoffman, Carl W., Major, USMC. *Saipan: The Beginning of the End.* Washington, D.C.: Historical Division, Headquarters, U.S. Marine Corps, 1950.

House, Highland II. *United States of America's Congressional Medal of Honor Recipients and their Official Citations.* Columbia Heights, Minnesota: Highland Publishers, 1980.

Huyssen, Ulrich. *The Violence of Fire.* Baker, Louisiana: Joy Publishers, 1979.

Ignatius, Paul R. *On Board: My Life in the Navy, Government, and Business.* Annapolis, MD: Naval Institute Press, 2006.

Jeffers, H. Paul and Dick Levitan. *See Parris And Die.* New York: Hawthorn Books, Inc., 1971.

Johnson, Lyndon B. *Public Papers of the Presidents of the United States: Lyndon B. Johnson, Containing the Public Messages, Speeches, and Statements of the President: 1966 (in two books); Book II—July 1 to December 31, 1966.* Washington, D.C.: U.S. Government Printing Office, 1967.

Johnson, Lyndon Baines. *The Vantage Point: Perspectives of the Presidency, 1963–1969.* New York: Holt, Rinehart and Winston, 1971.

Kasper, Shirl. *Annie Oakley.* Norman, OK: University of Oklahoma Press, 1992.

Katcher, Philip. *Armies of the Vietnam War, 1962–75.* London: Osprey Publishing Ltd., 1983.

Kerrigan, Evans E. *American War Medals and Decorations.* New York: The Viking Press, 1964.

Krulak, Lieutenant General Victor H., USMC. *First to Fight: An Inside View of the U.S. Marine Corps.* Annapolis MD: Naval Institute Press, 1984.

Lamb, David. *Vietnam, Now: A Reporter Returns.* New York: Public Affairs, 2002.

Lanning, Michael Lee, and Dan Cragg. *Inside the VC and the NVA: The Real Story of North Vietnam's Armed Forces.* New York: Fawcett Columbine, 1992.

Lucas, Jim G. *Dateline: Vietnam.* New York: Award House, 1966.

Mares, William. *The Marine Machine.* Garden City, NY: Doubleday & Company, Inc., 1970.

Marine Infantry Battalion (FMFM 6-3). Headquarters, U.S. Marine Corps, 2 June 1969.

Marine Rifle Company/Platoon (FMFM 6-4). Headquarters, U.S. Marine Corps, 10 August 1965.

Marine Rifle Squad (FMFM 6-5). Headquarters, U.S. Marine Corps, 6 April 1966.

Minor, Margaret and Hugh Rawson, ed. *American Heritage Dictionary of American Quotations.* New York: Penguin Reference, 1997.

Montross, Lynn, and Captain Nicholas A. Canzona, USMC. *U.S. Marine Operations in Korea, 1950–1953, Volume I: The Pusan Perimeter.* Washington, D.C.: Historical Branch, G-3 Headquarters, U.S. Marine Corps, 1954.

Moore, Harold G., and Joseph L. Galloway. *We Were Soldiers Once ... And Young.* New York: Random House, 1992.

Murphy, Audie. *To Hell and Back.* New York: MTF Books, 1949.

Nixon, Richard M. *No More Vietnams.* New York: Arbor House, 1985.

O'Sheel, Patrick, Captain, USMCR and Staff Sergeant Gene Cook, USMCR, ed. *Semper Fidelis: The U.S. Marines in the Pacific—1942–1945.* New York: William Sloane Associates, Inc., 1947.

Olsen, James S., and Randy Roberts. *Where the Domino Fell: America and Vietnam: 1945 to 1990.* New York: St. Martin's Press, Inc., 1991.

Palinkas, Lawrence A., and Patricia Coben. *Combat Casualties among U.S. Marine Corps Personnel in Vietnam; 1964–1972.* Bethesda, MD: Naval Medical Research and Development Command, 1985.

Palinkas, Lawrence A., and Patricia Coben. *Disease and Non-Combat Casualties among U.S. Marine Corps Personnel in Vietnam; 1964–1972.* Bethesda, MD: Naval Medical Research and Development Command, 1986.

Pearson, Willard, LTGEN, USA. *The War in the Northern Provinces, 1966–1968.* Washington, D.C.: Department of the Army, 1974.

Pike, Douglas. *PAVN: People's Army of Vietnam.* Novato, CA: Presidio Press, 1986.

Pike, Douglas. *The Viet Cong Strategy of Terror.* A monograph written by Douglas Pike for the United States Mission, Viet-Nam, 1970.

Professional Knowledge Gained From Operational Experience in Vietnam: 1965–1966 (NAVMC 2614). Headquarters, U.S. Marine Corps, 24 February 1967.

Professional Knowledge Gained from Operational Experience in Vietnam: 1967 (FMFMRP 12-41). Headquarters, U.S. Marine Corps, 8 August 1989.

Rawlins, Lieutenant Colonel Eugene W., USMC, and Major William J. Sambito, USMC, ed. *Marines and Helicopters: 1946–1962.* Washington, D.C.: History and Museums Division, Headquarters, U.S. Marine Corps, 1976.

Russell, Lee E. *Armies of the Vietnam War (2).* London: Osprey Publishing Ltd., 1983.

Santelli, James S. *A Brief History of the 4th Marines*. Washington, D.C.: Historical Division, Headquarters, U.S. Marine Corps, 1970.

Schwab, Stephen, and Irving Max. *Guantanamo, USA: The Untold History of America's Cuban Outpost*. Lawrence, Kansas: University Press of Kansas, 2009.

Scruggs, Jan C. and Joel L. Sweerdlow. *To Heal A Nation*. New York: Harper and Row, 1985.

Sharp, Ulysses S. G. Adm, USN, and Gen William C. Westmoreland, USA. *Report on the War in Vietnam (As of June 1968)*. Washington, D.C.: U.S. Government Printing Office, 1968.

Smith, Harvey H. *Area Handbook for North Vietnam*. Washington, D.C.: U.S. Government Printing Office, 1967.

Smith, Harvey H. *Area Handbook for South Vietnam*. Washington, D.C.: U.S. Government Printing Office, 1967.

Smith, Larry. *The Few and the Proud*. New York: W.W. Norton and Company, 2006.

Stevens, Paul Drew, ed. *The Navy Cross in Vietnam: Citations of Awards to Men of the United States Navy and United States Marine Corps, 1964–1973*. Forest Ranch, CA: Sharp and Dunnigan, 1987.

Stoner, Gregg. *The Yellow Footprints to Hell and Back*. New York: iUniverse, Inc., 2008.

Strecker, Edward A., and Kenneth E. Appel. *Psychiatry in Modern Warfare*. New York: The MacMillan Company, 1945.

Thomas, G.C. General, USMC (Ret.) and R.D. Heinl, Jr., Colonel, USMC, and A.A. Agerton, Rear Admiral, USN (Ret.). *The Marine Officer's Guide*. Annapolis, MD: United States Naval Institute, 1956.

Thompson, Sir Robert. *Defeating Communist Insurgency: The Lessons of Malaya and Vietnam*. St. Petersburg, FL: Hailer Publishing, 1966.

Thompson, Sir Robert. *No Exit from Vietnam*. New York: David McKay Company, Inc., 1969.

Truong, Nhu Tang. *A Viet Cong Memoir*. New York: Vintage Books, 1985.

Uhlig, Frank Jr., ed. *1969 Naval Review*. Annapolis, MD: United States Naval Institute Press, 1969.

Vezina, Meridith R. *The History of Marine Recruit Depot San Diego*. San Diego, CA: MCRD Historical Society, 2004.

Walt, Lewis W. *Strange War, Strange Strategy*. New York: Funk and Wagnalls, 1970.

Westmoreland, William C. *A Soldier Reports*. Garden City, New York: Doubleday and Company, 1976.

Wheeler, Keith. *We Are The Wounded*. New York: E. P. Dutton & Company, Inc., 1945.

Periodicals

"5 High School Seniors Enlist." *Greenville Advocate*, March 28, 1967.

Bartlett, SSgt Tom, and MSgt Wes Ward. "Boot Camp '66." *Leatherneck*, Volume XLIX, No. 8, August 1966.

Bartlett, SSgt Tom, USMC. "Corpsman!" *Leatherneck*, June 1966.

"Bobo, The English Bulldog, Follows Master Into Marines." *Charleston News and Courier* (Charleston, SC), April 5, 1968.

Boffey, Philip M. "Vietnam Veterans' Parade a Belated Welcome Home." *New York Times*, November 14, 1982.

Buehner, Kristin. "Call it Love." *The Globe Gazette*, May 25, 1998.

Burrows, Larry and Co Rentmeester. "Marines Blunt the Invasion from the North." *Life*, October 28, 1966.

"Combat-Ready U.S. Marines Land Near North Vietnam." *Greenville Advocate*, March 8, 1965.

"County Marine Dies in Action in Vietnam War." *Greenville Advocate*, April 3, 1967.

Curtis, TSgt. Paul C. "You ... a D.I?" *Leatherneck*, Vol. XL, No. 7, July 1957.

De Borchgrave, Arnaud. "The Battle for Hill 400." *Newsweek*, October 10, 1966.

"DI Force Increases." *Marine Corps CheVron* (MCRD San Diego base newspaper*)*, February 18, 1966.

Duncan, David Douglas. "Inside the Cone of Fire at Con Thien." *Life*, Vol. 63, No. 17, October 27, 1967.

Eldred, Tom. "Ex-Clayton principal found dead." *Delaware State News*, September 5, 1998.

Esterline, Warren. "Hospital Corps Begins 68th Year." *The Camp Pendleton Scout*, June 18, 1965.

Gagnon, Lisa. "The Ultimate Sacrifice: Darke County's Doug Dickey Killed in Vietnam." *Daily Advocate*, July 4, 2003.

Gagnon, Lisa. "Darke County holds dedication ceremony." *Daily Advocate*, June 10, 2003.

Harmon, George T. "Two Charlestonians Among Veterans Of Vietnam War To Receive Medals." *Charleston News and Courier* (Charleston, SC), February 24, 1968.

Jones, Woody. "Dickey Quiet Youth: 200 Gather As Tiny Rossburg Remembers Its Vietnam Hero." *Journal Herald*.

Koon, Warren. "Bill's Bo Becomes Marine." *Evening Post* (Charleston, SC), April 4, 1968.

"Larry J. Larson Killed in Vietnam." *The Carmel Pine Cone*, April 6, 1967.

Leinster, Colin. "The Two Wars of General Lew Walt." *Life*, May 26, 1967.

Lucas, Jim G. "Grim Side Of Paddy War: Casualties 'Light'—For Some." *The Pittsburgh Press*, February 28, 1967.

"Mailcall." *Leatherneck*, February 1968.

"Marine, Rifle Still Number One." *Marine Corps CheVron* (MCRD San Diego base newspaper), June 3, 1966.

"Marriage of Lt. Harry Wortman To Marine General's Daughter, Mary Barney Vogel, Announced." *Rockford Star*, September 9, 1945. Provided by Michelle Tom (Digital Archivist, Beloit College Archives), email to author, May 19, 2014.

Martin, GSgt Bruce. "Million Dollar Flight." *Leatherneck*, September 1969.

"Marvin Cole Honored." *The Lincoln Echo*, Volume 20, Issue 5, August 2011.

"MC Resorts to Draft." *CheVron* (MCRD San Diego base newspaper), September 24, 1965.

Morris, George. "Finding Family: Vietnamese child raised in BR rediscovers relatives in native country." *The Advocate* (Baton Rouge), May 5, 2013.

"'My Rifle': Freedom Fighters' Creed." *Marine Corps CheVron* (MCRD San Diego base newspaper), 6 May 1966.

Neher, LCpl D.A. "40 Special Instructors Give DIs Helping Hand." *Marine Corps CheVron* (MCRD San Diego base newspaper), May 13, 1966.

Parker, Maynard. "Infrared Cameras Spotted Enemy Swarming at Night." *Life*, Vol. 61, No. 18, October 28, 1966.

"Rockford Officer Decorated." *Rockford Star*, September 9, 1951, provided by Michelle Tom (Digital Archivist, Beloit College Archives), email to author May 19, 2014.

Rose, PFC Tom. "For Her Husband." *Leatherneck*, April 1968.

"Services Held For Sgt. Moore." *Evening Post* (Charleston, SC), March 11, 1968.

Snow, Keith. "In Search of Captain Dooley." www.eclectica.org/v2n3/snow.html, accessed 18 September 18, 2015.

Szydik, JO2 Frederick P., USN. "FMSS." *Leatherneck*, September 1969.

Tiede, Tom. "A Soldier Comes Home, His War Well-Fought." *Greenville Advocate*, March 30, 1967.

"Vietnam Decorations Go to 15 Here." *Marine Corps CheVron* (MCRD San Diego base newspaper), May 6, 1966.

"Vietnam Warriors: A Statistical Profile." *Veterans of Foreign Wars of the United States Magazine*, March 1993, Vol 80, No. 7.

Wheeler, Keith. "Marines in Battle Do Not Die." *Chicago Times and North American Newspaper*, 1944. Author's files.

Endnotes

Prologue

1 William Dorsey, interview by author, 8 April 2005.

1. An American Family

1 Shirl Kasper, *Annie Oakley* (Norman, OK: University of Oklahoma Press, 1992), p. 237.
2 Leona Dickey, interview by author, March 24, 2005; April 7, 2007; March 9, 2007.
3 Col Robert D. Heinl, Jr., USMC, *Soldiers of the Sea* (Annapolis, MD: U.S. Naval Institute Press, 1962), p. 444.
4 Carl W. Hoffman, *Saipan: The Beginning of the End* (Washington, D.C.: Historical Division, Headquarters, U.S. Marine Corps, 1950), p. 245.
5 Audie Murphy, *To Hell and Back* (New York: MJF Books, 1949), pp. 273–4.
6 Dennis Dickey, interview by author, March 30, 2005.
7 Tim Barga, interview by author, June 5, 2005.
8 Roger Young, interview by author, July 26, 2005.

2. A Distant War

1 Jack Shulimson and Maj Charles M. Johnson, USMC, *U.S. Marines in Vietnam, 1965, The Landing and the Buildup* (Washington, D.C.: History and Museums Division, Headquarters, U.S. Marine Corps, 1978), p. 12.
2 See U.S. Marine Corps photo: A183780.
3 For a copy of the photograph of General Karch that morning distributed by the Associated Press and World Wide Photos see: Jack Shulimson and Major Charles M. Johnson, USMC, *U.S. Marines in Vietnam, 1965, The Landing and the Buildup* (Washington, D.C.: History and Museums Division, Headquarters, U.S. Marine Corps, 1978), p. 12.
4 BGen Frederick J. Karch, USMC (Ret.), interview by Maj Jack K. Ringler, U.S. Marine Corps Oral History Program; interview conducted at Henderson Hall, Headquarters Marine Corps,

15 January 1972. Transcript of interview furnished by Oral and Video History Section, History Division, Marine Corps University, Quantico, VA.

5   "Combat-Ready U.S. Marines Land Near North Vietnam," *Greenville (OH) Advocate*, 8 March 1965, p. 1.

3. The Buddy Program

1   Lyndon Baines Johnson, *The Vantage Point: Perspectives of the Presidency, 1963–1968* (New York: Holt, Rinehart and Winston, 1971), p 142.; GEN William C. Westmoreland, *A Soldier Reports* (New York: Doubleday & Company, Inc., 1976), p. 132.

2   Jack Shulimson and Maj Charles M. Johnson, USMC, *U.S. Marines in Vietnam, 1965, The Landing and the Buildup* (Washington, D.C.: History and Museums Division, Headquarters, U.S. Marine Corps, 1978), 235–6.

3   Leona Dickey, interview by author, 24 March 2005.

4   Bob Birt, interview by author, 22 March 2016.

4. Platoon 394

1   Marine Corps Recruit Depot Command Chronology #2, dated 26 August 1966.

2   Jack Shulimson and Maj Charles M. Johnson, USMC, *U.S. Marines in Vietnam, 1965, The Landing and the Buildup* (Washington, D.C.: History and Museums Division, Headquarters, U.S. Marine Corps, 1978), p. 240.

3   Jack Shulimson, *U.S. Marines in Vietnam, 1966, An Expanding War* (Washington, D.C.: History and Museums Division, Headquarters, U.S. Marine Corps, 1982), p. 10n; Adm Ulysses S. G. Sharp, USN, CinCPac, and Gen William C. Westmoreland, USA, ComUSMACV, *Report on the War in Vietnam (As of 30 June 1968)* (Washington, D.C.: U.S. Government Printing Office, 1968), pp. 95, 100.

4   Lyndon Baines Johnson, *The Vantage Point: Perspectives of the Presidency, 1963–1969* (New York: Holt, Rinehart and Winston, 1971), p. 246.

5   Mike Gravel, ed., *The Pentagon Papers: The Defense Department History of United States Decisionmaking on Vietnam, vol. 4* (Boston: Beacon Press, 1972), pp. 299, 314, 527–8.

6   "MC Resorts to Draft," *Marine Corps CheVron* (MCRD San Diego base newspaper), September 24, 1965, pp. 1–2.

7   Jack Shulimson, LtCol Leonard A. Blasiol, USMC, Charles R. Smith, and Capt David A. Dawson, USMC, *U.S. Marines in Vietnam, 1968, The Defining Year* (Washington, D.C.: History and Museums Division, Headquarters, U.S. Marine Corps, 1997), pp. 557–8.

8   Marine Corps Recruit Depot Command Chronology #2, dated August 26, 1966.

9   Meredith R. Vezina, *The History of Marine Recruit Depot San Diego* (San Diego, CA: MCRD Museum Historical Society, 2004), p. 80.

10   For a comprehensive description of Marine recruit training in the 1960s, see: *The D.I.: A Builder of a Few Good Men*, 15 min., (Official U.S. Marine Corps documentary (MH-11082) about Drill Instructors); and, *This is Parris Island*, 40 min., (Official U.S. Marine Corps documentary (CMC-TFR 1–63 (Revision Two) about recruit training at Parris Island, SC).

11   William Mares, *The Marine Machine* (Garden City, New York: Doubleday & Company, Inc., 1970), p. 4.

12   TSgt Paul C. Curtis, USMC, "You … a D.I.?" *Leatherneck*, July 1957, p. 24.

13   Larry Smith, *The Few and The Proud: Marine Corps Drill Instructors in Their Own Words* (New York: W.W. Norton & Company, 2006), p. 157.

14 Letter from Douglas Dickey to Harold and Leona Dickey, dated April 24, 1966, courtesy of Dennis Dickey.

15 Keith Fleming, *The U.S. Marine Corps in Crisis: Ribbon Creek and Recruit Training* (Columbia, SC: University of South Carolina Press, 1990), 27.

16 Smith, p. 158.

17 Letter from Douglas Dickey to Harold and Leona Dickey, dated April 15, 1966, courtesy of Dennis Dickey.

18 H. Paul Jeffers and Dick Levitan, *See Parris And Die* (New York: Hawthorn Books, Inc., 1971), p. 81.

19 Bob Birt, interview by author (in person, Ansonia, Ohio), June 18, 2006.

20 Letter from Douglas Dickey to Harold and Leona Dickey, dated April 21, 1966, courtesy of Dennis Dickey.

21 Gregg Stoner, *The Yellow Footprints to Hell and Back* (New York: iUniverse, Inc., 2008), p. 77.

22 Mares, p. 54.

23 LCpl D. A. Neher, USMC, "40 Special Instructors Give DIs Helping Hand," *Marine Corps CheVron* (MCRD San Diego base newspaper), May 13, 1966, p. 4.

24 Letter from Douglas Dickey to Harold and Leona Dickey, dated 30 April 1966, courtesy of Dennis Dickey.

25 Ibid., May 7, 1966.

26 "Vietnam Decorations Go to 15 Here," *Marine Corps CheVron* (MCRD San Diego base newspaper), May 6, 1966, pp. 1, 4.

27 Letter from Douglas Dickey to Harold and Leona Dickey, dated May 7, 1966, courtesy of Dennis Dickey.

28 Ibid.

29 Letter from Douglas Dickey to Harold and Leona Dickey, dated April 12, 1966, courtesy of Dennis Dickey. (Note: Although Doug dated this letter April 12, 1966; based on the postmark and the chronology, he meant to date it: *May 12, 1966*).

30 SSgt Tom Bartlett and MSgt Wes Ward, USMC, "Boot Camp '66," *Leatherneck*, Number 8, August 1966, p. 35.

31 Letter from Douglas Dickey to Harold and Leona Dickey, dated May 23, 1966, courtesy of Dennis Dickey.

32 Ibid., May 17, 1966.

33 Ibid., May 15, 1966.

34 Ibid., May 22, 1966.

35 Ibid., May 26, 1966.

36 For Marine Corps shooting qualification course see: *U.S Marine Corps Rifle Marksmanship and Data Book (For U.S. Rifle 7.62-MM, M-14)*, NAVMC 42-GS (Rev. pp. 1–66).

37 Edson Range actually has a 500-meter line, which is about 48 yards longer than a standard 500-yard range. See: "Marine, Rifle Still Number One," *Marine Corps CheVron* (MCRD San Diego base newspaper), June 3, 1966, pp. 4–5.

38 Letter from Douglas Dickey to Harold and Leona Dickey, dated May 26, 1966, courtesy of Dennis Dickey.

39 Ibid., May 23, 1966.

40 Ibid., June 19, 1966.

41 Letter from Douglas Dickey to Norman Dickey, dated June 30, 1966, courtesy of Norman Dickey.

42 Kemper F. Cowing (compiled by) and Courtney Ryley Cooper (edited by), *"Dear Folks At Home - - -" The glorious story of the United States Marines in France as told by their Letters from the Battlefield* (New York: Houghton Mifflin Company, 1919), p. 3.

43 Letter from Douglas Dickey to Harold and Leona Dickey, dated June 27, 1966, courtesy of Dennis Dickey.

44   Ibid.

45   Ibid., June 29, 1966.

46   Ibid., July 31, 1966.

47   Ibid., August 3, 1966.

48   Ibid., August 11, 1966.

49   Ibid., August 14, 1966.

5. I Corps: "Marineland"

1   *A Marine's Guide To The Republic Of Vietnam*, MCBul 3480 (Prepared by G-2 HQ FMFPAC, May 11, 1966), p. 52.

2   BGen Edwin H. Simmons, USMC, "Marine Corps Operations in Vietnam, 1965–1966," (Reprinted from *Naval Review 1968*), *The Marines in Vietnam, 1954–1973, An Anthology and Annotated Bibliography* (Washington, D.C.: History and Museums Division, Headquarters, U.S. Marine Corps, 1974), p. 58.

3   Capt Robert W. Whitlow, USMCR, *U.S. Marines in Vietnam, 1954–1964, The Advisory and Combat Assistance Era* (Washington, D.C.: History and Museums Division, Headquarters, U.S. Marine Corps, 1977), pp. 132 n, 133 map.

4   BGen Edwin H. Simmons, USMC, "Marine Corps Operations in Vietnam, 1967," *Naval Review 1969* (Annapolis, MD: United States Naval Institute Press, 1969), p. 114.

5   Mike Gravel, ed., *The Pentagon Papers: The Defense Department History of United States Decisionmaking on Vietnam*, vol. 3 (Boston: Beacon Press, 1971) p. 422. See also: Jack Shulimson and Maj Charles M. Johnson, USMC, *U.S. Marines in Vietnam, 1965, The Landing and the Buildup* (Washington, D.C.: History and Museums Division, Headquarters, U.S. Marine Corps, 1978), p. 9.

6   Gen William C. Westmoreland, USA, *A Soldier Reports* (Garden City, NY: Doubleday & Company, Inc., 1976), p. 124.

7   Gen Lewis W. Walt, USMC, *Strange War, Strange Strategy* (New York: Funk & Wagnalls, 1970), p. 200.

8   Colin Leinster, "The Two Wars of General Lew Walt," *Life*, May 26, 1967, pp. 77–84.

9   Walt, p. 20.

10   Ibid., p. 27.

11   Gen Wallace M. Greene Jr. on-camera interview, *Vietnam: A Television History*, Episode 4: "LBJ Goes to War," 60 min., WGBH Boston, 1983, VHS.

12   Shulimson and Johnson, p. 69.

13   Ibid., pp. 69–83, 238.

14   Ibid., p. 238.

15   Maynard Parker, "Infrared Cameras Spotted Enemy Swarming at Night," *Life*, October 28, 1966, p. 35.

16   Edward Doyle, *The Vietnam Experience: The North* (Boston: Boston Publishing Company, 1986), p. 44.

17   Parker, p. 35.

18   LTGEN Willard Pearson, USA, *The War in the Northern Provinces, 1966–1968* (Washington, D.C.: Department of the Army, 1974), p. 98, chart 4.

19   Walt, p. 141.

20   Shulimson, p. 176.

21   Walt, p. 140.

22   Lyndon B. Johnson, "Remarks at the Parliamentary Luncheon, Canberra, Australia," October 21, 1966," *Public Papers of the Presidents of the United States: Lyndon B. Johnson, Containing the*

Public Messages, Speeches, and Statements of the President: 1966 (in two books); Book II—July1 to December 31, 1966 (Washington, D.C.: U.S. Government Printing Office, 1967), p. 1242.

23 BGen Edwin H. Simmons, USMC, "Marine Corps Operation in Vietnam, 1968–1972," *The Marines in Vietnam, 1954–1973, An Anthology and Annotated Bibliography* 2nd ed. (Washington, D.C.: History and Museums Division, Headquarters, U.S. Marine Corps, 1985), p. 156.

24 Ibid., p. 156. According to General Simmons, 19,733 Marines were killed and 67,207 were wounded during World War II. While, according to his figures, 14,615 Marines were killed and 88,589 were wounded in Vietnam.

25 BGen Edwin Simmons' on-camera comments in *A Fellowship of Valor: The Battle History of the United States Marines*, 150 min., A&E Home Video and the History Channel, 1998.

6. 1st Battalion, 4th Marines: God, Country, Duty, Corps

1 Kenneth W. Condit and Edwin T. Turnbladh, *Hold High the Torch: A History of the 4th Marines* (Washington, D.C.: Historical Branch, G-3 Division, Headquarters, U.S. Marine Corps, 1960), pp. 47–50.

2 Col Robert Debs Heinl, Jr., USMC, *Soldiers of the Sea: The United States Marine Corps, 1775–1962* (Annapolis, MD: United States Naval Institute, 1962), p. 252.

3 Condit and Turnbladh, pp. 111–7.

4 Ibid., p. 236.

5 James S. Santelli, *A Brief History of the 4th Marines* (Washington, D.C.: Historical Division, Headquarters, U.S. Marine Corps, 1970), p. 36.

6 Ibid., p. 41.

7 Jack Westerman III, (LtCol Westerman's son), interview by author, March 24, 2007. See also: Dick Culver, "Black Jack Westerman," www.bobrohrer.com/sea_stories/black_jack_westerman. pdf, retrieved February 26, 2014.

8 The man was identified as Major Morgan McNeely.

9 Lynn Montross and Capt Nicholas A. Canzona, USMC, *U.S. Marine Operations in Korea 1950–1953, Volume I, The Pusan Perimeter* (Washington, D.C.: Historical Branch, G-3 Headquarters, U.S. Marine Corps, 1954), pp. 132–5.

10 Andrew Geer, *The New Breed: The Story of the U.S. Marines in Korea* (New York: Harper & Brothers, 1952), p. 163.

11 Jack Shulimson, *U.S. Marines in Vietnam, 1966, An Expanding War* (Washington, D.C.: History and Museums Division, Headquarters, U.S. Marine Corps, 1982), p. 189.

12 LtCol Jack Westerman, USMC, tape recorded interview by Marine Corps field historian, December 7, 1966. Oral and Video History Section, History Division, Marine Corps University, Quantico, VA, File #269-A.

13 1st Battalion, 4th Marines, Command Chronology, September 1966, dated October 3, 1966, p. 6.

14 "155 V.T." refers to 155mm artillery rounds, armed with a Variable Time (V.T.) fuse. The V.T. fuse causes the artillery round to detonate in the air above the target rather than detonating once it hits the ground. This "air burst" is much more devastating to troops in the open because it showers the area from above with shrapnel—it literally begins to "rain shrapnel" on the enemy. Westerman had his Marines dig "down and back" so that they would have protection in their fighting holes from the shrapnel coming down at them from the air bursts—while the NVA soldiers would be caught helpless in the open.

15 LtCol Jack Westerman, USMC, tape recorded interview.

16 1st Battalion, 4th Marines, Command Chronology, September 1966, dated October 3, 1966. Westerman reports his figures twice in his command chronology: on pp. 12 and 15.

17 Paul Drew Stevens, ed., *The Navy Cross Vietnam: Citations of Awards to Men of The United States Navy and The United States Marine Corps, 1964–1973* (Forest Ranch, CA: Sharp & Dunnigan Publications, Inc., 1987), pp. 181–2.

18 For casualties suffered by 1st Battalion, 4th Marines, during the battle, see: 1st Battalion, 4th Marines, Command Chronology, September 1966, dated October 3, 1966, journal pages for September 16–19, 1966. For individual names, see: "Casualty Reports" on: http://1stbn4thmarines.net/Battalion/casualties.htm, retrieved on August 23, 2018.

19 LtCol Jack Westerman, USMC, tape recorded interview.

20 Copy of 1st Battalion, 4th Marines, "Welcome aboard" letter furnished to author by David Gregg.

21 Department of Defense Form 214 for Captain Harold John Edwin Deibert, USMC, dated February 28, 1971, provided to author by the Deibert family.

22 Donald W. Rohleder was 23 years old and a native of Maryland.

23 3rd Tank Battalion, Command Chronology, October 1966, Enclosure (4), Tank Combat Operations, p. 4, also Enclosure (12), Supporting Documents, 3rd Tank Bn SITREP Number 270 for the period 130001H October 1966.

24 Letter from Douglas E. Dickey to Harold and Leona Dickey, dated October 13, 1966, courtesy of Dennis Dickey.

25 "mules" refers to the M274 Military Mule, a small 4-wheel drive vehicle used to transport equipment and supplies. The vehicle was basically a 4'× 9' platform powered by a four-cylinder air-cooled engine. Mules were used instead of Jeeps to transport smaller loads, particularly within infantry units.

26 Bob Birt, interview by author, March 22, 2016.

27 Paul Dickey, interview by author, April 7, 2005.

28 Shulimson, p. 41.

29 LtCol Leonard A. Blasiol, USMC, Charles R. Smith, and Capt David A. Dawson, USMC, *U.S. Marines in Vietnam, 1968, The Defining Year* (Washington, D.C.: History and Museums Division, Headquarters, U.S. Marine Corps, 1997), p. 344.

30 3rd Tank Battalion, Command Chronology, October 1966, Enclosure (3), Intelligence, p. 1.

31 1st Battalion, 4th Marines, Command Chronology, October 1966, p. 5.

32 Letter from Douglas Dickey to Harold and Leona Dickey, dated November 5, 1966, courtesy of Dennis Dickey.

7. Norman

1 Harold "Norman" Dickey, interview by author, March 31, 2005.

8. Company C

1 LtCol Robert E. Kelley, USMC (Ret.), interview by author, March 14, 2008.

2 1st Battalion, 4th Marines, Command Chronology, November 1966, p. 6.

3 Col Robert Debs Heinl, Jr., USMC (Ret.), *Handbook for Marine NCOs* (Annapolis, MD: Naval Institute Press, 1979), pp. 578–82.

4 Letter from Douglas Dickey to Harold and Leona, dated November 12, 1966, courtesy of Dennis Dickey.

5 For unexplained reasons, probably just routine administrative oversight, the Truoi River area is spelled "Troui" with the "u" and the "o" transposed throughout the official reports and operation orders.

6   LtCol Alfred M. Allen, MC, U.S. Army, *Internal Medicine in Vietnam, Volume I, Skin Diseases in Vietnam, 1965–72* (Washington, D.C.: Office of the Surgeon General and Center of Military History, United States Army, 1977), pp. 102–19; see also: Lawrence A. Palinkas, PhD, and Patricia Coben, *Disease and Non-Battle Injuries Among U.S. Marines in Vietnam* (Bethesda, MD: Naval Medical Research and Development Command, 1986), Table 1.

7   Letter from Douglas Dickey to Nellie B. Schlecty, dated November 22, 1966, courtesy of Norman Dickey.

8   Ibid., December 5, 1966.

9   Steve Pruitt, interview by author, July 10, 2013.

10   For the tactical locations of the 10 CAC teams, see: 1st Battalion, 4th Marines, Command Chronology for November 1966, Tab G (Situation Reports), and Tab H (Operation Order 008-66).

11   1st Battalion, 4th Marines, Command Chronology for November 1966, Tab F: S-3 Journal. See journal entries #23–25 for period 140600–150600 November 1966; and entries #2,4,5 for period 150600–160600 November 1966.

12   Letter from Douglas Dickey to Harold and Leona Dickey, dated November 29, 1966, courtesy of Dennis Dickey.

13   Ibid.

14   Ibid., December 5, 1966. Note: the letter is dated "5 Nov 1966." However, by the postmark on the envelope (8 December) and the information and references in the body of the letter, it is clear that Doug mistakenly wrote November when he meant December—a common mistake people make at the beginning of a month.

9. Okinawa

1   The six main Marine bases were named after Major Henry A. Courtney, Jr., Private First Class William A. Foster, Private Dale M. Hansen, Sergeant Elbert L. Kinser, Private Robert M. McTureous, Jr., and Private First Class Albert E. Schwab.

2   See the "Casualty Summaries" http://thewall-usa.com/summary.asp, retrieved September 12, 2013.

3   Charles A. Runnels, interview by author, April 10, 2005.

4   Larry Normand, interview by author, May 19, 2013.

5   Isabelle Hudson, interview by author, January 29, 2013, November 1, 2013.

6   SSgt Tom Barlett, USMC, "Corpsman!" *Leatherneck*, June 1966, p. 39.

7   Greg Nichols, interview by author, May 9, 2008.

8   LCpl Warren Esterline, USMC, "Hospital Corps Begins 68th Year," *The Camp Pendleton Scout*, June 18, 1965, p. 6.

9   Ibid.

10   JO 2 Frederick P. Szydik, USN, "FMSS," *Leatherneck*, September 1969, p 33.

11   Keith Wheeler, *We Are The Wounded* (New York: E. P. Dutton & Company, Inc., 1945), p. 36.

12   Ibid., pp. 28, 36–7.

13   U.S. Marine Corps, *Amphibian Vehicles, FMFM 9-2* (Washington, D.C.: Headquarters, U.S. Marine Corps, September 17, 1964), pp. 182–3.

10. The Special Landing Force

1   U.S. Marine Corps, *Advanced Force Base Operations in Micronesia, FMFRP 12-46* (Washington, D.C.: Headquarters, United States Marine Corps, 21 August 1992), p. 41.

2   "Marriage of Lt. Harry Wortman To Marine General's Daughter, Mary Barney Vogel, Announced," *Rockford (IL) Star*, September 9, 1945, provided by Michelle Tom (Digital Archivist, Beloit College Archives), email to author May 19, 2014.

3   "Rockford Officer Decorated," *Rockford (IL) Star*, September 9, 1951, provided by Michelle Tom (Digital Archivist, Beloit College Archives), email to author, May 19, 2014; see also: U.S. Marine Corps Biography sheet on Colonel Harry D. Wortman, USMC, provided by Annette Amerman (USMC Archives, Quantico, VA) email to author, May 12, 2014.

4   Jack Shulimson, *U.S. Marines in Vietnam, 1966, An Expanding War* (Washington, D.C.: History and Museums Division, Headquarters, U.S. Marine Corps, 1982), pp. 188–9.

5   Maj Gary L. Telfer, USMC, LtCol Lane Rogers, USMC, and V. Keith Fleming, Jr., *U.S. Marines in Vietnam, 1967, Fighting the North Vietnamese* (Washington, D.C.: History and Museums Division, Headquarters, U.S. Marine Corps, 1984), p. 152.

11. HMM-363: "The Lucky Red Lions"

1   Bill Collier, *The Adventures of a Helicopter Pilot: Flying the H-34 Helicopter in Vietnam for the United States Marine Corps* (Sandpoint Idaho: Wandering Star Press, 2014), p. 69.

2   Jack Shulimson, *U.S. Marines in Vietnam, 1966, An Expanding War* (Washington, D.C.: History and Museums Division, Headquarters, U.S. Marine Corps, 1982), p. 368.

3   HMM-363 Command Chronology Report for Period January 1–18, 1967, dated January 17, 1967, pp. 1–7. The four Marines killed in the accident from HMM-363 were: 1stLt Gary D. Shields (pilot), 1stLt Robert P. Schena (pilot), Cpl Ernest H. Wilson (crewman), and LCpl Patrick L. Wood (crewman). The six Marines from 1st Shore Party Battalion killed in the crash were: LCpl Timothy D. Berry, LCpl William F. Coyne, LCpl Richard E. Fuchs, LCpl Alan R. Moore, PFC Francis L. Langley, and PFC Sandy L. Ross. All of the men's bodies were recovered. See casualty cards posted on; www.virtualwall.org/js/Profile.htm, retrieved on August 28, 2018.

4   Marine Aircraft Group 36, Command Chronology for January 1967, dated February 7, 1967, Enclosure II, "Narrative Summary," paragraph B and paragraph E.4, pp. 1–2.

5   HMM-363 Command Chronology Report for Period 19–31 January 1967, p. 2.

6   LtCol William R. Fails, USMC, *Marines and Helicopters, 1962–1973* (Washington, D.C.: History and Museums Division, Headquarters, U.S. Marine Corps, 1978), p. 9.

7   Tim O'Toole, interview by author, April 16, 2015.

8   Collier, pp. 140–41.

9   Fails, p. 137.

10 LtGen Keith B. McCutcheon, USMC, "Marine Aviation in Vietnam, 1962–1970," *The Marines in Vietnam, 1954–1973, An Anthology and Annotated Bibliography* 2nd edition, (Washington, D.C.: History and Museums Division, Headquarters, U.S. Marine Corps, 1985), p. 293.

11 Gen Lewis W. Walt, USMC, *Strange War, Strange Strategy* (New York: Funk & Wagnalls, 1970) p. 145.

12. Two Brothers

1   USS *Vancouver* (LPD-2) Deck Log Book for January 1–31, 1967, see entry for January 26, 1967. Retrieved from National Archives on May 28, 2014: http://media.nara.gov/dc-metro/594258-navy-deck-logs/batch-v/vancouver-lpd-2-1967-01/vancouver-lpd-2-1967-01.pdf

2   Letter from Norman Dickey to author, postmarked July 14, 2013.

3   Letter from Douglas Dickey to Harold and Leona Dickey, dated January 27, 1967, courtesy of Dennis Dickey.

4   Letter from Norman Dickey to Harold and Leona Dickey, dated January 28, 1967.
5   Letter from Norman Dickey to author, postmarked July 14, 2013.

13. Exercise *Mud Puppy III*

1   1st Battalion, 4th Marines, Command Chronology, February 1967, March 4, 1967, p. 10.
2   See: *BLT 1/4 Op Order 1-67: Mud Puppy III*, dated January 31, 1967.

14. Operation *Deckhouse VI*

1   Maj Gary L. Telfer, USMC, LtCol Lane Rogers, USMC, and V. Keith Fleming, Jr., *U.S. Marines in Vietnam, 1967, Fighting the North Vietnamese* (Washington, D.C.: History and Museums Division, Headquarters, U.S. Marine Corps, 1984), p. 53.
2   For geographic details of Duc Pho District, see U.S Defense Mapping Agency 1:50,000-scale map sheets: 6739 II, 6738 I, 6738 II, 6838 III, 6838 IV.
3   U.S. Marine Corps, *Professional Knowledge Gained From Operational Experience in Vietnam, 1965–1966. NAVMC 2614* (Washington, D.C.: Department of the Navy, Headquarters, U.S. Marine Corps, February 24, 1967), pp. 263–376.
4   Lawrence A. Palinkas, PhD, and Patricia Coben, *Combat Casualties Among U.S. Marine Corps Personnel In Vietnam: 1964–1972 (Report No. 85-11)*, San Diego, CA: Naval Health Research Center, May 1985), p. 9. See Table G: Combat Casualties by Wounding Agent, U.S. Marines in Vietnam, 1964–1972. Specifically, 27.5% of total casualties were attributed to mines/booby traps; and 26.9% of total casualties were attributed to bullets. Also, 54.9 % of all amputations were attributed to mines/booby traps while bullets, the next largest cause of amputations, accounted for 10.4 % of all amputations.
5   Telfer *et al*, p. 56.
6   Ibid., p. 57.
7   Copy of naval message provided to author by David C. Gregg during in-person interview on May 17, 2017. The message is dated 140540Z Feb 67. In naval message format, the message reads: "IF WE RECEIVE FIRE, LET'S DRAW BLOOD. I DON'T LIKE RPT THAT STATES: QUOTE NEGATIVE RESULTS UNQUOTE. BLACK JACK SENDS."
8   1st Battalion, 4th Marines, Command Chronology, March 4, 1967. See Journal entry #10, Journal Sheet 160600H to 170600H.
9   1stLt Jim G. Lucas, "Marpi Point," *Semper Fidelis: The U.S. Marines in the Pacific: 1942–1945*, edited by Captain Patrick O'Sheel, USMCR and Staff Sergeant Gene Cook, USMCR (New York: William Sloane Associates, Inc., 1947), pp. 223–5.
10   The most famous American war correspondent was Ernie Pyle. Pyle reported World War II from the front lines. He believed the real story was the spirit of average GIs who fought and bled on the front lines of the war. While other reporters haunted the command posts and headquarters trying to get scoops form generals and admirals, Pyle reported the war from muddy foxholes, talking to soldiers. He lived with the riflemen. He "celebrated the uncelebrated." Ernie Pyle died the way so many of the soldiers he loved died. He was killed in a hail of Japanese machine-gun fire on April 19, 1945 during the battle to take Okinawa.
11   Jim G. Lucas, *Dateline: Viet Nam* (New York: Award House, 1966).
12   Jim G. Lucas, "Grim Side Of Paddy War: Casualties 'Light'—For Some," *The Pittsburgh Press*, February 28, 1967, p. 1.
13   1st Battalion, 4th Marines, Command Chronology, March 4, 1967. See Journal entries #3 and #18, Journal Sheet 200600H to 210600H.

14 Lucas, "Grim Side Of Paddy War ..." p. 8.
15 Larry Wilson, interview by author, 1 June 2013.
16 Email from Ralph Grant to author, 1 December 2016.
17 Defense Department Photo (Marine Corps) A191129.
18 "Marvin Cole Honored," *The Lincoln Echo (Fort Smith, AR)*, August 2011, Volume 20, Issue 5.
19 Lionel Lawson, interview by author, 26 February 2013.
20 Lucas, *Dateline: Viet Nam*, p. 212.
21 Letter from Doug Dickey to Harold and Leona Dickey, dated March 1, 1967, courtesy of Dennis Dickey.
22 Letter from Doug Dickey to Carol and Lloyd Trittschuh, dated March 6, 1967.
23 Marine Medium Helicopter Squadron 363, After Action Report Operation DECKHOUSE VI, March 12, 1967, p. 4.
24 Ibid., p. 5; see also: Battalion Landing Team 1/4, Combat After Action Report Operation DECKHOUSE VI, March 9, 1967, p. 16.
25 Battalion Landing Team 1/4, Combat After Action Report Operation DECKHOUSE VI, March 9, 1967, p. 17.
26 Ibid., p. 6.
27 Ibid., pp. 21–2.
28 Lucas, "Grim Side Of Rice Paddy War ..." p. 1.
29 Ibid., p. 12.
30 Program entitled "MEMORIAL SERVICE For The Men Who Gave Their Lives For Their Country During OPERATION DECKHOUSE VI, USS VANCOUVER LPD-2, 4 March 1967." Enclosed with Doug Dickey's letter to Harold and Leona Dickey, dated 15 March 1967, courtesy of Dennis Dickey.
31 Battalion Landing Team 1/4, Combat After Action Report Operation DECKHOUSE VI, March 9, 1967, p. 31.

15. Subic

1 Greg Long, interview by author, April 11, 2005.
2 Col John F. Juul, USMC, (Ret.), interview by author, October 1, 2013.
3 Battalion Landing Team 1/4, Combat After-Action Report, Operation Beacon Hill I, dated April 9, 1967. See Paragraph 11.a.: "Personnel Losses," p. 15.
4 1st Battalion, 4th Marines, Command Chronology, March 1967, dated April 9, 1967, Section II, Paragraph F: "Morale, Postal Affairs, Liberty, R&R, PX," p. 4.

16. A Purple Heart

1 Larry Burrows and Co Rentmeester, "Marines Blunt the Invasion form the North," *Life*, October 28, 1966, pp. 30–40; Arnaud de Borchgrave, "The Battle for Hill 400," *Newsweek*, October 10, 1966, pp. 46–48.
2 3rd Battalion, 4th Marines, Command Chronology for March 1967, dated April 4, 1967, p. IV–4.

17. Operation *Beacon Hill*

1 Letter from Douglas Dickey to Vera (Dickey) Moore, March 18, 1967.
2 For details on the struggle to get the restrictions against preemptive artillery strikes in the DMZ lifted, see: Gen William C. Westmoreland, USA, *A Soldier Reports* (Garden City, NJ: Doubleday &

Company, Inc., 1976), pp. 196, 201; and LtGen Willard Pearson, USA, *The War in the Northern Provinces 1966–1968* (Washington, D.C.: Department of the Army, 1974), p. 12.

3 Maj Gary L. Telfer, USMC, LtCol Lane Rogers, USMC, and V. Keith Fleming, Jr., *U.S. Marines in Vietnam, 1967, Fighting the North Vietnamese* (Washington, D.C.: History and Museums Division, Headquarters, U.S. Marine Corps, 1984), p. 10.

4 1st Composite Provisional Bn was located at grid YD213741. For location of Gio Linh firebase, see 12th Marines Command Chronology for March 1967, dated April 10, 1967, p. 1-III-1.

5 1st Battalion, 12th Marines, Command Chronology for period February 1 to February 28, 1967, dated March 3, 1967, Significant events entry for March 26: "At 0716 Battery C-1/12 and Battalion Command group displaced to vicinity of GIO LINH."

6 12th Marines Command Chronology for March 1967, dated April 10, 1967, see Tab D: Journal: At 1330 on March 1, 1967, entry reads: "1235 General Walt visited Gio Linh CP [Command Post]. The entry for 1345 reads: "Received call from Gy Jerrel (OP Chief) that General Walt directed "C" Brty to displace because he (General Walt) was afraid they might be overrun."

7 According to the 12th Marines Command Chronology for March 1967, dated April 10, 1967, the US Army unit at Gio Linh was Battery B, 6th Battalion, 27th Artillery; see "Unit and Task Organization," p. 1-III-1. The battery was equipped with M107 self-propelled howitzers.

8 Telfer *et al,* p. 155.

9 Statement by Maj William M. Thurber, USMC, Marine Corps field historian, Oral and Video History Section, History Division, Marine Corps University, Quantico, VA, File #932A.

10 Battalion Landing Team 1/4, Combat After Action Report (Operation Beacon Hill I), dated April 9, 1967, pp. 4–5.

11 Private Nguyen Van Hung, quoted in: David Chanoff and Doan Van Toai, *Portrait of the Enemy* (New York: Random House, 1986), p. 48.

12 David Lamb, *Vietnam Now: A Reporter Returns to Vietnam* (New York: Public Affairs, 2002), 95.

13 Letter from Douglas Dickey to Vera Moore, dated March 18, 1967. Letter courtesy of Vera Moore.

14 Kent Hansen, interview by author, September 4, 2007.

15 Sgt James M. Couch II, USMC, interview by Marine Corps field historian, November 30, 1967, Oral and Video History Section, History Division, Marine Corps University, Quantico, VA, File #1878A.

16 For a description of the action, see the unit journal for 1st Battalion, 4th Marines, enclosed in the battalion's Command Chronology for March 1967. With regard to Company B's action, see journal entries #14 and #23 for period, 220600 to 230600 March 1967.

17 2ndLt Salvador Martinez, interview by Marine Corps field historian, Oral and Video History Section History Division, Marine Corps University, Quantico, VA, File# 3948A.

18 Fred Gaffen, *Unknown Warriors: Canadians in Vietnam* (Toronto, Canada: Dundurn Press, 1990), pp. 36–7. The number of Canadians who served in Vietnam may be as high as 30,000. The number is difficult to verify because many gave U.S. addresses when they enlisted and U.S. Government records are somewhat difficult to cross reference with regard to citizenship and service in Vietnam.

19 Silver Star Medal Citation for 2ndLt John S. Szymanski, United States Marine Corps; see also Letter from Capt Robert D. Kelley, USMC, to Mrs. John S. Szymanski, dated April 2, 1967.

20 Colin McClelland, interview by author, February 23, 2013.

21 Carl H. Martin, interview by author, August 26, 2015.

22 David Rumsey, interview by author, May 26, 2016.

23 Sgt Jimmie L. Blick, USMC, interview conducted at Marine Corps Schools, Quantico Virginia. Oral and Video History Section, History Division, Marine Corps University, Quantico, VA, File #2181-1B.

18. Easter Sunday

1   3rd Marine Division Command Chronology for period March 1, 1967 to March 31, 1967, dated April 19, 1967, p. 31.

2   Email from Jennifer Burke, Public Affairs Specialist, Selective Service System National Headquarters to John B. Lang, dated October 11, 2018. For more on the Marine Corps' use of the draft during the Vietnam War see: LtCol Leonard A. Blasiol, USMC, Charles R. Smith, and Capt David A. Dawson, USMC, *U.S. Marines in Vietnam, 1968, The Defining Year* (Washington, D.C.: History and Museums Division, Headquarters, U.S. Marine Corps, 1997), p. 580.

3   Richard Van Vactor, interview by author, May 28, 2013.

4   Jerry Idziak, interview by author, May 9, 2013.

5   Marine Corps Landing Force Development Activities, Marine Corps Schools, Quantico, VA, *U.S. Marine Corps Rifle Squad FMFM 6–5* (Washington, D.C.: Headquarters, U.S. Marine Corps, April 6, 1966), pp. 336–339.

6   Dennis Heider, interview by author, July 23, 2017.

7   Haywood J. Swearingen, interview by author, May 5, 2014.

8   Keith Snow, "In Search of Captain Dooley," www.eclectica.org/v2n3/snow.html, accessed September 18, 2015.

9   Phillip Key, interview by author, April 13, 2017.

10   Mike Helton, interview by author, March 17, 2018.

11   Carl H. Martin, interview by author, August 26, 2015.

12   Larry Wilson, interview by author, June 1, 2013.

13   David Rumsey, interview by author (in person, Ansonia, OH), June 18, 2006.

14   Steve Pruitt, interview by author, July 10, 2013.

15   BGen Edwin H. Simmons, USMC, "Marine Corps Operations in Vietnam, 1967," *1969 Naval Review,* Frank Uhlig Jr., ed., (Annapolis, MD: United States Naval Institute Press, 1969), p. 136.

16   Maj Gary L. Telfer, USMC, LtCol Lane Rogers, USMC, and V. Keith Fleming, Jr., *U.S. Marines in Vietnam, 1967, Fighting the North Vietnamese* (Washington, D.C.: History and Museums Division, Headquarters, U.S. Marine Corps, 1984), p. 118.

17   Ibid., pp. 229–231.

18   Larry Normand, interview by author, May 19, 2013.

19   LtCol William R. Fails, USMC, *Marines and Helicopters, 1962–1973* (Washington, D. C.: History and Museums Division, Headquarters, U.S. Marine Corps, 1978), p. 65.

20   Bill Collier, *The Adventures of a Helicopter Pilot: Flying the H-34 Helicopter in Vietnam for the United States Marine Corps* (Sandpoint, ID: Wandering Star Press, 2014), p. 106.

21   "Todd Ryan's Story About Operation Beacon Hill," an unpublished statement written by Todd Ryan and given to David Gregg before Ryan died in October 2009. David Gregg provided this to the author on 19 May 2017.

22   Greg Nichols, interview by author, May 9, 2008.

23   Tim O'Toole, interview by author, April 16, 2015.

24   Email, Lionel Lawson to author, June 26, 2013.

25   David C. Gregg, interview by author, May 17, 2017.

26   Email from Carl H. Martin to author, dated August 25, 2015. See attachment to email, "Corporal Lee's Story as Told to Me by Him."

27   Carl Martin, interview by author, September 24, 2015.

28   Silver Star Medal citation for Corporal Douglas W. Lee, USMC.

29   PFC Tom Rose, "For Her Husband," *Leatherneck,* April 1968, p. 65.

30   Dr. Ronald R. Bouterie, LCDR, USN (MC), interview by Major Gary L. Telfer, Marine Corps field historian, on board the USS *Princeton*, April 1, 1967, Oral and Video History Section, History Division, Marine Corps University, Quantico, VA, File #932A.

31 Larry Wilson, interview by author, June 1, 2013.

32 Keith Wheeler, "Marines in Battle Do Not Die," *Chicago Times and North American Newspaper*, 1944, author's files.

33 David C. Gregg, interview by author, May 19, 2017.

34 Tom Tiede, "A Soldier Comes Home, His War Well-Fought," *Greenville (Ohio) Daily Advocate*, Thursday, March 30, 1967, Opinion page, p. 4.

35 1st Battalion, 4th Marines, Command Chronology, March 1967. See Journal entry #16 for 260600H to 270600H March 1967 for Operation Beacon Hill, 1st Battalion, 4th Marines.

36 LtCol Leonard A. Blasiol, USMC, Charles R. Smith, and Capt David A. Dawson, USMC, *U.S. Marines in Vietnam, 1968, The Defining Year* (Washington, D.C.: History and Museums Division, Headquarters, U.S. Marine Corps, 1997), Appendix J: Tables of Organization, p. 766.

37 1st Battalion, 4th Marines, Command Chronology, April 1967 dated May 6, 1967, paragraph II. B: "Problem Areas/New Developments." And Paragraph II. C: "Personnel," pp. 3–4.

38 1st Battalion, 4th Marines, Combat After Action Report (Operation Prairie IV) dated June 7, 1967.

39 Telfer *et al*, p. 155.

40 1st Battalion, 4th Marines, Command Chronology, April 1967, dated May 6, 1967, "Items of Significant Interest," page 7.

41 Telfer *et al*, p. 10.

42 Robert Sheridan, interview by author, August 22, 2007.

43 Letter from PFC Gary L. Hudson to his parents dated March 30, 1967. Enclosed as part of "Diary of Vietnam: Gary Lee Hudson 2272112, 1st Bn. 4th Marines C-Co FPO, San Francisco, California, December 5, 1966 to December 10, 1967." This is a collection of letters assembled and edited by Gary's father, courtesy of Isabelle Hudson and Larry Normand.

19. The Gold Star

1 1918 newspaper editorial supporting the adoption of the Gold Star as a mourning symbol for those killed in action, as quoted in: Holly S. Fenelon, *American Gold Star Mothers Inc., 1928–2010: A History* (Doylestown, PA: Platform Press, 2010), p. 30.

2 Lisa Gagnon, "The Ultimate Sacrifice: Darke County's Doug Dickey Killed in Vietnam," *Daily Advocate (Greenville, Ohio)*, July 4, 2003.

3 Steven Dickey, interview by author, May 31, 2005.

4 Richard Birt is one of Bob Birt's distant cousins.

5 Diane Birt, interview by author, June 4, 2005.

6 Letter from Douglas Dickey to Norman Dickey, dated March 18, 1967, courtesy of Norman Dickey.

7 Letter from Leona Dickey to author, dated December 14, 2007. Leona Dickey enclosed a number of poems and letters she had written over the years in this letter, including the poems, *Rose Garden*, and *The Medal*, which is included in Chapter 20.

8 "5 High School Seniors Enlist," *Greenville (Ohio) Advocate*, March 28, 1967, p. 1. The five young men who enlisted were: Dale Burk, Samuel Stiles, Tom Brumbaugh, Robert Kimball, and Jack Phillips.

9 According to the Garst Museum in Greenville, Ohio, the casualties from Darke County are listed below, in order of loss. All were members of the U.S. Army except where noted otherwise: James V. Pottkotter (November 1, 1965), Sammy A. Barga (May 17, 1966), Gene M. Lutz (USMC) (May 20, 1966), Donald E. Byrum (June 28, 1966), Gerald F. Trittschuh (August 2, 1966), Robert L. Fowble, Jr. (November 3, 1966), James M. Klink (November 3, 1966), Jack E. Beam (December 21, 1966), Douglas E. Dickey (USMC) (March 26, 1967), Hubert C. Carter

(December 8, 1967), Gerald B. Greendyke (February 3, 1968), Robert E. Floyd (April 31, 1968), David A. Brown (April 26, 1968), Wayne A. Painter (May 27, 1968), Gene F. Morrison (USMC) (June 3, 1968), Dale E. Badgley (June 3, 1968), Jonathan L. Stoops (USMC) (June 6, 1968), Gerald F. Subler (USMC) (September 30, 1968), Melvin R. Green (November 29, 1968), Terry R. Heiser (May 12, 1969), John W. Richard (May 21, 1969), Merle W. Haben (September 21, 1969), William L. Wilhelm (September 6, 1970), James W. Fulk (August 12, 1972), Douglas P. Lefefer (USAF) (MIA: November 5, 1969—Body not recovered June 29, 1978).

10   Casualty statistics as recorded on: The Vietnam Veterans: The Wall-USA, website: http://thewall-usa.com/summary.asp, retrieved August 26, 2013.

11   Holly S. Fenlon, *American Gold Star Mothers Inc., 1928–2010: A History* (Doylestown, Pennsylvania: Platform Press, 2010), p. 51.

20. A Marine Hero is Honored

1   John Ferling, *The Ascent of George Washington: The Political Genius of an American Icon* (New York: Bloomsbury Press, 2009), p. 29.

2   *United States of America's Medal of Honor Recipients and their Citations* (Columbia Heights, MN: Highland House II, 1994), p. 3.

3   John C. Fitzpatrick, ed., *The Writings of George Washington, Volume 24: February 18, 1792–August 10, 1782* (Washington, D.C.: United States Government Printing Office, 1938), pp. 487–489.

4   Douglas E. Dickey was nominated for the Medal of Honor in the letter: Commanding Officer, 1st Battalion, 4th Marines, to Secretary of the Navy, dated April 19, 1967. Letter signed by LtCol Theodore J. Willis. The letter includes statements from: Second Lieutenant Larry A. Dickerson; Lance Corporal William L. Dorsey; Hospitalman Third Class Gregory R. Long; Private First Class Gary L. Hudson; Corporal Walter B. Smith; and Lance Corporal Charles A. Runnels.

5   Act of July 25, 1963, Public Law 88, p. 77.

6   "County Marine Dies in Action in Vietnam War," *Daily Advocate (Greenville, OH)*, April 3, 1967, p. 1.

7   Paul R. Ignatius, *On Board: My Life in the Navy, Government, and Business* (Annapolis, MD: Naval Institute Press, 2006), p. 174.

8   Commandant of the Marine Corps letter to Colonel H. E. Spielman, USMC, Marine Corps Aide to the Secretary of the Navy, dated April 3, 1968.

9   Lisa Gagnon, "Darke County holds dedication ceremony," *Daily Advocate (Greenville, OH)*, June 10, 2003.

10   Vera (Dickey) Moore, interview by author, April 13, 2005.

11   Copy of *Vietnam: The War This Week* episode featuring the story on Douglas Dickey. 16mm film provided to the author by Dennis Dickey.

12   Woody Jones, "Dickey Quiet Youth: 200 Gather As Tiny Rossburg Remembers Its Vietnam Hero," *Journal Herald* clipping furnished to author by Norman Dickey. Date and other publication data are not on the clipping. See also the program titled: "Douglas Dickey Memorial Services, Sunday, May 19, 1968—4 P.M. Rossburg, Ohio, 45362" furnished to author by Norman Dickey.

13   Dennis Dickey, interview by author, March 30, 2005.

21. Veterans

1   Stephen Crane, *The Red Badge of Courage* (New York: Barnes & Noble Books, 1992), p. 183.

2   Rick Eilert, *For Self and Country* (New York: William Morrow and Company, Inc., 1983), p. 63.

3   Ibid., 41.

4   Ibid.
5   1st Battalion, 11th Marines, Command Chronology, February 1967, p. 6.
6   Warren Koon, "Bill's Bo Becomes Marine," *Evening Post (Charleston, SC)*, April 4, 1968, p. 15.
7   George T. Harmon, "Two Charlestonians Among Veterans Of Vietnam War To Receive Medals," *Charleston News and Courier* (Charleston, SC), February 24, 1968, p. 13.
8   "Services Held For Sgt. Moore," *Evening Post (Charleston, SC)*, March 11, 1968, p. 2.
9   "Bobo, The English Bulldog, Follows Master Into Marines," *Charleston News and Courier (Charleston, SC)*, April 5, 1968, p. 13.
10   Eilert, p. 273.
11   Jack Shulimson and Maj Charles M. Johnson, USMC, *U.S. Marines in Vietnam, 1965, The Landing and the Buildup* (Washington, D.C.: History and Museums Division, Headquarters, U.S. Marine Corps, 1978), p. 117; Jack Shulimson, *U.S. Marines in Vietnam, 1966, An Expanding War* (Washington, D.C.: History and Museums Division, Headquarters, U.S. Marine Corps, 1982), pp. 283–4.
12   For details on medical evacuation flights, see: GSgt Bruce Martin, USMC, "Million Dollar Flight," *Leatherneck*, September 1969, pp. 26–31.
13   Jack Westerman III, interview by author, March 24, 2007.
14   LtGen Harold G. Moore, USA, and Joseph Galloway, *We Were Soldiers Once ... And Young* (New York: Random House, 1992), p. 337.
15   George Morris, "Finding Family: Vietnamese child raised in BR rediscovers relatives in native country," *The Advocate (Baton Rouge)*, May 5, 2013, p. 1D.
16   Ulrich Huyssen, *The Violence of Fire* (Baker, LA: Joy Publishers, 1978), p. 23.
17   Tim O'Toole, interview by author, April 16, 2015.
18   Richard M. Nixon, *No More Vietnams* (New York: Arbor House, 1985), p. 128.
19   Jan C. Scruggs and Joel L. Swerdlow, *To Heal A Nation* (New York: Harper and Row, 1985), 58.
20   Ibid., p. 67.
21   At the time the Vietnam War Memorial was built, the official records listed 57,939 casualties. Administrative reviews since the memorial was built have continually added more names as records have been updated; see Jan C. Scruggs and Joel L. Swerdlow, *To Heal A Nation* (New York: Harper and Row, 1985), p. 16.
22   Scruggs and Swerdlow, p. 96.
23   Philip M. Boffey, "Vietnam Veterans' Parade a Belated Welcome Home," *New York Times*, November 14, 1982, p.1.
24   Scruggs and Swerdlow, p. 153.

22. Rally Point

1   *FMFM 6-5: Marine Rifle Squad* (Washington, D.C.: Department of the Navy, Headquarters United States Marine Corps, April 6, 1966), p. 334.
2   Stephen Irving Max Schwab, *Guantanamo, USA: The Untold History of America's Cuban Outpost* (Lawrence, KS: University of Kansas Press, 2009), p. 193.
3   On-camera footage of Larry Dickerson speaking at the Ansonia American Legion during the first reunion of 2nd Platoon, Company C, 1st Battalion, 4th Marines. Footage courtesy of Dennis Dickey.
4   Corporal James D. Rader was killed in action on December 6, 1967. While Dickerson apparently knew him, the other members of the platoon had left before he joined the platoon.
5   Corporal Joseph Klein was killed in action on June 5, 1968. While Dickerson apparently knew him, the other members of the platoon had left before he joined the platoon.

23. A Brotherhood

1   www.masoncity.net/pview.aspx?id=17911&catid=477, retrieved on March 4, 2017.
2   David Ver Helst, interview by author, February 6, 2017.
3   Jack Ver Helst, interview by author, February 6, 2017.
4   Letter from Capt Robert D. Kelley, USMC, to Mr. Ray F. Ver Helst, dated April 2, 1967. Letter provided by David Ver Helst.
5   "Mail Call," *Leatherneck* (February 1968), p. 15.
6   Kent Hansen, interview by author (in person), March 5, 2017.
7   Kristin Buehner, "Call it Love," *The Globe Gazette (Mason City, IO)*, May 25, 1998, p. A1.
8   Ibid.
9   Ibid.
10   Ibid.
11   Ibid.

24. The Last Casualty

1.   Tom Eldred, "Ex-Clayton principal found dead," *Delaware State News*, September 5, 1998, pp. 1–2.
2   Gen G. C. Thomas, USMC (Ret.); Col R. D. Heinl, Jr., USMC; RADM A. A. Ageton, USN (Ret.), *The Marine Officer's Guide* (Annapolis, MD: United States Naval Institute, 1956), p. 4.
3   Maj General John A. Lejeune, USMC, Commandant of the Marine Corps, "Relations Between Officer and Men," Marine Corps Order No. 29, August 14, 1920.

25. A Living Memorial

1   Robert "Bob" and Mona Larson, interview by author, August 28, 2016; "Larry J. Larson Killed In Vietnam," *Carmel (CA) Pine Cone*, April 6, 1967, p. 1.
2   Digital recording of Larry Larson's tape from Vietnam, recorded on board the USS *Ogden* on March 18, 1967, provided to the author by Bob and Mona Larson on August 22, 2016.
3   Richard Van Vactor, interview by author, May 28, 2013.
4   Ibid.
5   Phone conversation with Mr. Patrick Owens, historian for the Picatinny Arsenal Historical Office, November 20, 2013.
6   Certificate for "Award for Outstanding Recruiter" for March 1963; and December 4, 1963 memorandum from Marine Corps Recruiting Station Buffalo, New York, noting Sgt Szymanski as a "Top Hatter" among the recruiters because he recruited 200 percent of his quota for November 1963. Furnished to the author by Loretta Szymanski.
7   Loretta Szymanski, interview by author, November 2, 2013.
8   Truong Nhu Tang, *A Viet Cong Memoir* (New York: Vantage Books, 1985), p. 268.
9   David Lamb, *Vietnam Now: A Reporter Returns* (New York: Public Affairs, 2002), p. 77.
10   James S. Olsen and Randy Roberts, *Where the Domino Fell: America and Vietnam 1945 to 1990* (New York: St. Martin's Press, 1991), p. 275. See also: Edward Doyle and Terrance Maitland, *The Vietnam Experience: The Aftermath: 1975–85* (Boston: Boston Publishing Company, 1985), p. 36.
11   While a midshipman at the U.S. Naval Academy, the author was sent to the USS *Oklahoma City* (CG-5) for at-sea training during the summer of 1979. While on board, he participated in the U.S. Seventh Fleet operation to rescue refugees from Vietnam in the waters off Vietnam.

12   Joan Baez, *And a Voice to Sing With* (New York: Summit Books, 1987), pp. 274–281.

13   Richard Nixon, *No More Vietnams* (New York: Arbor House, 1985), p. 17.

14   "Marvin Cole Honored," *The Lincoln Echo (Fort Smith, AR)*, Volume 20, Issue 5, August 2011, p. 1.

15   Patsy Puckett, interview by author, February 28, 2014.

16   David Flaherty, interview by author, April 12, 2017.

17   Email from Lisa Burke Snyder to 2nd Platoon group address, dated June 27, 2013.

18   Vicky L. Young, interview by author, February 1, 2017.

19   Debbi Nance, interview by author, September 28, 2015.

20   According to the National Archive's POW database, Private Douglas C. Lee was a member of the 23rd Infantry Regiment and was captured in Belgium on December 18, 1944 and repatriated from Stalag 4B on May 17, 1945.

21   Sandy Evans, interview by author, September 1, 2015.

22   Marcie and Dave Koziczkowski, interview in person by author, June 21, 2014.

23   "Vietnam Warriors: A Statistical Profile," *Veterans of Foreign Wars of the United States Magazine*, March 1993, Vol 80, No. 7, p. 20.

24   David Douglas Duncan, "Inside the Cone of Fire at Con Thien," *Life*, October 27, 1967, p. 42B.

25   David L. Anderson, *The Columbia Guide to the Vietnam War* (New York: Columbia University Press, 2002), p. 283.

26   During World War II, group therapy was touted as an effective treatment for those suffering from psychiatric effects of combat. Specifically, the benefits of group therapy included removing the feelings of isolation, and minimizing the feelings of difference. "Optimism, patience, and understanding are afforded." See Edward A Strecker, and Kenneth E. Appel, *Psychiatry in Modern Warfare* (New York: The MacMillan Company, 1945), p. 41.

27   Greg Long, interview with author, March 4, 2015.

28   Larry Alley, interview by author, March 2, 2017.

29   Mike Helton, interview by author, October 17, 2018.

30   Email from Tim O'Toole to author, October 20, 2018.

31   Ibid., December 1, 2018.

26. The Legacy

1   Jimmy Carter, "Congressional Medal of Honor Remarks on Presenting the Medal of Honor to Lt. Col. Matt Urban, U.S. Army, Retired. July 19, 1980," *Public Papers of the Presidents of the United States: Jimmy Carter, Volume 2* (Office of the Federal Register, National Archives and Records Service, General Services Administration, 1980), pp. 1379–80.

2   Larry Alley, interview by author (in person, Newark, DE), June 14, 2007.

3   Leona Dickey, interview by author, March 24, 2005.

Index